THE DURRELLS

The Story of a Family

THE DURRELLS

The Story of a Family

RICHARD BRADFORD

BLOOMSBURY CARAVEL
LONDON · OXFORD · NEW YORK · NEW DELHI · SYDNEY

BLOOMSBURY CARAVEL
Bloomsbury Publishing Plc
50 Bedford Square, London, WC1B 3DP, UK
Bloomsbury Publishing Ireland Limited,
29 Earlsfort Terrace, Dublin 2, D02 AY28, Ireland

A catalogue record for this book is available from the British Library

Library of Congress Cataloguing-in-Publication data has been applied for

ISBN: HB: 978-1-4482-1809-7; eBook: 978-1-4482-1811-0

2 4 6 8 10 9 7 5 3 1

Typeset by Deanta Global Publishing Services, Chennai, India
Printed and bound in Great Britain by Clays Ltd, Elcograf S.p.A.

To find out more about our authors and books visit www.bloomsbury.com
and sign up for our newsletters

For product safety related questions contact productsafety@bloomsbury.com

To Janna C Van der Stelt

And in memory of Elie Robert-Nicoud;

Husband, Father, Grandfather, Writer, Friend

CONTENTS

ACKNOWLEDGEMENTS

I owe enormous thanks to D. J. (Dai) Howells, who has given over a great deal of time in helping me with this book.

Ulster University provided me with a research grant to enable me to visit archives after I had used up the generous payments already made by Bloomsbury Caravel. Regarding the latter my editor Jayne Parsons has as usual been patient and kind. Thanks are due also to Lisa Verner of Ulster University for her administrative assistance. Penny Stenning has offered useful advice. Without the help of Mark Sampson this book would not have appeared. I owe him a great deal for his meticulous comments and attention to detail.

I'm grateful to Catherine Kirby who arranged for papers kept at Jersey Zoo to be moved for my consultation at the Jersey Archive in St Helier.

Archivists at Southern Illinois University, Bibliothèque d'Auxerre and The British Library deserve thanks.

Amy Burns made it possible.

INTRODUCTION

We know of the Durrells from their own writings, most famously Gerald's *My Family and Other Animals* on their years in Corfu, and from the image of them created by TV and film coverage and adaptations of their work. Louisa and Lawrence, the parents, were moneyed colonialists, he a senior engineer working on infrastructure projects in India until his death in 1928, aged only forty-three. Louisa returned to England with her four children and lived in Bournemouth before deciding to move the family to Corfu in the early 1930s. She and her children hated England because they were no longer part of the governing class, or caste. Corfu, she had heard, was an echo of the empire, governed by Britain for nearly half a century after the Napoleonic Wars and still sympathetic to Britain for improving its roads, drains, water supply and so on. The Durrells went there to relive their colonial past and found that most of the indigenous population treated them with aghast fascination, and expatriate Britons saw them as a disgrace to the homeland. Gerald leaves this out of his book. Alcohol was a feature of their carefree island lifestyle, presented by Gerald as one aspect of their ability to assimilate to a culture where consuming wine and spirits was as routine as eating. In truth it was symptomatic of a collective desire to escape from uncomfortable aspects of their lives. Louisa had been an alcoholic since India and after 1939 each of her beloved sons drank themselves to death, albeit at varying speeds.

Lawrence and Gerald are of course the most famous Durrells. Both were exceptional in their chosen fields, the first as an experimental literary writer and the second as a zoologist and conservationist. They were an improbable double act and history does not provide a comparable pairing, though the hypothesis of James Joyce as the elder brother of an animal-loving version of P. G. Wodehouse comes close. Their siblings, Margaret (Margo) and Leslie, will always be perceived through the distorted lens which Gerald turned upon them in *My Family*. Leslie is the comic villain of the book and he went on to resume the role in real life. The Durrells' maid in Corfu, Maria Condos, went with them to England where Leslie had an affair with her. She became pregnant and he abandoned her and their child Anthony and took up with Doris Hall, landlady of a local pub and off-licence. They emigrated to Kenya to 'farm' and eventually fled after Leslie's true source of income was revealed. He had been using fraudulent investment schemes to steal money from well-off expatriate widows. Having returned to London he worked as a caretaker in an insalubrious block of flats and died of a heart attack in a pub in 1982. None of the family attended his funeral. Margo tried but was too ill at the time. Margo's departure from Corfu was almost as fantastical as Gerald's depiction of the place. She fell in love with an Imperial Airways engineer who spirited her away from the advancing Germans in a flying boat. For much of her later life Margo acted as the thread that kept the otherwise disparate parts of the family together, usually by ensuring that at the very least they wrote to each other regularly. She failed with Leslie who on several occasions tried to make contact with his brothers, but both snubbed him. Compared with Lawrence and Gerald, Margo and Leslie seemed to exist in a different universe, as indeed did their omnipresent mother. Louisa? Well, Louisa was loved unreservedly by all of her children but more as a mystery than a mother they actually knew and understood. Throughout their lives and in their writings she hovered over them, adored but not properly comprehended.

Gerald, post Corfu, became celebrated as a pioneering naturalist and conservationist. He began by keeping stray animals at his mother's house in Bournemouth, worked for a while in Whipsnade Zoo, and at the end of the 1940s, making use of a generous legacy from his late father – who bequeathed the family more than £800,000 in today's terms – started bringing animals in danger of extinction back to England. His first trips were to the Cameroons and, dissatisfied by the manner that his new pals were treated by conventional zoos, once more used the family house and garden as a home for everything from gorillas to poisonous snakes, much to the perturbation of the neighbours. After failing to gain permission from various councils in southern England to found a zoo he leased the house and grounds of Les Augrès Manor on Jersey, which endures as a monument to his ideals. For one thing, he revolutionised the notion of the zoo, transforming it from a source of prurient entertainment which gave no attention to the intrinsic instincts and rights of animals to a means of preserving threatened species. His zoo, later Trust, on Jersey earned him the esteem of establishment figures dedicated to animal conservation, notably the Princess Royal and Sir David Attenborough. The costs for the upkeep of the Trust and his foreign expeditions were met by profits from his writing. *My Family and Other Animals* (1956) sold more than 300,000 copies in its first year, has never gone out of print, was for a long time a set text on O level English Literature and has been subjected to numerous film and TV adaptations. It is supposed to be based on recollections of what happened to the Durrells in Corfu but it is made up largely of lies. Why did Gerald do this? The answer might be found in his many unpublished notes where he expresses unreserved contempt for writing as an activity he is obliged to undertake to pay for his animal-focused mission. Most of all he did not like writing about people; compared with animals he felt that they – we – did not deserve the effort. Consequently, he transformed the thwarted expectations of Corfu into a carefree pantomime. In their light-hearted spontaneity the characters of the book do indeed resemble 'other animals'.

The facts of Gerald's achievements as a conservationist are indisputable, but what is evident and overlooked is the question of what motivated his concern for, indeed obsession with, animals. From a young man determined to protect vulnerable species he became in middle age a figure who loathed the species of which he was a member. In the manuscript of his unpublished autobiography colour and delineation of objects seem to preoccupy him from early infancy onwards. The natural world is apparently his most comfortable environment but it soon becomes evident that he would prefer the company of those who are part of it – from insects, through birds and beasts to fish – to those who, he subtly implies, have intruded upon it – us. Aside from the narrative of the draft Gerald allows himself lengthy philosophical reflections on his disdain for human beings. He was a depressive whose affection for animals reflected his unease with the human condition and this eventually ruined his first marriage. Jacquie was just a little too human. Some of the passages from his unpublished notes are by equal degrees poignant and dismaying, showing how different he has become from the pioneering conservationist of his early years. In his sixties Gerald treats the universe of non-humans with what amounts to tormented envy: he wishes he were more like them than the way he is. Compared with Gerald's mindset the more extreme figures of the Green movement, Extinction Rebellion and Just Stop Oil appear serene. *Myself and Other Animals* came out under Gerald's name in 2024. It is edited by his widow Lee, his second wife, and while it is promoted as his unpublished autobiography, albeit mainly by implication, it is anything but. It includes only brief passages from archived manuscripts kept in Jersey but strangely leaves out the most revealing and sometimes unsettling aspects of the real Gerald preserved in the archive. If you wish to encounter this truly peculiar individual see below.

Lawrence never forgave his mother and father for maintaining the Raj tradition of sending sons to school in England, a country he first experienced aged eleven and continued to loathe for the rest of his life. It was he, recently married to Nancy Isobel Myers, who persuaded his mother to take his siblings to Corfu in 1935. The move was not, as Gerald describes it, a reckless romantic instinct by Louisa but a decision made on behalf of the rest of the family by Lawrence as their only means of avoiding what he called 'the English death', the lowbrow introverted culture of a nation obsessed with its place in the world. Lawrence's first two novels, *Pied Piper of Lovers* (1935) and *Panic Spring* (1937), were written two decades before his brother's *My Family* but were equally autobiographical, telling of their main character's childhood in India and Britain and eventual move to the Mediterranean. Notably, however, none of the family comes with him and any form of raucous comedy is replaced by reflections on what kind of philosophical quietism – available apparently only in Egypt and the Greek islands – will compensate for the vileness of England and the British Empire. After 1939 Lawrence became a twisted refection of his brother; both hated their past but while Gerald took refuge with animals Lawrence became an acclaimed practitioner of the kind of writing that few humans would choose to read, notably in *The Alexandria Quartet* and *The Avignon Quintet* – elitist, inaccessible books that the intellectual hierarchy felt would protect them from the incursions of mass culture. He was certainly ranked as a leader among the highbrow division of writers. In keeping with tradition the Nobel Committee revealed its 1962 shortlist half a century later in 2012. Lawrence and Robert Graves had come in close behind John Steinbeck. In 2008 when a special Folio Society edition of the *Quartet* was published the influential critic Michael Wood wrote that it is celebrated both as 'a masterpiece' in its own right and because it is 'unreadable.' He is right, at least in the sense that it is unreadable, and how that affects its standing as great literature is a different issue. What Wood ignores is the question of why Lawrence chose to follow the example of figures such as Joyce, Beckett and Gertrude Stein. The answer I believe is that he found his own temperament and experiences unsuitable as raw material for stories that might be regarded as accessible and realistic. The most sufferable aspect of his life involved his work in various parts of Europe and in Argentina for the Foreign Service and the British Council. He claimed that these jobs kept him above the breadline so that he could pursue his true vocation as a writer. In truth, he was a part-time agent for SIS/MI6. This, one might assume, was nothing to be ashamed of, particularly during the Cold War, but what unsettled Lawrence was that the daily experience of subterfuge – pretending to be something you're not – mirrored key aspects of his private life. His closest friend was the American writer Henry Miller and they shared an obsession with a special supplement to the surrealist, improvisational modes of 1920s modernism: a fanatical preoccupation with sex as the wellspring of significance. One might regard this as an acceptable aesthetic stance but both men were also addicted to infidelity for its own sake, Lawrence especially. Sometimes his extra-monogamous activities triggered a desire to humiliate his partners, on some occasions resorting to violence. Add to this his enormous self-regard as an artist and intellectual, amounting to a snobbish contempt for ordinary people, regular bouts of antisemitism (despite his second and third wives being Jewish; though he did grow to loathe the former), and his treatment of his second child in an unspeakable manner, and we are left with a man who, understandably, chose inaccessible fiction as a hideaway from the truth.

A NOTE ON SOURCES

The sources of quotations are provided in the main text. These will come largely from interviews or published works, and the principal sources for unpublished material are archives, including those in Southern Illinois, Auxerre, The British Library and Jersey.

The majority of unpublished material on Gerald and other members of the Durrell family is deposited at Jersey Zoo. On request, this was taken for viewing to the Jersey Archive in St Helier; hence my bracketed references to this as '(Jersey Archive)'. Although a good deal of this relates to Gerald a considerable amount held in this same collection includes documents, correspondence included, that provide insights into the activities and attitudes of others, his brother Lawrence in particular.

Regarding material typed or written by Gerald, I have provided dates only when these are available on the documents themselves. In other cases I have used the term 'Jersey Archive, undated' and made use of circumstantial evidence, where available, to estimate the date on which the document was composed.

The biographies of Lawrence by Bowker (1996) and MacNiven (1998) and of Gerald by Botting (1999) (full details in Bibliography below) have been exceptionally useful. I am grateful to all three authors.

1

A Strange History

Family trees are supposed to offer a visual substitute for what might be lost in verbal accounts. The various twists and turns of death, divorce, birth, illegitimacy, remarriage, nationality, etc., are fixed on the page like the trunk and branches of a crudely drawn sapling. For the Durrells, however, two centuries of incessant peculiarity defy both description and illustration.

The famous four children of the Corfu era were Lawrence (Larry), Gerald (Gerry), Margaret (Margo) and Leslie. Their father Lawrence Samuel died near what is now the India–Pakistan border in 1928 and Louisa, their mother, led or was kept by the family, depending on who you believe, until her death in Bournemouth in 1964. Despite the siblings advertising her as Irish – her maiden name was Dixie and her ancestors hailed from Cork – she had little connection with the country. She was born in India in 1886, and her maternal family originated in Bloomsbury and Brighton, mostly. Her mother Georgina Boustred was also born in India.

Louisa married Lawrence Samuel Durrell in 1910. His mother was Dora Maria Johnstone whose family, of English origin, had lived in India since the early 1840s and she had married Samuel Stearn (or possibly Stearne) Amos Durrell in Lucknow in 1883. He was the only one of the Durrell family forebears who could claim a direct family link with Britain. He was born in the tiny hamlet of Hacheston, Suffolk, in 1851, but his background is anything but straightforward. His baptismal certificate is marked 'illegitimate', because his mother Mahala Durrell's husband William had died seven years before he was born. His biological father was a farmer, Samuel Geater Stearn, with whom Mahala had lived unmarried since her husband's death. William Durrell had commanded the coastal vessel *Reformation* and for reasons that are unclear he shot himself in the head while off the Yorkshire coast.

Samuel Amos Durrell, Mahala's son by the sixty-three-year-old Stearn, who was himself married with three legitimate adult children, joined the army, aged eighteen, in 1869 and in 1876 he was posted to India. In 1874 he had married Emma Cooper in Portsea. She would die in Allahabad during the hot season of 1881 of one of the diseases to which newly settled Europeans were prone when confined to stifling unhygienic quarters as temperatures averaged more than 36 degrees Celsius for months on end. Two of their children had succumbed to one of these during their first year on the subcontinent. One other, a daughter, survived but nothing more is known of her and none of the Durrell siblings ever spoke of their spectral great aunt.

Samuel married Dora Maria (aka 'Big Granny') Johnstone in Lucknow in 1883 and in 1884 she gave birth to Lawrence Samuel, patriarch of the Durrell family of recent history. He would marry Louisa Florence Dixie in 1910. They had known each other for some time; he had studied at the Roorkee Thomason College of Civil Engineering and the Dixie family was established in the city in the spacious and airy 'Manor' which looked as if the gentry of Britain and France had over the previous two centuries collaborated in something weirdly and grandly eclectic.

The degrees awarded by Thomason College did not quite carry the social prestige of British universities but by the late nineteenth century India had become the proud bastard child of the imperial home country, the Jewel in the Crown as it was commonly known. Its white expatriates were the biological sons of empire while the indigenous population was tolerated, even sometimes respected, by virtue of caste, wealth and cultural westernisation. Thomason men did not study classical literature but they graduated as experts in the building of bridges, railways and canals. The economic infrastructure installed in India by Britain caused the region to race ahead as the first non-European avatar of the industrial revolution, and the colonists might have offered a proprietary smile at making the rigid caste system a central mechanism of organisation, mirroring the homegrown state of class inequality.

Wealthy colonial entrepreneurs, often retaining contacts with Britain, would routinely send their (male) offspring to public school and then Oxford or Cambridge with the expectation that they would return to impress their state of superiority upon a part of the empire that reeked of feudalism, where many could still be treated as second-class citizens or sometimes subhuman.

The Durrells belonged to a confused and indefinite social stratum. Samuel, the English immigrant, had become a warrant officer – sergeant – soon after his arrival and following distinguished service during the Boxer Rebellion in China he'd been mentioned in dispatches and afterwards promoted to the rank of Honorary Lieutenant, a position generally reserved for indigenous soldiers in the army of the Raj, those judged able enough to manage a platoon but not quite deserving of the social status of a fully commissioned officer. By the end of his military career Samuel had attained the status of Honorary Major, by equal degrees a compliment to his abilities and a reminder that he would never be properly middle class. Most others who had such posts, he was reminded regularly, were Indians.

Samuel dwelt in a social hinterland. Just below him were the Indian higher-caste bourgeoisie and above him was the elevated position shared by the Indian minor aristocrats and the colonists who administered and ran the Raj. It was for this reason that he sent his son Lawrence first to La Martinière Christian Boys School in Lucknow and then encouraged him to enrol at Thomason College. It was a step on the ladder towards a status denied to him but which he hoped his eldest son would attain.

Lawrence Samuel held the rank of District Engineer on the Indian National Railway, earning 600 rupees or around £48 per month. At current rates this would amount to between £50,000 to £60,000 per year, a decent amount for a middle manager based in Britain. One would have thought that the reduced cost of living on the subcontinent would have enabled him to live very comfortably but like his father he found himself caught in the middle. He certainly could not afford the kind of colonial mansion in which Louisa had grown up, and Jullundur (Jalandhar), where the couple spent their first few years, was a town built primarily for those who worked on and serviced the railway. The roads were unpaved and every house was a bungalow. The Durrells took the best available, more spacious than those occupied by their Indian neighbours but still with one storey only; this in itself was a sign of being at the bottom. They did not quite have a first floor but prided themselves on windows in the roof which could be opened with cords to allow cooler air to circulate; status of a sort.

There was a small garden at the front where Louisa planted some flowers, a miniaturised replica of the luxurious lawns and beds of her childhood. At the back, their servants took care of a vegetable patch and a few chickens. Two miles away was the Jullundur Cantonment, the military station. Permanence was its theme, with soldiers' barracks hidden behind neo-classical quarters, occupied by officers and their families, and built from locally hewn limestone and surrounded by beautiful gardens in which the ruling classes, their wives and children could enjoy their status; separate and superior. The Durrells were not particularly religious but sometimes they would spend Sunday mornings in the Victorian Gothic Anglican Church of the Cantonment. It too was a stone-built structure, airy, and in midsummer refreshingly cool. They were also admitted to the Officers' Club. Most members were gentlemen soldiers but civilians judged to have attained similar professional status were eligible. It was a curious arrangement in that Lawrence and Louisa would spend afternoons taking tea and cocktails there, playing cards, going to dances and then returning home to where some of those who cooked for club members, served them drinks, even cleaned up after them, were the Durrells' not too distant neighbours.

Lawrence Samuel was by all accounts a man who saw the empire as philanthropic, a means of improving those parts of the globe as yet uninfluenced by the unique qualities of Britishness. Larry recalled that during dinner he would often pause, stare at nothing in particular, slap the table and shout, 'We must go on!' Louisa, conversely, could best be described as batty. Soon after their engagement she announced to Lawrence that she believed in ghosts. She had not only adapted her Christian faith to their benign existence but had made friends with some ghosts in particular. She talked to them, though was a little coy, when Lawrence asked, on disclosing the identity of her departed companions.

The Durrells' servants were variously Hindus and Muslims who took the existence of a spirit world for granted and on several occasions the Muslims expressed their fear that in the woods at the rear of the bungalow there were 'efreets'. These were demonic presences at once frightening but distressed; they'd heard them crying in the night. She settled their fears by wandering into the forest after dark with a lantern, imploring the spirts to 'Come on, come on' as though calming a frightened child. Family legend had it that the servants treated her with warm affection thereafter. Whatever had haunted the woods seemed now at rest.

The Durrells' first child, Lawrence George, was born in the Jullundur house on 27 February 1912. Three months earlier a ceremony had been conducted in Delhi, a Durbar, in which India came as close as it ever would to being a voluntary constituent of the British Empire, with the native princes and other nobles swearing their allegiance to the crown. King George V and Queen Mary presided over official events between 7 and 16 December 1911 and only one Indian aristocrat, Maharajah Sayajirao III, indicated dissent by approaching the royal couple without his jewellery on and turning his back on them following a cursory bow. The rest of his class were dutifully obeisant, along with approximately 700,000 Indians who flocked to see the British King-Emperor of their country. On 14 December George V presided over a parade of almost 60,000 troops, 95 per cent of which were volunteers from the indigenous population.

All of this seemed to reinforce Lawrence Samuel's vision of imperial grandeur and though we have no record of his comments on the birth of his son it seems likely he felt that his offspring would inherit and benefit from his labours as part of the colonial enterprise. He sent Lawrence George, aged eight, to St Joseph's School, Darjeeling. The boy had received some home schooling but St Joseph's was the Indian equivalent of an English preparatory school, run by a Catholic order of priests and nuns but eclectic in its admissions policies. All denominations were welcome and the institution wished to establish itself as a multi-denominational launchpad for men of regard and authority. Its pupils would finish their education in Britain, graduate from the old universities and return to what was instilled in them as their home. Lawrence Samuel predicted that Lawrence George would, after completing his education in England, rejoin the family as MA (Oxford or Cambridge) and make a claim to an elevated social status so far denied to their forebears.

But Lawrence George – let us now call him Larry, as did those closest to him from his youth onwards – did not want any of that. He spoke much later of how from his dormitory in St Joseph's he could see the Himalayas but nowhere in his recollections does he disclose an affection for the institution, or for that matter his family.

In his later years Larry spoke occasionally and obtusely of his time in India and shortly afterwards in England, but leaving aside the accuracy, or otherwise, of his recollections, the most emotionally charged impression will be found in his first novel, the autobiographical *Pied Piper of Lovers* (1935). The novel opens with Walsh Clifton, Larry's alter ego, witnessing the death of his mother in what might be India or subtropical Burma. The Durrells spent almost a year in Burma, Lawrence Samuel having been appointed to work on the proposed Indian–Burmese railway. Larry was only a few months old and his later claims to remembrances of the place are one element of his tendency to rewrite his past either as fiction or a personal mythology. Larry was four when his then only sibling, his sister Margery Ruth, died of diphtheria in 1916 aged just over six months. He never mentioned her either in print or conversation and for the rest of the family she seemed not to have existed.

Clifton's mother dies in childbirth after being attended by a well-meaning if less than competent English doctor, a woman. To friends, much later in his life, Larry would often claim to have a direct memory of his birth (MacNiven, 1998, p14), involving the doctor's misuse of forceps that left him with an unevenly shaped head. Louisa had wanted her first child to be delivered by a native doctor. She did not regard non-European medics as professionally superior but she felt that Indians improved upon cold science with their instinctive sensitivity to the local natural world. Lawrence Samuel, the rationalist, insisted on an English practitioner and was disappointed when a newly qualified female doctor arrived late soon after Louisa had gone into labour.

It is implied in the novel that Clifton's mother dies because the English doctor is disengaged from the organic, largely Buddhist culture of the locality. Clifton is of mixed race, his mother an Indian woman married to an Englishman. The child – a projection of his creator – survives and blame for the ghastliness of it all is aimed clearly at John Clifton, his father, the epitome of unflinching colonialism.

John Clifton is determined that Walsh will be sent 'home' to England. His salary now enables him to pay fees for a decent preparatory school in London which, he is convinced, will prepare his firstborn for a scholarship to a prestigious public school and then to one of the old universities. Lawrence Samuel prepared an identical route for his eldest son. In 1923 he decided that Larry's and the family's future would be secured by a rite of passage provided for those with sufficient money and entitlement to secure it. Two years earlier he had left the railway and founded his own business, Durrell and Co., which would provide subcontinental engineering enterprises with expertise, raw material and locally recruited manual labour. The company flourished as a contractor for the Bengal–Nagpur Railway and Lawrence Samuel was convinced that Larry would return from England as a fully constituted gentleman, perhaps with a degree in Greats, ready to preside over the family enterprise. His lack of any qualifications in engineering would be a grand irrelevance; he would, like a politician, be patrician overseer rather than simply a manager.

On 18 March 1923, three weeks after his eleventh birthday, Larry boarded the SS *City of London* at Calcutta, along with his mother and his six-year-old brother Leslie. In several interviews and through Walsh in *Pied Piper of Lovers* he recounts the voyage as an odyssey of adventure and delight which concludes with disenchantment. The Indian Ocean is a magical blend of lazuline sky and a lighter blue sea, and passing through the Suez Canal the whiteness of the sand almost blinds him. In the Mediterranean, the ship takes Larry close enough to the coasts of Italy and Spain to ignite a devotion to a continent that seems contentedly lavish. It was late spring and the landscapes he gazed at through his father's binoculars appealed to him so vividly that he made a vow to explore them after the turmoils of adolescence. And then he had sight of the legendary white cliffs of Dover, which reminded Larry of yellowing teeth. They might once have been pristine, glowing, but something had gone wrong and his first impression of England proved an accurate forecast of what he would encounter in London.

Lawrence Samuel joined them in the summer of 1923 and he and Louisa were beguiled by the imperial capital. She loved the pristine order of the way people lived in the West End and in the suburbs; in particular, the symmetry of the Georgian and Victorian terraces, the quiet organisation of nature in the squares of the city and the gardens proudly exhibited by householders on the edge of the metropolis. Suddenly her quasi-mystical love of the uncultivated environment had become a little house-trained. Lawrence Samuel was overawed by the mechanics of the place. The underground and surface railways seemed to operate, along with the trams and the road systems that hosted the new invention, the motor car, like the actions of a clock. It was, he thought, an exemplar of Britishness, the modus operandi for making far more efficient the world in which he, a senior railway engineer, played a part.

Lawrence Samuel returned to run the businesses in India in September and Larry was placed in a nondescript school in Tunbridge Wells – we have no record of whether it depended on fees or was an elementary school funded by the local authority. Nothing survives of his academic performance and all we know of this period comes from his private reflections and the observations of Walsh on how his first year in London deepened his sense of loathing for the place. Rain was regular in India, but it was warm, a supplement to a subcontinent bathed in other forms of heat. In England Larry found the dark, wet, cold environment vindictive and appropriate. It matched the mood of the place.

In early summer 1924 'Big Granny', Dora Maria Durrell arrived, though from where is unclear. Her husband Samuel Stearn had died in 1914 and at some point she had returned to England. Louisa followed Lawrence Samuel back to India and Dora Maria oversaw the schooling of the two boys. Larry was placed in the independent St Olave's and St Saviour's Grammar School, just south of Tower Bridge. It was the kind of institution where lower-middle-class clerks and businessmen sent their offspring, in the expectation that the homespun conventions of obedience and ambition would be supplemented by good, hard teaching: the objective was a university education. Leslie was packed off to the Caldicott, a Wesleyan Methodist school where it was hoped that his tendencies towards impulsive bad behaviour might be constrained. Much later Larry disclosed that his younger brother had become feral;

'[he] lashed out with his fists when crossed ... Fighting became an end in itself for Leslie.' On one occasion a fight left him with a ruptured eardrum and semi-permanent deafness. He called this period, for both of them, their 'Pentonville Period'; both schools, he felt, had left an imprint on them comparable with London's hardest prison (private archive of Professor Keith Brown, Oslo University).

In 1926 Larry was moved from St Olave's and St Saviour's to St Edmund's, a school close to Canterbury but of no significant difference from his earlier one. What records we have indicate that his academic performance at the latter was outstandingly average, his most notable achievement being punctuality. He often took the train to London to enjoy the atmosphere of the streets surrounding Southwark Cathedral, but not because of their innate charm. The cathedral itself is a magnificent, heavily restored survival of the Great Fire but by the 1920s everything around it was made up of dour nineteenth-century red-brick terraces and offices. Larry was fascinated by its ghosts, notably John Gower, one of England's earliest poets who lived in the area and is interred in the cathedral, and Shakespeare who held court nearby in the Globe Theatre. We know this only from Larry's own reflections made much later in his life in which he implies that his creative inclinations were more significant than the drab routines of schoolwork. In fact, his story of his attempt to hunt down the spirit of Shakespeare comes exclusively from his interview with Malcolm Muggeridge in 1965. As we will find with Larry, he existed as much in a cameo of recollections and memoirs as in what most of us would treat as real time. In 1940 he told Michael Dibdin that 'My identity was foxed all the time by counter-identities ... I wasn't an Indian, but I wasn't English either. I'm not real. I was a series of afterthoughts ... I'm a complete fake really!' (Bowker, p25). Often he presented himself as owing as much, temperamentally, to his 'Irishness' as the colonial split personality of England and India. But before we dismiss this as exhibitionism and gamesmanship, we should consider how Larry's early life prompted him to snatch at fragments of everything for certainty, a panicked search for security in an unnerving vacuum. In 1986 in an interview with the BBC cricket correspondent Christopher Martin-Jenkins he told of how he had grown to love cricket in his first two years in England. He added that he had regularly played truant from school to watch county and test matches at the Oval, the cricket ground south of the Thames. Jack Hobbs's hundredth century in 1926 and Harold Larwood's bouts of 'bodyline' fast bowling during the same summer had, he reported, filled him with awe. As well they might, given that Hobbs had scored his record century against Somerset in Bath in 1923 and Larwood's destructive bowling sessions had taken place in the Ashes series in Australia in the 1930s.

Larry went on to offer Martin-Jenkins a lyrical tour of cricket's role in the culture of a country, England, that he otherwise claimed to despise. At St Edmund's he would lie in the long grass between pastures and playing fields outside the school. Above him were the buildings of Victorian Gothic and Tudor which over seventy years had weathered so tastefully as to be mistaken for the real thing. In his hand was an edition of the work of Canterbury's challenger to Shakespeare, Christopher Marlowe. The music of Marlowe's verse was counterpointed against the distant rhythm of leather against willow and polite applause coming from the school cricket ground whose pagoda-like pavilion reminded him of grander buildings in India. Walsh, his fictional alter ego, seems to have a less obliging view of his new home. 'But far above everything else it was teaching him to put up with the life of a narrow, ignorant, and conservative society in which none of the rules (unwritten) and regulations (printed) were not wholly idiotic.' Who should we believe: Larry who began his blatantly autobiographical novel when he was sixteen at his next school, a crammer in West Wratting, Cambridgeshire or Larry the middle-aged dissembler who had earned himself the esteem of the cultural establishment by writing fiction that rarely made sense?

Consider how he would have felt when sent to England in 1923. Some children might have dealt with it as a great adventure, an odyssey comparable with that of other boys sent to boarding school, except this involved a voyage halfway around the world to a place he had known of only through myths and rumours, rather than taking a train to another county. Think also of his siblings. He was the only one who had witnessed the presence of his younger sister, dead after less than a year. Leslie was six when they set off together, only to be separated on their arrival in London. Margaret (b.1919) was only just three when he left and he would not see her again until 1925, briefly, following which she returned to India with Louisa a year later. During the same period in England, he met his youngest sibling Gerald (b.1925) who was brought to London briefly by their parents and who as a one-year-old had no memory of their encounter or the visit.

At this point we should give some attention to Gerald, or as I will hereafter call him, Gerry. Like his elder brother he was known to those closest to him by his casual name after infanthood. As most are aware their careers took them in different directions, Larry to approbation as a novelist and Gerry as a zoologist who wrote books only to support his dedication to threatened species. Despite this they had something in common. Their lives, as far as we can recover them from what they wrote or said about their pasts, were largely works of fiction. Gerry's experiences of India lasted less than the first three years of his life; he would with the rest of the family leave the subcontinent for good in 1928.

Much later he left a remarkably detailed report of his birth, including his mother's pre-natal experiences. Louisa was only five feet tall and suddenly began to gain weight. Embarrassed, she refused to leave the house but Lawrence Samuel urged her to seek company among other expatriates, most of whom enjoyed the effects of overeating. He added that if she felt uneasy about 'waddling' to the club he would hire her a howdah, an enclosed bed-like compartment carried on a small elephant. In response to the suggestion she said, 'Well, I look like one!' Her pregnancy was not discovered until after its thirtieth week and to celebrate her release from some apparently incurable state of obesity she drank at least a bottle of champagne a day until after Gerry was born. 'To this I attribute the fact that I have always drunk excessively, and especially champagne' (Jersey Archive, undated; notes from his incomplete memoir). He was, he recalled, the largest despite being their final child – though he 'slipped like out of her like an otter'. In his notes Gerry tells of how his mother's family were from the Irish gentry, the so-called Ascendency, without explaining why the Dixies had exchanged their privileged West Brit status for what amounted to a life as lower-rank colonialists. Like Larry, Gerry enjoyed telling of their Irish background, ignoring their very limited links to the country – somewhere between fabled and non-existent – as a testament to the contrariness of the Durrells.

Elsewhere in his sketches Gerry recalls being surrounded by 'sharply etched vignettes of brilliant colour', of ayah, his nanny, refusing to wake him in the morning until 'the strains of Harry Lauder on the gramophone' entered the room. His favourite breakfast was 'rice boiled in buffalo milk with sugar' and he enjoyed so much being dressed by his ayah in 'little suits made of tussore ... the lovely colour of it – a very pale biscuit brown – and the delicious soft silky feel of it and the rustling sound it made' (Jersey Archive, undated). When we gather together the circumstantial coordinates of this point in Gerry's life we find he would have been no more than eighteen months old. What a memory he had, at least if we treat memory as an adjunct to invention. He was no more than two and a half when he first encountered a zoo in Jamshedpur, recording much later the 'ammonia-like smell' of the tiger and leopard cages, the 'screams' from the groups of monkeys, and the 'melodious songs' of the various captured birds (Jersey Archive, undated). The cages seemed even to his infant perception far too 'tiny' and unclean. As an adult, when he recorded his impressions, he was certain that he would have closed the place down, which was creditable, had a Jamshedpur zoo existed in the 1920s.

He tells also of 'Uncle John' Dixie, Louisa's 'favourite' brother, employed by the government to shoot man-eating tigers and lions and rogue elephants. One day he brought the family two Himalayan bear cubs, charming when tiny but vast and deadly as full-grown creatures. In Gerry's account the cubs were, for the safety of the family, sent to a nearby zoo.

Much of Gerry's unpublished account of his early life unravels as a fantasy when we compare what he says with verifiable fact, with some exceptions. 'It seemed that we had adopted them but they hadn't adopted us. It was their country. Oh yes, of course. But you know we loved it too – I used to watch them – so beautiful – they had India [and] we had each other and the Club' (Jersey Archive, undated). Larry assumed that his father would return to Britain to monitor his eldest son's attempts at academic advancement but he would never see him again. By early 1928 Lawrence Samuel had begun to suffer regular headaches and bouts of dizziness, not helped by his steady intake of whisky. On 16 April he died in Dalhousie of what was officially described as a cerebral haemorrhage and was buried the following day. He was only forty-three. Louisa, still in London, could not attend the funeral and would never return to India. Instead, she entered a state of eccentric English widowhood, while Larry, still only sixteen, was by consensus called to duty as head of the family. Only Larry had spent more than brief periods in England and none would ever go back to India. In July Louisa was officially granted the full estate of her late husband, coming to 246,217 rupees; then the exchange rate would have bought her about £19,000, today just under a million. A clause of the document allocated £150 (roughly £8000 today) exclusively to Larry to cover the costs of his continuing education. None of his other children received anything beyond what Louisa might offer them at her discretion, and she would eventually set up trusts for each. The will does not survive but the reported special treatment of Larry is plausible because Lawrence Samuel was dedicated to securing a respectable professional or social position for his eldest son, somewhere, but he knew that Larry had a deep contempt for traditional schooling. Before his death he would also have learned that early in 1928 Larry had left St Edmund's with dismal reports on his performances and would need to use family finances to pay for private tutoring. Between 1927 and 1930 he attended the private crammer in West Wratting, Cambridgeshire, a small village where the collective economy of farming was supplemented by an overpriced fee-paying academy for boys who had failed or dropped out of mainstream schools. At St Edmund's his teachers had informed him that he would stand no chance of entering Oxford or Cambridge and, commendably, his West Wratting tutors confessed to him that irrespective of how much he paid them they could not improve on his prospects. He later claimed that while he was not unintelligent, he was temperamentally averse to being taught anything. 'At seventeen or eighteen I was anti-everything ... I should have liked to have gone to Oxford, if only to give my father some pleasure.' But he thinks again: 'above all my subconscious was set on proving to my father that it was unfair to send me back to prison. So, in spite of my capabilities, I fluffed all the exams; three, four, five times' (*The Big Supposer*, pp29–31). In the last sentence he implied, while omitting, 'deliberately'. In his comments and interviews on his early years, especially in *The Big Supposer*, Larry regularly contradicts himself, at least in terms of what we can surmise from other sources. The 'exams' he refers to include, he claims, university entrance examinations but all records of his time at St Olave's and St Edmund's indicate that he was encouraged to leave because they judged him unsuitable as a candidate for either of the old universities. The West Wratting crammer made its money by rescuing middle-class boys from intellectual and professional oblivion. It prepared teenagers for entrance examinations for the junior civil service, the officer class of the Colonial Office or, at best, for training at Dartmouth (naval officers) or the Royal Military Academy Sandhurst (army officers). Larry chose not to put himself forward for any of those.

Gerry's feelings on the death of his father are unrecorded in interviews or print. In his archived notes for a future memoir he says little more than 'I must confess that my father's demise had little or no effect on me, since he was a remote figure ... I was on much greater terms of intimacy with my mother' (Jersey Archive, undated). Larry said nothing at all, at least on record. All we have are Walsh's private ruminations in *Pied Piper* on his father's death. 'He felt guilty ... because he was capable of feeling nothing but his overwhelming numbness.'

In late 1928 the rest of his family arrived in London for good. It was a curious decision on Louisa's part since Lawrence Samuel's estate would have enabled her to live as part of the colonial gentry, in decent quarters with servants, for the foreseeable future. Instead, she took a lease for herself and her three children – not Larry – on an enormous house in Alleyn Park Road in Dulwich, a Victorian villa with a fourth-floor accommodation for servants, which she advertised for and employed. Quite soon it was evident that the building was an expensive and unnecessary requisite to colonial role-playing. Next, she took a self-contained single-storey flat in the Queen's Hotel in Upper Norwood. It was in grandiose contrast with the rest of the building, made up of long-term bed-sitting room residents – mostly retired spinsters or army officers – or others such as travelling salesmen who took short-stay single rooms. Émile Zola lived there while in exile from France after he claimed that Alfred Dreyfus had been wrongly convicted of treason. Zola photographed Queen's in 1899 and it looked much the same when the Durrells moved in almost three decades later. It appears to be an untidy melange of residential properties from various historical periods.

Some of the frontages carry a hint of retro-Georgian style while others jump forward to the ornate quasi-Gothic manner of the nineteenth century. The impression is that the hotel resulted from these houses being knocked together but in truth it was planned and built as a single project. The hotel was completed in 1854 and it was meant to evoke the architectural development of London over the previous century and a half. It would serve wealthier visitors to the recently relocated Crystal Palace, an exhibition centre for the numerous wonders of Britain and its empire. Shortly after its opening its most distinguished regular guests were the Emperor Frederick III and the Kaiser Wilhelm II of Germany who would each occupy at least two floors. The former had married Queen Victoria's eldest daughter and often visited his mother-in-law, and the latter was Victoria's grandson. It is almost certain that the spacious single storey occupied by the Durrells was what remained of the maisonettes used by German royalty. There is no evidence that Louisa or her relatives or children were aware of this but they did notice the decaying grandeur of their new home. The wallpaper was elaborate and the lavish Wilton carpets were track-worn with regular use. It bespoke an empire past its best and Louisa's choice of it as her place of retreat from India was inadvertently appropriate.

Larry sometimes stayed overnight at the hotel but during the years following his departure from West Wratting in 1930 he lived nomadically. He visited mainland Europe on several occasions, developed a love for France and an intermittent affection for Amsterdam where the official ban on brothels, pimping and prostitution was rarely if ever enforced. For a while he took rooms in Bloomsbury repeating his exercises in literary ghost-hunting, this time exchanging Shakespeare and Marlowe for Verlaine and Rimbaud who were rumoured to have lived in Old Compton Street. No one was sure of the exact street let alone the number but Larry found a smoke-blackened property advertising 'rooms' for rent, sensed their long-departed spirits and moved in. Allegedly, his French predecessors spent most of their time downing extra-strong absinthe, smoking hashish and starting fights with those who visited to discuss poetry with the two legendary rebels. By 1930 the eighteenth-century terrace was the equivalent of a slum inhabited by the near-destitute but for Larry it retained a mood of sweet decadence. The rent was slight and

Larry spent no more than two nights a week there, returning occasionally to his mother's home at Queen's for somewhere heated and habitable to concentrate on his writing.

He supplemented his lump sum from his late father's estate by working for rental agencies, collecting overdue payments from an extraordinary range of occupants, including grocers, tailors, poverty-stricken families and brothel keepers. After learning to drive – tests at the time were not a requirement – he routinely took his mother's car without permission, sped around the more dismal areas of London where he collected rent, and one night, having been to the pub for several large whiskies, crashed the vehicle into a lamppost. The damage was relatively slight but Louisa responded by banning him completely from the hotel. 'You can be as bohemian as you like,' she stated, 'but *not in the* house.' He was obliged to spend five days in his slum and repented. Larry did his best to produce poems and between 1929 and 1931 wrote seven that would appear in print and which he included in his *Collected Poems* of 1980. They are brief, hybridised blends of the unfocused modernism of the period and the mannered lyricism of the previous century. They seem, like their author, unaffiliated and lost.

Once more, all we know of Gerry during this period comes from the notes for his autobiography. He reports that he often spent nights in his mother's bed, principally to offer her protection against the ghosts that seemed to outnumber the living guests. He tells also of how when Larry was absent, voluntarily or by Louisa's command, confirmation of 'other' presences would come via noises from his room. They had brought from India Lawrence Samuel's massive teak rolltop desk and it was the platform for Larry's typewriter. From the outside of Larry's bedroom Gerry, his mother and on one occasion Margo would listen to the clatter of the top being opened and closed again. One evening they also heard the noise of the typewriter keys. When Louisa, strengthened by several gins, opened the door and switched on the light she and her son found the desk closed and the room empty. There was no other door. Was Larry ever told of his spectral proxy? He never spoke or wrote of it.

Equally mysterious and dubious is the figure of Tabitha. Her 'big eyes' were 'brown and glossy as horse chestnuts'. She was 'gentle and gay', her 'smile engulfed you with love' and 'she smelt gorgeous as well'. 'I loved the days I spent with her,' recalled Gerry. He tells of how they first met in the garden of the hotel but leaves us to wonder if she was a fellow resident or from somewhere close by. Wherever she lived he was made her guest, introduced to her squeaky 'wind-up gramophone', and taught by her the Charleston and the waltz. The impression left is that she is close to his age, if a little precocious, except that we eventually learn that his 'visits to her flat were ended' when 'Mother got to hear of Tabitha's business associates'. These were 'gentlemen' who would spend time 'in her bedroom, talking business'. Tabitha the louche full-grown woman, maybe prostitute, seems designed to raise eyebrows among readers of Gerry's story of his childhood. He was only five. Even by the time he wrote the unpublished memoir in his late sixties he had still not quite banished the fantasist, the creator of delusions that turned his family into a legend, born out of his own *My Family and Other Animals*.

Louisa's only friends at the hotel were the Brown family, similarly middle class and now rather down at heel. The widowed Mrs Brown, whose Christian name remains unrecorded, was around Louisa's age and the daughter of the doughty Victorian matriarch Grandmother Richardson. Mrs Brown's only significance in the odyssey of the Durrells is her decision to move her family to Bournemouth in March 1930. She remained a regular visitor to the capital and convinced Louisa that the resort was to London what the French Riviera was to Paris, a region with an azure sea and gorgeous sunshine.

In early summer 1931 Louisa bought Berridge House, a gloweringly ugly nineteenth-century residence in Parkstone, a suburb of the town inhabited by those snobbish and rich enough to detach themselves from the vulgarity of a place which could be reached on the train by the lower orders. Larry was torn between laughter and tears. Berridge House was set in four acres with an orchard and two tennis courts; the grounds required the attention of three full-time gardeners. Above ground were four floors of sitting, living and dining rooms and six bedrooms; in the basement a parquet-floored ballroom, not used since the 1870s, was offered to Gerry as his private indoor playground. A year after she moved in Louisa realised that she could not afford to keep the place and bought the smaller 18 Wimborne Road, less than a decade old, affordable and closer to the centre of Bournemouth. Louisa decided to call it Dixie

Lodge in honour of her family, a curious choice given that the previous residence seemed more manorial, albeit grotesquely.

Summer visitors to the town might have been young but its permanent residents were mostly retirees and for Larry it appeared to be an oddly expanded version of the Queen's Hotel, or 'a living cemetery' as he put it. He hated what his family had become and despised himself for his apparent inability to get away from them. Both Bournemouth houses regularly hosted mysterious 'aunts', though it remains unclear as to their actual biological relationship with Louisa and her children. It is certain that neither the late Lawrence Samuel nor Louisa had brothers or sisters in Britain though it is possible that second or third cousins from previous generations endured from before members of the Durrell or Dixie family departed for India in the mid-nineteenth century. Aunts Fan, Nora, Patience and Prudence crop up often in recollections and books by Gerry and Margo but rather like figures at a séance without introductions or surnames. Much later, in the essay collection *Spirit of Place* (1969), Larry would subject them to a calculatedly lazy brand of satire, as if they were too ludicrous to command much attention. He edited out his brief walk-on appearance in the Durrell pantomime. After the rest of the family had moved to the south coast he found himself stranded in a room whose cultural resonances lost the competition with damp, the lavatory shared with many others in the building, and rats. So he bartered his radical self-image for more comfortable quarters in Bournemouth. Soon he would return to London as a committed bohemian but first he followed his mother's advice to find paid work and applied for a job as a porter at Bournemouth railway station. Louisa was overjoyed and commended him for securing a more respectable means of supporting himself than collecting rent from people unable to pay it. He would try to write every evening in Wimborne Road having spent the day carrying luggage for visitors from the capital. He was, however, reprimanded by the station master for refusing to wear a porter's uniform. His preference was an Edwardian long coat borrowed from the local drama society and a vividly colourful bow tie. The prophet of the Comte de Lautréamont was, it seemed, reincarnated as an employee of London and South Western Railway.

In early 1932 Larry decided to commit himself to London in the hope that he would make contact with the circles of writers and artists he'd heard of while working as a rent collector in Bloomsbury. The trouble was he did not know where to go or for that matter who he was searching for as a contact. Soho, he had heard, was London's version of Paris's Montparnasse, the haunt of figures such as Malcolm Lowry, Dylan Thomas and the painter Nina Hamnett, each as much notorious for their appetite for sex, alcohol and drugs as their artistic achievements, at least during the straightlaced interwar years. Larry regularly visited the Fitzroy Tavern and the Marquis of Granby conveniently close to his new lodgings in Tottenham Court Road, and much as he tried to begin conversations with arty-looking seemingly resolute drinkers or the celebrities he hoped to meet it seemed that he was chasing shadows.

The only person with a tenuous link to London's literary culture who he succeeded in befriending was Cecil Jeffries. Jeffries had published nothing but had made several attempts at becoming an independent publisher of modernist writing. He owned a hand-press and in 1931 brought out a very slight poetry collection by his friend called *Quaint Fragments* under the imprint of Cecil Press. It was dedicated to Larry's mother and there is no record of it ever being displayed in a bookshop or bought by anyone, though by the time that Larry had established himself as a novelist of global eminence the edition was treated as gold dust by rare book collectors.

In spring 1932, soon after his failed attempts to track down members of London's decadent cognoscenti, Larry began to make connections with those in the cultural underclass of the West End, some enthralling and others bizarre.

Those involved still dispute the nature of his first meeting with Nancy Isobel Myers. Even in her memoir *Amateurs in Eden*, Nancy's daughter Joanna Hodgkin concedes that it recedes into 'vagueness'. Nancy had for some time been pursued by 'Roger', surname never disclosed, a fellow student at the Slade School of Art, but at some point, probably in 1932, she had come across a man driving a smart Hillman saloon car. This in itself would not have been uncommon in London at the time but he looked like he'd stolen it, having childlike features and being the height of a fourteen-year-old. Larry was little more than five feet two inches tall. There is no record of why they spoke to each other but they did and Larry soon began to refer to her as the 'lamp post': at five foot eight she loomed over him. She was beautiful, graceful in movement and virtually everyone she met commented on her uncanny resemblance to Greta Garbo. They were almost exactly the same age and what attracted her most to him was his determination to rebel, to make art out of hopelessness. Consequently, she moved in with him briefly to a bedsit in Soho and then to Guilford Street, Bloomsbury.

At the opening of Chapter 11 of *Pied Piper of Lovers* we are told of Walsh Clifton that 'if he found them to be wayward and irresponsible people during those first few weeks, he marvelled at the haphazard and disordered habits of their lives … he was at least profoundly grateful to them for the frank kindness and generosity they showed him' (p207).

The 'they' referred to are a loosely fictionalised assembly of the individuals with whom Larry and Nancy spent their time in the less salubrious districts of Soho, Notting Hill and Bloomsbury.

His associations with these figures began shortly after they first met, when he was playing jazz piano at the Blue Peter nightclub in Upper St Martin's Lane near Leicester Square. He had been taught the basics of reading music in India and had only rudimentary skills on the keyboard, but he could improvise, especially if joined by a double bass player and drummer. The club had a licence to sell alcohol but it attracted cultural rebels and general dissolutes because of its reputation as a place where hashish could be purchased and consumed. Harold Nicolson was a regular customer. Despite being married to Vita Sackville-West, Nicolson enjoyed numerous homosexual relationships and one night, when Larry exchanged jazz for dance tunes such as 'Smoke Gets in Your Eyes' and sang them well enough, Nicolson walked to the stage and spread his arms around the young pianist's shoulders. Nancy was pleased for Larry that Nicolson found him attractive, mostly because she was aware of her boyfriend's concealed pomposity. Larry's avowed contempt for what he called Britain — Pudding Island — was matched by his elitist aspirations.

Two weeks after that the club was raided by the police. Larry escaped through a window in the men's lavatory. He waited for Nancy outside a theatre where she had taken on a walk-on role and they went to the Windmill Café in Great Windmill Street. Ostensibly the café was a coffee bar but spirits were available to regulars. Larry was distracted from his conversation with Nancy by the spectacle of a man of about his age – in fact, they were born within months of each other – smoking a cigarette in an ivory holder and dressed as though he had been reincarnated from the pre-First World War generation. Also, he was busily correcting galley proofs of what appeared to be verse which prompted Durrell to introduce himself as a recently published poet. The man, slim, fox-faced and red-haired, replied that he, John Gawsworth, was a publisher, writer and patron of the literary arts. Still only twenty, Gawsworth explained that following his time at Merchant Taylors' School he had worked at Charlie Lahr's bookshop in Red Lion Square and for the publisher Ernest Benn, earning a modest amount of money which he supplemented with family funds to set up his own press. Moreover, he was the authorised champion of M. P. Shiel (born Matthew Phipps Shiell), the erratic writer and 'officially' crowned King Felipe of Redonda, a mile-long uninhabited rock off the Leeward Islands which Gawsworth and Shiel maintained was a sun-drenched tropical paradise. Gawsworth had, he added, recently been appointed by Shiel as the Laureate of Redonda. Larry later commented that 'I was a complete novice and a provincial and the meeting was an important one for me, for in John I found someone who burned with a hard gem-like flame – the very thing I wished to do myself' (Archive, University of Paris X, Nanterre University, undated). Read between the lines and Larry is admitting to being attracted to an alchemist, a fraud. Gawsworth charmed him with stories of his literary apprenticeship, when he had been introduced to Yeats and Hardy (who died when he was fifteen), and his ongoing acquaintance with the grandmaster of modernism, T. S. Eliot, and the apologist for progressive sexuality and eugenics Havelock Ellis. He was lying about all of this but Larry was beguiled. Although the promised introductions to Gawsworth's list of intellectual celebrities never came about Durrell was, through him, admitted to a circle of eccentrics and artistic deviants.

Charlie Lahr's bookshop was London's answer to Paris's Shakespeare and Company, or at least it wanted to be. Instead of Sylvia Beach hosting Joyce, Hemingway, Fitzgerald, Pound et al., Lahr made do with the likes of Count Potocki de Montalk, New Zealand-born poet and pretender to the throne of Poland. In 1932 Potocki was imprisoned for publishing obscene literature, notably 'Lament for Sir John Penis', and after that he became an enthusiastic advocate of fascism. Other, less freakish visitors included Mulk Raj Anand, born in India seven years before Larry, and destined to become one of the country's foremost thinkers and novelists. He had completed his doctorate at Cambridge two years before he met Larry and the latter was exhilarated by encountering someone from the place where he'd grown up who was intellectually superior to the majority of Englishmen he'd met so far.

George Barker impressed him as both his near replica and guide. Barker's parents were from humble backgrounds. His father had fought as a private in the First World War, earned himself a field commission and risen to Major but on his return to London taken work as a butler at Gray's Inn. His mother was from rural Ireland. After taking a degree at Regent Street Polytechnic, Barker kept himself with menial work, lived in a horrible bedsitting room and devoted his time to writing poetry. He had, he told Larry, been invited to meet T. S. Eliot of Faber, who stated that his verse impressed him; he would eventually publish it. Like Anand he was a political radical and both men supported communism and the independence of states colonised by Britain.

Born in Canada, George Woodcock had come to England in his early teens. He had turned down his wealthy grandfather's offer to cover his tuition fees for Cambridge and when he met Larry at Lahr's was working as a clerk at the Great Western Railway. He introduced Larry to anarchism, which Woodcock regarded more as a state of mind than a political conviction; politics, in his view, was by its nature repressive. Woodcock's books on anarchism combine radicalism with benevolence – he was throughout the Spanish Civil War outspokenly anti-fascist but during the Second World War he registered as a conscientious objector. Larry was beguiled by his new friend; they were almost the same age but Woodcock seemed to have attained an extraordinary level of philosophical gravity. Woodcock also warned Larry against the men who had impressed him but who he should avoid. Gawsworth was, in his view, 'one of the most rat-like human beings I have ever known, full of grievance and always ready to bite', and Potocki was an 'old-style authoritarian reactionary' (Bowker, pp45–47). His warning was shrewd given that by the mid-1930s Potocki was an unashamed supporter of Hitler's antisemitic policies.

Evelyn Waugh knew none of Larry's new circle of friends but his second novel *Vile Bodies* (1930) catches perfectly the state of aimlessness and pretension which informed this world of young intellectuals in London during the early 1930s. Nancy introduced her boyfriend to Peter Bull, youngest son of Sir William Bull, MP for Hammersmith. Bull was educated at Winchester and already a rather portly all-day drinker when, aged twenty-one, he made his first stage appearance at the Shaftesbury Theatre. Bull was a friend of the Hon. Nicholas Phipps (unrelated to the aforementioned Matthew), a fellow Wykehamist also launching his career as an actor, who reminded many of Noël Coward, if only in appearance. The third Wykehamist was George Wilkinson. Like the others Wilkinson was heir to a minor aristocratic title, a baronetcy, and son of the owner of the Curwen Press which specialised in expensive delicately produced art books. At school he concentrated on fencing, treating conventional academic study as largely avoidable. In London he spent as much time as possible at the First Edition Club in Pall Mall, whose title belied any actual literary associations; its principal attraction was the availability of unrestricted drinking hours.

In 1932 Larry and Nancy moved from the cramped Guilford Street bedsit to Wilkinson's more spacious floor of rooms at 6 Fitzroy Square, Fitzrovia. Soon afterwards Wilkinson's girlfriend Pamela Black, a beautiful auburn-haired actress, made up a foursome on the square. Wilkinson himself never published anything but he saw himself as guide and mentor for his ambitious bohemian friends. He would eventually convince Larry that Corfu was his ideal destination and he oversaw the practicalities when the rest of the Durrell family later moved to the island. Without his calm assistance Larry's second volume of verse, *Ten Poems* (1932), would probably never have gone into print. Larry had already shown and read many of the poems to Gawsworth who damned each with exceedingly faint praise – 'splendidly musical – bless you!' – but condemned them overall as an act of plagiarism, specifically from Gawsworth's own dismal, privately printed *Kingcup*, but we should not take seriously Gawsworth's dismissal of it. At the time literature of any kind was, for the latter, part of a ludicrous fantasy world. His brother was a Jacobite Earl, he wore a regal cloak regularly on his strolls through West London and on the anniversary of the execution of Charles I he would buy a white rose and place it reverently at the base of the king's statue in Whitehall. He, like Potocki, delighted in the rising tide of fascism in Europe. Both men perceived Jews as subhuman, complicit in the Bolshevik Revolution and the murder of the Czar and his family. For them, poetry and other arts were the exclusive possessions of noblemen and neither was troubled by such bothersome matters as democracy. Gawsworth attempted on several occasions to seduce Nancy who, while not flattered by his attentions, was willing to sideline her distaste for him for the sake of participating in a farcical, almost otherworldly ritual of tolerating his forays; she was after all an actress. At the Café Royal Gawsworth challenged Larry to a duel for her hand. No weapons were available so they agreed to verbal combat and Gawsworth eventually conceded defeat after the two men had drunk too much to be able to string together a coherent sentence.

In 1932 Larry endured a week as the straight man in a pantomime. Somehow his mother had learned of his relationship with Nancy, and it was later evident that she was aware that they were cohabiting as an unmarried couple and at her behest he arranged for the two of them to visit his family in Bournemouth.

According to Nancy's taped 'memoir' of 1972, which was never published, Larry painted for her a picture of his closest relatives as variously dysfunctional and deranged. Louisa was, he avowed, both mentally ill and alcoholic. She had wasted his father's savings on shockingly expensive almost palatial properties. Drinking gin from breakfast onwards Louisa had neglected Larry's siblings who had become feckless and anarchistic. Nancy was fascinated and puzzled. On the one hand Larry seemed to be warning her about what she would encounter in Bournemouth and perhaps was even attempting to persuade her to cancel or postpone the visit. But at the same time, she wondered why he felt it necessary to apologise for the oddities of his family while he seemed entranced by a circle of similarly eccentric exhibitionists in London.

The apparent anomaly tells us much about Larry's emerging disposition. He was becoming a disciple of anything mutinous and subversive, with the proviso that Englishness was anathema to both. The Durrell house in Bournemouth closely resembled a middle-class version of Wodehouse's Blandings, where the lack of order or restraint was matched by cosy self-caricature. Larry was afraid that Nancy would be charmed by the parochial eccentricity of his family so he attempted to add to it a touch of his own abhorrence. He failed completely as Nancy's recollection of the visit testifies.

> The rooms ... had a certain amount of comfort – a rather disarray sort of comfort. I mean, they had a few easy chairs and a sofa in the sitting room and the floors were carpeted and things. It all seemed a little bit makeshift somehow. But I remember I loved the house – the sort of craziness about it, people sort of playing at keeping house rather than really keeping house. You felt they weren't forced into any *mould* like people usually are – every sort of meal was at a different time, and everybody was shouting at everybody else, no control anywhere. (Botting, p24)

She goes on to tell of the seven-year-old Gerry – who was 'too sensitive' to go to school – that he 'looked a bit like Christopher Robin'. Leslie, she recalled, was equally unorthodox. He was fourteen, 'never very quick-witted', and Nancy suspected that Larry took against him for letting down the family intellectually: 'Larry would make him look a fool any time he liked, and any time Leslie crossed him he used to absolutely flay him,' by which she meant he would verbally belittle his younger brother.

There was episode in which Larry 'hopped into bed' with Nancy and shortly afterwards 'Gerry hopped into bed too'. None of them saw this as anything other than familial conviviality, at least until Louisa burst into the bedroom and said she had never been so disgusted in her life. "'What a way to behave!" she said, shouting. "*Out* you go, *out* you go this minute, out you *both* go, five minutes and you must get out, I'm not having Gerry corrupted!'"

Nancy was not sure how to respond. Clearly, Louisa implied that she and Larry had lured her infant son into the culture of depravity they brought with them from London. But at the same time the Bournemouth house was made up of abnormalities. As Nancy pointed out:

> Mother [Louisa] used to drink a lot of gin at that time, and she used
> to retire to bed when Gerry went to bed ... and she'd take a bottle of
> gin up with her when she went. So, then *we all* used to retire up there,
> carrying a gin bottle to bed. (*Ibid.*)

Multiple occupation of the same bed, often with shared bottles of gin,
seemed to be a routine habit in the Bournemouth household and in
the light of this Louisa's accusation that Gerry would be 'corrupted' by
joining Larry and Nancy appeared ridiculous. Nancy implies in her
recollections that Louisa treated her as a dangerous outsider. She was
having sex with one member of the Durrells and might therefore be
capable of infecting the rest with these practices. For Louisa, the notion
of teenage siblings sharing a bed with each other, their parent and a bottle
was magically untainted by hints of sex because all of this happened in
the weird fairyland of Dixie Lodge. Larry and Nancy threatened this
fantastic idyll.

Larry too felt apprehensive about Nancy's presence in Bournemouth,
but for reasons quite different from Louisa's unease, and he drove
her back to London as soon as he could. He had a temperamental
commitment to metropolitan depravity – seeing it as a collateral element
of experimentalist art – and he feared that extended involvement with
his family's innocent parochial version might draw the attention of his
girlfriend to how both shared something of the absurd.

In the capital they decided to set up a photographic agency called
Witch Photos, a deliberate pun on words designating choice and satanism.
Photography as an art form had gained ground at the same time that
modernism had influenced all other long-established aesthetic genres,
and Larry and Nancy wanted to make money from portrait photographs
while wearing this new form of expression and representation as a
radical fashion accessory.

They rented a loft in Millman Street and furnished it with a large
imitation-leather armchair for their subjects plus a rolltop desk and
some antiquated furniture for an untidy bohemian set. Behind the
camera tripod was an enlarger, developer, light-sensitive paper and one
Pike (Christian name unknown), who unlike Larry and Nancy knew
how to produce photographs. They had few customers, most notably

A. J. A. Symons, recommended to them by Wilkinson. Symons was about to complete his bizarre *The Quest for Corvo*, part biography of Frederick Rolfe, the self-styled Baron Corvo, part autobiographical reflex by Symons on his own obsession with Rolfe. Symons wanted several photographic portraits of himself to emphasise the self-possessed nature of his book and Pike, following Larry's instructions on how to catch various expressions of displacement and loss, got to work. But something went wrong with the loading of the film plates and the use of the developing acid, and Symons came out resembling a figure from a Dalí painting. He returned for a second sitting. Their friend Peter Bull came for portraits, for no other reason that he needed framed likenesses of himself in a Savile Row suit to boost his acting career. Their other customers were drawn to the studio because of Nancy's association with the stage. Sometimes she had worked in Soho nightclubs when plays weren't available and Witch Photos became a magnet for men who dealt in pornography. Dancers and waitresses were brought in to pose in underwear or naked and Larry, Nancy and Pike did the work.

Financially they were secure enough but the enterprise caused them disquiet, particularly for Nancy. She had made use of family legacies to set it up and on the 8 May her family gave her a silver fox fur for her birthday. She sold it to purchase sophisticated photographic equipment. Pike did his job without comment but for Larry and Nancy the profitability of erotica seemed to have overridden their zeal for the aesthetics of photography.

In the late summer of 1933 Larry, Nancy and Pam and George Wilkinson set off from London in Louisa's Hillman saloon for the Sussex coast. They had no specified agenda or clear objective – each seemed to enjoy the uncertainty of whether it was a day out or if they might stay over somewhere. Pam later recalled that they talked about finding a 'beamy' centuries-old cottage which they might rent for a few days, and when they drove towards the quaint village of Loxwood, about halfway between London and Sussex coast, they came across a half-timbered detached house with a spacious garden. It was called Chestnut Mead, stood about a mile from other properties, and on the 'To Let' sign was the owner's address in nearby Loxwood, to which they drove. Still, at this point, none of them was quite certain of their short- or long-term

27

plans, or so those who later recalled these events claimed. But if we read between the lines of their recollections, we detect a subliminal consensus. They did not explicitly decry or distance themselves from the chaotic bohemianism of the rundown districts of the West End with its dissolute eccentrics, some making claims on aristocratic legacies or forging new credos for writing, painting or living. Privately they knew that most of those they mixed with were no-hopers and they did not wish to share a collective destiny of underachievement.

So, while none of them would confess to it, they conformed. Chestnut Mead was well-appointed with two study bedrooms which George and Larry could claim as their own. The furnishings were unostentatious but comfortable and the owner had stored enough logs and coal to keep each of the large open fires burning for the winter. They agreed to rent the cottage for at least twelve months and Nancy and Pam slipped into the roles routinely allocated to the women of the house: tending the garden, cleaning and cooking. They did, however, ensure that Larry and George listened to their caustic opinions on art, society and politics.

Europe was becoming more polarised between far-right nationalism and communism and while many of their friends in London had espoused extremism as a stamp of idiosyncrasy Pam and Nancy urged their partners to take seriously the prospects for their continent and their country, and think about something other than art. They were indulged and ignored, and during autumn and winter, in what Larry had renamed as Little Songhurst Cottage, the two men spent long hours in their private studies typing away on works that were resolutely conceited and apolitical. Nothing survives of Wilkinson's attempts at literary writing – we do not know if he was attempting verse, prose fiction or something else, but he confided to Larry that it was an exercise in self-absorption. Larry committed himself to what would become his first significant work to go into print.

Pied Piper of Lovers would be published by Cassell in 1935 almost a year after Larry completed it – in Little Songhurst Cottage. It is, as already stated, autobiographical, but at the same time speculative, even delusional. Larry continually edits his life as if he were composing a memoir in the manner of alternative history novels. Notable examples of the latter include Robert Harris's *Fatherland* (1992) in which Germany triumphs in Europe in the Second World War and Kingsley Amis's *The Alteration* (1976) where Luther foreswears rebellion and becomes Pope. Like the historical novelists Larry follows the authentic narrative, in this case his own life, while choosing to alter the actual history at key points. Notably, he begins with causing his mother's death before he ever meets her, during his birth. There are fragments of truth in this given that his was a difficult birth, though as an infant he suffered the effects more so than Louisa. Or so he claimed. The strange mythology of his early childhood, such as the servants feeding him with warm blood from freshly killed chickens every morning to strengthen him, was circulated by Larry during his adulthood, after he had completed *Pied Piper of Lovers*. Altering truth for his novel would become his personal and creative fiat, and eventually, in his most celebrated work, he would abandon completely all notions of credibility and coherence. Pieces such as *The Alexandria Quartet* owed little allegiance to the world as we routinely apprehend it.

Typing in his first-floor study in the cottage Larry set about reshaping his past and allowing words to overpower facts. He turned himself into an orphan and with a slight nod towards actuality denied existence to his siblings without having to kill them. Like his author, Clifton was the first-born child, but his parents would not live on and procreate, and he would spend his teens and early adulthood alone in England. Larry's only concession to verity was his creation of Clifton's aunt Brenda, a rather stuffy Edwardian relic who reprimands him for apparent moral degeneracy. Brenda is a hybrid of Louisa and the weird assembly of female relatives who were drawn to the hapless Durrell household.

During the year at Little Songhurst he limited his visits to his mother's house to around one every month, and rarely if ever did he stay the night. He was weaning himself off his family's influence and his reluctant emotional dependency on them, enabling himself to become temperamentally closer to Clifton, his invention, his man without a family. The episodes in London are close enough to a memoir, with adjustments. Clifton's artistic dedication is to music, the composition and performance of jazz, and while Larry sometimes played jazz piano in clubs there is no hint that Clifton ever has literary ambitions. So once more we find Larry taking a step back from his life without fully removing himself from it.

Clifton's lover, Ruth, though hazily sketched, is based in part on Nancy. The principal difference between them is that Ruth is terminally ill and we know that soon after the novel ends Clifton will be entirely alone. Was Larry indulging a slightly morbid fantasy? Nancy read the novel as it progressed and confessed to some feelings of disquiet. Larry had never disguised the fact that Clifton was a reflection of himself but he was less forthcoming about why he had chosen to refashion the figures who surrounded him and his creation by getting rid of them.

The only other significant female character is Isobel, with whom Clifton has a relationship. She is probably the most compelling figure in an assembly of flawed creations and she can hold her own with the men in arguments on everything from money to the nature of existence. Intellectually she outranks Clifton, and their parting is quite moving. She loves him yet pities his immaturity and inadequacies, knowing that it will be best for each of them if he is allowed to deal with his quandaries alone. It is a compliment on Larry's part to the woman he was with. He will not patronise her by dragging her into Clifton's struggles with his self-inflicted predicaments; she can leave if she wishes to. Nancy's middle name is Isobel.

During the spring of 1934 Larry was revising the novel and George Wilkinson confessed that he had wasted the previous eight months completely. While he matched the incessant tap-tap rhythm of his friend's typewriter in the room below all that resulted were overflowing wastepaper baskets, the contents of which he burned in the downstairs fireplace before anyone, Pam included, could read what he had decided was worthless.

In May he announced that he had given up, without expanding on what he had decided to abandon or if he would ever return to the enterprise. He and Pam got married in a nearby registry office and told Larry and Nancy that their honeymoon would be a bicycle trip through continental Europe. They hoped to reach Corfu before the close of summer and left the cottage at the beginning of June. Shortly afterwards Count Potocki arrived unannounced, in ceremonial costume, and accompanied by his American mistress, known only as 'Madame'. She was dressed like an extra from the 1926 film adaptation of *The Great Gatsby*, except at fourteen stone she might have seemed out of place, as would her variously sullen and shrieking teenage son. Potocki claimed for himself and his entourage the rooms previously occupied by the Wilkinsons. If any doubts remained about Larry's attachment to the bohemians of London these were dispelled the following day when he left the cottage for good without speaking to Potocki and moved in with his mother in Bournemouth.

Nancy, heroically, helped Potocki and his new family to settle into a nearby property and then followed Larry to Louisa's house. Neither of them would ever meet the Count again and nor would they regret the loss. At the close of *Pied Piper* Clifton hints that England holds nothing for him. 'I feel I've been imprisoned for a long time.' Customarily critics treat this as the declaration of Larry/Clifton that the smug insularity of middle-class Britain stifles anyone with artistic or intellectual ambitions. But one has to wonder how Larry really felt about a country that provided a home for the many pretentious delinquents whose company he appeared to treasure in the early 1930s.

Larry's debut novel draws upon a particular strand of modernism that has, with the assistance of Anthony Julius, caused an explosive debate. As Julius pointed out, the representation of Jews as endemically loathsome figures in T. S. Eliot's major poems was excused, defended by apologists for the poet, as 'art speaking for itself'; in short, the poems dramatised antisemitism but did not endorse it or express the prejudices of their author. Which is, of course, nonsense. Accept this argument and you allow for 'literary' texts to foreground a limitless amount of foul prejudices while allowing them protection within the grey area of aesthetics.

Compared with *Pied Piper of Lovers* Eliot's work comes across as relatively philosemitic. Between page 182 and page 222 there are eleven representations of Jews as physically or morally abhorrent. It would be bad enough if two or three Jews had been picked out for abuse but within over twelve thousand words at least nine separate individuals are chosen, or rather invented, as grotesques. Those who were in some sort of discreditable trade, mostly landlords, are described as predatory, animalistic figures who 'grappled' their 'hard hands' together and made 'grasping demands'. Typically, Jewish women had 'black, weary-looking eyes, [with] their bodies under their coloured coats supple as greyhounds'. A Jewish prostitute has a 'pinched little Jew-face ... dark and attractive' and the fact that Clifton is sexually stimulated appals him, fills him 'with a senseless rage, a fear for his own body ... he turned from her in a bitter disgust ...' Clifton's own landlord is 'both a businessman and a Jew – a formidable combination under any government'. In a nightclub 'Mrs Gluckstein, the Queen Bee' retreats to an alcove as revellers arrive, taking her dog with her. There the two of them 'carried on their exchange of witticism'. Evidently, Mrs Gluckstein and her dog have a good deal in common. A group of Jews share a complexion described as 'sallow' and 'pallid', and 'their coats were padded out about the shoulders to give them the appearance of physique which they did not possess'. Once more, the implication is that beings of a lesser breed can disguise themselves as human.

During the interwar years the presentation of Jews in literature as variously suspect and subhuman was the badge of honour for writers making claims on radicalism. Eliot was the chief felon with Pound not far behind, but figures such as Orwell and Hemingway were almost as bad. Larry had read Eliot's poems of the 1920s. The following passage is from 'Gerontion':

My house is a decayed house
And the Jew squats on the windowsill, the owner,
Spawned in some estaminet of Antwerp,
Blistered in Brussels, patched and peeled in London.

Pied Piper of Lovers is a strung-out prose version of this and Larry evidently wanted to join the club of artists for whom antisemitism was a routine gesture. It is difficult to explain this collective obsession. Perhaps the stereotypes of Jewishness – notably involving greed and financial advancement – were seen as an anathema to art and creativity. Equally, the extreme modernists might have treated Jewishness as an unfortunate inheritance, comparable to the time-worn artistic conventions they were so determined to undermine. Either way Larry's participation in this loathsome consensus is self-evident.

In Bournemouth, his sense of having returned to the cul-de-sac of family life was abated by his chance meeting in H. G. Commin's bookshop with Alan Thomas. Thomas was assistant manager to the shop's owner, Ernest Cooper, and as he and Larry talked about books and writing they sensed a curious empathy, despite on the face of things having little in common. Thomas came from a Quaker family and still adhered to his own brand of pacifist Christianity. He was almost six foot five, which meant that speaking with Larry usually caused both to have to sit down. Larry entered his height on his passport as five foot four; in truth he had added two inches. Larry's cultivated persona as an extrovert – mirrored in his invention, Clifton – was the antithesis of Thomas; well-mannered and the epitome of order and rectitude. Nonetheless Larry was fascinated by his new acquaintance's confession that he was a self-advocated medievalist, who could read Old and Middle English and who took delight in a culture because it was so obscure and esoteric. Larry did not share any of his interests but he was impressed by Thomas's refusal to grandstand his eccentricities. Thomas was authentically odd.

Thomas introduced him to Patrick Evans, another young man from a Quaker background but who had rebelled against all forms of religion. He had studied at Oxford and still lived in the spacious late-Edwardian mansion his mother and father had built inland from Bournemouth on the edge of the New Forest. The three men shared an interest in jazz piano which mutated into the composition of irregular and obscene limerick poems. They spent much of their time drinking in local country pubs, particularly those with pianos and indulgent landlords.

Nancy found Larry's new friends agreeable enough but was dismayed by his apparent contentment with fecklessness. He had sent the typescript of his novel to Cassell, one of the more prestigious London publishers, yet seemed unconcerned with whether or not they would reply to him. So far, they had not even acknowledged the receipt of the work.

Between July and October 1934, Larry and Nancy decided on how to shift themselves out of their state of limbo. Or, to be more accurate, a sequence of letters during this period from the Wilkinsons determined their future and that of the entire Durrell family, though neither Pam nor George were at the time aware of the repercussions of their correspondence. By early July they reported on their experiences cycling through the Austrian Alps and from then through to late autumn they charmed Larry and Nancy with what amounted to weekly instalments of a Baedeker telling of northern Italy, the Balkan states, mainland Greece and then a ferry ride to the island of Corfu, barely twelve miles from the coast. In September they'd found a house to rent, close to the sea, and George's presentation of the area as a flawed idyll reads rather like an adult version of Gerry's *My Family and Other Animals*. He reports that the panorama of colours – the azure sea and a sky that flickered with gold at sunset – could only be savoured at the price of relentlessly hungry mosquitos. Unlike in England, it never seemed cold and because of this, everywhere stank horribly: open-pit lavatories were unavoidable. But they were having a sailing boat built for £8, roughly the cost of two pairs of custom-made shoes. Why walk when you can simply float from beach to beach, he asked his friend.

George commented that he had completed almost 20,000 words of a book and felt that the trip across Europe, and then Corfu, had enabled him to crystallise his previously unclear ambitions. He wanted to be a travel writer. Reading his letters Larry and Nancy agreed and sadly their encouragement is all that remains of his project. Gradually and incessantly Larry and Nancy ransacked their friend's enthusiasm. Larry began to read everything available in local libraries on Minoan civilisation and the state of the islands during classical antiquity while Nancy became obsessed with the remains of Byzantine wall painting in the region. On 7 September George had asked, a little flippantly, 'Why not come out?' and for the remainder of the year a hypothesis matured into a plan.

When Larry replied to George the latter thought that his friend had treated the invitation as tomfoolery given that Larry had declared that 'all would come', adding that a suitable school would have to be found for Gerry. George had spent months listening to Larry's complaints about his family, implying they variously embodied the worst aspects of Englishness, the imperial heritage included, and that he wished to separate himself from them and the country as soon as he could. Flabbergasted, George replied, 'D'you all intend coming (!) and how many is all?' Yes, Larry stated, every one of the family would come to Corfu. He was taking with him a coterie of figures struggling to cope in southern England to an island that was economically backward and in other respects an eclectic legacy of occupations by various European powers, notably the French, the British and the Venetians.

Nancy and Larry decided to marry in Bournemouth Registry Office in January 1935, an event surrounded by numerous fascinating stories. Larry's later comment that he chose not to inform Louisa because he was desperate to avoid the flamboyance she would insist on is credible enough; as is Nancy's claim that she kept it from her parents for the same reason. The rest of the legend, cultivated over the years by Larry, comes across as a short story again in the manner of Wodehouse. Alan Thomas, who unlike others from the period in England would remain a close though absent friend of Larry, was initially invited to be best man yet Larry changed his mind when he foresaw the registrar mistaking the tall, angular man as the groom rather than the little man dwarfed by Nancy. Larry explained this to Thomas and asked if he knew someone 'a bit shorter' in the area who could stand in. He recommended Jack Watts, whom he knew as a regular at Commin's bookshop. Larry agreed and found that Watts was a figure he'd known from his time in Bloomsbury before he met Nancy, when both men had involved themselves in behaviour that few would openly admit to. Nonetheless Watts and Thomas accompanied Larry to the registry office but the latter asked them to wait while he briefly visited a travelling circus which advertised performances by dwarfs. He asked the manager if one of these little people might be loaned or rented to him as to serve as best man because Watts, though slight, was too tall. The answer was no. When they arrived at the registry office Larry pulled a copy of Rabelais' poems from his pocket and insisted that all oaths should be sworn on it rather than the Bible. The registrar reprimanded him for demeaning this 'deeply serious thing' and soon afterwards the groom realised that he had left the ring on Louisa's mantelpiece. Interviewed by her daughter Joanna Hodgkin for *Amateurs in Eden* Nancy stated that, apart from the marriage being held in secret, the rest was a myth spun by Larry. He seemed addicted to fiction, literary or otherwise.

There are ludicrously contrasting accounts on how the decision was reached that the entire family should go to Corfu. Bowker affirms that Larry persuaded his mother that 'life in Corfu was cheap and pleasant, and that they would enjoy themselves much as they had in India, living an independent life among peasants' (p55). Gerry, in *My Family and Other Animals*, dramatises an exchange between Larry, Louisa and Leslie in which the first rages against the English climate as the cause of physical and spiritual decay.

> It was Larry, of course, who started it ... 'Why do we stand this bloody climate?' he asked suddenly, making a gesture towards the rain-distorted window. 'Look at it! And if it comes to that, look at us ... Margo swollen up like a plate of scarlet porridge ... Leslie wandering around with fourteen fathoms of cotton wool in each ear ... Gerry sounds as though he's had a cleft palate from birth ... And look at you [Louisa]: you're looking more decrepit and hag-ridden every day. (p8)

In *Amateurs in Eden* Joanna Hodgkin reports that Louisa at first objected to uprooting the family from England but fell into line once she realised she was outnumbered, even by Leslie – generally feckless but now filled with enthusiasm. They had lived in England for just six years, and in that time moved house frequently and had put down no real roots. Nancy quotes Louisa as saying,

> Well, I'm not going to stay here if you're going to Corfu. What d'you expect me to do, with all these children? We're coming too! (*Amateurs in Eden*, pp146–7)

Another version of who decided on what can be found in Gerry's notes for his autobiography in the Jersey Archive in which he discloses that Louisa's taste for gin was more than a recreational indulgence and that his elder brother 'feared for her.' She was an alcoholic, prone to bouts of depression and maniacal behaviour. Larry did not exactly rejoice in taking his mother and siblings with him to the eastern Mediterranean, but he feared that if left alone with the children in Bournemouth, the family would face poverty and destitution without someone who could at least offer guidance on simple matters such as how the house was heated and cleaned: him. None of the others involved in the move from England to Corfu mention the role played in this by Louisa's alcohol dependency, but it is evident from Gerry's autobiographical fragments that each of them was aware of it.

Before Gerry published *My Family* there was no public account of the Durrells' journey to Corfu and thereafter the book was accepted as the truthful story of this eccentric English family abroad. Margo had packed 'a multitude of diaphanous garments, three books on slimming, and a regiment of small bottles each containing some elixir guaranteed to cure acne'. Leslie, along with a couple of rolltop pullovers, brought with him an extra pair of trousers in which he had wrapped two First World War-vintage revolvers and instead of clothing found space in his baggage for a book called *Be Your Own Gunsmith* and a large leaky can of oil to service his collection of firearms. Larry's clothes were crammed into a briefcase while his two large trunks bulged with books, and Louisa 'sensibly' divided her luggage between clothes and cookbooks. Gerry, in his account, took only those items he 'thought necessary to relieve the tedium of a long journey': a jam jar full of caterpillars, his dog, a butterfly net and four books on natural history (pp10–11). He pays no attention to Nancy's baggage, or to be more accurate she herself has already attained the status that will endure for the entire book: non-existent.

According to Gerry in *My Family* the whole family took the ferry to France and went from there to Switzerland, then Italy and then via a short boat trip to mainland Greece, a route only slightly different from the romantic odyssey of the Wilkinsons. This was a lie. Larry and Nancy left Tilbury on 2 March 1935 on the P&O liner SS *Oronsay* for Naples, they took the train to Brindisi and from there the overnight ferry to Corfu. The rest of the family boarded the Japanese SS *Hakone Maru* in London, a cargo ship with upper deck cabins for passengers, which called at Gibraltar and then docked at Corfu roughly a week after Nancy and Larry had arrived on the island.

The legend of the Durrells will forever be shadowed by Gerry's account of the years in Corfu, even more so given that the film and television adaptations have, for a massive global audience, eclipsed Larry's reputation as a literary artist. Amusingly, the thirty-one-year-old cash-strapped naturalist who wrote *My Family* proved to be as talented a fiction writer as his acclaimed brother, notably because he claimed to be telling the truth.

2

A Dysfunctional Family

The Durrells' life in Bournemouth was presented by those closely involved in it or by observers in so many different ways that we will probably never have a trustworthy picture of what went on. Alan Thomas recalled, much later, 'There never was more generous hospitality. Nobody who has known the family at all well can deny that their company is "life enhancing"' – yet along with this there will be 'furious arguments and animated conversation ... going on long into the night' (Botting, p23). Molly Briggs, a cousin of the Durrell siblings on their father's side, commented to Botting that while Gerry was 'a beautiful little boy, really, and great fun', Leslie had coached him in bad behaviour. 'Both Gerry and Leslie ran rings round Aunt Lou and were quite unmanageable.'

> Leslie drove Aunt Lou mad at this time, staying in bed till midday and slouching about. He never settled to anything, never saw anything through ... my sister and I didn't like him very much. Sometimes he would condescend to play with us, but you never knew from one minute to the next how he would behave. He would suddenly turn nasty for no reason at all. (*Ibid.*, p26)

How exactly Leslie began to acquire his collection of firearms when in his mid-teens remains a mystery but the revolvers that Larry stated he took to Corfu were real enough – First World War-vintage, 455-calibre pieces that could down a bull at fifty yards – as was his Winchester 1907 semi-automatic rifle, and his Lee–Enfield bolt-action 303. During the interwar years firearms regulations were flexible to say the least. The Firearms Act of 1920 stated that only those 'under fourteen' or 'drunk or insane' could be restricted in the possession or use of guns. Leslie enjoyed target shooting as a compensation for the lack of wildlife in Bournemouth and its environs, though according to neighbours the pet dogs of the locality sometimes mysteriously disappeared.

Both Gerry in *My Family* and Hodgkin in her memoir on Nancy present Louisa during this period as quaintly batty and happy to indulge the various foibles and eccentricities of her children, even those approaching early adulthood. They say little of Leslie but imply that his mother was content enough with his hobby. Larry spent his time writing, Gerry collected insects and frogs – so why would she be distressed that Leslie had become a Hampshire gunman?

Read though the various fragments and reflections, in print and unpublished, and one occasionally glimpses something more disturbing beneath this superficial display of amiable chaos. Louisa cooked obsessively, almost always Anglo-Indian dishes that she had memorised from sketchbooks by servants from her time in the subcontinent. Visitors were amused, fascinated, and also puzzled. Why did she not offer the family traditional British meals – roasts, stews, bacon and eggs – perhaps even to emphasise the difference between the conservative cuisine of England and the adventurous, spice-laden dishes of South Asia? Nancy, much later, began to suspect that her obsession with Indian food reflected a slight mental imbalance. Her late husband Lawrence adored curries as part of the culture of the Raj. Now he was buried there Louisa couldn't quite detach herself from her life with him before the limbo of widowhood in England. He, and India, were essential parts of who she was and her preoccupation with the food of her childhood and her married life was all she had left.

Several times she went into a mental institution and on each occasion Gerry, the youngest and most vulnerable child, remained at home in the care of a Miss Burroughs, a freelance governess whose effect on him, still only seven during Louisa's first absence, can best be described as life-changing. According to Gerry in his unpublished notes Miss Burroughs insisted that he must be protected from adults who might visit the house uninvited. She seemed to assume that there was the possibility of a kidnapping and she had double locks fitted on all external and internal doors and made sure that he was unable to move from one room to another without her permission. To visit the lavatory, he would need to summon her by ringing a school playground bell she'd placed at his disposal. The garden was out of bounds and he, as he put it in his memoir, had been 'kidnapped' by her. At night he had no choice but to urinate onto joints between the wooden floor beneath rugs. His closest friend was his nervous mongrel Simon, but Miss Burroughs insisted that Simon must be confined to the garden. She believed that all dogs carried fleas and germs and Gerry's only contact with his pet came when he heard him whining at night, still denied access to the house. This ceased for good when the noise from the chimney-sweeper's motorcycle panicked Simon to flee into the road where his head was crushed under the front wheel of a neighbour's car. Miss Burroughs cooked for the family in a manner that contrasted startlingly with Louisa's subcontinental cuisine. Breakfast involved unerringly bland porridge; fruit, jam or compote additions were forbidden. Dickensian gruel-like broth was standard fare for lunch, and recently invented tinned convenience foods did for dinner with ungenerously buttered bread. Margo and Leslie borrowed food from friends. Their bedrooms were spared from her maniacal regime of double-locked imprisonment and they spent as much time away from the family home as they could.

Leslie's obsession with guns intensified during his mother's months away, particularly when Miss Burroughs cast her menacing shadow over the household. He and Margo felt like outsiders, mercifully spared the attention of the strange governess yet largely avoided by their elder brother who never visited the Bournemouth house when Louisa was absent. No one spoke of her problem or its cause, then or later, and the only surviving record are the unambiguous disclosures in Gerry's memoir. She was perpetually anxious and depressed, which contrasts with Alan Thomas's presentation of her as a jocular eccentric. But Gerry also explains why the behaviour could be perceived differently, depending on whether one was part of the family group or an occasional visitor to the house. She was a severe alcoholic. The fun-loving character who sometimes took a gin bottle to bed was in truth a woman who buried her despair in drunkenness from breakfast-time onwards.

One of the most unsettling passages in Gerry's account of his childhood is of when he slept alone with Louisa, very different from Nancy's story of amiable bed-sharing and gin-swigging. 'At the end of the day I would have my bath and then ... I would climb into the bed I shared with Mother ... Then Mother would come to bed and I would curl up against her warm body in its silk nightgown and frequently I would wake to find myself pressed up against her in a state of arousal' (Jersey Archive, undated). He would just have reached puberty and he does not comment on how he feels retrospectively, decades later about feelings verging on incest. The quotation comes from his early-1990s notes and he says nothing of whether Louisa played any part in causing his erection.

Gerry refers to his mother's disappearances as her 'rest cures', a polite way of disclosing that while her mood swings and depressions would continue they might in the short term be alleviated by her being dried out. The first of these took place in mid-October 1932. We don't know the name of the institution that received her but records survive of her other, preferred destination (Jersey Archive). She had booked and paid for a passage on the Ellerman Line's SS *City of Calcutta*, which would sail for India from Liverpool on 29 October. The only other ticket for the journey was for Gerry. It requires no expertise in psychoanalysis to draw conclusions on the mental state of a woman who could not bear the loss of her husband and their shared life in India and who now planned to return there with their very young son. Evidently, they did not sail but we know nothing of whether Louisa disembarked voluntarily or if someone else intervened.

Who choreographed the nightmare of the Durrell years in Bournemouth, notably the removal of Louisa and the installation of Miss Burroughs? Gerry says nothing of this in his autobiographical fragments but the circumstantial evidence leaves a clear enough trail. The various cousins and more distant relatives had no authority regarding the organisation or financing of family business, and nor did any known lawyer. Aside from Louisa, who was self-evidently incapacitated, the senior member of the family was Larry.

The individuals who set off for Corfu in 1935 were in their ways idiosyncratic but certainly not in the way Gerry presented them in *My Family*. They were damaged and, apart from Larry, perplexed.

The story of the Durrells going south as a collective enterprise is a distortion of the truth. Aside from the fact that Nancy and Larry and the others took separate routes, Larry had originally agreed only to allow Louisa and Gerry to join them in Corfu, in fear that without him she would drink herself to death in England or endanger the lives of his siblings, Margo and Leslie, whom he expected would stay. He planned to employ a permanent housekeeper, an improvement on the hideous Miss Burroughs about whom Leslie and Margo had complained. But Margo reported to the headteacher at Malvern School that she was leaving to move abroad, and Leslie did the same at Pangbourne College in Berkshire where he had recently become a boarder. Each informed Larry that they would go too and he was left with no choice. He arranged for the house to be sold. The Durrell expedition to the Ionian Sea was a mixture of accidents and expediencies.

Larry and Nancy arrived first but there is no reliable record of the date. We know they were held up in Brindisi because from the Hotel Internazionale in the city Larry wrote to Alan Thomas of their being delayed by an attempted military coup in Greece. Larry ridiculed the events, claiming that the leader of the rebels – probably General Nikolaos Plastiras – had been smuggled from Italy to Athens 'disguised as a cargo of garlic', and that thereafter boat traffic to the Greek islands was suspended. The letter was dated as 14 March, by which point most of the rebels had been defeated. Larry also claimed that he had found the skipper of a small boat who promised to land them at Corfu town during the following night despite the fact that military action had engulfed the area. The authenticity of this is questionable, given that the coup was over by 11 March and had affected only the mainland rather than the islands. The remainder of his letter to Thomas reads like an adventure story, with the couple heading recklessly, joyfully, into a chaotic war zone. He portrays the attempted coup as a farce with live ammunition. The Greeks, he reports, were the wild romantics of Byronic lore, too passionate about their shared legacy to actually shoot at each other. He tells of shells fired deliberately into the sea to avoid damaging naval vessels and rifles and machine guns discharged only into the air 'so as not to hurt their friends'. Perhaps the rascal boatman who offered them passage to the island was part of the fantasy (Lawrence Durrell Archive, British Library, undated). They reached Corfu town within a week of the letter of the 14th, booked into the Pension Suisse in the old town and reserved bedrooms for the rest of the family who would arrive a fortnight later.

The buildings in the town reflected its unsettled history, with medieval fortifications and political residences dating from the fourteenth to the late eighteenth century, periods when it had been an outpost of the Venetian nobility. The more delightful houses looked as if they had been transported from the banks of the Grand Canal. These would have been the streets onto which Larry and Nancy disembarked in spring 1935. A few years after the Venetian period residencies were built by the French during the occupation in the Napoleonic Wars and following that the British took over and imposed an orderly infrastructure of macadam roads and piped water. During the Second World War many of the Greek, Italian and French buildings were damaged or destroyed.

Larry wasn't looking forward to the arrival of his mother and siblings but Louisa handed him a letter that would change his life significantly. It was from his recently acquired agent Spencer Curtis Brown who informed him that Cassell had accepted *Pied Piper* with an offer of a £50 advance. He telegraphed his acceptance the following day, searched for champagne in bars and shops, found none and made do with the Greek sparkling wine *afrodi* and a bottle of ouzo. Even before he saw the disappointing reviews, he regretted writing the book, but it was in print with a prestigious publisher; he was on his way. He and Nancy had stayed only two nights in the Pension. They then moved to a villa which the Wilkinsons had found for them on the coast about three miles south of Corfu town. Larry greeted his family at the docks, though how he knew of the exact details of their arrival remains a mystery since neither he nor the Wilkinsons had a telephone. He left them at the Pension and promised to make enquiries about finding them a house, and he wrote to Pat Evans 'Like the blue fart that she [Louisa] is, she says the heat is too much, the flies too many, and the Greeks too insanitary I'm afraid she might go back any day. What a waste of money!' (*Ibir*

43

Even though it was still early spring, and cold, Louisa insisted that the rooms at the Pension were infested with lice and mosquitos. Margo, aged sixteen, cried every day, for no other reason than that she found herself in a foreign land that offered her no more than the essentials of existence. She no longer went to school and no one wished to answer her occasional enquiries in English. Leslie became a little demented, first screaming at the young man at the Pension reception that he must have 'paper!' Shown copies of month-old national dailies from France and Britain he shrieked that he wanted 'paper' for the lavatory which his family shared with others on the same floor. Rage caused him to unpack one of his guns and fire randomly at gulls and wood pigeons perched on roofs opposite their rooms.

In *My Family* Gerry tells of a Mr Beeler, 'the hotel guide', who made enquiries about house rentals and disappointed Louisa by failing to find a place with a bathroom. Beeler was an invention but Gerry introduced him as a prelude to a very real figure, Spyros Chalikiopoulos, or Spiro as he would become in the mythology of the Durrells in Corfu. In *My Family* the family are pestered by taxi drivers intent on swindling them, only to hear 'a deep, rich vibrant voice'. '"Thems been worrying yous?" he asked Mother ... "Yous wants someones who can talks your own language ... thems bastards ... if yous will excuses the words ... would swindles their own mothers. Excuses me a minute and I'll fix thems."' Spiro was sitting in a spacious open-top Dodge saloon, which dated from the mid-1920s but was probably the most spectacular car on the island. It was certainly the only one built in the United States. As Spiro explained to his English 'family', the vehicle testified to his sophisticated recent history. He had spent six years in Brooklyn and Chicago, doing jobs that seemed suspect and tantalising, and he was indeed known on the island as Spiro Americanos. Spiro found them a house with, as Louisa demanded, a bathroom, a bungalow villa only a mile from Larry and Nancy's more spacious villa. But each of the family had a bedroom and the small garden was beautifully ordered and well-tended by whoever had previously rented the place. In *My Family* Gerry called it the 'strawberry-pink villa', surrounded by olive groves, cypress trees, exotic fruit bushes and overlooked by a 'sky still brighter blue for our arrival'.

The family was divided physically and in other respects too. Larry visited Louisa's house around once a week though he later commented in interviews that he rarely saw the rest of the family at all, except at Christmas. Things changed in October when Larry decided to move to Kalami, a hamlet of about five houses on the northeast coast as far from his mother as it was possible to be. Proportionately, in England, it was the equivalent of exchanging the coast of Kent for Lancashire. Shortly afterwards Louisa and the three children moved to Kontokali, about four miles down the coast road from Corfu town. The house was, and still is, a beautiful three-storey mansion, echoing the architectural heritage of the Venetian family who built it more than a century earlier. The grounds were extensive, more than an acre, and scattered with olive, lemon and orange groves, cypresses, banana trees, vines, palms and bamboos. These had originally been planted in a regimented form, separated by paths and small lawns, but by the time the Durrells arrived the various parts had become a near-impenetrable jungle. It was here that most of the authentic events reported in *My Family* occurred. Barely three hundred metres down the hill on which it stood was the stone beach and wooden jetty from which Gerry would make his seaborne excursions. He had his own bedroom where he stored and investigated creatures he had collected from the overgrown garden, the beach and the sea. These and the 'Daffodil Yellow Villa' contributed to the mythology of the family. According to Gerry in *My Family*, Larry was there permanently during the Durrells' time in Corfu while in truth he only visited the property on brief occasions. Nancy is removed from the book completely.

Larry soon became unsettled by aspects of Corfu's culture which contrasted with its Grecian and Venetian parentage. Britain had run the island from 1815 to 1864 and many of the locals had taken a liking to their largely benevolent governors. The indigenous gentry were Anglophiles and styled their habits and customs on what they knew of the English middle and upper classes. The supper parties to which Louisa was invited appeared to be a caricature of what she'd known in London and Bournemouth, with vaguely familiar dining etiquette and dress offset by a difficulty with the language. On one occasion she was sent an invitation which stressed the informality of the evening by asking her to come 'undressed ... in the family way'. Spiro surprised

Larry by announcing his affection for '*fermaro kai issia*', which he translated as 'block and wallop'. He meant cricket, which had been introduced to the island in 1823 with a match between the Royal Navy and the British Garrison. The Corfiots were intrigued by a game which appeared as complex and idiosyncratic as chess. Corfu town in 1935 had the longest-established cricket pitch and club in Europe outside England. Many enthusiasts were expatriates, but Corfiots attended regularly as players and spectators. It was all rather quaint and eccentric but Larry felt also that essential features of Pudding Island had followed him to the Ionian one. This was one of the reasons why he and Nancy chose to live so far from the Corfu town, the cosmopolitan base for mostly British expatriates. Louisa told her eldest that Spiro had declared that 'Honest to Gods, Mrs Durrell, you cut me open you find a Union Jack inside'.

Other things too urged Larry to move into the hinterland. He was exasperated by his family and sometimes treated his junior siblings with disdain. Nancy recalled that Leslie irritated Larry continually and that in response the latter would tell Leslie 'what a fool he was, how he'd wrecked his [own] life, slapping him down all the time'. She added that when he got angry with Larry, 'he used to point one [of his guns] at him and threaten to shoot him'. After one incident the family handed him to the so-called 'field police, a very low category of person' (Botting, p37). Gerry's story of Leslie's comic episodes with misfiring and unloaded guns in his failed attempts to shoot snipes were lies. His brother's fixation with firearms reflected something far more disturbing, notably his elder brother's tendency to humiliate him.

There is a much-quoted passage in *My Family* in which Larry accidently spills Gerry's jar of leeches. This certainly happened but it did not, as Gerry reported, result in an amicable exchange between the brothers. Larry felt that Gerry's interest in leeches was abnormal and infantile. He smashed the jar deliberately during his brother's attempt to release the wriggling parasites into the garden. Over the previous two nights Larry was unable to sleep, convinced that his seemingly maniacal sibling was using him as an experiment, hoping to find out what would happen when he released the creatures to suck Larry's blood while he slept.

Theodore Stephanides would play a unique role in the experience of the Durrells in Corfu. His was a friend of the Wilkinsons and they told him of their neighbour Lawrence Durrell; of how they had shared a cottage with Larry and Nancy in England, and that he was due to have his debut novel published in London and was working hard on his next, *Panic Spring*. So far, so good. Theodore was familiar enough with expatriates – mostly English – with literary and artistic ambitions. But the more George told him of Larry, and his family, the more he became entranced by the similarities between his and their backgrounds.

Theodore, then thirty-nine years old, had been born in Bombay in 1896. His father, Philip, was Greek by birth but had lived in India since his infancy and worked for the Ralli Brothers, a company of merchants. The Rallis were second-generation Greeks who had made a small fortune on the subcontinent and Philip married the elder daughter of the family who had been born and educated in London. Summers in Bombay were often unbearably humid and the Stephanides and Ralli families would spend these months in the cooler hill stations of Darjeeling and other parts of West Bengal. Philip Stephanides retired and moved with his family to Marseille in 1907 – three years before Louisa married Lawrence Samuel Durrell and settled in the same region of Bengal that had been the summer destination of the Stephanides.

At their first supper, hosted by the Wilkinsons, Larry and Theodore exchanged accounts of their childhoods which seemed to be slightly revised versions of the same story. Theodore disclosed that English was his first language, the one he learned and spoke in the household of his childhood, with Greek as something he was taught by his mother and his nanny prior to the family move from Marseille to Corfu in 1908. Larry valued the company of a man who shared his sense of a confused, blended heritage. Theodore was, like many other Anglophile families on the island, indulged as a respectable hybrid. His Greek was beautifully fluent and correct yet touched into national borrowings from the 'Queen's English' of the Raj. Nonetheless, he volunteered to fight with the Greek army on the Macedonian front against the combined forces of Germany, Austria and Bulgaria. He went on to serve as an infantryman in the bloody Greco-Turkish War of 1919–22, after which he was imprisoned and court-martialled for refusing to accept the return of

King Constantine I to the Greek throne at the close of 1921. Theodore was an outspoken supporter of the deposed prime minister Eleftherios Venizelos, who advocated liberalism and democracy.

In 1922 he went to Paris to study medicine at the Sorbonne and returned to Corfu as a general physician with a specialisation in radiology along with expertise in astronomy and freshwater biology. He had translated some of the finest modern Greek poetry into English for publication and he wrote verse himself in the language he felt most suitable to the genre, Shakespeare's. The term 'renaissance man' is a hackneyed cliché but Theodore comes close enough to justify its use. On the opening page of Larry's travel book *Prospero's Cell* (1945) we find, 'Other countries may offer you discoveries in manners or lore or landscape; Greece offers you something harder – the discovery of yourself.' Given the nature of the book this would usually be taken as an existential rumination, but from what we know of Larry's encounter with Theodore, the word 'harder' hints at resignation. Perhaps Theodore confronted him with the 'yourself' he wished for but had not yet attained.

In *Autumn Gleanings*, Stephanides' own memoir of Corfu in the 1930s, Larry is presented as a formidably committed artist:

> Lawrence had the happy knack of being able to compose his works straight onto the typewriter and at tremendous speed ... In those days at least ... he seemed able to turn a tap in his brain on and off at will ... Sometimes I would wake up at two or three in the morning and hear the faint, distant early click of his typewriter in his room. (p43)

This, we just assume, is the authentic Theodore, given that it is his personal account of things. A very different one – a distracted eccentric – appears in *My Family*. At the close of Chapter 13 he talks with young Gerry about the nature of toads. Theodore ponders their life expectancy. "'Well, it's difficult to say ... um ... there are no statistics to go on," he pointed out, his eyes twinkling, "but I should imagine that ones as large as these might well be twelve or even twenty years old'" (p258). Throughout the account Theodore's statements are attended by Gerry's presentation of him as rather batty ("'Ah ha!" said Theodore, and smiled in his beard'). Following the spectacle of a toad swallowing a large worm

Theodore observes, "'I wonder," said Theodore meditatively, his eyes twinkling – "I wonder if one could teach toads to swallow *swords*? It would be interesting to try'" (p259).

There is no resemblance at all between this figure and the one Larry portrays as his intellectual cohort, the embodiment of existential self-restraint and cautious sagacity.

Who do we believe? All those involved are now dead but we should note that none of the accounts of Theodore's personality and temperament, including the persona which emerges from his own writings, remotely resemble the figure depicted in *My Family and Other Animals*, whose eyes 'twinkle' at least twice during each of his appearances.

The Theodore of Gerry's recollections, or perhaps his imaginings, would be the one who became a central performer in the Durrell mythology. In the screenplay of the 2016–19 TV adaptation, written by Simon Nye, we witness Theo played by Yorgos Karamihos, a Greek actor with classically handsome features who is close enough in years to the actual Theo of the mid-to-late 1930s. His good looks are supplemented by his wacky eccentricities. Like the original, Nye's version is of a polymath; but in this interpretation he is not properly competent in any of his specialisations. One scene is largely consistent with the mood of the book but goes even further than Gerry as a misrepresentation of what actually occurred. In the TV adaptation Theo performs an appendectomy on the youngster with a textbook in one hand and scalpel in the other; his knowledge of medical science is only rudimentary. In truth Stephanides was a fully qualified and respected medical practitioner.

The authenticity of Gerry's stories of Corfu in *My Family* and the two other volumes of the trilogy is questionable, at least to the extent that the joie de vivre of family life is not too evident in the recollections of others. But while Gerry created the myth that fed the appetite of film and TV producers from the 1960s onwards, he was not the only fantasist involved. Larry completed *Prospero's Cell* in Alexandria in 1943. It too was an account of Corfu as he had known it less than a decade earlier and while the two men could not be expected to offer identical accounts the differences are extraordinary. There are hardly any 'animals' in Larry's book and his family barely seem to exist either. His recollections are of the period when he and the rest of the Durrells were co-residents of the island and while he was not particularly overjoyed by their company his complete editing of them out of the book reminds one of Stalin's purging of his past by erasing enemies from photographs. Perhaps this is why Gerry, twelve years later, got his own back by turning his elder brother into an arrogant and unsuccessful writer. On page 98 Larry does tell of how 'my brother', out shooting rabbits, runs into a man who confesses to being 'from the prison'.

'Where are you going?'
'Home. I get every weekend off.'
'What is your sentence?'
'A life sentence. I am a murderer.'

The episode, involving Leslie, is retold farcically by Gerry but we must be careful before assuming that the younger Durrell simply offers his own version of something grounded in fact, because Larry creates from it an exchange that might have come from Beckett's early fiction. The 'brother' unnamed and the bizarre murderer/convict, allowed 'every weekend off', seem more a product of the imaginative grotesque than an authentic recollection. The sibling seems almost a metaphysical presence who ventures only once into the story unaccompanied by other relatives. Larry's story of the Corfu years, which is treated as non-fictional, is as weirdly counterfeit as his brother's.

It deserves more attention because it reveals how the life of the Durrell family is made up of accounts by two competing versions of Walter Mitty. For Gerry, the family are performers in his pantomime of nostalgic innocence, while Larry rids himself of them and becomes the singular figure in an existential odyssey. He also, like Gerry, expels Nancy but perhaps for different reasons; by the time he completed the book she had left him, with their first child. The only figure allowed to travel from reality to the book is Theo, but as I've stated Larry played with the truth. Theo was certainly not Gerry's protean buffoon but nor was he Larry's introverted bohemian:

Fine head and golden beard: very Edwardian face – and perfect manners of Edwardian professor ... Tremendous shyness and diffidence. Incredibly erudite in everything concerning the island.

Firm Venezelist and possessor of the driest and most fastidious style of exposition ever seen. (Notebook for *Prospero's Cell*,, British Library Archive)

Some might claim that Larry's representation is a case of artistic licence, flattering Theo by making him a little more enigmatic. But elsewhere in *Prospero's Cell* it becomes clear why Larry has distorted the truth: the new Theo is a far more suitable member of the cast in his portrayal of the island as an aesthetic nirvana. The personae and gods of ancient Greece – 'Periander, tyrant of Corinth', his 'brutish son Lycophron', the 'Corcyrean nobles', 'Diodorus the Sicilian', etc. – feature not only as a show of Larry's erudition. He brings them into the present, as figures who endure as part of the place's magical legacy, at least for the few who see themselves as entitled enough to share it. Thus we come upon 'Count D', who dwells in a magnificently decaying mansion hidden from the main road by dense woods. The Count is presented as convincing enough but his lack of a surname or full title serves to place him also in the past, a remainder of some aristocratic lineage long displaced by the wars and political traumas of the European continent. We spend quite a while with the Count who gradually provides Larry with a cathartic revelation. He claims, with persuasive details, to know that Corfu was the true setting for Shakespeare's *The Tempest*, that the play was based on fact, records to which the Bard had access. He even implies that Shakespeare might have visited the place himself, as inspiration for the play's blend of exotica and mystification.

The Count is the most exhilarating figure in the book, but he never existed. Larry made him up.

There is an intriguing passage in which the Count, his acquaintance Zarian (a historian, and also an invention), Theo and Larry debate a question raised by the latter: "And I?" I say. "What sort of picture will I present of Prospero's island?"' (p116). The Count replies in an inscrutable manner, including many classical references, and suggests that, like Shakespeare, he must make Corfu part of his imaginative landscape, so that writing about it becomes the equivalent of accessing the intimate memories available only to those who know it.

Theo interrupts the exchange, 'suggests a stroll, and soon we are walking down the avenues of cypresses together', and they reach lawns where an unkempt nymph stands on her rotunda. 'Her loins fall away in their heavy inevitable lines to her shapely feet ... The breasts ride superbly.' The Count comments: 'An old man's love ... Look at her. There you have desire which is quite still, retained inside the mind as form and volume' (p117).

Placing Theo alongside him in this transfiguration of fact as fiction enables Larry to go further than realise some kind of artistic ambition. He is rewriting his recent past and removing from it the parts that in varying ways displeased and shamed him. The statue of the nymph, at once alluring yet absent, is as close as he comes in the book to an engagement with sexuality and one can't help feel that Nancy was on his mind as he wrote the passage. She was by everyone's account superbly attractive but now an image frozen in his memory like a statue and not a living presence in the book.

For many, *Prospero's Cell* was Larry's early literary manifesto, a commitment to place, memory and imaginative legacy at the expense of truth-telling or realism. I see it as symptomatic of a man for whom writing was a substitute for those aspects of his personality, and his sense of the world, he preferred to avoid.

Bearing in mind the statue of the nymph – stimulating, naked and impersonal – we might consider other events regarding Larry and Nancy's marriage. In 1937 she became pregnant and was shocked and appalled by his desire of a termination. His reasoning was erratic and narcissistic – a child would be more than they could afford at present, would distract him from his artistic vocation, and hers as a painter, might even have to have Greek nationality; the latter was an utterly spurious claim – and he arranged for her a back-street abortion, performed by a qualified physician in Corfu town but no less distressing for that.

Less than six months afterwards Larry and Nancy went to Paris, and Larry went on to London ostensibly to contact his agent and interested publishers and to meet T. S. Eliot. There he also had drinks and dinner with the British ballet dancer Veronica Tester and her friend and fellow dancer the Australian Dorothy Stevenson. Both were, by profession, athletically slim; and they were pretty. We do not know where or how Larry came across them but they evidently got on well because he insisted that they come to stay at his house in Corfu the following spring.

They arrived in early summer 1938, to Nancy's astonishment – he had not told his wife of their existence let alone the invitation – and moved into the house.

Sunbathing and swimming naked had been Larry and Nancy's occasional routine since they had moved in, despite the fact that local fishermen would throw stones at them for the importation of unreligious decadence. Dorothy and Veronica were even more conspicuous and rebellious. Apart from bathing unclad on the largely hidden beaches they insisted on walking between the house and the shoreline and relaxing in the garden and on the terraces without clothes. Nancy knew that Larry was sleeping with them but said nothing of this until after they had split up in 1942. In 1939 he confessed to her that he had been unfaithful with Dorothy Stevenson 'behind a rock'. In truth he had slept with four other women, including Veronica, in her bedroom in the Corfu house, and with two other women in London.

The comedic dramatisation of Corfu by Gerry would dominate public perceptions of the Durrells but *Prospero's Cell* involves something much worse; cruel self-regard would be the most apt description. It was almost understandable that Larry would exclude his family from the book. They were not really suitable companions in his story of existential and artistic self-discovery. Nancy had to go because any hint at her as part of his life there would oblige him to confront her tolerance of his greedy narcissism. He had certainly loved her. Most men would be unable to resist devoting themselves to a woman of such beauty and intelligence, but Larry wanted more. Nancy was his enticing and reliable mainstay but he enjoyed playing the field as a hedonist. His persona in the book is that of the inheritor of and participant in a classical and Renaissance culture and he did not wish to stain this image with a hint that he might be a modern version of Falstaff.

Shortly after this arrival in Corfu Larry introduced himself, albeit by letter, to a man who would become his involuntary mentor, morally and aesthetically. A few months earlier he had read Henry Miller's *Tropic of Cancer* (1934). It was banned in the United States, Miller's home country, until 1964, roughly the same period that D. H. Lawrence's *Lady Chatterley's Lover* was forbidden from publication in the UK. Each book is celebrated as breaking down the barriers between the actualities of existence, the sex lives of humans, and what can be said of these in literature. This cannot be denied but nor can the fact that as literature they are substandard. Each writer is so determined to rage against convention that they overlook matters such as credibility or an appealing storyline.

Lawrence proselytised his notion of sex as a form of metaphysical transformation while Miller's novel is a strenuous exploration and celebration of excess; including prostitution, sexual abuse, physical deformities and extremities, obsessive debauchery, etc. The main characters are: Collins, who is gay; Carl, who lives in squalor, is seemingly bisexual and prefers sex with those younger than himself; Fillmore, the diplomat, who enjoys, masochistically, the attentions of Ginette whom he has made pregnant, but eventually abandons; Carl's inamorata, 'the rich cunt, Irene'; Macha, the debauched Russian 'princess' with 'the clap'; Tania (probably based on Anaïs Nin), with whom Miller, the autobiographical narrator, is obsessed ('O Tania, where now is that warm cunt of yours, those fat, heavy garters, those soft, bulging thighs? There is a bone in my prick six inches long. I will ream out every wrinkle in your cunt'); and Van Norden, who earns Miller's respect as the most unappealingly debauched man in the story evidenced in his habit to append the label 'cunt' to every woman he attempts to seduce, successfully or not.

Dickens's characters are sometimes regarded as cartoonishly unreal and *Tropic of Cancer* comes across as Dickens rewritten by a humourless pornographer.

Larry first wrote to Miller via the British consul in Corfu in August 1935. He comments entirely on *Tropic of Cancer* and it would be an understatement to describe the letter as a case of fawning adulation. In Larry's opinion, it is 'the only really man-size piece of work which this century can really boast of. It's a howling triumph from the word go.' Compared with this novel the work of figures such as Eliot and Joyce is 'whim-wham and bagatelle'. '*Tropic* is something they've been trying to do since the war. It's the final copy of all those feeble, smudgy rough drafts – *Chatterley*, *Ulysses*, *Tarr* etc.' Miller replied almost the same day, from 18 Villa Seurat, Paris, the city in which his novel is set.

Your letter rocks me a bit too. You're the first Britisher who's written me an intelligent letter about the book. For that matter, you're the first anybody who's hit the nail on the head.

Miller stressed that he does not take Larry's praise as empty flattery. Rather that he is the first to have detected his true intent.

> The phrase that struck me particularly, in your letter, was – 'I seem to recognize it as something we were all ready for.' That's just it. The world *is* ready for something different, something new, but it seems that it requires a war or some colossal calamity to make people realize it.

A life-long friendship was born. They would correspond and meet when they could on a regular basis until Miller's death in 1980. The first tangible outcome of their relationship was Larry's *The Black Book*, begun shortly after his exchange with Miller in September 1935 but not published until 1938. It takes up where *Pied Piper* left off, or to be more accurate it recycles the material of his debut as an enthusiastic but flawed imitation of Miller's novel. The narrator is Lawrence Lucifer who is living on a Greek island and the story is his recollection of his years in England. Novels as bad as this have gone into print but none can quite outdo its awfulness. *Panic Spring* was Larry's second published novel but he wrote it after he had completed *The Black Book* and the latter occupied much of his attention over the years between its writing and its eventual acceptance by the Obelisk Press three years later. It features in most of his letters to Miller, to whom he sent a draft, and Larry seemed to take a kind of masochistic pleasure in suffering the same fate as his hero, specifically having produced a book that would appal and be rejected by the mainstream literary establishment and censored by law. The decision by Obelisk, albeit a small independent house, to risk taking it on was greeted by Larry more with resignation than triumph: he was, it seemed, not quite the outlandish equal of his mentor. Proof of his ability to outrage and disgust everyone could only be shown by unanimous letters of rejection.

With surrealist visual art shapes, faces and figures speak to each other in a warped yet sometimes beguiling conversation. In literature the correspondent result can come close to unadulterated incoherence, and this is what we find in *The Black Book*. There is some sexual grotesquery, with a nod towards Miller, but at least the latter's book is painfully readable. Larry seemed to be using impenetrable modernist techniques to smother any suspicion that the story might actually be fathomable.

There is some irony here given that Miller in *Tropic of Cancer* used his tale of bacchanalia and debauchery as a triumphant confession. Miller was as bad, often worse, as the characters in his book but this only became evident to Larry after they met in Corfu. Larry had begged him on several occasions to visit him on the 'magical' island and he did so on the eve of the declaration of the Second World War, in July 1939, two months before the Nazis invaded Poland. Miller was sufficiently impressed by the episode to turn his recollections into a book, *The Colossus of Maroussi* (1941), but he leaves out details of his first in-person encounter with Larry. He was met at the dock in Corfu town by Larry and Spiro, in his taxi, who drove them to lunch at the Kalami house. Nancy received him graciously – Miller had become her husband's source of inspiration – but she was a little surprised that he had brought a companion, an English girl, still in her mid-teens, called Meg Hurd. Miller explained that she had been his psychoanalytic patient in Paris, which struck the Durrells as odd since he had not even any amateur interests in psychoanalysis, let alone qualifications. In truth he had been, as we would put it today, grooming her. It was, the Durrells agreed, none of their business, at least until Larry introduced Miller to the shrine of Arsenius, within walking distance of the house. Miller was entranced and insisted on undressing and having sex with Meg on the monument as the Durrells, horrified, watched.

Miller and Larry visited mainland Greece and on their return the former announced to Nancy that when he visited the Acropolis in Athens he had 'felt so inspired to communicate with God' that he'd had 'an overwhelming desire to masturbate', and had done so. Nancy pretended not to have heard, or properly understood, what he had said.

Miller certainly played a role in the break-up of Larry and Nancy's marriage, though with no intention on his part. He was, perhaps to his credit, a candid and unapologetic grotesque. The life he lived was replicated with exacting honesty in his fiction. This, for Larry, presented a severe dilemma, mainly because despite himself he was entrapped in the hypocrisies of the English middle classes, a state of mind he loathed but could never quite escape from.

During their 1937 visit to Paris and London Larry and Nancy had spent time, briefly, with Anaïs Nin, and when Larry had gone to London alone he began his liaisons with the dancers Stevenson and Tester. These remained secret and Nancy only got to know of them on their arrival in Corfu. He was beginning to treat her harshly, telling her when she ventured opinions on his writing or behaviour simply to 'shut up!' The journey, albeit briefly, had introduced him to the experience of being a minor literary celebrity. In Paris they shared the apartment block with Nin, Miller, the American painter Betty Ryan, the French–Russian artist Chaïm Soutine and the Austrian writer Alfred Perlès. This was the Paris of the avant-gardists – Hemingway, Fitzgerald, Joyce, Stein et al. of a decade before. And Larry felt he belonged to it, to the extent that he returned briefly to London, this time with Nancy, and over a manic three-day period played host to Miller, T. S. Eliot and Dylan Thomas, and introduced each of the trio to the others. It sounds impressive but it was embarrassing, mostly because throughout this period Thomas was perpetually drunk – he arrived for the meeting in his socks because it was only when he reached the pub that he realised that he had left his shoes at his hotel – and the two others, Eliot and Miller, could not quite overcome their longstanding contempt for each other.

But the performance was sufficient for Larry to turn himself into an immoralist, a literary adventurer whose personal misbehaviour was licensed by his artistic radicalism. Following his seductions of the two ballerinas during his first London visit he attempted on his second to persuade the American artist Buffie Johnson to sleep with him. She made it clear that she found the prospect repulsive.

Larry's attempts to conceal his licentiousness from Nancy were by now becoming workaday and ineffective. Nin, though married, had been having an affair with Miller from 1930 onwards when he began work on *Tropic of Cancer* while he too was married to his wife June. Nin, who had once been an artist's model, paid part of the rent for Miller's apartment at 18 Villa Seurat and would eventually finance the publication of the first edition of his novel. The sex network of Nin, Miller and their respective partners was not restricted to the four of them and Miller's letter to a friend on the nature of his book tells us much about his literary and moral raison d'être. 'I start tomorrow on the Paris book: First person, uncensored, formless – fuck everything!' Larry, feeling that he was now a member of this club, made advances to Nin, which she rejected with polite but, for him, insulting humour. It was not that Miller actively encouraged Larry to become a sexual bohemian – he was too anarchistic to accept the notion of indoctrination – but Larry had become obsessed with him. The idea of becoming part of the world you had created in fiction was for Larry a necessary stage in his initiation as an artist, and this was part of his dilemma. From his teens Miller had been a non-conformist, personally and politically. He grew up in a rough area of Brooklyn, abandoned third-level education after a semester, joined the Socialist Party of America, a quasi-communist organisation, and was recklessly unfaithful to his first wife. He was the living antithesis of all the standard conventions of American society. Larry had never quite detached himself from the staidness of 'Pudding Island', England, and this included Nancy. True, she was an artist and a woman prepared to accept the nomadic lifestyle of her writer husband. But she was also Larry's anchor to a world he proclaimed to hate but which he was too anxious to fully lose. She would, he knew, be due considerable financial inheritances and she was the intermediary between him and his own family which he professed to find embarrassing but which he knew he could never abandon.

The Paris–London trips marked the end of Larry and Nancy's marriage. She decided, after his second visit to London, to go skiing in Switzerland for an indeterminate period. She went alone and it was clear that she simply wanted to be away from Larry. Her family supplied her with the necessary equipment and clothing and she calmed herself: just snow, without people she or Larry knew. In January 1938 she moved on to Innsbruck, Austria, and Larry joined her at her hotel, unannounced. He wrote to Miller: 'Now we tear each other's hair out in the very room where the poet Goethe made his celebrated stay in this pearl of a town.' He was lying. Nancy received him politely but with resignation rather than passion. It was not that Larry was attempting to convince Miller that his marriage to Nancy was robust and vigorous – Miller had no interest in the dependability of relationships – but rather he wanted to cast himself as the kind of debaucher who featured regularly in *Tropic of Cancer*. In his letters to Miller Larry is calculatedly deceitful. His family are, as in *Prospero's Cell*, perpetually absent and Nancy becomes the kind of woman Miller would recognise from his own fictional universe: 'And my wife, who is divinely mad' (20 November 1936). In truth Nancy was his stabilising presence. On 27 January 1937 he tells Miller of the circumstances in which they met. 'I hymned and whored in London – playing jazz in a nightclub, composing jazz songs ... Never really starved, but I wonder whether thin rations are not another degree of starvation. I met Nancy in an equally precarious position and we struck up an incongruous partnership: a dream of broken bottles, sputum, tinned food, rancid meat, urinals, the smell of the lock hospitals.' The 'dream' might be more accurately treated as a grotesque delusion because Larry and Nancy's time in London was never like this. When Miller got to know Nancy the sexual goddess of Larry's letters was replaced by the real version; calm and pragmatic. During their early correspondence Larry believed that the figure he invented for himself was close to the characters in the weird, lurid fabric of Miller's fiction. There is a touch of the plaintive in his own ambition to reinvent himself as a replica of his hero.

When war was declared by France and Britain following Germany's invasion of Poland, Miller became desperate. Three years earlier Orwell, on his way to fight for the POUM in the Spanish Civil War, had called on him in Paris. Miller treated Orwell's dedication to the long-term struggle against fascism in particular and authoritarianism in general with sanguine amusement, lending him a scarf as protection against the biting cold of Catalonian winters. He explained to Orwell that war was irrelevant to art, that he was wasting his talents by involving himself in Spain. By the summer of 1939, several months before war was declared and when those who thought it likely treated the Maginot Line as impregnable, Miller became neurotic about his visits to Paris; he confessed to Anaïs Nin that his presentation of himself as a pacifist aesthetician was a sham, admitting that his true commitment was to craven hedonism. En route to his months of sexual misadventure in Corfu and mainland Greece he went first to the Marseille docks to find a direct seaborne means of reaching the Ionian Sea – a curious choice – but he was determined to avoid any areas of mainland Europe that might fall prey to Germany. Even the most pessimistic figures west of Germany still felt at this point that the appeasement policy of Chamberlain and the French would postpone war indeterminately. Miller was short of funds and his decision to sail around Italy rather than taking trains through still open borders was proving expensive. Nancy, begged by Larry, paid for his journey from her family trust fund.

It is unfair to claim that Larry based his own attitude to the outbreak of war on Miller's but there are certainly parallels. Certainly, Larry looked into the possibilities of serving in the Royal Navy, but no more than that. He made no formal enquiries. During the period when it was still possible to travel between London and Paris without fear of being bombed or shelled, he became hyperactive, feverish in his attempts to join the cultural hierarchy. He tried to arrange meetings with Eliot as often as possible, cultivated the support of the poet Anne Ridler as his supporter, made friends with George Barker for the same reason, and encouraged Nin to write to Eliot and Faber to present him as a second-generation Ezra Pound. He, with Nancy, even visited people they had known before Corfu and presented himself as a writer on the brink of greatness. Along with this he found time to have an affair, for two weeks, in Paris with the American journalist Thérèse ('Tessa') Epstein.

Larry had always been impatient to find esteem within the literary establishment but his near-obsessive attempts to place his poems with Faber, and by implication receive admission to the circle governed by Eliot, was abnormal. Fiction writing was not well paid but verse, even with the most distinguished publishing houses, brought in little more than pocket money. It was as though he sensed that the cultural ascendency of western Europe was under threat. He did nothing to personally defend it but he appeared determined to become part of it before its demise. The notion of an artist as exempt from the customary ordeals – death and suffering – to which war subjected others is evident in a letter that Miller wrote to Larry on 8 October 1938. Just over a week earlier Neville Chamberlain had acceded to Hitler's demand that Sudetenland, part of Czechoslovakia, belonged to Germany. Miller fled to Bordeaux for no other reason that it was as far west as possible from what was happening in central Europe. 'Zero hour,' exclaimed Miller. 'I am sadder and blacker now than I was at 21 Years of age!!!' Three years after that the United States entered the First World War. He was largely unconcerned with the likely loss of American lives. What depressed him was that war would once more sideline art as the preoccupation of those who were part of the social and cultural elite. 'What licks me, to put it simply, is this – how can people resume life after an experience such as we went through? How can they have the faith and the courage to take up their tools?' By 'people' he meant writers, by 'life' he meant writing, by 'faith', 'courage' and 'tools' he meant the impetus of literary creativity. He cared nothing for the enormous loss of life that the First World War had brought about. It appalled him only as the stalling of the aesthetic momentum of the best, and he feared it was about to happen again.

In May 1940 Larry had been taken on as an English instructor at the British Council in Athens. Previously he had worked with them in the Information Services, a farcical post which involved distributing politely phrased propaganda on the wonders of democracy produced on multigraph duplicators which had to be dried out on a clothesline. His role as an English instructor went beyond language teaching and included lessons on how English literature and British culture in general had since Shakespeare contributed to the improvement of global civilisation. His classes were popular, something which rather inspired him given that Britain, France and most certainly Greece were at the mercy of a new brand of populist barbarianism. There had during the summer of 1940 been an increase in Italian troops on the Albanian border with Greece. Italy had occupied Albania more than a year earlier and it seemed certain that Mussolini was set on drawing Greece into his new Roman Empire. He would declare war on the country officially on 28 October 1940. Miller had disembarked from the *Exochorda* in New York in January 1940 and throughout the year Larry and Nancy shifted between states of despair, resignation and panic. She had found herself pregnant in December 1939 and flew from Athens to London with Imperial Airways in February 1940. She hoped to stay with her family at least until the birth of the child but two months later Larry asked her to return, stating that travel between Britain and Greece might soon become impossible. Hodgkin writes that the decision was mutual, that Larry 'hated being alone' but equally 'life in wartime Bournemouth had no doubt started to pall for Nancy' (p255). The hypothetical 'no doubt' is telling because the only evidence of which of them influenced the other is a privately held letter from Larry pleading that 'I love you; and miss you horribly' (*Ibid.*). She crossed the Channel and took trains through France, Switzerland and the Balkans. The conventional route, via the *Orient Express*, had been abandoned in 1939 given that it was impossible to cross borders between nations at war with each other. It was extraordinary for a pregnant woman to find her way alone across Europe in spring 1940. In France, the railway journey to Paris would in itself have been unsettling and hazardous, crossing countryside in which units of the British Expeditionary Force and the French Army were encamped. The British would begin to evacuate troops from Dunkirk less than a month later.

Penelope Berengaria Durrell was born to Larry and Nancy in Athens on 4 June, the day on which the last of the Allied troops were rescued from the French beaches. The Italian assault on Greece on 28 October was resisted by a Greek army made up of a small number of regular soldiers and an impressive recruitment of private citizens who had no experience of armed service. The Italians were far better armed and equipped but they were lacking in morale and determination: many conscripts who had supported Mussolini's plans for a new Italy found his imperial ambitions preposterous. By late autumn 1940 most Italian units had been driven back into Albania. Nancy and Larry saw this war of attrition as a sign that their life with Penelope on the mainland or on one of the islands might continue. Despite Larry's record of infidelity, the new child seemed to turn him into a contented husband and father. He wrote to friends on how changing nappies delighted him and of his delight in his daughter's nicknames as 'Pinky' and 'King-Pu', a reference to her apparently limitless capacity to defecate.

For almost nine months the region remained in a state of phoney war with Italian forces encamped on the Albanian side of the border. Mussolini, his political advisors and senior military officers prevaricated on what to do next, fearful that another defeat by a supposedly weaker army would drain morale completely from a country already divided on the outcome of Il Duce's grandiose imperial ambitions. Things changed suddenly on 6 April 1941 when the Germans invaded on five fronts from the north mainly via Bulgaria and Macedonia. It took them little more than three weeks to occupy all of mainland Greece.

At the beginning of the invasion Larry and Nancy were in Kalamata on the south coast. Larry had recently been appointed to a position with the British Legation. His post was unspecified but those at the Legation recognised that his fluency in Greek and familiarity with the region would enable him to pick up on locally circulating rumours. He was an irregular spy, and later he would be taken on again in this role. After a few weeks he left the Legation for a teaching job with the British Council, prompting the move to Kalamata. The Council was sponsored by the Foreign Office ostensibly as an educational body but in truth was a means of promoting British interests abroad, which terrified Larry. He had no diplomatic immunity and faced the prospect of being arrested or at best interned as a British government representative in a country now at war with Germany. Britain had begun to send equipment to Greece before the invasion along with a small expeditionary force of British, Australian and New Zealand forces. By 30 April 7,000 members of this unit had been captured only a few miles from where they landed on the southern coast.

On 12 April Nancy cabled her family asking for the emergency transfer of £50 to supplement their dwindling resources. All that concerned them was to escape with Penelope. A week later, on the 18th, news reports announced that Alexandros Koryzis, the prime minister, had died of 'heart failure'. His predecessor, the dictator Ioannis Metaxas, had died from cancer in January after the country had swept back the Italian forces. Koryzis, a political moderate, seemed to embody a new dawn for Greece but the spark of optimism was extinguished once his actual cause of death became common knowledge. He foresaw inevitable defeat by the Germans and shot himself in the head.

The British Vice-Consul in Kalamata was a wealthy Greek banker called Panos Kostopoulos who informed Larry that a ship would soon be leaving for Crete, then occupied by a large force of Allied troops. Alexis Ladas, a family friend of the Corfu period, drove them speedily along the 55 kilometres to the port in a borrowed open-top Mercedes, a hair-raising experience given that the mountain road was crammed with British and Greek army lorries headed in the other direction. They arrived at noon on the 22 April, six hours before their vessel was due to leave. Appalled, they found that the 'ship' was a caïque, a shallow-hull

63

fishing boat rigged with sails, supplemented for power by an ancient diesel engine. It was a trawler designed for use in the calm shallow waters close to the fishing villages of the coast, and Crete was more than 160 kilometres away. The sea was busy with similar crafts and on the following day – under cloudless blue skies – German Stuka dive bombers attacked them relentlessly. There is no record of the number of deaths but it is thought that at least five vessels were sunk. That same night Theo set out for Crete from Piraeus on the collier *Julia*. He had served as a medical officer in the Greek army over the previous year and feared, justly, that his background as a political radical would bring him to the attention of the Nazis. His ship was hit by Stukas before reaching Crete, two died, and he treated others who were seriously injured. On reaching the island he heard a German radio broadcast which triumphantly announced that the Greek 'warship' *Julia* had been sunk with all crew and passengers lost.

After several days of hugging the rocky coastland of the mainland the caïque's captain set out for open water and Crete. The boat was listing precariously to port and with little wind the overworked diesel motor emitted a trail of sparks and black smoke, offering Luftwaffe pilots an easy target. Luckily, they were not attacked and after two days reached the island of Cythera, still some distance from Crete. The villagers were in a state of panic and confusion, their news of the front coming from an armed party of Cretan soldiers who had deserted from the Albanian front. They were told that the Italians had been repulsed but accounts of the more recent attack by the Germans were second-hand and conflicting in nature. The deserters were not so much cowards as political subversives without a cause. They knew they had been defending Greece but were uncertain of what kind of nation it would be even if it survived the onslaught of various fascist powers. Many of the most influential political figures were royalists, and some favoured an unelected dictatorship, and many a combination of the two. Indeed, once the soldiers found that their own boat was irreparable, they talked of seizing the caïque to get them to the main island of Crete. Their objective, they explained, was to assassinate an army general who had served briefly against the Italians and who they believed was a fascist sympathiser and traitor.

Eventually the villagers and deserters found common cause in sympathising with the caïque refugees, slaughtered one of their last sheep and fed them as much as they could, for the remaining part of their journey. Larry, Nancy and Penelope had, like all other passengers, been ordered to abandon virtually all of their belongings before leaving the mainland. They had little more than the clothes they were wearing and some now inedible pieces of bread. Penelope was carried in the wicker basket which once contained the loaves.

There is no record from Larry or Nancy of how long it took them to reach the port of Chania on the northwest coast of Crete and nor is there a reliable account of how long they stayed on the island. This is understandable given that each of them was undernourished, in fear that their ramshackle boat would list too far to one side and take in water or lose power completely. And once they disembarked their search for temporary accommodation was interrupted by machine-gun fire and bombs from Luftwaffe aircraft. All we know for certain is that they managed to board an Australian transport steamer, whose name no one can recall. It set sail for Egypt only hours before the Greek government officially surrendered to Germany.

Most of the others on board were Australian troops, with very few officers. They had brought with them from Crete as much wine as they could beg, buy or steal and remained drunk until the bottles were drained. They were, however, easy-going, kind-hearted sorts who broke into the stores and supplied Nancy with enough Carnation Milk to keep Penelope going for the rest of the voyage.

Larry's novel *The Dark Labyrinth* (1958; first published as *Cefalu*, 1947), written several years after his brief experiences on the island, is set in Crete and involves an assembly of unappealing middle-class British cruise-liner tourists who visit the place shortly after the end of the war. As usual Larry's portraits of these 'Pudding Islanders' are relentlessly cruel and they find themselves trapped in the eponymous labyrinth facing the wrath of a vengeful minotaur. The message is simple enough: they – the self-absorbed English – had it coming.

Larry later referred to it as his 'divorce novel', and so it was, involving a vile and inaccurate presentation of Nancy as Alice Liddell, art student and beautiful narcissist.

Bowker states that 'they hung around in Crete for some six weeks' (p136), a gross exaggeration. He probably assumed that Larry needed at least this amount of time to absorb the culture of the place for his representation of it. In truth the 'Crete' of the novel is Corfu remodelled, with a hint of Rhodes where he completed it. Its subject was the countrymen he had always loathed and the wife who had now joined his numerous targets for contempt. Alice becomes pregnant by a Jewish lover, has an abortion, leaves Baird (Larry), and Baird is instructed by several Mediterranean women that he can now enjoy a real sex life, released from the selfishness of Anglo-Saxon womanhood.

The departure from the Greek islands by the other members of the Durrell family was far less colourful. Even before war was declared Louisa was informed by her financiers in London, Grindlays Bank, that when hostilities began it would be likely that it would be impossible to transfer funds to her in the eastern Mediterranean. On 1 June 1939 Louisa, Gerry, Leslie and their Corfiot maid Maria Condos took the boat from Corfu to Brindisi. Maria joined them not as a family servant – not quite. Leslie, twenty-two, had been having an affair with Maria – we do not know her exact age – for two years, and shortly before the Italians occupied Albania her strict Orthodox family learned of this and declared to Louisa that they intended to execute her son for dishonouring their virgin child. Leslie, a long-term fan of firearms, carried one of his revolvers with him daily and kept it under his bed at night. He treated the vendetta as an adventure but Louisa found the Condos family as terrifying as the Nazis and promised that Maria would be married into the family in England. The Condos family of Corfu never learned that Maria was pregnant when she left for Britain with the Durrells.

From Brindisi they took the train north and at the Swiss border the group was described on the entry card as 'ONE TRAVELLING CIRCUS AND STAFF'. Along with the four members of his family Gerry had insisted that they took with them a pigeon and an owl, a linnet, a seagull, two magpies, six canaries, four golden finches, three dogs, two toads and two tortoises. Or so he claimed in his later notes on the Durrell family mythology.

Margo stayed on for a further seven months. She insisted that she would never leave the 'White House', and would, if necessary, disguise herself as a local peasant, though it seemed not to occur to her that the

Germans might wonder how an impoverished farm girl could return each evening to a spacious house more often the preserve of wealthy expatriates. In December she met Jack Breeze, an engineer on one of the flying boats that still moved troops and resources between Greece and North Africa. Soon after Christmas 1939 Jack secured for her a place on a flying boat to North Africa. In England in 1940 the two of them would marry and soon afterwards Jack was posted to Mozambique, and she went with him. He was not in the RAF but employed by Imperial Airways, a non-military airline, yet like merchant seamen he was regarded as a legitimate target by the enemy. Jack and Margo ended up in an Italian POW camp in Ethiopia. There, she gave birth to their first son by caesarean section. She named him Gerry, as a pledge of affection for her favourite brother.

Spiro, who had, throughout their time in Corfu, acted as the Durrells' general helpmate and chauffeur, had been overawed by the albeit brief presence of Henry Miller. He had read nothing of his, nor much of anything else in English, but Larry explained that this American was a superstar who had changed the nature of literary writing and Miller himself delighted Spiro by reading aloud some of the most outrageous passages from *Tropic of Cancer*. When he arrived in New York in January 1940 Miller found a letter from Spiro's son Lillis stating that his father had died shortly before Christmas. 'My poor father died with your name in his mouth which closed forever. That last day, he had lost his logic and pronounced a lot of words in English as "New York! New York! Where can I find Mr Miller's house?" He died as poor as he always was' (Haag, p165).

Spiro, or 'Spyros', the comedic luminary in Gerald's Corfu trilogy, died at the close of 1939 but for fans of *My Family*, in book form and televised, and indeed for Gerry when he wrote it, he became immortal. In the second volume of the trilogy, *Birds, Beasts and Relatives* (1969), Gerry closes with a sequence of letters between members of the family composed soon after they left the island. Margo writes to Louisa before boarding a boat from France and quotes from a 'Most odd' letter from Spiro.

Dear Missy Margo
This is to tell you that war has been declared. Don't tell a soul.
Spiro

Botting (p71) quotes this as authentic, but Gerry had made it up. By the time that Britain declared war on Germany, 3 September 1939, Louisa, Gerry and Leslie were already back in England, concerned exclusively with their future, and no longer in any contact with Spiro. Margo would leave later but she too had long ceased to communicate with him. Once Gerry began *My Family* and reinvented Spiro for the project, he did not even know he was dead and seemed not to care.

In *My Family* Louisa, Gerry and Leslie are having problems leaving the island because of a suspicious customs official and are rescued by Spiro. "'Wells, I'll says goodbyes,' he began and his voice wavered and broke, great fat tears squeezing themselves from his eyes and running down his furrowed cheeks. "Honest to Gods, I didn't mean to cry," he sobbed, his vast stomach heaving, "but it's just likes saying goodsbye to my own peoples. I feels you belongs to me'" (p372). He was not present, already ill with the terminal condition that would cost him his life before the end of the year. Maria was there but she is not mentioned anywhere in the book.

3

All Over the Place

By August 1939 Louisa had found a flat in a terraced Victorian house in Kensington High Street. The building had once housed a mid-nineteenth-century middle-class family but had since been turned into self-contained single-storey lets. Gerry had his own bedroom next to Louisa's and down the hall Leslie and Maria shared a room and awaited the birth of their child. Gerry does not mention them in his unpublished memoir. The various family, cousins and even more distant relatives sometimes called to welcome Louisa back to the home country but neither she nor they spoke of her son and his Greek companion, both of whom were asked to stay out of the way when others visited. They were told that 'Maria' was his Greek bride, shy of company because of her lack of English.

At the end of the year Louisa bought a reasonably spacious suburban house at 52 St Albans Avenue, Bournemouth, her long-term retreat on the south coast. Gerry, Leslie and Maria went with her and in 1940 they were joined by Margo. Leslie and Maria's child, Anthony, was not born in the house but recalls from his mother that she slept in a bunk in the kitchen at least until Louisa found her a job at a laundry in nearby Christchurch where he was raised by her in a council house. Anthony kept his mother's surname and claimed never to have met his father.

He knew something of a figure from his early childhood in Bournemouth but was never sure if this ghostly presence came from direct recollections or was part of a story told to him by his mother.

We cannot be certain of whether Louisa and Margo were exclusively responsible for getting rid of Maria and her son or if Leslie was consulted on her removal. He certainly did not object to her being sent away. He only found that she was pregnant in early 1945 when Margo saw her hanging out the washing in the Bournemouth garden. 'That's funny' commented Margo, 'she's pregnant, and I said to Mother, "I think Maria's pregnant," and she looked immediately round for a double gin' (Haag, p176). Leslie was the last member of the family to be informed that he was due to be a father but he soon forgot about Maria and their impending child. Earlier in the war he had been turned down as a volunteer for RAF aircrew because the medical board found him to be partially deaf in his right ear. He spent the remainder of the conflict doing unskilled work in a local factory which produced parts for the major aircraft manufacturers and had continued with this when he found that Maria was pregnant, seemingly unconcerned with her future or that of the baby. Most of his wages went on drink.

Anthony (Tony) was born to Maria in September 1945. Margo, who had now moved into St Albans Avenue with Jack Breeze whom she'd married in Bournemouth, arranged for Maria to be taken into a 'home' for pregnant unmarried women run by the Catholic Church. Margo told Botting that 'she [Maria] kept marching up and down the street with the baby in a pram, telling all and sundry it was a Durrell baby, another Bournemouth Durrell boy, which was rather embarrassing for the family' (p103). She added that while Gerry and Larry never set eyes on their nephew they 'were adamant that Leslie shouldn't marry the girl… Though they could both be very unconventional… they could also be very prudish and correct, surprising though that may sound' *Ibid*.

In those days the foot soldiers of the Roman church responsible for dealing with the likes of Maria – usually nuns with some knowledge of nursing and midwifery – assumed it their natural right to seize children of single mothers for adoption by respectable families. Maria and Tony managed to stay together either through her belligerence or because her affiliation to the Greek Orthodox Church somehow spared her the jurisdiction of the nuns. The former is most likely because, according to Margo, the only member of the family to keep in touch with Maria, she continued to adore Leslie, referring to him as her 'Roula Mou', Greek for closest darling, even though he showed no interest in her or his son. Tony and Leslie would never meet. Indeed, Tony's only brief association with his father's family came in the late 1940s when Margo arranged for him to see the house in St Albans Avenue, conveniently when every other resident was out. Tony knew nothing of his uncle Gerald or his fascination with animals and recalls only that in the absence of humans the house seemed to be spilling over with other creatures, chimps and rabbits crawling over the furniture and snakes peering at him from open chests of drawers.

By 1947 Margo had used what remained of her father's trust fund to buy a house of her own, directly opposite Louisa's home in St Albans Avenue. She and Jack Breeze had two children, but she was quietly consulting a solicitor regarding grounds for divorce. Jack was now a pilot for the British Overseas Airways Corporation, flying Avro Tudors, pressurised airliners based on late-design Lancaster bombers. He drew a line between his glamorous way of life and parochial Bournemouth, visiting the latter as little as possible and instead welcoming the attention of singers and dancers in the London clubs he attended while still sporting his pilot's uniform.

Margo's own contribution to the Durrell folk tale, *Whatever Happened to Margo?* (1995), opens with her decision to buy the house in 1947. Like her siblings she cultivated a taste for making the past conform to her preferred version of what actually occurred. While she is honest enough about Jack and their children Gerry and Nicholas the story of her St Albans Street bed-and-breakfast reads like a prose version of a *Carry On* film screenplay. Her customers include a couple of gorgeous young nurses who choreograph nightshifts at the local hospital with home visits by stylishly attired gentlemen; probably doctors but we are never certain. One tenant is an artist, a painter of nudes, whose models, along with the nurse's visitors, lead neighbours to complain that Margo is running a brothel. Uncle Gerald pops in from time to time, sometimes accompanied by a monkey or marmoset, causing the neighbours to suspect that the activities in the B&B are even more weird than they first thought. All of this might have occurred but no one who recorded or spoke of the Durrells' lives at the time mentions anything like it.

71

During the final months of Maria's pregnancy Leslie proposed to Doris Hall, who kept a pub and off-licence several streets away from St Albans Avenue. She was eleven years older than him and the couple had been having an affair since the time that Maria had moved in with the Durrells. Leslie had sex with Maria in spare bedrooms of the Durrell house mostly during the daytime while spending evenings at Doris's pub and staying over with her after closing time. She agreed to marry him shortly after his disclosure of the inheritance from his father, part of which he invested in a fishing boat, berthed in Poole harbour. Evidently, he was attempting to recreate something of Corfu on the Hampshire coast. The vessel was in good order, fully equipped with trawling nets and a sail, if necessary, but relying mainly on a diesel engine. Leslie took her out alone on her maiden voyage but ran aground on rocks which punctured her timber keel. He managed to clamber out without injury, but his boat was effectively destroyed by being smashed against the rocks in subsequent tides. He had not thought to take out insurance.

In his memoir Gerry recalls that his only proper education came via a private tutor called Harold Binns, based in Bournemouth. He had already been refused admission to a local minor private school. The headmaster asked all ex-colonial potential pupils to open the interview by reciting The Lord's Prayer, but Gerry had never even attempted to read the printed version out loud. Binns, apparently, adopted a rather cavalier attitude to poetry as a sideline to other pleasures, aesthetic and sensual, but his self-presentation as suave libertine was belied by the deep scars on his face. He had, according to Gerry, served in the First World War as a subaltern barely into his twenties. The actual Binns clashes somewhat with Gerry's presentation of the debonair war veteran. Beyond Gerry's notes we know that he translated the Spanish novel *A True Hidalgo* into English (1911) and that his own *Outline of the World's Literature* came out in 1914. He was thirty when his translation of the Spanish novel was published, would have been thirty-three when the First World War began and more than sixty when Louisa hired him as her son's tutor in 1942; a man who 'would thrust a book into my hands and gallop out of the room trailing eau de Cologne like a bride's train behind him'.

Gerry's tendency to romanticise his past became evident in *My Family* and even those who knew it was partly fictionalised forgave him because it was a good story which hurt no one who was in it. Had the memoir gone into print at a time when his actual life was mostly public property it would have struck people differently. Certainly he sentimentalises his early years but by contrast his later reflections on existence per se are unsettling to say the least.

Late in 1942 he received his call-up papers and reported for the army medical examination in Southampton. His account of it in his notes much later is heartily comedic, with him responding to the doctor's order to 'follow my finger' by shifting his head and torso left to right without moving his eyes. Next he encounters Dr Magillicuddy, a farcical Scot who inspects his sinuses and observes, 'It's like gazing into Edinburgh Castle. If anyone wanted to clean that up, they'd have to excavate your skull with a pickaxe.' He failed and was given the option of working in a munitions factory or on the land. He chose the latter and in his own account 'set off on my bicycle' to find a farm that suited him best. Clearly the Hampshire branch of war personnel and recruitment took a laissez-faire attitude to the activities of those outside military service. Gerry introduced himself to the manager of the riding school at Longham, a village on the Stour barely two miles north of the inland Bournemouth suburbs. The owner, Mr Brown, was summoned; a red-faced, short, stocky man who in Gerry's recollection never appeared in anything but riding jacket, jodhpurs and flat cap. Gerry persuaded Mr Brown that he would muck out the stables, groom the twenty-two horses and be lead rider for those who paid Brown for use of his horses on the forty acres of adjoining land. In return Brown would pay him a cursory wage and, crucially, send a letter to the authorities stating that he was helping to 'run the farm', suggesting that the place produced foodstuffs rather than offered recreation to the local middle classes. Prior to this neither Gerry nor anyone else refers to him as ever having ridden a horse.

Within a year Gerry had 'a horse of my own' called Rumba, though he leaves it unclear as to whether the creature had been allocated to him for his exclusive use by Brown or if, by some means, he'd bought it. He tells of how he and Rumba formed an affectionate relationship, enjoying each other's company in the empty pastures and woodland paths which surrounded the riding school. Rumba even introduced him to what would become his 'favourite pub', situated deep in the forest away from roads that might carry motor vehicles. How this magical, unnamed hostelry remained in business, isolated from roads and the village itself, is a mystery.

He tells also of how all of Brown's customers, whom he guided through the surrounding countryside, were women; most of them were beautiful and he had several brief affairs. He does not flatter himself by suggesting that his teenage attractiveness or seductive strategies caused the women to fall for him; rather he presents the idyll of riding through the woods in seclusion, united in love of the natural world, as an irresistible aphrodisiac for each of them. This, it seems, was when he lost . his virginity. He was indeed rather better-looking than his elder brother Larry: taller, with a classically handsome face and striking blond/brown hair that he would sweep back in the manner of a film actor.

Shortly after VE Day, in late May 1945, Gerry left the farm for good, returned to his mother's house in Bournemouth and began to make a list of his enthusiasms and objectives. It was brief and inconclusive, involving only his determination to support himself in some way doing what he had loved in Corfu and, when possible, since then: scrutinising and helping all non-human living creatures. He had no idea of how he might sustain this commitment as paid work, but he began by sending a letter to the Zoological Society of London. He found their address at the local library but had no idea of to whom within the society he should address his enquiry. He wrote on the envelope 'The Zoological Society of London' and began his longhand letter with 'Dear Sir'.

Today, unprompted enquiries to eminent institutions from figures with no qualifications (Gerry was honest in his disclosure of never having taken let alone passed a formal examination) would be treated at best with a polite rejection. However, England in 1945 seemed rather more kind and less inhibited. A secretary at the Zoological Society was amused, even impressed by what appeared to be the daring sincerity of one Gerald Durrell and passed on the letter to the then superintendent of Regent's Park Zoo, Geoffrey Vevers. He too was struck by the young man's determination to devote himself to wildlife and replied, inviting him to attend an interview in London, at which Gerry 'prattled away interminably about animals, animal collecting and my own zoo', the last meaning his collection of frogs, snakes, rabbits et al. in Louisa's house.

Gerry was informed that at present there were no vacancies at London but was offered a position as 'student keeper' at Whipsnade, the Society's 'country zoo' in the Chilterns (Jersey Archive, undated).

Founded in 1931, Whipsnade was the first zoological park in Britain though there were several others in continental Europe and America. Unlike conventional zoos its animals were placed in spacious enclosures designed to recreate their situation in the wild. Confinement in cramped cages was all but forbidden. Whipsnade occupied more than 500 acres of pasture and woodland that was once the estate of a long-abandoned country house. Lions and tigers roamed freely across a landscape which, but for the climate, resembled that of the South African bushveld. Separated by secure wire fences, for their own safety, zebra, antelopes and giraffes spent their lives in an area of more than forty acres, through which ran a clear stream. Gerry had read about African safaris, and while despising those designed for hunters, he felt that he had become part of one, barely thirty miles north of London.

Whipsnade village was then a scattering of charming cottages. The only substantial buildings were the sixteenth-century church of St Mary Magdalene and the local pub. When Gerry arrived on 30 July 1945 the population was less than 200, two of which were Mr and Mrs Charlie Bailey, with whom Gerry had arranged to lodge. They lived in a tiny thatched, oak-beamed cottage and like most of the locals Charlie had been a farm labourer before being recruited by the zoo. He worked with the elephants, who too had their own spacious domain.

This was Gerry's first experience of the British working classes, but Mrs Bailey provided him with dinners far superior to anything he'd come across in ration-strapped Bournemouth. There was an abundance of game available in the locality for a man with a shotgun and most evenings he was fed well with pies and stews made up of rabbit, pheasant, pigeon, partridge and sometimes wild duck. The Baileys treated him as a member of the family but were puzzled. His accent was the King's English, the kind that they heard from news readers on the wireless home service, but not in the locality. Tentatively Charlie asked what he was doing, being paid hardly enough to keep himself in a job that offered few prospects. Gerry explained that he had always been interested in animals

75

and had kept them at his mother's house in Bournemouth, but that he could hardly expect to keep wild carnivores or deer in a moderate-sized back garden. Whipsnade was his route to expeditions in Africa, South America and various parts of Asia where he hoped to work to protect species in danger of extinction. Charlie nodded, assuming that his new lodger was agreeable enough but mad.

Gerry's boss was the zoo superintendent Captain William Beal, a former army veterinary officer who before the war had served in various parts of Africa where the imperial forces relied on horses for transport and cattle for food. He, like Bailey, was intrigued by a young man of evidently upper-middle-class origins who had volunteered to work as little more than a labourer in the middle of nowhere. Gerry explained to Beal that he had kept animals before and the captain gleefully replied that the ones he would now deal with were capable of eating him.

His official job title was 'student keeper', an accurate description of his status as an apprentice with no experience. In the idiom of zookeeping he was more often referred to as the 'odd-beast boy', an ambiguity that left one wondering if the boy or beast was odd.

His earliest friend was Jill Johnson, an eighteen-year-old who took care of the Shetland ponies and the huskies. Jill was a local girl who like everyone else noticed that Gerry's accent and mannerisms made him something of an outsider. Six months later he was also befriended by Lucy Pendar, roughly the same age as Jill and the daughter of the zoo's chief engineer. She was still at school but worked part time at Whipsnade at the weekend and some evenings. Both women recall that Gerry was quite good-looking, charming and enigmatic, spending most of his spare time absorbed in books on global wildlife, particularly endangered species. They talked of him with Botting, and one is struck not so much by the clash between their accounts and Gerry's remembrances in his later notes as by the fact that he concentrates on aspects of his life which for them seem to be fantasies. For example, he writes of how he attempted to ravish a 'town girl' in a hazel grove which normally housed dormice. Most of her clothing was, he reports, scattered around the grove but she refused to take things further because he seemed as distracted by the surrounding creatures as he was interested in her. He tried again in the same spot with 'an adorable girl with a Devonshire accent' but she too felt unsettled by the location: 'they [the mice] might be watching'. He was briefly successful with a local policeman's daughter who ran Pets' Corner, where children could touch or cuddle smaller creatures. Gerry and his adorable girl would lock the enclosure at lunchtime and '[poke] the living daylights out of each other at every opportunity'. In Botting's account neither Jill nor Lucy remember him with any girls at all. They themselves were quite attractive and rather puzzled by his lack of interest in them as anything other than friends. They were routinely chatted up by virtually all other young men they met. From Gerry all they received were lengthy quotations from rather unromantic poems, mostly by Housman.

Eventually he moved out of the Bailey house into a huddle of old cottages called the Bothy. It was owned by the zoo and housed keepers on the most basic wage. He now had privacy but at a cost: one room with a bed and desk, and a lavatory and bath shared with others in the same cottage. In his Jersey Archive notes of forty years later he implies that this would be his ideal place for seduction. The local pub, the Chequers, was next door and he could ply his dates with drinks there before they retired to his room. However, Jill and Lucy remember him as a recluse, and no one else recalls him entertaining guests. His existence was monk-like, his only companions a pile of books on threatened species and his notes on how he planned to rectify the cruelties visited upon the natural world by humans.

At around the same time Gerry had his first-long term affair, allegedly. The exact dates are uncertain because all we have is his own unpublished account, but 1946 or 1947 are likely given that we know that he visited London on several occasions to seek advice on wildlife from Peter Scott, pioneering conservationist and son of the Antarctic legend. According to Botting, it 'seems likely' that Gerry attempted to contact him but in his notes Gerry tells of how he and Scott once went for lunch at a Bloomsbury restaurant made known to him by Larry as the favoured meeting place for bohemians of more than a decade earlier. Of what they spoke we know nothing. Later that same day he states that he met a woman he refers to in his notes as Juliet, at least seven years his senior – he was twenty-one or -two; she was certainly not 'classically beautiful' but had a 'beguilingly memorable face, dark eyes and glossy brunette hair'. She was, he casually remarked, married but separated, and she had two children. Nothing is known of whether the meeting was accidental or otherwise.

The story of their relationship is recorded in Gerry's memoir notes, as well as in a brief comment by Margo to Botting in an interview, both four decades later: 'Juliet was Gerry's first real affair, his first complete realisation of love and sex and all that,' she recalled (Botting, pp106–7). We should note that Margo only felt able to comment on the nature of her brother's 'first affair' because Botting had quoted to her passages from Gerry's own notes on it. Gerry had never spoken directly to her of Juliet at the time of their liaison and nor had he mentioned her to any other member of the family. Juliet was, it seems, an alluring if very ghostly presence, given that neither of the two women he later married, Jacquie and Lee McGeorge, knew anything of her either.

There is in the Archive a record of another relationship which he had during the same period, though it seems that he wrote of it much later. It involves a Scandinavian girl called Kirsten who appears to be studying zoology and doing work experience at the zoo. She causes him to indulge in reflections on the metaphysical particulars of sex.

The thought that because I got pleasure I should *give* pleasure never occurred to me. The fact that I didn't know *how* to give pleasure was of course an important factor. I was taught a stern lesson by a lovely girl called Kirsten from Sweden ...

Kirsten appears to be sexually egalitarian, beyond what would be expected of a young woman at the end of the 1940s, but when Gerry discloses his own thoughts something about him emerges that is unsettling. 'I was so excited I could have raped an elephant or possibly two, if they'd been side by side and I had a stepladder.' Obviously, he kept this to himself because afterwards she continues, saying to him, 'You give me pleasure and out of my pleasure will come your pleasure.' He replies to her, 'You mean like a butterfly out of a chrysalis?' She does, but once more his private contemplations are shocking. 'The preliminaries were so wonderful that I was hard pressed not to rape her.' He seems to treat sex, at least with fellow humans, as an uncomfortable postponement of the type of oblivion that does not worry animals.

He slipped back into death as if it were his natural home, with a glad to be back sigh ... The tigers rippling like a golden sea with black wave tips. The leopard moving under a tapestry of spots. (Jersey Archive, undated)

One must wonder whether the confessional, disquieting account by Gerry of how Kirsten affected him – involving 'rape' as something both casual and naive – can be reconciled with his story of his time with Juliet. In their earliest conversation, as recorded by Gerry, he asked what she did and Juliet replied, 'I paint horses', which created for Gerry the image of this enchanting woman, a shire horse, a brush and a bucket of paint. But she corrected him: 'No ... I paint pictures of them – for their owners. Pedigree horses, of course.' 'Can I come and see your etchings some time?' he asked (Jersey Archive, undated). Soon we find him being invited for lunch at Juliet's townhouse, bringing her a dozen gull's eggs and viewing her paintings ('she wasn't as good as Stubbs ... but damned near it'). They go to dinner in a restaurant close by (Mayfair, it is implied, but we cannot be sure) and he stays the night, moving in the next day and exchanging his Aunt Prue's house in Chelsea, his occasional London base, for Juliet's home. Where, one wonders, are her two children? Does Gerry ever meet them, and what are they called? One suspects that the whole thing is a fantasy because her disclosure at the opening that she has children and a husband is engrossing, but after a while Gerry seems to tire of it, much in the way that the lazy author of a short story forgets what he invented at the beginning of the first draft.

According to the autobiographical notes, Gerry's affair with Juliet lasted around eighteen months, up to and during the period of his wildlife expeditions to the British Cameroons in 1947. Following his return from one of these he went straight to her house intending to propose marriage to her. (Was she now divorced? His jottings say nothing of this.) He found a note on her dressing table in which she declared that 'we're growing too fond of each other'. The melodramatic resonance is striking if not quite credible: the note is in the *bedroom*, left for him even though she had no knowledge of when he was likely to return and if she would be at home when he did, though seemingly he has a key to the front door. It comes across as the closing scene from a Hollywood romantic drama, which is probably what Gerry had in mind as he made it up.

At Whipsnade in 1946 Gerry reached twenty-one and his share of his father's trust fund was opened to him, a gross sum of £3,000 (worth roughly £105,000 in today's money). He now had funds to support his foreign expeditions, and according to his diary notes he spoiled Juliet with several hundred pounds. On what – who knows? He met the botanist and ornithologist John Yealland, who had helped Peter Scott in the founding of the Wildfowl Trust at Slimbridge in Gloucestershire. How or where they met is not clear, but it has become part of the Durrell legend that they were probably introduced to each other by Scott. It is an alluring narrative, with the precocious young enthusiast summoned to the court of Britain's most celebrated zoologist. But it is based entirely on unsubstantiated speculation, even wish fulfilment. Botting once more is to blame in that Scott's name features eight times in the passage on this period of Gerry's life; the only evidence that they might have met is based on them living in London at the same time, as did Clement Attlee and George VI, neither of whom were on speaking terms with Gerry.

Yealland would later become Curator of Birds at London Zoo and while it is not clear what he and Gerry discussed when, in Botting's terms, they formed a 'team', it is implied that their decision to visit the British Cameroons, then still a part of the empire on the west-central African coast, was mutually agreed. What no one mentions is the fact that while Yealland was admirably experienced and carried the kudos of having worked with Scott he was also, when he met Gerry, a middle-aged family man who relied for his upkeep largely on salaried posts. In other words, Gerry's recently acquired resources meant that he would dictate the destinations and itinerary of the visit.

Eventually Gerry would turn this expedition and later ones into his first book, *The Overloaded Ark* (1953), which itself was a formal compendium of talks on the project he had delivered for the press over the previous four years. It is a charming piece of writing made up of the minute particulars of the various species he collected and quirky tongue-in-cheek anecdotes of an Englishman abroad. Strikingly, it is clearly a rehearsal for what made him famous three years later, *My Family and Other Animals*. Both draw upon the raw material of actuality – respectively the goings-on in the Cameroons and Corfu – but are largely fiction.

In his debut work he treats the members of the indigenous population with the kind of begrudging respect that was commonplace during the years of imperial decline – decent types in their own right but a bit different. In the letters he wrote to his mother from the Cameroons between 1947 and 1948 something far more distasteful emerged. When he first set up a camp outside the township of Victoria, he described to Louisa his conversation with a local man who promised to help him locate some unusual creatures, notably a large freshwater crab.

Me: Good morning (very British).
Native: Good morning, sah (taking off a filthy rag which is his hat).
Me: We look for small beef [the local idiom for any small animals].
      You have small beef here?
Native: Sah?
Me: Small beef ... SMALL BEEF.
Native: Ah! Small beef, sah? Yes, we hab plenty sah, plenty. (Letter to
      Louisa, 1947, otherwise undated, Jersey Archive)

He goes on to describe how the 'native' and his similarly unnamed companion offer to carry Gerry and Yealland piggy-back across a neighbouring swollen river. The two locals sink up to their necks while Gerry and Yealland cling on for their lives and the passage could be treated as a parody of Kipling at his worst.

One day he comes upon a hunter who has a rare bird to sell. The man is probably part of the broad range of tribes known as Bantu but Gerry is unconcerned with his affiliation. He is evidently angry that he must communicate with such a 'primitive' figure, 'sitting down on the ground, hat on the back of his head, cigarette in his mouth, explaining to the crowd how clever he had been to capture the creature'. When Gerry approaches and speaks the man replies, but does not stand, remove his hat or his cigarette. Gerry orders him, to '"Get up, take your hat off, take that thing out of your mouth and then say good morning properly!" I snarled ... He obeyed like a naughty schoolboy' (*Ibid.*).

When he and Yealland set off into the wild country with a group of local 'carriers' in 1948, he fears that the hastily employed group are 'cut-throats' and fears for their future, even that the two of them might be 'eaten three miles out of Mamfe'. The locals fight among each other to carry the smallest load and give the general impression of being at best barbaric.

Compare his account of the native population with his descriptions of animals – particularly in the letters, if less so in the book – and it is evident that he has an empathetic affection for the latter while regarding the human beings of the region as scum.

Most of the creatures they collected were birds, chimps, monkeys and baboons, plus a few tortoises, bats, frogs and gigantic insects. What is striking about Gerry's description of them is that he treats them as friends. 'The Yellow Baboon (whom I have called George) ... stands about two feet high and is as tame as a kitten. When you tickle him under the armpits he lies on his back and screeches with laughter ... If dinner is late, it is always due to George having upset the soup or something' (letter to Louisa, 1948, otherwise undated, Jersey Archive). This brings to mind Gerry's encounter with the unnamed hunter whose temperamental peculiarities – hat remaining on head, cigarette in mouth, etc. – he regards as fully deserving of his contempt. Similarly, the 'Red-eared Monkey is simply sweet ... it makes a delightful twittering noise ... Its fingers are long and bony like an old man's, and it looks so sweet.' Or, as he might have put it, so unlike the foul individuals, the 'carriers' who helped him catch it and who he feared might be 'cut-throats', even cannibals.

Anthropomorphism is, for some, idiosyncratic, even charming – but when the delight in animals replaces respect for other humans, what can one feel but unease? Especially when the degraded humans are Black.

A few days later he tells of how when feeding and washing the monkeys, 'all skittish, leaping and gambolling like rabbits ... stamping their feet when frightened', he feels fatherly regarding his newly acquired 'family'. Then he describes the evening, of

how I found my watchnight asleep, tied his legs to the chair and then shouted for him so he leapt up and fell on his face; how a villager tried to strangle his wife down by the river, and how the staff had to down, lay the man out, hold his wife down, and throw his mother-law into the river as she was having a wonderful attack of Victori hysterics. (*Ibid.*)

Sometimes he tells of discussing with locals the 'thrilling' and 'ludicrous' prospect of 'Home Rule for the Cameroons', but this taxes his patience. We should pause before branding Gerry as a racist if only because virtually all other white people in the late 1940s took it for granted that the indigenous peoples of what was left of the empire were in various ways their subordinates. As we will see, the extraordinary thing about Gerry was that while in maturity he adopted broad-minded liberalism regarding people of colour, his egalitarianism involved a different kind of discrimination: he came to treat all members of the human race as inferior to animals (see closing chapter).

In June 1948 he and Yealland were joined by Ken Smith of Whipsnade and Cecil Webb of the London Zoo. Both regarded Gerry as an amateur and Yealland as his more experienced but subordinate accomplice. There then followed a laughable competition between the two teams to see who could track down and capture an angwantibo. The creature was rare and reclusive, and in appearance charming, one of the world's smallest primates, with almost no tail and a facial expression that brings to mind that of a fearful kitten. Webb, a dedicated conservationist, was concerned only with securing enough of the species to breed them in London Zoo and so ensure a guarantee against their extermination in the wild. Gerry had already agreed to deliver his own captured animals to London, but he was obsessed with overtaking Webb in their pursuit of the same objective. He wrote to Louisa: 'I am going up to ... Mamfe where he [Webb] is now. I shall then take pleasure in telling him that we have now got (3) Angwantibo!!!!!!!!!' (*Ibid.*)

Gerry certainly cared about animals, but one suspects that his affection for them was a substitute for something lacking from his relationships with other members of the human race. He took an immediate dislike to Webb mainly because he saw him as his competitor and in his diaries and letters even Yealland is tolerated as an unfortunate prerequisite for the expedition rather than a colleague, let alone friend. The figure who overwhelms him is Cholmondeley (pronounced Chumley), who demands a form of rough-house respect with his huge arms and massive chest, larger than Gerry's, and a face that resembled the misshapen visage of a retired boxer.

> [He] paused briefly to shake my hand in the most regal manner before walking into the house as if he owned it. He gazed around the living room of our humble grass hut with the air of a middle-European monarch inspecting a hotel bathroom suspected of containing bed bugs. Then, apparently satisfied, he ambled over to the table, drew out a chair and sat down.

Then, after taking one of Gerry's cigarettes and lighting it in a proprietorial manner, he 'crossed his legs again and lay back in his chair inhaling thankfully and blowing great clouds of smoke out of his nose' (undated contemporaneous notes, Jersey Archive). He also enjoys sugary tea and has a fondness for the bottled beer that Gerry and Yealland had brought from England. According to Botting, Gerry 'parted with this extraordinary character with much regret'.

Cholmondeley was a chimpanzee. Most of the species are about four foot eleven and weigh around one hundred and ten to one hundred and twenty five pounds but Gerry's new friend was bigger than that, closer to Gerry's height of five foot nine and close to one hundred and forty pounds, roughly the size of a small gorilla.

Gerry tells of how prior to entering his house Cholmondeley had to be released from a timber crate, have a steel collar removed from his neck and the chains that bound his arms, unlocked. The local assistants had imprisoned him this way and for Gerry he now becomes a quasi-human presence with whom he shared cigarettes, tea and beer; he was no longer an animal who was treated cruelly by others involved in the expedition.

Gerry and Yealland freighted their collection of animals, birds and insects onto the merchant ship *Tetela* and docked at Liverpool on 10 August 1948. They unloaded almost two hundred creatures, most of which would be transported to London and Whipsnade zoos, though Gerry arranged for two crates of smaller animals, mostly primates, to be transported to the family home in Bournemouth. There was some press coverage and although Yealland was already a fairly well-known zoologist, Gerry, the 'expedition leader', was piloted from utter obscurity to sudden fame.

Why exactly he requisitioned a private collection of African creatures has never been explained, by Gerry or anyone else, but he took over another of the ground-floor rooms and fenced in part of the garden as home for his chimpanzees. They were cute and harmless, but they were not part of an endangered species and there was no obvious reason for their relocation in a parochial English seaside town favoured by retirees.

During the months of late autumn Gerry held court in St Albans Avenue for Louisa and Margo, Leslie and Doris who lived nearby, and quite a number of neighbours who had read of the heroic activities of Louisa's youngest son. The fact that the family doctor, Alan Ogden, had diagnosed Gerry as suffering from a particularly vile form of malaria crystallised his image of having returned from an exotic, life-threatening experience. His stories were based partly on what actually occurred during his time with Yealland, but he spiced them up with tales of frightening encounters with lions and crocodiles, neither of which he came across in the Cameroons. Nevertheless, his audiences were captivated, especially when he arranged for one of the chimps to apparently escape and mix with the audience. Knowingly or not, Gerry was rehearsing for talks that he would soon give for BBC Radio.

In his memoir notes he tells of how he tried to look up young women he'd known in the town before he left for Whipsnade, a difficult task given that there is no account by him or anyone else that he met any teenage girls of his age in Bournemouth. Magically, however, 'Ursula' glided into his life. They spoke first at a 'friend's' birthday party, where she addressed him as 'the bug boy'. He had seen her a few days earlier on a double-decker bus in the town, his attention drawn to her dark curly hair, huge eyes and long, magnificently shaped legs, a 'willowy coltish figure that turns young men's thoughts to lechery'. According to Botting, Ursula Pendragon's real name was Diane though he does not disclose how he discovered this. Gerry says nothing of her name in his notes though he does refer to her as an ex-public school girl from a wealthy family whose vast Regency house was a mile or two beyond the suburbs of Bournemouth. In Gerry's story of this encounter, he persuaded Jack Breeze, Margo's ex-husband, to drive him to meet her at a country pub in a vintage Rolls-Royce which, bizarrely, Jack had recently purchased. Jack agreed to wear his BOAC pilot's uniform and pretend to be the Durrell family chauffeur. At the time Jack had moved away from Bournemouth and whatever car he might have owned was unlikely to have been a Rolls. New models – Silver Wraiths – cost more than the salary of a stockbroker at this time and older models were painfully expensive because of the cost of spares and servicing. Botting did his best to drag some recollection of Ursula, or Diane, from Margo but all he recovered was her vague memory of a 'young dolly bird with blonde hair who sat around in a droopish fashion which was very irritating to the rest of us' (Botting, p141). She does not remember her name, but the 'dolly bird' sounds very different from Gerry's portrait of Ursula/Diane.

Gerry's second expedition to the Cameroons began in late 1949. This time his companion was Ken Smith, thirteen years older, a senior keeper at Whipsnade and eventually superintendent at Paignton Zoo. It was the then owner of Paignton, not yet a public zoo but a private animal park, Herbert Whitley, who provided much of the advance funding for the expedition. Gerry had spent almost half of his inheritance on the first trip and had not made up the difference with payments from the institutions that took the animals. He needed to protect himself from what might amount to self-inflicted bankruptcy.

Again, he set off from Liverpool docks, this time on the freighter *Reventazon*, in January 1949, shortly before his twenty-fourth birthday. They returned in early August on the banana boat the SS *Tetela*, the same ship used for his first voyage. This time there were even more reporters from the national press awaiting them. All of the popular dailies sent correspondents, with the *Daily Express*, which averaged four million sales per day, substituting political news for a simple front-page headline: 'Two Men Sail in With New Noah's Ark'. They unloaded 139 crates. Eighty-one contained mammals, mostly primates, forty-two held reptiles and a further sixteen were filled with land crabs and birds. The holdings were sold to various zoos for a total of £900, not quite a profit but a decent investment for Gerry given the celebrity status bought for him by the project: the populist *Star* singled him out as 'the Jungle Hunter'.

The press did not know what had actually gone on during this second journey to the Cameroons. There were, as usual, the darkly comic adventures of the Englishmen abroad in the empire. On several occasions Gerry drank too much of a local spirit, *mimbo*, and awoke unclear of the events of the previous day. He made friends with 'the Fon', a tribal chieftain who preferred gin to *mimbo*, and he maintained an affectionate relationship with Charlie, a chimp who would hang himself around Gerry's shoulders when the latter cycled to the coastal resort of Victoria several miles from the basecamp of the expedition. Within a few months Gerry's new pal would find himself in a crate on the dockside in Liverpool, to the amusement of dockers. He would then be taken by lorry to London Zoo and never see Gerry again.

On 30 April 1949 Gerry, Smith and a team of local hunters set out in canoes on the river Mamfe where, local intelligence had informed them, there was a small colony of hippos. The capture of one of these animals would ensure the profitability of the expedition. No one spoke of their tactics because they were pre-established and discomforting. Adult hippos were too gigantic and powerful to be caught with nets and even if they used a heavy-duty sedative dart the animal would be impossible to control when recovered. They could attempt to detain a calf, if small enough, but it was well-known that fully grown bulls and cows would attack anyone who attempted to seize their youngsters.

Gerry had a .450 hunting rifle, powerful enough to bring down an elephant with a well-placed headshot. They came across a cow and a bull with a very young calf and he decided that the cow would be the most dangerously defensive. He missed her completely with his first shot but his second went into her skull. With three fully manned canoes Gerry involved himself in a stand-off with the bull, asking his hunters to howl as he fired shots in the animal's direction. Eventually the bull fled downstream, and the team went back to look for the calf. There was no sign of it, but a large crocodile rose to the surface where the hippo was last seen. Gerry reloaded and dispatched the crocodile with another shot to the head. In his diary Gerry expresses remorse for killing the full-grown hippo while feeling 'enraged' by the crocodile he assumed had killed the calf. He goes on to claim that they found the remains of the latter in the belly of the dead crocodile after they cut it up for meat for the locals.

Quite soon the carcass of the hippo cow became a magnet for a group of hungry predators, 'a pack of animals, fighting, tearing, screaming and pushing'. One member of the mob, species undisclosed, became obsessed, 'a game old thing ... [she] at last swam back to shore, weeping and moaning ... I got her a large bit of meat and gave it to her ... Bathed her wound as well as I could. Now every time she sees me, she starts dancing and clapping her hands' (Gerry's diary, 1949, otherwise undated, Jersey Archive). Mary 'has a habit of lying on her back and looking at you daringly'. She has a 'passion for clothes' and is apt to steal shirts from others, particularly the Western adventurers. Mary is a large chimp but the unnamed female desperate for meat from what is left of the shot hippo is a local human being. Read both accounts and it is evident that Gerry regards the 'pack of animals', people, who tear apart the dead hippo as inferior to the actual animals, such as Mary, whom he often befriended.

4

Larry in Egypt

Clea was the final volume of Larry's widely praised *Alexandria Quartet*, published in 1960 but opening with a passage echoing the experiences of Larry, Nancy and Penelope in May 1941. Durrell, his wife and child, about twenty other refugees from Greece and the Balkans and the crew members of the Australian transport steamer slipped through the anti-U-boat boom into Alexandria harbour at around 4 a.m. on 1 May.

The weather was unwelcoming and nothing like the supposed late-spring delights of the south Mediterranean coast, as presented in travel guides. The city itself seemed to be crouching. Balconies and promenades were largely deserted following a month of relentless attacks by Stuka dive bombers. In the novel Larry touches on this but very reluctantly. There is an irony in Larry's encounter with the official who checked the identity and papers of those disembarking. He was a sergeant in the Military Police and, while no one at the time recalled his name, Larry, for years later, entertained listeners with his account of their exchange. Passports, then and now, did not record the occupation of the traveller but the sergeant looked up and asked, 'Lawrence Durrell, writer?' 'Yes,' answered Larry. 'Friend of Harry Miller, once resident in Villa Seurat and author of *The Black Book*?' The policeman said that they'd met once in Paris, that he thought his most recent novel wonderful and welcomed him to war-torn Alexandria.

The conversation has become part of the Durrell legend and while the sergeant 'John Brown' existed (Joanna Hodgkin names him as such in her account, though Haag refers to him as 'Braun'), there is no evidence that he was part of the Miller/Nin circle or had direct connections with the cultural intelligentsia of London or Paris. Brown himself, while allegedly a man with literary ambitions whose name appears above some magazine poems published in 1941, is never heard of thereafter. Perhaps he was killed in action; who knows? A month later Larry did spend time with a serviceman/writer of mythical status, Keith Douglas. Or so he said. After he wrote *Clea*, he told the critic George S. Fraser that he had based Johnny Keats, 'the Greek God' who impresses Darley, on Douglas. To Fraser he implied that Douglas – cut down in his prime yet resonating with eternal dimensions – was a necessary aspect of his, Larry's, life; from him, he insinuates, the classical timeless settings of *The Alexandria Quartet* drew some inspiration.

Once more Larry was basing the folklore of his writing on a lie. In Egypt in 1942 Larry took on an editorial role in the recently formed highbrow literary journal *Personal Landscape*. Publishing and printing resources in the country were scarce but somehow Larry – along with other expatriates Robert Liddell, Gwyn Williams, Terence Tiller and Dorian Cooke – managed to find London-based sponsors. Larry wrote to T. S. Eliot to see if Faber would take it on as a Middle Eastern outlet and asked him for a contribution. Both requests were declined but somehow the eight issues of the magazine which appeared were lavishly presented, attractive enough for wealthy residents of the city – Egyptians and non-Egyptians alike – to purchase. Their interest, or otherwise, in English poetry was irrelevant; the volume was in its own right conspicuously luxurious. Larry contributed some verse along with manifestos on the nature and function of poetry, largely self-contradictory gibberish that made Ezra Pound seem an example of common sense.

Keith Douglas contributed poems to three issues, mainly because he met up with the sub-editors Robin Fedden and Bernard Spencer when he was stationed very briefly in Cairo before serving on the front line against Rommel's forces, which had come as close as sixty miles west of the Egyptian capital. He never communicated with Larry.

According to MacNiven, Douglas had met Spencer in Cairo but his suggestion that Larry's recreation of him in *Clea* is based on personal acquaintance is questionable. Nancy said nothing of him to her daughter

Joanna Hodgkin – a curious omission, given that Douglas had become the most famous British poet of the Second World War when Hodgkin wrote *Amateurs in Eden*.

The day after their arrival in Alexandria Larry, Nancy and Penelope were loaded into lorries with rough seats and canvas rear-coverings for their journey to Cairo, along with sailors, other servicemen and groups of refugees from various parts of Europe. After a few days in hotels Larry and his family found themselves a self-contained ground-floor flat in the Gezira Guest House, located in Zamalek, an island separated from the rest of the city by two branches of the Nile, which in many ways reflected the atmosphere and lifestyle of Corfu. It was largely uninhabited until the mid-nineteenth century when the French created an exotic botanic garden fed by the river. This became the magnet for a large number of wealthy Europeans, along with a few members of the Egyptian aristocracy who turned the island into something fantastic and bizarre. The dispossessed royal Muhammad Ali built the Gezira Palace in a manner that blended Ottoman luxuriance with Italian neo-classicism. Smaller but no less ghastly cocktails of borrowed grandiosity followed and by the time the Durrells arrived the island had become a pantomime of easy-going colonialism. The British had their own polo pitch, cricket ground, bowling green and golf club, all surrounded by colourful and exotic plants that might have decorated the Raj.

Three bridges connected the island with the rest of the city, but their shortness belied extraordinary contrasts. The surrounding metropolis was the hub of tensions between various sects, political factions and ideologies that had imposed themselves on Egypt over the previous millennium, complicated by Napoleon's occupation in the early nineteenth century followed by the Ottoman Viceroy and then British control from 1882 to 1956. Most significantly the city beyond the island was rife with poverty and political unrest stirred particularly by groups who wished to turn the country into an Islamist republic, some of which attempted to form alliances with the Nazis.

The sprawling metropolis was, for a middle-class English expatriate, a horrible place to live, which is why Larry looked for accommodation on the island. His personal history was repeating itself in that while he claimed to despise the dreary solipsism of Englishness, he found himself unable to avoid it during his periods abroad, first during his India childhood, then in Corfu and now in Egypt. He found some solace in arrivals from Greece, first Alexis Ladas who had obtained the last seat on a flight from Greece, then David Abercrombie, whom he'd known in Athens, and most importantly Theodore Stephanides, who had escaped by boat and was treating wounded in an auxiliary hospital first used in the First World War and reopened for the same purpose in 1940. The ancient beds that had held wounded of the disastrous Gallipoli invasion of 1915 now did so for those injured in Tobruk.

Larry had little money, but he had telegraphed Louisa shortly before leaving Corfu requesting funds, which arrived at a bank account opened by Theodore in Cairo roughly a month after they arrived in the city. Two weeks later they moved to a more luxurious three-bedroom apartment at 14 Saleh Ayoub, part of a nineteenth-century mansion in Zamalek. But rather than looking for paid employment Larry busied himself by setting up an intellectual and literary circle. The editors of *Personal Landscape* were part of it, as were Hugh Gordon Porteus – poet, sinologist, connoisseur of horsemeat and organ music – and John Speirs, who was dedicated to instilling in students at Cairo University, where he taught English, the mantra of F. R. Leavis that great novels are the source of moral improvement.

Betsy and Jon Uldall, phoneticians both and connected with the university, joined the group. Betsy was American and very good-looking, and Larry attempted to seduce her on frequent occasions.

Bernard Burrows, who Larry had known in Athens, introduced him to Freya Stark. She was forty-eight, nineteen years older than Larry but her magnetism and reputation dispensed with the age difference. There is no evidence that they had an affair, but it is clear enough that Stark's mission as an Arabist had an entrancing effect on him. She is sometimes compared with T. E. Lawrence except that Lawrence's obsession with the culture of the Middle East was largely a reflection of his private uncertainties. His famous *Seven Pillars of Wisdom* (1926) is more a romanticised fantasy about the Arab world than an accurate account of it. Conversely Stark was employed, secretly, by the British Foreign Office to promote political ideals that were versions of those upheld by the democratic states of the West. She founded the Brotherhood of

Freedom, an organisation which promoted the ideal of Egypt as a largely secular democracy. Her motive was to undermine the various radical groups that ranged from communism to fundamentalist Islamism.

Despite Stark's appeal as a proselytising reformer, Larry was attracted to aspects of Cairo which she either ignored or attempted to improve. When he ventured beyond the island he came across a metropolis that seemed to be an outrageous, debauched version of Paris. Street vendors supplemented their standard merchandise of chocolates, cigarettes, privately distilled spirits and fake high-quality wristwatches with an hour in a nearby tenement with their virgin sister or, if the customer was inclined, a boy not yet in his teens. Business was brisk with British private soldiers and NCOs. Officers made use of higher-calibre services at the city's classiest hotel, Shepheard's, founded by an Englishman in 1841 and a century later still opening its doors almost exclusively to middle- and upper-class westerners. After British officers had said goodbye to their prostitutes, they might well have encountered esteemed politicians on neighbouring staircases. The hotel was thought sufficiently grand to host the Greek government-in-exile and it became a meeting place for other Greeks who saw it as an antechamber for the eventual liberation of their country. Alexis Ladas had become a regular and he introduced Larry to the bizarre fabric of the hotel's bars and restaurants. In terms of etiquette and conventions of dress little seemed to have changed since the 1920s and 30s but beneath this respectable surface the hotel enabled the patrician expatriates and serving officers to enjoy a cosmopolitan version of what the squaddies paid for in the rough parts of the city. Theodore told Larry that the boundaries between class and rank were erased at the Agusa General Hospital where he worked and where all servicemen shared queues for treatment for venereal disease. Enlisted men outnumbered officers, but not by much.

Larry's Saleh Ayoub apartment was expensive but he had sufficient resources from the funds sent by Louisa to avoid seeking regular employment and this enabled him to enter the circle of the Uldalls, Speirs, Porteus and eventually Stark. The assembly drew in would-be poets who were stationed in the city with various British and imperial units: George S. Fraser, John Waller, Hamish Henderson and the New Zealander Erik de Mauny. Surprisingly John Gawsworth, one-time Soho debauchee, drunk and occasional associate of Larry and Nancy, was now in Egypt with the RAF, digging trenches at landing strips rather than flying aircraft.

Soon the assembly of uniformed wordsmiths was making use of the cheap printers of the city to bring out an extraordinary number of English-language magazines. *Citadel* and *Parade* trod a narrow line between scandal sheets and literary weeklies. Fraser and D. J. S Thompson's *Orientations* was tenaciously eccentric and read by hardly anyone, unlike Gawsworth's *Salamander* which, astonishingly, sold in its thousands to military personnel. It was probably the only miscellany of poetry which held the attention of the non-officer class, mostly educated at school only up to the age of fourteen. Gawsworth was an advocate of no-nonsense straight-talking verse epitomised by the likes of Rudyard Kipling, and Larry did not submit any copy.

The Egyptian Gazette was founded by British expatriate journalists in 1880 and still publishes a daily copy in English. Its heyday was during the British occupation of Egypt and Palestine in the mid-twentieth century and when there was an expeditionary force of Anglophone soldiers based in the region during the Second World War its sales matched those of the *London Evening Standard*. Like the *Standard* it aimed for popularity by mixing short news items with opinionated commentary and gossip columns. Larry contributed to the latter with his 'Yorick's Column'. The Shakespearean resonance of the title was a goodbye note to high culture, given that Yorick tells largely of the escapades of his Aunt Norah, widow of Sir Percival Staggers, who is by parts a satirical portrait of the English aristocracy at its most ludicrous and a middle-aged sex maniac. The soldiers loved Yorick's tales of his mad, filthy relatives and Larry earned on average £15 a month for his efforts, at today's rates about two thirds of the UK state pension.

Financially things improved further in early August 1941 when Larry was interviewed for the post of Foreign Press Officer at the British Embassy. Walter Smart, the Oriental Counsellor, knew him slightly and had the decisive vote on the panel. He would be on £600 per year, two and a half times his fluctuating income from the *Gazette*.

Though Nancy and Penelope lived well his appointment marked what would be the final year of their time together as a family. Few reliable records of what Larry got up to during this time survive but George Lassalle, an MI5 man attached to the embassy, reported to Bowker that at everything from informal cocktail parties to dances, 'When an attractive woman entered the room, he would leap up like a puppy-dog and clutch at her breasts ... A frolic everyone involved found entertaining' (Bowker, p153). We have to take in on trust that the subjects of his groping were 'entertained' by his activities.

Nancy and Penelope took the train for Jerusalem in mid-July 1942, ostensibly as part of the evacuation eastward of British civilians following Rommel's early successes in the first battle of El Alamein. In truth Nancy used this 'flap', as it was known, as a cover for what would be their permanent separation.

They exchanged some correspondence but in early September, from Jerusalem, Nancy announced that she would never return to him, and that Penelope would always remain with her. On this last she insisted that were he to attempt to gain legal access she would produce evidence of his numerous record of infidelities. A few weeks later he persuaded her to meet him in Jerusalem, but she was as abrupt and obdurate as she had been in her letters. Joanna Hodgkin describes a side of Larry that his friends and MacNiven overlook. Mary Bentley had been the fiancée of Group Captain Dudley Honor when the Durrells first met them in Cairo. She had taken the train to Jerusalem with Nancy but returned shortly afterwards. Larry persuaded Dudley to fly him to Palestine for his meeting with Nancy.

Hodgkin tells of a letter that Nancy wrote to Penelope much later. Their daughter was far too young to understand what was going on between her mother and father during the early 1940s – aside from being aware of Larry's prolonged absences – so when she was in her teens Nancy offered her an account, allegedly from notes she had made at the time. When Nancy refused to discuss any kind of reconciliation during his visit to Jerusalem he was 'scorched with words, muddled with words, bewildered with words and his ever-changing expectations ... When Larry is crossed, he lashes out with all the guns he can think of – "Nothing but a dirty Jew" to me – but this only hurt me because he was saying it' (Hodgkin, p277). She goes on to explain that Larry's residual antisemitism was his last resort before turning to violence. When distaste grew to hatred he would hurl antisemitic abuse against people, usually women, who had no connection with Judaism. Nancy had witnessed it before but when directed against her it showed that she had driven him into a corner. He no longer had a rational or emotional case for the repair of their relationship, so he was now humiliating himself. Even before she left for Jerusalem he had given up on granting his wife the courtesy of even discussing an issue, however trivial, on which they disagreed. His routine response was 'Why don't you shut up?' (Hodgkin, p277).

Soon after Nancy left him Larry was moved by the UK Diplomatic Service from Cairo to Alexandria. His duties were the same but the atmosphere of the city that had greeted him on his arrival fed the appetite for lecherous hedonism which marriage had held slightly in check. Before leaving Cairo, he went to a party in a grand building that had once been a club catering for Egyptian diplomats and was now referred to as 'Orgy Hall'. Larry had already charmed a large number of female administrative and secretarial staff at the embassy, and now with drink flowing appeared to have become a magnet for most single women in the room.

A large Australian infantry lieutenant, who had done two tours on the front line, was embittered by the spectacle of a well-dressed civilian having more success with the girls than men in uniform and advised Larry to go 'home to your mother'. A verbal exchange turned rapidly into a fist fight and Larry was rescued by colleagues. For some time afterwards he impressed anyone willing to listen with his account of how his matchless sexuality had led to a rough-house version of a duel. The event is worth mentioning because it occurred Soon after his meeting with Nancy where, once more, he insisted remorsefully that he had only been unfaithful to her twice, in Corfu. In truth, and despite his pleas to her to return to him, he had wasted no time after her departure in attempting to seduce any woman he met, often successfully.

They were not divorced until shortly after the end of the war in Europe in 1945, largely because Larry hindered attempts by their solicitors to prepare a mutually agreeable settlement. Up to 1944 he was still sending her letters imploring her to reconsider her decision to end the marriage. He first met Yvette – later Eve – Cohen at a party in Alexandria in 1943 but they did not begin a relationship until the following year and his decision to turn this into something formal and permanent, eventually marriage, occurred at the same time that he assented to divorce from Nancy. As we shall see he was not exchanging one monogamous commitment for another. He had enjoyed being a bachelor and was equally attracted to his own version of an 'open' marriage with Nancy – open to him more than her. He wanted the best of both worlds but by the time Egypt moved towards post-colonial independence after the war he realised that he could no longer depend on Eve's status as his unofficial partner. She was a Jew in a predominately Muslim region, technically stateless and without papers, and it became apparent to both of them that the marriage was an unavoidable expediency. It might seem that he was rescuing his new love from a potential social vacuum, but we should bear in mind the fact that he did not simply exchange Nancy for Eve. While he was attempting to recharge his relationship with the former and enchanting the latter, he was also busying himself as a Lothario.

On 25 December 1943 he tells Miller of how he 'work[s] in a little tower – very smart and quaint' which in itself was slightly dishonest because the building was his home rather than his office, a quirky example of nineteenth-century orientalism in the centre of the city. In his next letter, little more than a month later, he seems to have forgotten what he wrote on Christmas Day: 'I have furnished myself a Tower ... where I have finished one book of verse' (8 February 1944). In the first letter he also announces that 'Nancy is in Jerusalem with the child. We have split up' – which was accurate enough, unlike his explanation for the break-up: 'just the war I guess.' Adding that: 'The women are splendid – like neglected gardens – rich, silk-and-olive complexions, slanting black eyes and soft adze-cut lips, and heavenly figures like line drawings by a sexual Matisse. I am up to my ears in them – if I must be a little *literal*'. He continues:

But one has never had anything lovelier and emptier than an Alexandria girl.

Their very emptiness is a caress. Imagine making love to a vacuum ... When they make love it's like two people in a dark room slashing at each other with razors.

Given that he idolised Miller as a Lothario one might wonder if he was fantasising about his own profligacy for his hero. He rejoices in these seemingly limitless opportunities for emotionless gratification very soon after he told Miller that the war had separated him from Nancy.

He first mentions Eve Cohen to Miller in a letter believed to be of early May (otherwise undated) 1944 and he refers to her as 'Gipsy Cohen'. Perhaps he had informed Miller of her actual first name in letters now lost. She is, apparently, the ultimate embodiment of desensitised Alexandria sexuality. She 'serves me up sex lives of Arabs, perversions, circumcision, hashish, sweetmeats, removal of the clitoris, cruelty, murder'. By this he means that when they have sex, she entertains him with detailed accounts of local rituals. As for Eve herself:

> It has been incredible to find a woman whose sex responses start upwards from the soles of her feet – without any corrupting Anglo-Saxon nonsense. It has cured me of English women for good and all ... Sex now as a non-possessive form of friendship much more moving ... than the old Anglo-Saxon rout of ideas *about* everything.

He seems, hazily, to be recommending the kind of sex he is having with Eve as exhilarating because it is emancipated from such abstractions as emotional attachment or commitment. Clearly enough it enables him to break free of the cumbersome nature of 'Anglo-Saxon' intercourse and one suspects he is casting a vengeful eye towards the memory of Nancy, though he had no complaints about his relationship at the time aside from the tiresome restrictions of monogamy. However, he seems not quite to have freed himself from the pitiable attractions of Anglo-Saxon womanhood because in the same letter he admits to a fling with 'a lovely English wren [WRNS, Women's Royal Naval Service] and a girl [also English apparently] with the hips of an acrobat'. The habit of sleeping with one's own sort is difficult to break: 'But it's all really quite meaningless.' Presumably one of Eve's attractions was her indifference to Larry's fatigued infidelities with English women, of which she was aware.

In his following letter (23 May) he tells Miller of his debauched experiences with 'more beautiful women than any place else ... the mixture Coptic, Jewish, Syrian, Egyptian, Moroccan, Spanish ... Sexual provender of quality ...' Neither Eve nor anyone else commented on Larry's activities, then or later, and we have to take his reports to Miller on trust. All that can be said with any confidence is that the letters are remarkably similar to the sexualised prose of his friend's fiction.

He also refers also to recent news on the activities of Xan Fielding, whom both knew from Greece, and Larry's recent acquaintance from Cairo, Patrick Leigh Fermor. Of Fielding he states, 'There is lots of amusing and exciting news I would give you about ... Fielding, but I'm afraid censorship wouldn't let it pass' (*Ibid.*). From 1942 onwards Fielding had been a member of the Special Operations Executive (SOE), an organisation created at the beginning of the war. It was allied to MI6 as an overseas spying agency but went farther than that and was allowed to operate as an armed guerilla group whose members could pursue operations, including assassinations, behind enemy lines without uniforms and in disguise. Fielding had already worked alongside resistance groups in Crete, involving both firefights and the supplying of arms. He was once captured but managed to escape before being handed over to the Gestapo. At the time Larry wrote to Miller he was about to be parachuted into the south of France to contact Maquis units which would receive arms and explosives prior to the imminent Allied invasion of northern France. Fielding was captured again and was rescued from a firing squad execution by the intervention of a local resistance group. Although Larry did not disclose anything specific to Miller of Fielding's activities – as he stated, 'censorship wouldn't let it pass' – the fact that he knew of them shows that his ostensible role as press officer was a cover for other enterprises. Only someone connected with the embassy branch of the intelligence services would have any knowledge of Fielding's work with SOE, particularly his imminent parachute drops into France.

He also mentions Patrick Leigh Fermor to Miller, offering his friend a tantalising if fragmented account of Leigh Fermor's wartime adventures. He too was a member of the SOE, had accompanied Fielding on several operations in Crete and was often parachuted into Greece and the Balkans to communicate with the resistance groups, some of whom were battling against each other as often as they were the German occupiers.

Most famously he led a party that in 1944 captured and took to Egypt Major General Heinrich Kreipe, the German commander of the island.

During his time in Cairo Fielding established the unofficial headquarters of the SOE in a spacious mansion which he called 'Tara', close to Larry and Nancy's previous home in Zamalek. It became the base where SOE officers planned operations, doing so beyond the control of the conventional hierarchy of the military or the security services.

The building was also a magnet for reckless exiles, including figures from the Balkans and other parts of central Europe who attained an unofficial status as members of the SOE and accompanied British officers on missions into their regions. Most famously, the Polish Countess Sophie Tarnowska requisitioned several rooms for her group of Polish military men who had fled south after the occupation of their country in 1939. Drunken parties were rife and so was a determination among all involved to kill as many Germans as possible. There was a tacit agreement between the SOE and the SAS, founded in Egypt by David Stirling in 1941, that the latter would conduct raids against Rommel's Afrika Korps while SOE would concentrate on the eastern Mediterranean and the Balkans. Tara also opened its doors to SAS men, of all ranks.

Cairo was three hours away from Alexandria by train but between 1943 and 1945 Larry visited Tara every two weeks on average. His closest friends there were Fielding and Leigh Fermor. All had interests in philosophy and literature – Leigh Fermor was translating works by Villon prior to his mission to kidnap Kreipe – but it is wrong to assume that Larry made such regular visits to discuss verse. Officially Reginald Leeper, Ambassador to the Greek government-in-exile in Egypt, was the liaison between the British government and the SOE. In truth the latter obfuscated and distorted details of its activities for Leeper and used Larry as their informant on what the British authorities, military and diplomatic, thought it was up to. Leigh Fermor and Fielding liked him certainly but also treated him as their expedient stooge.

When one searches through Larry's correspondence during this period what is most striking is his sense of the war as an irritant. He complained about the attritional state of things in North Africa, especially when

Rommel was persistently victorious, but he was not overly concerned with the fate of the British settlement in the Middle East.

In September 1941, four months after Larry arrived in Egypt, he set off on a tour of various sites that embodied the country's religious and cultural heritages, including the pyramids. He returned to Cairo shortly before the Japanese attack on Pearl Harbor, followed Soon afterwards by Hitler's declaration of war against the United States. This was the turning point in the history of the Second World War. Following Germany's invasion of the Soviet Union the latter had formed an alliance with Britain against the Nazi forces and on 11 December the United States joined the UK and the Soviets in a broader confederation against the Axis. Western and central Europe was still occupied by Germany but the combined power of three superstates would ensure the defeat of Hitler's; it was a matter of when, not if. Throughout Cairo there was a widespread feeling of exuberance; the war was certainly not over but its outcome was settled. Leigh Fermor remembers Larry at the time as 'a man who pumped oxygen back into the air ... of wit, intelligence, charm, comic sense, a vast array of interests and a staunchless fluency'('Observations on a Marine Vulcan', *Twentieth Century Literature*, Fall 1987, p305). He also recalls that he talked energetically of the 500-page draft of his new book, provisionally entitled *The Air-Conditioned Nightmare*, that he had put together during his journeys, and that he was obsessed with setting off for Mexico, India, China or Tibet. The war, it seemed, was other people's business.

By May 1943 the Axis forces were defeated in North Africa and the Allies had begun their invasion of southern Europe with landings in Sicily and the Italian mainland. Larry wrote to Miller a year later:

Well, the last few days we've driven out through Bourg El Arab, and slipped down through the battlefields to a long beach where the real Mediterranean comes up in great green coasters and the sky is smothered down to violet, all lambent and turning your body in water to a wonderful rose. The sea citron-green cold and pure with sandy floor; for the first time in four years I felt I was in Greece. Bathing naked. (Larry to Miller, May 1944, otherwise undated)

He weaves into this evocation of the seemingly timeless, transcendent landscape something more immediate: 'empty rounds of ammunition, dirty bandages, twisted wrecks of enemy tanks, lumber.' Months earlier bodies and body parts would have been strewn across this terrain but Larry chooses to assimilate recent events to antiquity. 'Strange atmosphere this deserted battlefield with the sea inking in the edges of the sky and the old fortress glowing like a jewel.' He closes, 'Wonder when it will all end?' but after reading the letter one has the impression that for him it is not taking place.

He knew of developments in the ongoing conflict in Europe from Fielding, Leigh Fermor and others in the embassy working in intelligence but aside from the distracted references to battlefield wreckage the letter, at over two thousand words, is concerned primarily with Alexandria as a hotbed of sexual diversity, a city in which various branches of the Occident and the Orient released otherwise suppressed erotic energies, especially for his benefit.

> It's funny the way you get woman after woman: and exactly what it adds up to I don't know: each more superficial than the last Gaby, Simone, Arlette, Dawn, Penelope ... but only Gipsy Cohen burns black and fierce under her Tunisian eyebrows; the flavour is straight Shakespeare's Cleopatra; an ass from Algiers, lashes from Malta, nails and toes from Smyrna, hips from Beirut, eyes from Athens ... And breasts from Fiume.

Critics have been reluctant to treat Eve as the model for the eponymous heroine in the opening novel of Larry's *Alexandria Quartet*, *Justine* (1957). Most feel that it would be unjust to reduce the novel's famously incomprehensible modus to an autobiographical interpretation. Justine, as a character, is not quite 'there' in the conventional sense of our being able to apprehend figures in realist novels. Rather, she becomes inseparable from the notion of Alexandria itself as multifaceted and dangerously alluring. Equally, it is wrong and misleading to treat *Justine* purely as a work of art; in truth it is an offshoot of Larry's personality and temperament.

Read his reports to Miller from his time in Cairo and Alexandria, then look at the novel and you feel that boundary between Larry the man and Larry the fiction writer melts away. The letter I quote from above resurfaces in the opening pages of *Justine*.

> The symbolic lovers of the free Hellenic world are replaced here by something different, something subtly androgynous, inverted upon itself. The Orient cannot rejoice in the sweet anarchy of the body – for it has outstripped the body (p14).

Sex is the topic to which the prose returns addictively, as if the figure telling the tale, the elusive Darley, is desperate to avoid references to anything else: it is clear enough that the setting of the novel is Alexandria in the 1930s and 40s but the war is hardly ever mentioned.

Larry kept copies of his letters to Miller and sometimes we find almost verbatim borrowings for the novel. In *Justine*, 'The sexual provender [in Alexandria] which lies to hand is staggering in its variety and profusion' (*Ibid.*). To Miller (23 May 1943): 'Alexandria is, after Hollywood, fuller of more beautiful women than any place else ... Sexual provender of quality ...'

Larry blinded himself to the Second World War and while we cannot condemn an individual for their wish to avoid something awful this tendency becomes more perturbing when it informs a literary work. It is a commonplace to praise *Justine* as wonderfully experimental in terms of its refusal to focus clearly on a narrative or the particulars of time and place. But consider this from a different perspective. Larry's artistic breakthrough was a reflection of his state of mind. He was bohemian, a narcissist who, unable to wish the war out of existence, compensated by creating a fantasy in *Justine*.

Larry's naming of Eve as 'Gipsy' was not disparaging in that he was entranced by her as a figure who did not really belong anywhere. Her father was a small-time businessman who moved to Alexandria from Tunisia in his early twenties where he met her mother, whose family had arrived in the city at roughly the same time. Both were Jewish and could trace their roots back to the expulsion of Jews from Spain in the fifteenth century. Her father's family were North African Sephardim, while her mother's had spent the previous four centuries in Istanbul; in Egypt they continued to speak Ladino at home, a blend of Hebrew and Old Spanish.

They did not quite qualify as members of the urban middle classes – during the 1930s and 40s antisemitism was rife in Egypt – but they lived comfortably enough. After the relationship ended Larry frequently portrayed Eve's father as a kind of downmarket Shylock, a moneylender who traded from the steps of buildings in the less salubrious areas of the city. In truth, he was a respectable merchant and the family adhered to the various mantras of propriety and correctness that Larry had encountered in southern England.

There is no evidence that he even met Eve's parents. Their first names never appear in letters or other documents and his only known involvement with them involved his attempt to rescue Eve from what appeared to be their attempt to have her locked up.

She left school at sixteen, worked for a while as a secretary and was expected by her family to exchange this brief dalliance with independence for life as a wife and mother. Instead, she established herself as a freelance journalist and sold enough copy to local newspapers to pay rent for a small bedsit in the city.

She and Larry first met at a party attended mainly by diplomats, writers, journalists, artists and various other expatriates. He was attracted to her partly because of her stunning appearance – at least if we believe his descriptions of her as sensuous and exotic in letters to Miller – and also because she was the only person there who could claim to be a genuine embodiment of the polyglot nature of a place that was neither entirely European or African, the Orient or Occident.

They talked, felt a tinge of mutual attraction and made no specific plans to meet again. But Larry had left her his phone number and little more than a week later they arranged a late lunch in the legendary Pastroudis, a mixture of a patisserie and a bar. They ate pastries and drank coffee with shots of brandy and that evening their affair began.

The cause of Eve's parents' displeasure remains unclear. It might have been her apparent behaviour as an independent woman, or as they saw it, a libertine. Larry was certainly not her first lover but there was something quintessentially Western and decadent about him. While he lived alone it was common knowledge in Alexandria that he had a wife and child and the Cohens contacted a psychiatrist of dubious repute with the intention of gaining evidence that their daughter's activities were symptoms of insanity, sufficient to have her sent to a lunatic asylum. This all sounds absurd but Larry was genuinely alarmed and contacted a friend from Athens, Paul Gotch, who worked for the British Council and lived with his wife and daughter in Tanta, a city approximately halfway between Alexandria and Cairo. Gotch agreed to offer her refuge in his house and Larry saw her off on the train. She would remain on good terms with the Gotches but stayed in Tanta for only two weeks and then returned to Larry's flat in Alexandria. Stories of how they lived during 1943–4 vary according to the teller but it is clear enough that Eve was genuinely fearful of the outcome of her parents' pursuit of her. She told Larry that even before they met on the few occasions she stayed at the family home her father had locked her in a room and sometimes struck her when she attempted to leave. In *Justine* the eponymous heroine and Darley share a sense of terror. Their affair is secretive and tense because Nessim, Justine's husband, is intent on vengeance. Eve was not married but her father behaved like Nessim, as if she belonged to him.

Despite stating to Miller that 'if I could get to some Greek island and live in real poverty with somebody like Gipsy Cohen I could work like a fiend' (May 1944, otherwise undated), Larry's perception of Eve as a long-term permanent partner is questionable. Soon after the war in Europe ended, he took up a post in Rhodes, then occupied by Britain as a military protectorate. He assured Eve that she would join him, but she was effectively stateless. Egypt, as a sovereign state, did not exist. It had a government but was still controlled by an unsteady coalition between Egyptian and British armed forces. She had no passport; she could only obtain one by marriage and Larry at the time had still not given up on some form of reconciliation with Nancy, principally as a means of maintaining access to their daughter even though he cared little if anything for his estranged wife In mid-1945 he asked Robert Liddell, poet, novelist and lecturer at Alexandria University, to marry Eve as a temporary expedient; Liddell, appalled, turned and left the room without replying.

This sounds by parts desperate yet commendable, but we should remind ourselves that while Larry treated Eve as magical, his attentions were not fixed exclusively upon her. She seemed unconcerned with his one-night stands; they bolstered his persona as a wayward bohemian.

But some things he kept quiet from her because they would have exposed him as a calculating deceiver. Roughly a year before he pleaded with Liddell to offer Eve an escape route from Egypt Larry had an affair with the English ballerina Diana Gould, then touring Egypt. She was from a wealthy West London family, and was attractive in an elegant, sharp-featured, very English way. She was in terms of background and appearance the complete antithesis of Eve who, two months after he met Diana in 1944, Larry was celebrating in letters to Miller as a woman who 'burns black and fierce under Tunisian eyebrows' (May 1944). Diana was in Alexandria throughout the spring of 1944, though she sometimes travelled by train with the rest of the dance company for appearances elsewhere. Throughout this period Larry courted her in a mannerly upper-class way, arranging for verses to await her in her dressing room after performances; these were composed specifically for her in longhand, praising her beauty rather as seventeenth-century lyric poets turned their work into exercises in seduction. She found him attractive and was rather flattered by the attentions of a dedicated literary writer and member of the Foreign Service. He appointed himself her guide to Alexandria and the surrounding area. After spending their first night together, they walked by the shore of Lake Mariout just outside the city. Each was awestruck by the pure blue freshwater lake meeting the cloudless dawn sky with only a slight notion of dry land. He promised to write her a poem on the spectacle and did so, in 'Delos: For Diana Gould'. The piece would appear much later in print in his *Collected Poems*, but he left her a manuscript version, again in longhand, a week after he wrote it. Next, he asked her to marry him and she put him off by claiming that Robin Fedden, who also worked at the embassy, had already taken her out and she wanted to see more of him. She was lying. Fedden was a friend, and no more than that. She was fully aware that Larry had a wife and child in Palestine and while she had never met Eve in person, she knew of her. Fedden played along with her masquerade at least until she left Egypt. Later in 1944 she would meet the acclaimed violinist Yehudi Menuhin, begin an affair and marry him in 1947 following his divorce from his first wife.

One has the impression that wartime Egypt was the scene of carefree debauchery, especially for those not directly involved in the conflict.

Figures such as Xan Fielding, Patrick Leigh Fermor and Billy Moss, one of the youngest of the SOE officers, devoted their spare time to cultivating new ways to attack the Nazis. Surely Larry must deserve the title of libertine-in-chief. Eve never commented on his affair with Diana Gould and he did an outstanding job of keeping her a secret. He had sex with her at her hotel but the city was a hive of gossip and he must have entered and left the establishment in disguise. He eagerly reported to Miller that Eve was his 'favourite' but at the same time he attempted to seduce any presentable woman he met. He closed a letter of late May 1944 with an explanation of all he desired: 'Simple needs this time. A girl who really fucks with the heart and soul and buttocks ...' He was not referring to Eve in particular, or anyone else for that matter. 'A girl' would be anyone who moved within his compass of erotic ambitions. Notably he did not say anything to Miller of Diana, probably because she was a little too bourgeois to suit their double act of radical immorality.

Larry left Alexandria for Rhodes on a heavy-duty motor launch on 30 May 1945, three weeks after Victory in Europe had been declared. He arrived in Rhodes old town and recorded his impression in *Reflections on a Marine Venus* (1953). Most of the once magnificent buildings were either flattened by German bombing or disfigured by shells and gunfire. Around eighty percent of the indigenous population had fled for the remote parts of the island or mainland Greece. The only people left seemed to be forlorn Italian troops – many others had been shot by the Germans after the Italian surrender – and German prisoners of war who were filling in shell holes and hauling half-sunk fishing boats ashore. The British military and diplomatic corps ran the island and Larry was welcomed as a senior member of the latter to his room at the Albergo della Rose, the most prestigious and largely undamaged hotel on the island; the German High Command had used it as their headquarters. As yet Larry had not been appointed officially to a post on the island but was confident that one would soon be offered. That he would sail from Alexandria without even resigning from his job there causes one to suspect that his relationship with the' Foreign Service was at once unofficial and furtive, with his movements decided upon by a Service within a Service.

On his first morning at the Albergo he ran across the garden to the beach, dived into the sea and felt that he'd been taken back in time to the Corfu years.

On 20 June Larry went back to Alexandria on a merchant steamer and when he arrived set about redrafting and sometimes forging documents, with the assistance of his colleagues, to ensure that Eve Cohen was established as his 'Administrative Secretary' and given diplomatic immunity from what might have been her original nationality. His own role was provisional; in Egypt his post was designated as 'Press Attaché', to be confirmed with a designated role when he returned to the island. They sailed for Rhodes together and moved into a spacious double-room suite in the Albergo.

Throughout the rest of 1945 Larry underwent something close to an explosion of hubris. His position as Press Attaché to the Consulate was confirmed and he also became the liaison officer between the Foreign Service and the British military. He told friends that he now felt like Governor of the Dodecanese islands, of which Rhodes was the capital. He was responsible for editorial control of all of the local newspapers – Greek, Italian and Turkish – in that their working editors had to seek his approval for content, especially since the precarious relationship in Greece between the communists and other political groups was aggravated by the defeat of the Germans, and civil war loomed. Matters were complicated by the fact that while the Dodecanese islands were, culturally, affiliated with mainland Greece, their political and administrative status remained ambiguous. They would not become formally united with the country until 1947, against the vociferous objections of Turkey; a considerable minority of the population regarded themselves as Turks. Larry, fluent in English and Greek, and more recently competent in Turkish, hosted numerous press conferences on the future of the islands.

In keeping with his feeling of self-importance he requisitioned the Mercedes staff car previously used by the island's commander Otto Wagener and, with a British army driver, set off around the island, pausing to inspect fishing villages, ancient ruins and spectacular, empty beaches. As in Corfu he resumed his habit of bathing naked, now with Eve, while their driver relaxed with a cigarette in the open-top car.

Larry behaved as if he owned the place and greeted guests, mostly from his Egypt days, as the newly restored Colossus of Rhodes. Fielding and Leigh Fermor came, as did his Cairo friend Romilly Summers, the painter John Craxton and the war photographer Mary Mollo. He asked the latter to do portraits of him in various striking locations, including the streets and buildings of the ancient city and his new office in the medieval quarter. His own room was luxurious and spacious and he was assisted by two secretaries and a personal assistant, though Eve was now more his surreptitious consort despite her forged appointment in Alexandria.

Larry and Eve swam in the Mediterranean every morning before he left for work – the hotel was only a hundred yards from the beach – but within three months of her arrival he thought it was best for them to have separate rooms. They met regularly enough, and had sex, but Larry had become concerned with his image as, in his perception, the most prominent figure on the island. It seemed improper to tarnish this with a blatant extramarital relationship.

A late edition of *Personal Landscape* had been published in London by Editions Poetry shortly after the end of the war in 1945. It contained nine poems by Larry along with pieces by figures he'd known in Cairo and Alexandria, including Keith Douglas, Robert Liddell and Gwyn Williams. Throughout the rest of the year, he was busy putting together a collection exclusively by him for Faber to be called *Cities, Plains and People* (1946). His editor was Faber's director T. S. Eliot with whom he had been in contact since before the war.

In July/August (otherwise undated) he replied to a now lost letter from Eliot and opened with an apparent response to Eliot's enquiry. 'You ask whether I think myself a poet?' We can never know for certain, but it is likely that Eliot wondered if he felt that his principal affiliation was to fiction or verse, given that he was striving for a reputation in both. Larry, however, seemed to treat it as an invitation to judge his poetic accomplishments.

I'm without doubt among the first three in contemporary England. You and Auden are the other two ... all the others are decorators of each other's bed-sitters. I wish this would become clear to a great number of people. (Faber archive)

Modestly, he does not grade the three – himself, Eliot and Auden – in terms of their relative qualities, presuming that Eliot will share his opinion on which of them deserves gold, silver or bronze. In truth his early work slipped between competent amateurism and incomprehensibility.

His role as master of a vacant classical paradise – Apollonius had thrived on the island – seemed to have taken grip of his delusions of literary grandeur.

At the beginning of 1946 Larry came across a slight but elegant building beshadowed by the headquarters of the British administration where he worked and close to the city's largest mosque. It was the gatekeeper's lodge of the old Turkish cemetery, made up of a kitchen, sitting room, bedroom and bathroom, all in good order and comfortably furnished. He moved in, without bothering to ask permission from anyone.

The cemetery contained the graves of grand memorials to the eminent Muslims of the island and while some children from the Turkish quarter would spit at the building before running away – showing their distaste at the incursion of 'infidels' – adults kept a respectful distance. All of this was seen by Larry as acceptance of his eminence; it was also his revenge against 'the suffocating beastliness of Islam ... [its] bigotry, cruelty and ignorance' (*Reflections on a Marine Venus*, p53). Larry had the building officially renamed as Villa Cleobulus, after the Rhodes poet and radical Hellenic philosopher, a man who embodied secularism long before the birth of monotheism. To establish himself as new ruler of the island commonwealth Larry ordered a group of Royal Engineers to build him a spacious wooden table around the massive trunk of the baobab tree, probably a thousand years old, that seemed for most visitors to the cemetery to embody the post-classical history of the city. At first Eve remained in the hotel, visiting sporadically, but within months she joined him permanently as Jewish hostess at the gateway to the Muslim population's monument to their heritage.

Regular guests for dinner were Fielding, Leigh Fermor and his girlfriend Joan Eyres Monsell, along with the British Chief Medical Officer Ray Mills and his wife Georgina; the latter, like Eve, had grown up in Alexandria. Eve had brought the two couples together after Larry used his position to have her referred to Mills following a period of back pain. At least this was the ostensible reason. At the time opioids were diagnosed both for pain relief and as crude versions of what would become anti-depressant drugs. During the 1940s depression was either unrecognised or misunderstood by most members of the medical profession, but it was evident that Eve was experiencing unexplained bouts of melancholia and introversion. This would worsen greatly over the next few years but on Rhodes the jovial company of the Millses and Larry's other friends, plus the use of crude sedatives, seemed to enable her to control the condition.

Larry wanted to retain a position within the diplomatic corps. It was his only source of a regular income and, so long as he could persuade them that he was a specialist in eastern Mediterranean affairs, his guarantee of being allowed to remain in a region he felt to be his spiritual and creative nexus. Life at Villa Cleobulus was an idyll. He could deal with his duties by walking across the road and directly answering enquiries from the press, which were becoming far less frequent, while delegating other mundane tasks to his numerous members of staff. Then he could spend the rest of the day in the villa, writing and then dining and drinking with Eve and guests. He knew that all this would soon come to an end because of the decisions made in summer 1946 at the Paris Peace Conference. This did not involve Germany, which was for the time being an occupied region rather than a nation, but the destiny of territories torn apart over the previous six years was determined. The Dodecanese, occupied previously by several major European powers, would now be permanently united with the rest of Greece. But well before the close of the Paris Peace Conference Greece was in the depth of a civil war, which was a rehearsal for what might happen in the rest of Europe if the 'cold' war between the Soviet-dominated East and the liberal democracies elsewhere heated up. Moscow openly supplied the Greek Communist forces with arms and advisors and Britain and the United States did the same for a panoply of other groups, so long as they were not stridently left-wing. Larry had never held clear-cut political opinions and his equivocation and confusion now became all the more evident.

Friends, notably Diana Gould and Robert Liddell, reported to him of London as a horribly dull and melancholy place. Diana complained of incessant freezing fog and added that in 'this country there's no sex in the climate even' (11 January 1946, Southern Illinois University, Durrell Archive). The war, they implied, had encouraged reckless hedonism but its aftermath involved a puritanical Labour government determined to rule out fun, particularly for middle-class bohemians.

Larry was at first rather pleased with Labour's election victory but in late 1946 he wrote a confused letter to T. S. Eliot who was, he claimed, deluding himself that Britain was a 'Christian Society' while hypocritical Labour politicians were evidently in favour of a Soviet attempt to take over Europe (12 October 1946, Faber Archive). He was particularly horrified at the prospect of a Communist victory in the Greek Civil War. To Theodore Stephanides he wrote that there would be another European war 'within six years', with the majority of Western countries, perhaps with the help of the United States, fighting against 'Russian totalitarianism' for the control of the continent (October 1946, UCLA Archive).

Since the Corfu years he had cultivated an adoration for Greece. The landscape, climate and lifestyle were exquisite, and it could claim to be the cradle of European philosophy and culture. At the same time, it was, after the classical period, a fluid and often anarchic state, persistently occupied by other powers and apparently unable to organise itself as a sovereign state. For Larry its disarray was the key to its charm. Most of the people seemed content with feckless irresolution as a way of life and this was particularly evident in the islands, whose allegiances to the mainland were chaotic. But the Paris conference of 1946 had unified the mainland with its numerous offshore cousins and if the Communists took control of Athens, then the islands would become part of a socialist regime.

Larry had no plans to go beyond Rhodes – he was happy there with Eve in his ancient cemetery house, writing and entertaining. But he feared that once mainland Greece took full control of the island, and the Communists took control of mainland Greece, he would be summarily dispatched from his salaried position in paradise.

At the end of October 1946 Larry applied for a senior post in Athens, reasoning that even if the Communists did gain control of the country British diplomats in the capital would remain immune from the less disagreeable aspects of such a regime. He had what he assumed would be goodbye drinks and meals with the Leigh Fermors, the diplomat Patrick Reilly, Rex Warner the acclaimed writer and classicist, and the historian Steven Runciman, feeling that Athens could be his new home.

He did not get the job and returned to Rhodes despondent. It was clear that he would have to leave the island in about a year – the British contingent, diplomatic and military, was to be drastically reduced. Even if he secured another Foreign Office post Eve could not go with him. Now the war was over regulations were being tightened and married diplomats were no longer allowed to cohabit with their mistresses.

At the end of 1946 Nancy settled on terms for divorce, mainly because she wanted to marry the ex-soldier Mike Silver who had served with distinction in the Tank Corps. Their solicitors advised that the most expeditious means of ending the marriage would be for one party to admit adultery and since Larry's relationship with Eve was public knowledge in much of the eastern Mediterranean, he consented to be the guilty party. Nonetheless, laws drafted in the sanctimonious era of Queen Victoria seemed to demand prurience and humiliation in that it was required of Nancy to provide proof of Larry and Eve's relationship despite his admission of guilt. Her solicitor asked if she could offer photographs of her husband and his mistress 'together'. She could not and in the end Paul Gotch agreed to give sworn testimony that he had witnessed Larry and Eve sharing the same bedroom on numerous occasions. He had made this up but without his assistance the procedure would have gone on for years.

In the run-up to the finalisation of the divorce Larry revised and completed the novel *Cefalu* (1947 with Editions Poetry; later published as *The Dark Labyrinth*, 1958). The character of Alice Liddell is clearly based on Nancy, or to be more accurate Larry's spiteful misrepresentation of his soon-to-be ex-wife. She has an affair which eventually leads to the breakdown of her marriage with John Baird, a version of Larry which flatters the author enormously. Baird is of the lorded gentry, now forced by the loss of the family estate to become a wandering bohemian artist, betrayed by his wife but finding relief in his army career. He is parachuted into several Greek islands to help local resistance groups against their Nazi occupiers, as had done Fielding and Leigh Fermor while Larry enjoyed a hedonistic lifestyle well behind the front line.

113

He wrote to Miller in January 1947, 'I am very happy; being married sometime this month to Gipsy Cohen here in Rhodes.' But his opening mood of exhilaration seems to drift towards anxiety and equivocation. 'I hope it turns out alright but I find rather a lack of confidence in myself these days. Feel rather hysterical. Guess I haven't got over the loss of *my* small daughter yet – *that's* the real crux.' In the novel Alice denies Baird access to his child by having an abortion. If evidence is needed to show that the parallels between fiction and fact are not accidental, they can be found in his letter to Theodore Stephanides in December 1945 shortly after he had agreed to be named as transgressor. He reports that while waiting for the papers to be served he was 'hacking out the last pages of my divorce novel' (December 1945, UCLA Archive).

5

The Meeting of Opposites

Larry and Eve left Rhodes for Athens in mid-March 1947. They had married in a civil ceremony in Rhodes on 26 February, a little later than he had anticipated in his letter to Miller. Larry once more hoped to find work with the diplomatic corps in the Greek capital but nothing was available.

By the end of March Eve had her British passport and the couple were advised to leave for London where Larry might find overseas posts with the Foreign Office or the British Council. They travelled to London via Cairo and Alexandria and accounts of what had occurred in the Mediterranean city differ radically, especially between Larry's two biographers, Bowker and MacNiven. Each had access to some archive material, most significantly letters by Larry, but it is evident that their contrasting versions of events resulted from Larry's tendency to tell different stories for different people. According to Bowker, they went through a Jewish Orthodox marriage ceremony. To mollify Eve's parents, who never wanted her to marry him, Larry bribed an embassy friend to emboss the certificate with a 'grand red Embassy seal', whatever that was, but the only record of this comes from Artemis Cooper's memoir, based on Larry's tale to Cooper (Bowker, p183). In MacNiven's version, coming mainly from correspondence, no religious ceremony at all took place; Eve passed through Alexandria without communicating with her parents, and Larry never met his in-laws then or later.

I emphasise this discrepancy between what seemed to be and what might have been because it was a prelude to the brief coming together of the Durrells in England in 1947, when it became evident that the predominant family trait was a reluctance to tell the truth.

Larry and Eve first spent a week in London where he hoped to reconnect with what was left of his bohemian network of the pre-Corfu years. He tried the Blue Peter nightclub where he had played jazz piano, only to find that it no longer existed. The Fitzroy Tavern was still open, but he knew no one there and when he asked of Gawsworth, George Barker and Potocki he was met with glances of incomprehension. Some had heard of Dylan Thomas, but none knew why the mysterious stranger was asking of him or where he might be found.

According to Botting, Larry would often go shopping for books, mostly second-hand and unobtainable in the Mediterranean and Middle East, and one day came out of a shop with a parcel of volumes only to bump into his youngest brother almost nine years after they had last met. In Gerry's notes Larry insisted that he should visit his friend from wartime Cairo Hugh Gordon Porteus who now lived in the basement of a Georgian house in Chelsea.

In Gerry's Jersey Archive account the Porteus household contrasts sharply with the rather dour atmosphere of post-war London. A 'gaggle' – exact number unspecified – of 'nubile young women' would spread themselves alluringly across sofas and rugs while Porteus stirred a stew made largely from horsemeat and root vegetables. This would feed many, contained as it was in a large and now sealed brass bidet stolen from a Paris brothel, and suspended over a single gas ring. In Gerry's words 'Most of the girls were wearing very little else but diaphanous dressing gowns and bras and exciting lace panties underneath. The soup bubbled in the bidet. The horse steaks were lying in a row on top of a bookcase' (Jersey Archive, undated).

> 'D'you know,' said Hugh, gazing lovingly at the pride of purring lionesses, gurgling sweet nothings to each other, 'I think old Theo would enjoy this – I'll give him a ring and ask him round.'
> 'You mean Theo Stephanides?' I asked, considerably startled.
> 'Um,' said Hugh, 'a dear man.'

'But you can't subject Theo to this – this – what looks like a bordello,' I protested. 'He would shrivel away with embarrassment.'

'No, no,' said Hugh. 'Man of the world. All doctors are forever looking at naked and semi-naked women, lucky swines.' (Undated contemporaneous notes, Jersey Archive)

Consulting his wristwatch Porteus pulls a miniature organ out of a cupboard, asks for silence, and plays a number of tunes, mostly classical pieces. He then explains that this is a daily arrangement for the entertainment of a Mrs Honeydew who lives in the ground-floor flat above the basement. If she is satisfied with the performance she bangs on the floor with her walking stick, and on this occasion she does so.

After entertaining Mrs Honeydew Porteus plays 'The Blue Danube' at length for the semi-clad girls, who dance alluringly. One of them kisses Gerry and presses her body against him but his hopes of more to come are dashed by the unexpected arrival of Theo, then working as assistant radiologist at St Thomas' Hospital, Lambeth.

They [the girls] cooed around him like doves round a fountain. They pressed olives on him and cheese biscuits. They sat round him in a ring of delicious fragrance, palpitating at each word he spoke. (*Ibid.*)

Frustrated by the girls' magnetic attraction to Theodore, Gerry and Porteus spend the rest of the evening talking about zoology.

As a piece of fiction, it is far-fetched, but it is supposed to be an authentic recollection by Gerry of what occurred after his unexpected meeting with his eldest brother. One has to ask: what happened to Larry? After he took Gerry to Porteus' basement and introduced the two men to each other, did he leave? We do not know because he disappears from Gerry's story as if he'd entered it as some sort of otherworldly presence.

Larry mentions Gerry only in a letter to Miller (June 1947) where he reports that 'my youngest brother has turned out a zoologist as he wanted, and is leaving for Nigeria in September to collect wild animals and snakes for the English zoos'. When he wrote this Larry and Eve were staying in his mother's house in Bournemouth after a brief period in London, but in Gerry's notes he first met his brother in the capital in

September while waiting for his passport that would enable him to travel to Africa.

It is probable, likely even, that the rest of the family told Larry of Gerry's plan to visit Africa but at no point does he even suggest to Miller that he had actually met and spoken to his youngest brother. And if he had it is interesting that at no point does Gerry include in his notes any reference to the fact that Nancy has been replaced by Eve. While she might not have been with Larry when he emerged from the bookshop it is curious that he did not mention to Gerry, on their way to the Porteus basement, that he had a new wife.

In Bournemouth Larry introduced Eve to his mother, Margo and eventually Leslie. MacNiven reports that she 'was accepted without question' (p337), an observation based on his brief exchange with Margo almost half a century later. Eve does not feature at all in Margo's memoir *Whatever Happened to Margo?*; the latter focuses almost exclusively on the parade of utterly bizarre guests that pass through the boarding house she opened near the family home in St Albans Avenue. It is equally odd that Eve is absent from every page of Gerry's contemporaneous notes and from the draft for his memoir intended for publication put together much later. She, Larry and Gerry had crossed paths on several occasions during the late 1940s, and Eve was a memorable, outgoing individual. But since she had been excised from *My Family*, the book that made him famous, perhaps he felt uneasy about bringing her to life for later potential readers.

From Bournemouth Larry took the train to London several times: he visited T. S. Eliot, who encouraged him to press forward with his ambitions as a poet; tracked down and took lunch with his old friend George S. Fraser; and arranged to see the surrealist poet David Gascoyne, who he'd known and admired before the war and who had recently suffered a nervous breakdown and been confined to a mental hospital.

In June 1947 his numerous enquiries for work with the British Council resulted in his being summoned for an interview. At this he was informed that the only post available was as consultant and lecturer on British culture in an unspecified location abroad. He was unnerved by the prospect of going somewhere as yet to be decided, but, as the only applicant, was offered the job. He reluctantly accepted it and was informed a week later that he would be based in South America. Not once in his later interviews or in recollections by others does Eve appear as part of this story. Nancy had put up with being Larry's biddable other half, but by comparison her successor seems to have been reduced to the status of baggage.

Further evidence of Larry's political naivete comes in his letter to Miller of June 1947. 'England,' he declares, 'is really very pleasant, the easiest country in Europe to live in despite our groans; the Socialists have done a wonderful job on food distribution and price control.' The Labour government has, in his view, brought about the 'greatest benefit of the greatest number' and 'civil liberties haven't suffered as in Dictator countries'. A year earlier, in Rhodes, he was certain that the post-war government would turn the country into a version of the Soviet dictatorship. He seemed to be living in a bubble given that during the two years after the end of the war food rationing was as severe as it had been at any point during the conflict and during the period of his return to Britain. The Labour government set out in its manifesto to establish a welfare state to protect every citizen from 'cradle to grave', to create a National Health Service 'free to all at the point of access' and to nationalise all major utility industries. It would pay for this by raising taxation to a point higher than any in recorded history; 75 per cent for the comfortably-off middle classes. Outside the expanding Soviet bloc Britain was the only socialist democracy on the planet.

Larry immunised himself from all of this by mixing in London with those who had maintained a bohemian lifestyle from 1939 to 1945 by hiding their stores of wine and spirits and saving their cash reserves for anything else that was available on the black market. Porteus was an exemplar of this.

As usual England was Larry's transit camp, his crossroads to more exotic destinations; his brief visits enabled him to behold the bizarre spectacle of his family, seemingly dedicated to becoming all the more eccentric as years went by.

In July he was informed that he would be based in Argentina. It was then the world's fifth most prosperous country, having been spared the economic ravages of the Second World War which would leave most of

Europe in debt for several generations. He would not set off until the autumn and decided to spend the remainder of his time in the northern hemisphere pretending that things were as they had been in 1938.

He had known the Austrian writer Alfred Perlès in pre-war Paris. Perlès, an Austrian-born Jew, had fled to the US but was now living in Scotland, having been granted UK citizenship. His hosts were John and Gene Pick, the former being a poet, novelist, Quaker and conscientious objector who had spent most of the war working in the coal mines. The Picks and Perlès lived in a small Georgian farmhouse near a loch teeming with trout and Larry spent his time with them fishing. Later he commented that the experience was like Corfu in a cold climate. Once more there is no record of Eve's presence and it is possible that she stayed behind because they arranged to meet on the ferry to Calais at the end of July.

Their host in Paris was the publisher Maurice Girodias, whose Olympia Press had evolved from his father's Obelisk Press which had brought out Miller's *Tropic of Cancer*. Girodias lent Larry £50 and assured him that repayment was unnecessary. This covered around half of their three-week stay at a decent hotel in Notre-Dame-des-Champs, from which Larry ventured out and introduced Eve to the bars and bistros where he had enjoyed himself with Nancy, Miller, Anaïs Nin and others of the bohemian arts community of the 1930s. The atmosphere was evocative but ghostly. Unlike London the French capital remained unscarred by the conflict. It looked just as it did a decade before but the cosmopolitan artistic personnel seemed to have left.

On their return to London Larry and Eve moved into 10 Orme Square in Bayswater, one of the most prestigious locations in the city and made up of eighteenth-century and Victorian houses built for and by the wealthiest members of the aristocracy. Number 10 belonged to Bernard and Ines Burrows who were at the time abroad on diplomatic business. Larry had met them in Cairo but the fact that he hardly spoke of this raises a question as to why Burrows should offer his grand residence to a man who served the Foreign Office and British Council on only an impermanent, ad hoc basis. In 1947 Burrows had been appointed Head of the Foreign Office's Eastern Department, an important post given that 'Eastern' referred to the east Mediterranean and the Middle East, where the fragmented governance of numerous Arab states had become the focus of conflict between several of the post-war powers.

He was not an elected politician, but he was one of the most influential figures regarding Britain's foreign policy in the late 1940s and 1950s. At the time Larry and Eve were borrowing his house Burrows was talking with representatives of Egypt, Syria, Transjordan and Iraq on their response to what seemed the likely formation of a Jewish State in Palestine, then controlled by Britain. Burrows was not an active member of MI6 but he had a significant influence on the activities of the numerous agents who held spurious 'diplomatic' posts in various parts of the Middle East.

Access to records of individuals who worked for MI5 or MI6 is closed but as we shall see a private letter from a retired fellow agent confirms that Larry worked for the latter at various points in his career as a quasi-diplomat. Further to this it is interesting that Burrows would make himself and his home available to a man who was, on paper, a minor functionary in the Foreign Service. Larry was allowed to invite anyone he wished to the house and on two occasions he ushered the servants away and had Eve cook lunch for T. S. Eliot and Gwyn Williams. Impressed, Eliot thereafter exchanged his standard correspondence opening of 'Dear Durrell' for 'Dear Larry'. The Burrows returned at the beginning of October and Larry and Eve remained as their guests until the end of the month when they embarked on the *Brasil Star* from Liverpool. There is no record of what Larry and Burrows spoke of during the period in London and it is curious that a man whom Burrows had met only briefly in Egypt, at least according to explicit disclosures, should then be treated as a close and confidential guest.

One can only speculate on the reason for this and in doing so we must consider Larry's imminent posting. He had no knowledge or experience of Argentina, or for that matter of the country's Spanish and Italian legacies. What is evident is that throughout the Second World War and afterwards the nation was a microcosm of the political divisions and ideologies that had polarised Europe in the years before and immediately following the conflict. Juan Perón had been elected President in 1946 and his Labour Party seemed to have much in common with its British counterpart; both campaigned for the nationalisation of utilities, improved working conditions for the lower classes and a welfare state. Perón, however, enforced his policies in a manner that resembled German National Socialism under Hitler. Dissidents who questioned his programmes were subjected to harassment, physical violence and imprisonment without trial, including those affiliated to left-wing or liberal causes.

Beneath the surface of Argentine politics, during the war and afterwards, there was a widespread sympathy for the Axis powers of Italy and Germany and for Franco's dictatorship, which is why such a large number of senior Nazi military officers and officials found refuge in the country following the defeat of Germany. Ostensibly Larry's job would be to supervise the teaching of English history and literature at the University of Córdoba, founded by Spanish colonists in the early seventeenth century and one of the oldest universities in the Americas. The ancient city was made up of late Renaissance and Baroque buildings and treated as 'Argentina's Oxford'. The appointment flattered Larry, particularly since he had no university qualifications, but as well as giving lectures he was expected to send back reports on the mood of the place to the Foreign Office via Buenos Aires. Perón had a particular loathing for academics, who he suspected were a primary source of seditious ideas, and during his time in power more than two thousand were summarily dismissed from their posts, many from the prestigious University of Córdoba. It is clear enough that Larry was sent to Argentina as Burrows' watcher; his accounts would contribute to the Foreign Office's perception of Argentina being an unstable 'rogue state', carrying traces of European pre- and post-war dictatorships and reflecting the tensions of what the now ongoing Cold War.

At first Larry and Eve found Córdoba stultifyingly tedious. It is 450 miles from Buenos Aires and while economic and industrial growth in the early twentieth century had caused the city to expand far beyond its ancient academic centre it remained a metropolis in the midst of millions of acres of largely deserted pampas. There were a few agreeable restaurants in the old town but beyond that the bars and cafés served the working classes of the commercialised areas.

Relief came when Larry met Enrique 'Quique' Revol, a young writer, and thereafter spent evenings talking and drinking with Revol's friends, most of whom were from the Argentine gentry whose families were part of the seventeenth- and eighteenth-century Spanish colonial legacy. Most had private incomes and without the need to work spent much of their time composing verse and fiction. Revol introduced the Durrells to Jorge Ferreyra and his young and very beautiful wife Bebita. The Ferreyras had properties in various parts of Argentina and lived on a great deal of inherited wealth. Their ancient stone farmhouse, Casa Norman, was a few miles from Córdoba; modest in size but redolent of two centuries of entitlement.

Jorge was impressed by Larry's cultural associations, which he proudly advertised and exaggerated: he was, he announced, Henry Miller's closest friend, T. S. Eliot's confidant, Orwell's occasional correspondent, and sometimes acquaintance of the unfortunate Ezra Pound, now imprisoned for his Fascist sympathies.

The Durrells were invited to share the casa with the Ferreyras, where good-quality wine and food and the attendance of dutiful servants made life in the middle of nowhere almost bearable for Larry. He'd ridden before but now he became briefly addicted to the pedigree stallions kept in the casa stables. He rediscovered the limitless, featureless landscape that had dispirited him when he first arrived once the Ferreyra horses swept him and Eve across it as if they and their mounts were the only living creatures on the planet. The experience inspired 'High Sierra', one of his best poems and one of the few in which he exchanges arbitrary complexity for a more transparent lyricism.

The grass they cropped converting into speed
Made green the concert of their hooves
Over the long serene sierras turning
In the axle of the sun's eye
To legs as delicate as spiders' ...

Larry seems to have carried to Casa Norman a brand of casual privilege he'd enjoyed at the Burrows' mansion in the West End of London.

Typically, he would arrive at the British Council office between 9 and 10 a.m., appear to do an hour or two of administrative work and then disappear with the typewriter. It was evident to all that he regarded his salaried job as sponsorship for his true vocation as poet and fiction writer. After three months with the Ferreyras Larry made use of their upper-class connections to secure a spacious apartment on prestigious Boulevard Chacabuco. Its owner was spending a year in Buenos Aires and Jorge persuaded him that only a nominal rent was appropriate for a great artist working on a masterpiece. Once he had moved to the flat Larry did not bother to return the typewriter to his office and spent less time there than previously.

Larry's boss, the Director of the British Council in the city, was Alec Clifford, a man who treated the stately environment of Córdoba as his natural home. He was an evangelical Anglo-Catholic who admired scholarship and culture as the worldly cousins to piety.

Larry filled him with indignation. He was shocked initially by his junior colleague's lectures. Instead of offering the Argentines the English classics, including even the risqué audacity of Dickens, as moral and cultural archetypes, Larry talked of the likes of Dylan Thomas, T. S. Eliot and Auden, presenting them as personal friends who had happily vandalised tradition. His celebrations of new writing were improvisations, off-the-cuff monologues delivered with only rough notes and sometimes a glass of spirits in hand.

Clifford was equally appalled by Larry's behaviour outside the lecture room. A regular attender at his classes was Norma Campbell, a fellow British Council lecturer who was keen to learn from her associates. She was in her mid-twenties, pretty and shy, and quite soon she and Larry were seen regularly in bars and restaurants. They were having an affair and a friend of Clifford's was questioned much later on Larry's complaints about the boredom of life in Córdoba. 'What do you mean ... what a miserable life he had in this ass of the world of Córdoba? ... The s.o.b. was always drinking the best wines ... and eating the best food and riding the best horses and screwing the best señoritas in town ... You call that fellow poor Larry?' (Raúl Victor Peláez in an interview with Ian MacNiven, 2 April 1987; MacNiven, pp349–50).

The random, extemporised nature of Larry's lectures is evident in their eventual appearance, from his notes, in *A Key to Modern Poetry* (1952). There is a good deal of name-dropping. Psychoanalysts such as Freud, Jung and Groddeck are rounded up alongside the anthropologist James Frazer; Whitehead and Einstein from pure science are there and a token nod towards literary criticism goes to Wyndham Lewis and Edmund Wilson.

It is difficult to discern an overarching thesis and because of this the book might well appeal to advocates of contemporary cultural studies: it engages with all manner of issues but says nothing in particular.

Larry seems especially concerned with the space–time relationship and declares that, since Darwin, via Einstein, 'time as history [has] received its death blow ... time as process, as extension along a series of points, has been halted ... dammed up' (pp34–5). Death, it appears, is not quite as we once perceived it – something to be waited for – but rather a state of mind. This, for those who take it seriously, might be seen as something of a relief. But wait. Its manifestation in literature is Joyce's *Finnegans Wake*, which is circular, without an opening or a conclusion. It goes on, forever.

The choice between having to read Joyce's novel perpetually or accept the old-fashioned notion of death as termination might seem a grand existential dilemma, at least until we accept Larry's book for what it is: intellectually lazy drivel.

When he was not, as Peláez put it, 'drinking the best wines, eating the best food ... and screwing the best señoritas', Larry was toiling away on the stolen British Council typewriter, mostly on drafts of his play *Sappho*, a modern verse-drama that clearly felt itself worthy of comparison with Shakespeare, with extra helpings of figurative verbosity, reflections on the pains of writing and sex. It was largely incomprehensible and it is intriguing that T. S. Eliot responded to his drafts by indicating that Faber would be likely to publish it as a poem rather than try to sell it as a play. Eliot was probably shrewd enough to recognise that post-war London theatregoers had no appetite for further bouts of depression.

It was first performed in Edinburgh in 1961, to rapturous applause, mainly because the audience were devotees of Larry and modernism. The mainstream reviewers were unanimous in their assessment of it as at once grandiose and incomprehensible.

The correspondence between Larry and Eliot when the former worked on it are enlightening regarding both men. Eliot comes across as a figure too self-assured to be real, an embodiment of the pompous and the sublime. Typically, he picks up on a phrase which to him seems unsuitable but remains gnomic on why exactly he thinks it wrong. He will, however, proceed to magisterial comment, on writing per se. For example, after reprimanding Larry on a matter of style he praises him as someone who understands that 'poetry is merely prose developed by a knowledge of aeronautics' (Eliot to Larry, 11 July 1948, printed in *Atlantic Monthly*, May, 1965, pp62–3). Instead of treating this as affected nonsense, as most would, Larry played the game as Eliot's slightly impudent novice. 'Many thanks for your rather acid letter ... Me, I'm a romantic ... at the moment we need a sort of Stendhal for the stage' (Larry to Eliot, 6 August 1948, Faber Archive). Their dialogue comes across as something produced by a cruel satirist with an eye for pretension and an ability to brilliantly reproduce it.

In August 1948 Larry decided that he must find a way out of South America which did not involve him resigning from the British Council or dissociating himself from the diplomatic corps. He had made the best of Córdoba – enjoying the patronage of the Argentine gentry, good food and drink, extramarital sex and insubordination as a lecturer – but he was aware that living outside the cultural mainstream of Europe, Britain and America chipped away at his ambitions to become a literary celebrity.

Larry visited the doctor at the British Consulate and reported himself to be suffering from various forms of depression, panic and nervous distress. In 1948 mental illness of any sort was treated by the medical profession as a kind of self-directed melodrama. Larry was refused a medical discharge from his Argentine post and advised to either strengthen himself or resign.

He chose the latter and set sail with Eve for England on 4 December 1948. After disembarking in London, they took the direct train from Waterloo station to Bournemouth. The family home was as dysfunctional as when he left it for South America just over a year earlier. Margo's B and B, across the road from Louisa's house in St Albans Avenue, was keeping her and her two sons as well as could be expected for a soon-to-be-divorced woman with no qualifications and little work experience. Jack Breeze had disappeared and sent her no money. Her guests were mostly travelling salesmen or transient lower-middle-class clerks with insufficient money to rent even a bedsit. The atmosphere of the place was unusual to say the least given that as a hostess Margo was more resentful than welcoming. For much of her early life she had been used to having the cleaning done, bedlinen washed and food prepared by servants. Now she faced the prospect of doing all of these things for a household of paying residents, most of whom chose to eat out in basic local cafés after sampling two nights of their landlady's suppers, which seemed to involve stews made up of anything unrationed that the local butcher sold cheaply. Breakfast was unavoidable but equally wretched. Most Britons treated bacon and eggs as culinary gold dust, being still part of the harshly imposed food-rationing scheme: Margo overcooked whatever of it she could lay her hands on, offering those in the breakfast room the spectacle of a ruined early-morning delight. She managed by charging less than competing guest houses in the area.

Leslie was busily avoiding arrest, peddling any black market products that he could lay his hands on. These included illegally distilled spirits, which he would supply to Doris's off-licence for rebottling and re-flavouring as gin or whisky.

Larry hoped to be able to spend around a month with his mother, who continued to employ a maid and a cook. He still wanted to convince the British Council that his departure from Argentina was due to various nervous conditions that merited a change of post and region. He had reported that he would be taken care of by his family while awaiting news of another position. His case soon rebounded as he found that Louisa was receiving home visits from John Dixie, his cousin, who worked as a psychiatrist at the nearby Park Prewett Mental Hospital. His mother, he realised, was genuinely unstable and, feeling a little ashamed, he set off with Eve for London. This time some of his pre-war old cronies were around. John Gawsworth, the new King of Redonda, was holding forth regularly in the Old Crown in Museum Street, and other customers included George S. Fraser and the soldier-poet Ian Fletcher. He visited Eliot with a bottle of good wine to congratulate him on his Nobel Prize and called at Diana Gould's house with a signed copy of his *Black Honey* (a piece he had written on Baudelaire's Black lover, Jeanne Duval). He went without Eve. He knew that Gould's new husband, Yehudi Menuhin, was rehearsing; his attempt to seduce her was unsuccessful but they parted on good terms.

Soon afterwards, in spring 1949, Larry booked an appointment with one Arthur Gauntlet, a Kabbalist as he presented himself to his numerous wealthy clients. In truth, he was much the same as the astrologers who catered for the lower classes at circuses, except that he claimed to have access to 'metaphysical insights' involving 'determinism', 'predetermination' and other terms that impressed those who wanted to make palm reading intellectually respectable. What we know of the session comes from Larry himself, who later stated that his future was opened up to him: government service, continuous marital turmoil, problematic relationships with his family, and a life that involved constant shifts from one place to another ('Interpretation of the Horoscope', undated, Southern Illinois University, Durrell Archive). We don't know whether this was Gauntlet's prediction or Larry's weird reflections on it many decades later. There is no genuine record of what the former said and Larry was by now becoming prone to intellectual speculation.

He returned briefly to Bournemouth to see Penelope who had been placed by Nancy in the Lytchett Minster Boarding School in September 1947. Shortly before this Nancy had become pregnant by and then married Edward Hodgkin. It was the first time he had seen his daughter since 1942 and he brought her back to Louisa's house for a few days in an attempt at reconciliation. She hardly remembered him yet at the same time she was desperate for a secure alternative to the sense of abandonment that followed her mother's departure from the gates of her school several months earlier. Louisa, suffering an apparent nervous breakdown, was too unsettled to offer grandmotherly comfort and after less than a week Larry returned Penelope to her school and went back to London. He wanted to write though he knew that his plays would not attract mass audiences in the West End and nor would his novels become bestsellers. He needed a salary and yet again Bernard Burrows proved to be a generous benefactor. He knew of Larry's return from Argentina and by various means contacted him, inviting the Durrells once again to use his luxurious Orme Square house while he was abroad on diplomatic service.

Shortly after Larry moved into the Burrows house a letter arrived from the Foreign Office inviting him to attend an interview for a full diplomatic position abroad. He was puzzled and thrilled in that while he had worked alongside embassy and consular officials in Egypt and the Mediterranean, he was not on the so-called Foreign Office List, the directory of those with experience as diplomats; for this, service with the British Council did not count. Moreover, while the invitation contained a date, time and location in the Foreign and Colonial Office in Whitehall it did not specify the nature of the post and most confusing of all Larry could not clarify these omissions and peculiarities because he had not applied for a job.

Before he set off for his appointment, he received a telegram from Burrows explaining that he had invented the post and arranged for Larry to be summoned. He would be the only applicant for the position of Press Attaché at the British Embassy in Belgrade. The interview was a formality, involving perfunctory questions from the panel on post-war politics which Larry dealt with as if making conversation in a pub. He was offered the post; an initial three-year contract came with £5,000 per year along with various perks including accommodation, transport and anything he cared to charge to his employers, such as meals and drinks in restaurants. In today's terms he would be earning close to £150,000 per year. He would be able to save virtually all of this given that the government paid him for almost everything else.

Once again it was clear that Burrows had arranged the job; this time, so that Larry could serve as his listening post for what was happening in the Balkan states that had become the federation of Yugoslavia in 1918, an uncomfortable assembly of Serbs, Croats and Slovenes. At the close of the Second World War the partisan leader Josip Broz Tito had imposed a communist totalitarian regime on the region but over the next few years he refused to ally himself with Stalin's Soviet bloc countries of central and eastern Europe. Churchill coined the phrase Iron Curtain in 1946 but it was during the following year that it became evident that specific countries in the region were Moscow-controlled satellites. In 1947 most of them rejected the American Marshall Plan which was designed to fund the regrowth of war-damaged Europe. It was seen as an injection of investments into the private sector and the economic infrastructure that had been ruined by six years of conflict and Moscow made it clear that capitalist growth was no longer welcome in a multinational communist federation. Tito, however, prevaricated and sought the best of both worlds. Before the Marshall plan was even mooted he foresaw the economic and political polarisation of Europe and declared Yugoslavia an independent socialist state in 1945 while requesting from the United States financial aid for its economic recovery. The US began sending money in 1949, shortly before Larry's appointment as a Belgrade-based diplomat, and would continue to provide financial support to Tito's regime until 1953, a year after the end of Larry's three-year contract. The country was a wedge between the two sides in the early period of the Cold War: economically it resembled the hard-line socialist regimes of the Soviet bloc but at the same time it presented itself as a country inclined to form alliances with the West. It had relatively open borders with Italy, Austria and Greece.

As with Argentina, Larry's official post as press attaché distanced him from the full members of MI6 who worked in all British embassies and disguised themselves with suitably vague and innocuous job titles. He would attend meetings with Tito's officials, go to government events and dinners, speak to the British press and appear authentically as what he was supposed to be. Unofficially, he would offer reports on the state of things to Burrows, which included rumours and drunken disclosures he picked up from Tito's officials. He was also expected to mix with ordinary people, judge their mood and, crucially, assess the degree of popular support for Tito against those who would prefer their country to be allowed to recover from the conflict much as the Italians were doing across the Adriatic.

Before leaving London Larry was obliged to attend a four-day Foreign Office briefing on eastern Europe, with particular emphasis given to questions surrounding Tito: specifically, did it seem possible that he could become an ally of the West, albeit an undemocratic socialist one; or would he do a deal with Stalin?

Larry and Eve set off by train through France towards the Balkans, staying over in Paris for a few days, and then on to Trieste. On 20 May they boarded the train for Yugoslavia. In Belgrade they were given a small, functional flat used by British diplomats until they could find something more agreeable and during the first few weeks Larry wrote to

Miller and friends in England of his impressions of the country, which for the former he described as epitomising 'systematic moral and spiritual corruption' (June 1949). His erstwhile sympathies for socialism, albeit a radicalist fashion statement, were soon banished by his experience of ideology in practice. He wrote to correspondents of the lack of food and other essential resources, of a population seemingly fearful and ragged in appearance. Worst of all it was clear to him that the army and the secret police were ubiquitous controllers of behaviour. Everyone he spoke to outside his own circle of diplomats and expatriates appeared terrified by the potential consequences of their statements. All newspapers were subject to government censorship.

By the end of the year, he hoped that the British Labour government would be defeated in the forthcoming 1950 general election. He suspected that among the individuals who had transformed Britain after 1945 many wished to impose a brand of hardcore socialism similar to Tito's. Labour survived but by only five seats.

Within three weeks of their arrival Larry and Eve moved into 3 Puskinova Street, a grand, detached house in an area of the city once occupied by wealthy businessmen and their families. Now the locality was in a state of limbo, with most of its original occupants moved out and the buildings seemingly destined for use by the government. In the interim some were made available to Western diplomats.

Throughout his first year in Belgrade Larry bombarded Miller with letters lamenting his fate, mostly because he was compelled to spend his time among people whose nature and temperament he loathed. 'The character of these Middle Europeans is dull, self-pitying and Slav – like the Poles; heavy as gunmetal' (Larry to Miller, 13 January 1950). One suspects that he complains too frequently. Even though Tito had imposed an authoritarian regime upon the citizens of Yugoslavia, others – diplomats and visitors – could enjoy a beautiful landscape and an architectural melange which combined aspects of neo-classicism and Ottoman eclecticism. His work schedule was more than flexible: unless he had unavoidable meetings with the press or government officials he could do as he wished. Many years later he told of how, when on a visit to Trieste, he had found in a locked garage a spectacular German car of the late 1930s, a Horch straight-8, five litre, fitted with hand-crafted leather seats and capable of cruising at 85mph. It was silver-grey and, he also claimed, armour-plated. He allegedly purchased it for a nominal amount and since the garage was in the northern zone, administered by the Allies, drove it a few miles into the southern part of the city, not fully part of Yugoslavia but controlled by various agencies in Belgrade. He reported to his friend Anne Ridler of how he and Eve enjoyed their escapades in 'Herman', as he called the car. He claimed it had once been the property of Hermann Göring and that its very appearance – bespeaking grandeur, officialdom and power – guaranteed that the state police were sometimes sufficiently cowed to even salute it rather than check Larry's papers.

Aside from this letter there is no evidence that his story is authentic. MacNiven (p373) spoke to an embassy mechanic who recalled a vehicle that was similar to that of Larry's accounts but knew nothing of it being driven let alone owned by one Lawrence Durrell. Larry's story might have been true but its striking resemblance to his tale of finding a German general's car in Rhodes causes one to weigh coincidence against plausibility.

Little more than a year after his appointment he booked a flight for himself and Eve to the Italian island of Ischia, where they rented a villa next to an exquisite beach for much of June 1950. Friends from the Corfu years, Constant Zarian and his painter wife Takuhi, were residents and the two couples drank, ate and swam as if the threats to stability in Europe were the delusions of others.

Later in the year, around October or November, Larry began an affair with a Yugoslav ballerina referred to in correspondence only by her forename, 'Smilja' (Larry to Alan Thomas, December 1950, British Library Archive). The relationship concluded when Eve found out that she was pregnant.

Larry decided that the newly established British National Health Service would provide far better care for late pregnancy and birth than the shambolic hospitals of Yugoslavia. He contacted his mother and Mary Mollo, the photographer he had known in Egypt, and asked for advice. Mary suggested that he should rent a house close to a prestigious hospital outside London – free of charge and with no queues for attention by consultants and excellent midwives – and they agreed that Oxford was the best option. Hence, Larry rented a house in Headington, an Oxford suburb where the city's main hospitals – John Radcliffe, Nuffield and Churchill – are based.

Their daughter was born in the Nuffield on 30 May 1951, a week after Larry had arrived from Belgrade. According to Foreign Office regulations he was allowed three weeks' paid paternity leave, immensely generous given that at the time most mothers had pay deducted for the period they elected to miss work and fathers were not granted paid leave by law until the twenty-first century. Larry spent two extra weeks in Oxford with Eve, most of the time debating with her and others the name of their new child. Larry wanted to call her Sappho, the title of his forthcoming publication. Mary and Eve wondered if the child would be mocked at school for carrying forward the name of the first, allegedly, lesbian poet of the Greek classical era. Larry held firm on his insistence and gave way only to Mary's suggestion of Jane by allowing it as his daughter's second name. Eve had very little say in the matter.

When he was in Oxford Larry introduced himself to Francis John Mott, who a year earlier had published *Universal Design of the Oedipus Complex*. Like Georg Groddeck and E. Graham Howe, whom Larry also admired, Mott is presented by some as a creditable, unorthodox thinker who erased the boundaries between philosophy, psychoanalysis and mysticism. In truth he was intellectually deranged, borrowing half-understood praxes from Freud for his own notion of how the flow of fluids through our body conditions us psychologically and explains our destiny and position in the universe. Before the war he had published a tract comparing Hitler with Moses.

The two men became friends and after Larry returned to Belgrade he arranged for Eve and their daughter to stay as guests in the spacious Mott residence in north Oxford. Larry wrote to Miller of his excitement with becoming a pupil of Mott and his friend replied that Mott was dangerous and insane. Mary Mollo was also unsettled by Larry's apparent adoration for Mott and his willingness to place Eve and their daughter in his care. Larry ignored her and indeed asked his new mentor to become Sappho's godfather, despite the fact that neither man believed in God.

Since his time in Paris before the war Larry had become increasingly preoccupied with philosopher-psychoanalysts, notably Groddeck and E. Graham Howe who treated Freud as the gatekeeper to speculations on the nature of selfhood and consciousness that were by parts eclectic and bizarre. They were like children let loose in the sweetshop of radical ideas that arrived at the beginning of the twentieth century, ranging from Einstein's groundbreaking explorations of space and time to the philosophical implications of modernism.

Larry was attracted to these more eccentric disciples of the unorthodox because they put self-indulgence before rationalism and logic, always manipulating particulars of new thinking to suit their idiosyncratic inclinations. It is difficult to describe Larry's own cabinet of enthusiasm because it involved so many contradictions and anomalies but the following is not too inaccurate: Einstein, in his view, had come upon a scientifically respectable version of time travel and non-linear human existence; Freud's more deviant followers explained what prompted behavioural urges and habits via a mixture of make-do biology and agnostic mysticism; and de Sade, D. H. Lawrence and Freud, again, explained that sex, particularly for men, was by equal degrees vital and exempt from accountability. It is doubtful that he actually believed in these borrowings as clarifications of life as he lived it – except perhaps the sex thesis as a rationale for his infidelities – but they served him well enough as justifications for creating fictional worlds that bore little relation to any sane person's notion of reality.

Larry returned to Oxford from Belgrade in late August and on 1 September Eve and Sappho joined him on the *Orient Express* back to the Balkans. Once more Larry set about reorganising embassy duties to make room for his true vocation as a writer. Desperate to complete *Reflections on a Marine Venus* by Christmas, he sent it to his publisher in mid-January. He communicated regularly with the esteemed actress Margaret Rawlings, who was due to organise a public reading of *Sappho* in London on 21 January, and he was doing final corrections to *A Key to Modern Poetry* which would appear with Peter Nevill Publishers in London in April 1952.

Early in the New Year there were drastic reductions in Foreign Service salaries, partly as a result of the newly elected Conservative government's desire to save on public spending while maintaining the welfare and health legacy of Labour. Larry's £5,000, plus residential and travel expenses, was slashed to an all-inclusive £1,500. In England this would be enough for a thrifty person to live well enough but Larry in Yugoslavia was anything but thrifty, and nor was he particularly concerned with his duties. From the beginning of May he left with his family on a six-week camping tour through Macedonia into Greece and after that they established themselves on the Greek peninsula of Chalcidice until their return to Belgrade on 8 July.

MacNiven (p379) presents Larry's departure from Foreign Office service as his decision, made partly because he was finding it difficult to survive on a reduced salary and partly as a result of his enduring contempt for his work. Neither is likely given that £1,500 is better than nothing, which is what he was left with in October. Also, his final official duty was to play host to the official five-day visit to Belgrade of the Foreign Secretary Anthony Eden who wanted to reassure Tito that should Stalin threaten to drag Yugoslavia into what amounted to his Eastern bloc superstate he could rely on the support of Britain and her NATO allies. When Eden departed on 23 September, he publicly praised Larry and his team for their work. The following day he was released from his Foreign Office contract. Certainly, his three-year initial term of duty had expired but by convention initial contracts were seen as probationary periods. Bowker (p208) states that Larry was 'fired'. We will never know for certain who took the decision to part company with whom. What is clear enough now however is the true nature of his work. Much later when he was based permanently in France and earning his living exclusively as a writer he received a letter from the journalist and fellow novelist Frederick Forsyth (16 March 1971, Jersey Archive), whose debut volume *The Day of the Jackal* (1971) had sold millions and would earn the author a gigantic amount from the 1973 screen adaptation. It was first assumed that the plot, centred on an attempt by a French right-wing group to assassinate de Gaulle, was based largely on news reports and invention. But in his memoir Forsyth revealed that he had supplemented his twenty years as a journalist with regular work for MI6. He had based the novel on direct knowledge of communications between British and French intelligence services.

In the letter he discloses to Larry that he is writing to him because they had both been involved in the 'same business', which does not refer to their shared profession as writers. Forsyth explains that he has been commissioned to do a screenplay for a film on the unorthodox branches of British military forces during the North Africa campaign. He knew of Larry's friendship with Leigh Fermor and of the tensions between his group, the Special Operations Executive, and MI6. The very existence of the latter was not disclosed until 1994 and the fact that Forsyth felt able to discuss with Larry confidential details of it shows that they were part of the same espionage network.

Forsyth was particularly interested in the activities of the so-called Special Interrogation Group (SIG), an offshoot of SOE made up of German-speaking Jews from Palestine and other parts of the Middle East, which went behind enemy lines in Wehrmacht uniforms, attacked communication networks and kidnapped German soldiers who would be questioned on their recent activities – hence the term 'Interrogation'. It was a controversial organisation and Forsyth was aware that he could not expect Larry to testify – confess – as an associate. Nonetheless, he asked in the letter for details that would be informative but redacted if necessary. Particularly, fifteen SIG men had been killed in a German ambush and it was thought that the one member who survived was an informer. The commander of the unit, Captain Herbert Buck, was, Forsyth reminded Larry, a friend of his and had been too unwell with a stomach problem to go on the raid in which all but one had been killed.

It was evident that Forsyth knew from his associates in the intelligence services that Larry was part of a network of organisations – principally the SOE, SIG and MI6 – which worked together in the war and thereafter. In the letter it is clear that he had obtained what amounts to his correspondent's CV as a spy.

Within a month of Larry's departure from his job in Belgrade Eve started to alternate between periods of anxiety, elation and nervous depression. Every account of this is marked by a determined reluctance to consider the trigger for her condition. All MacNiven does is to shift our attention to Larry's cryptic, conceited assessment of things in a poem he wrote at the time:

So, marriage can, by ripeness bound,
From over-ripeness qualify
To sick detachment in the mind ('Letters in Darkness', in *Collected Poems*, 1980)

Most poems avoid literal interpretation – the form is by its nature capricious and oblique – and it is for this reason that Larry chose to use it as a strategy of avoidance. Consider: a woman whose husband was a serial adulterer, and who had suddenly chosen homelessness and potential poverty because this suited his whimsical state of mind; she had recently had a child by him and had exchanged her previous existence for what now appeared to be a state of limbo. Common sense would treat this as a recipe for a nervous breakdown, but why face such an uncomfortable truth when it could all be distilled into something resembling Yeats' mythical gibberish.

Given that Larry was no longer officially attached to the British diplomatic corps it remains open to speculation on how he managed to find transport for her and admission to the Psychiatric Division of the Military Hospital in Hanover. She was admitted on 4 December.

Reports reached Larry that his wife was a psychiatric depressive and prone to suicidal tendencies. He did not visit her in Germany; instead, he bombarded his friends with enquiries about jobs or loans for enterprises in the eastern Mediterranean.

Eve recorded her thoughts while in the Hanover hospital. 'I was constantly aware of *all* parts of the maelstrom which was terrifying me ... with the result that I only felt safe in the hospital' (Eve's 'Notes on Life', p3; unpublished manuscript held by Ian MacNiven). MacNiven interprets the keyword 'maelstrom' as Eve's own shrewd assessment of her self-diagnosed 'manic depressive' state; she was thus content to place herself in the care of the hospital psychologists before she felt well enough to rejoin her beloved Larry.

Sappho, however, offers a very different account of events (published after her death as 'Journals and Letters', in *Granta*, Autumn 1991). At the time she was only around eighteen months old but her 'recollection' is based on what her mother told her later.

According to Sappho Eve had to 'nurse' Larry for 'acute depression' in Argentina, a condition that was a euphemism for his heavy drinking. One sentence is not contained by inverted commas but it is clear enough that Sappho expects us to treat it as a direct quotation from her self-regarding father: 'No one could suffer as much as a great artist.' In Belgrade Larry had apparently become a threatening, often violent husband. When Eve removed her ring and said she would leave him, 'He wheezed with the shock and started to throw her around ... He became the devil. He refused to believe she had the will to leave him.' Sappho, from Eve, claims that her mother was not sent to Hanover because of a genuine mental disorder. 'She was having hallucinations' because of Larry's reign of terror. 'She was drugged and taken to a military hospital. They drugged her heavily to the point where her head was throbbing' (*Granta*, Autumn 1991).

Considered in relation to Sappho/Eve's report the 'maelstrom' was not in Eve's head but rather caused by her relationship with a man now some eight hundred miles to the southeast 'which was terrifying me'.

It is difficult to decide conclusively on which version of events to believe but in considering the conundrum we ought to take into account how MacNiven, Larry's authorised biographer, or more accurately hagiographer, deals with it. He does not deny or attempt to refute Sappho/Eve's story. He pretends that it does not exist.

Shortly before Eve's removal to Hanover Larry had asked George Wilkinson to find him a villa in Corfu, his old paradise, but in her absence said he now wanted to move to Cyprus. A small house was rented and Alan Thomas arranged for his papers, notebooks and unfinished manuscripts to be sent there.

Eve was discharged from the Hanover hospital in early January 1953 and while she was relieved to be allowed out, she asked to be spared her husband's company. She was permitted to very briefly join her daughter in Bournemouth where Louisa had been looking after Sappho since Eve had been diagnosed as mentally ill. Sappho:

While my mother was away, I was looked after by my grandmother but she disliked having to deal with my shitting (servants had dealt with it in India with her children). My father echoed her disgust and disapproval. She said that when my mother came back she was going to punish me for shitting in my pants (I still had to wear corduroy trousers to keep nappies up). On her return my mother was horrified to see my fright. (*Granta*, Autumn 1991)

On 26 January 1953 Larry disembarked at Limassol, Cyprus, with Sappho. They had left Eve in Trieste to 'rest' and see a consultant psychologist regularly but at the end of January, she would return voluntarily to Hanover for further intensive scrutiny and treatment. Eve would not join Larry and her daughter in Cyprus until February 1954, after begging the Burrows, whom she'd grown to trust, to find her and Sappho a place to stay in England should she suddenly decide to leave Larry with her daughter. By late July Larry and Eve accepted that their marriage was beyond repair and that she would join him on the island only for them to come to an agreement on the timing and nature of their formal separation.

In March 1953 Larry had bought a pretty, spacious but dilapidated house in the hamlet of Bellapaix, four miles from the sea, where, soon afterwards, he was joined by Louisa who would look after Sappho while he oversaw restoration by local builders and began work on what would be the first volume of *The Alexandria Quartet*. Once Eve had rejoined the family and the dreadful nature of their relationship was acknowledged Larry began to spend much of his time in the larger town of Kyrenia. He had rented a room there for a token amount and used it as a private bolthole for writing. He bought a fold-down bed and paid visits to his daughter, mother and soon-to-be ex-wife for short periods during the day.

He was not, however, entirely dejected. Before the arrival of Eve, he had met Marie Millington-Drake. She too was restoring a local property, far more grand than Larry's. 'Villa Fortuna' as it was eventually known would later become the Turkish Ambassador's summer residence. Marie's father was the wealthy diplomat Sir Eugen Millington-Drake, and her mother, Lady Effie Mackay, was daughter of James Mackay, 1st Earl of Inchcape. She was twenty-nine when they met, blonde, gratuitously eccentric and very beautiful, and would begin an affair with Larry before

Eve left him finally in late 1955, Marie resurfaces, undisguised, as 'Marie' in the memoir *Bitter Lemons* (1957), and with a little more camouflage as 'Martine' in *Sicilian Carousel*, a fiction/travel book hybrid (1977). The latter was a tribute to her: she had married Duke Gaetano Paternò Castello of Sicily and become Duchess of Carcaci. She died in 1973.

Of 1953–4 Bowker writes that 'Genius makes an uneasy bedfellow, and Durrell's genius was about to burst forth' (p210). Similarly, for MacNiven the period marks an artistic epiphany: 'The principal quarry for the events of the future *Quartet* had been Egypt; let Cyprus now be the crucible' (p385). Both seem to believe that the vocation of artist is an excuse for virtually all kinds of nasty behaviour and are thus incapable of perceiving Larry for what he was: a cruel, self-regarding egotist.

6

The Rise of Gerry

Following his return from the Cameroons in 1949, Gerry arranged with his fellow collector/zoologist Ken Smith that their next trip should be to South America, where there were just as many species unknown to Europeans and threatened by extinction. First, however, he took the train to Manchester to have talks with the managers of the Belle Vue Zoo. He hoped to persuade them to take in some animals from Africa and the Americas that their visitors had never seen or heard of but before he even spoke to them his life took a very different course.

He took a room at an unostentatious commercial hotel owned and run by John Thomas Wolfenden. Almost all the other occupants were young female members of the *corps de ballet* of the Sadler's Wells Opera Company. Several of them recognised Gerry from newspaper photographs, and one commented that he resembled a rather short, Anglicised version of the athlete and actor Johnny Weissmuller whose entire cinematic career was founded on his appearances as Tarzan and more recently in the *Jungle Jim* movies.

One other young woman present was Jacqueline, known familiarly as Jacquie, Wolfenden, nineteen-year-old daughter of the owner and stepdaughter of his recent wife. She was pretty, sharp-featured and bore a slight resemblance to Audrey Hepburn. Jacquie later recalled being irritated by this 'crowd of chattering females' who 'could do nothing more but talk about some marvellous being who apparently had everything any woman could desire ...' On the following Sunday afternoon, a mass of them 'cascade' through 'the living-room door dragging in their wake a rather delicate-looking Rupert-Brookeish young man ...Wonderboy himself' (*Beasts in My Bed*, pp7–8). Decades later in his notes Gerry records his first impression of her: '... pursed rosebud mouth like the anus of a baby goat' (undated contemporaneous notes, Jersey Archive).

Jacquie was studying opera and her meeting with Gerry altered his life completely and indeed the legacy of the Durrell family in general. She was well-enough read but preferred the prospect of a career in music to that of literature, either in terms of studying, teaching or producing it. Nonetheless she was brilliant in terms of her ability to pick out the mood and appeal of a good story and, crucially, to draw out the captivating from the otherwise ordinary in the way it was told. Larry was the 'serious' Durrell author but his brother created the legend of the Durrells, and Jacquie created Gerry the writer. Without her, *My Family and Other Animals* would not have been the book that it is. In his memoir notes Gerry wrote, 'She [Jacquie] is upright and honest – I am upright and dishonest. We are like two sides of a coin of legal tender' (Jersey Archive, undated).

During his first stay at the Wolfenden hotel, roughly two weeks, Gerry asked John's permission to take his daughter out on a date. She 'thought it might be amusing to spend an evening with such a "man of the world"' (*Beasts in My Bed*, p9) and they went out for dinner. Gerry told her he was soon off on another 'trek abroad' but that he would write and see her again in Manchester on his return, if she wished? She replied that she did, later reflecting that she found his promise 'more amusing than romantic'.

In January 1950 Gerry and Ken Smith set off on a steamer from Liverpool for British Guiana, a landmass on the northwestern part of South America but in all other respects part of the British colonial domain of the Caribbean; it would not gain independence until 1966. Both men were overjoyed by their first encounter with a geographical environment and climate that seemed far more exotic and diverse than anything they had encountered in Africa. White beaches soon gave way to muddy, tidal marshlands, bordered by plateaus, flat-topped mountains and savannahs. Its grasslands resembled the South African plains, while at their highest the Pakaraima mountains reached up to 2,800 metres. The variegated shapes, colours and landscapes of the globe seemed to have been crammed together into an area smaller than that of the United Kingdom.

The strange appearance of the region was matched by the peculiarities of its non-human inhabitants. Gerry had come across anteaters before but none that seemed roughly twice his size. The capybara belongs to the rodent family, but at around two feet in height and up to one hundred pounds in weight it puts the fear of God into those even mildly unsettled by rodents. Gerry's team managed to net an arapaima, which bears a slight resemblance to the European pike, albeit without the colourful appearance, but while the largest recorded pike was around five and a half feet long, arapaimas often reach seven to eight feet. They are among the world's largest freshwater fish, carnivores whose diet is limited mostly to other marine life but who looked as fearsome as sharks to Gerry and his companions. Tree porcupines, or 'pimple hogs' as Gerry christened them, were one more among the range of charming indigenous species, as was the beguiling 'paradoxical frog', named as such because at its tadpole stage it might grow to more than fourteen inches and then in maturity shrink to the size of other toads.

Gerry was transfixed and added to his catch a 'squirrel monkey', seemingly without an official Latin name, and a potentially deadly anaconda snake.

He also attempted to acquire Rita, of mixed African-Iberian and northern European origin dark-skinned and beautiful. She had ventured into Mrs Clarabelle's boarding house in Georgetown, Gerry and his team's basecamp, and in his diary he recorded some of their exchanges: 'My name is Gerry and you are the most beautiful girl in the world', to which she responded, 'And you are something else, man' (Jersey Archive, undated).

She had very pale, chestnut-coloured skin, the sort of shade you would get by mixing half a bar of Cadbury's chocolate with a pint of cream. Her hair was long, black, curly and as magnificent as a lion's mane. She was slender, with superb legs and wonderful hands ... We went to bed. (*Ibid.*)

Afterwards, he lectures her on the wonders of her locality.

> 'I never knew there were so many beautiful birds in Guyana,' she said, wonderingly. 'That's because you've been sleeping with the wrong men,' I pointed out. 'Sleep with a naturalist and he'll show you the wonders of the universe.' (*Ibid.*)

We will never know if Rita was real or part of the fantasy that Gerry sometimes wove into his notes on his expeditions, but even if she did exist there are two versions of her. The first, from the 1950 diary, is rendered in the characteristic mode of the era, as a delightful subject of the empire who sleeps with Gerry in the hope that he'll enable her to buy a bicycle. Much later she emerges in the passage quoted above as part of his planned autobiography written during the closing years of his life. The second Rita is an avatar for his lifetime mission as a zoologist, which informs every sentence of his draft for the memoir. Hence, the almost evangelical mode of his exchange with her after they've had sex. He explains to her the habits and mannerisms and indeed the beauty of the creatures that surround her and she experiences what amounts to an epiphany.

Despite his promise to write to Miss Wolfenden from South America he never quite found the time. Later he claimed that she was always on his mind during the expedition, while she stated that 'I was very busy gaining experience in public singing, and was, in fact, far too occupied even to think about what Gerry might be doing' (*Beasts in My Bed*, p10). Nonetheless she experienced 'shock to find him sitting in our living room one May afternoon, looking extremely fit and (even to my rather jaundiced eye) attractive'.

She was not, however, clear about the nature and cause of her attraction. He had, it seemed, a certain allure for other women – 'clumping carthorse blondes' or dance-hall girls as she later called them – but those capable of something closer to intelligence were less magnetised by his reputation as an explorer and animal lover.

She was a little more impressed when he persuaded her to come with him to Belle Vue Zoo, southeast of Manchester city centre. It had originally opened in 1836 as a spectacle for genteel classes of the early industrial revolution; those who wished for a diversion from the manufacturing townscape by gazing at exotic creatures imprisoned behind steel bars. For the first time in their brief acquaintance she encountered the real Gerry. As they wondered between the enclosures, he explained that 'zoos must be sanctuaries rather than enclosures'. 'His most cherished ambition in life was to create a special zoo where he could keep and breed some of these [most threatened] creatures in the hope that they would not be completely exterminated.'

> ... the thing that most impressed me was Gerry's relationship with all these creatures. Suddenly, this seemingly shallow young man became a different person. Gone was the diffident air as he walked solemnly up and down the lines of cages, giving each creature titbits and talking to them. He really cared about them and they, in a funny way, returned this love and interest with obvious trust. (*Ibid.*, pp11–12)

It was at this point too that Jacquie was aware that her feelings of beguiled irritation were, like those of the animals, turning into a special brand of affection.

Over the next three weeks Larry travelled across England negotiating with managers of zoos to secure places for his new guests from South America yet he never quite left Jacquie behind, leaving phone messages with her father and stepmother on what he was doing and sending her first-class letters that read like versions of the enchanting monologues on rescuing the threatened animals he'd offered her in Belle Vue.

Suddenly he arrived at the hotel in person, bearing a large bouquet of chrysanthemums, which he thrust towards her and asked, 'You wouldn't like to marry me, would you?' (*Ibid.*, p13). She was too stunned to reply immediately and before she could he grinned, turned and left the hotel reception.

The only first-hand account of what occurred during the next few months comes from Jacquie in her memoir, which I will summarise. Doing this, however, is the equivalent of describing 'what happens' in one of Larkin's or Betjeman's best poems. You can try to outline the crux of the thing while knowing that its true value has little to do with what it is about. Her voice and comic touch are just as bewitching as her story.

The marriage proposal might have been genuine or something more peculiar and consistent with Gerry's increasingly aberrant character. We will never know because Jacquie keeps us guessing. Thereafter he bombards her with letters – probably of endearment, but again this is not clear – and expensive presents. She seems captivated by this, much as one might be if invited to a party by an odd though seemingly harmless stranger.

Eventually Gerry returned to Manchester and asked if he could speak to Jacquie's father to 'explain it all personally'. She listens at the door apparently hoping to hear one of Wolfenden's periodic bouts of rage followed by Gerry's terrified departure. Instead, their exchange sounds amicable, often punctuated by laughter.

The following day Gerry invites her to Bournemouth to meet his family which, she implies, is a prelude to something like an enduring relationship.

By this time Louisa has sold what was once the main house and moved into Margo's property across the road, now transformed from a bed and breakfast to an assembly of flatlets occupied by individuals who seemed well-suited to their eccentric family of hosts: a jazz saxophonist and pianist who shared a bed; a man, allegedly from Sicily, who always dressed as woman; a terrified wife hiding from her violent husband; a portrait artist who only painted female nudes and never sold any of his works.

Jacquie was introduced to Louisa, whom she found 'very different' from how she'd imagined her to be: a 'tall, rather forbidding woman'. She does not explain how she had formed her initial impression but it is safe to assume that since she helped Gerry with *My Family and Other Animals* three years later, she was indulging their shared transformation as part of her recollection. Louisa was in fact 'a tiny, gentle person with merry blue eyes and silver hair' (*Ibid.*, p19). She wasn't, but she might have been had the fantasy of *My Family* aged a couple of decades.

Leslie struck Jacquie as likeable, mainly because he resembled a bit-part lovable rogue from post-war British comedies, someone like Sid James. Margo was, at least in Jacquie's portrait of her, faintly bizarre, as if a little detached from what others perceived as the world of actual events. 'Elder Brother Larry seemed the most formidable, but I probably wouldn't meet him yet as he lived abroad' (*Ibid.*).

Jacquie's father was away on business so they decided to return to Manchester for a few days, and after supper in the town, found that everyone in the house had gone to bed. They chatted in front of living-room fire before realising that it was past five in the morning. Falling over themselves to reach the unlit hall Gerry said to her 'very quietly', 'Well, will you marry me?' to which she replied, '"Yes, of course I will," and so the trouble was over' (*Ibid.*, pp21–2).

Almost, since they next found themselves racing for an express train south at Manchester Piccadilly station in case her father had already discovered her note of intent and was in pursuit of them with his shotgun.

Once back in Bournemouth they marshalled the services of the Durrell family in the arrangement of the wedding, with Margo taking command, accompanying Jacquie to choose a ring, ordering a single-tier cake ('As a reward for her efforts we ordered large slabs of cream gateau which Margaret devoured with obvious pleasure') and organising events at the local Registry Office. Leslie offered alcohol of dubious origin for the modest reception. Larry had sent a letter expressing his approval, though no one could explain how he had learned of and responded to the event so rapidly. Jack Breeze, Margo's first husband, strolled in and was asked to be best man.

'You poor thing,' said Jack, 'how did you get embroiled with the Durrells?' Raising one of his bushy eyebrows, he asked, 'You didn't have to, did you?' and then roared with laughter. (*Ibid.*, p27)

They were married on 26 February 1951, moved into a flatlet in the Durrell property and then looked for work. Gerry found a position for both of them in Margate, at a cross between a disorganised menagerie and a seaside amusement park. In March when they went there, it was all but empty and they were expected to take care of the place, clean out cages and other areas in return for accommodation, food and no salary.

Within three weeks they were back in Bournemouth and Jacquie came up with an idea. 'Larry Durrell was quite a successful author and had, from all accounts, always encouraged Gerry to write. If one Durrell could write and make money at it why should another one not try?' (*Ibid.*, p30). She had made up the claim that Larry had prompted his brother to write, and in the mid-1960s when she concocted this story Gerry had sold far more books and made more money from them than had the esteemed author of *The Alexandria Quartet*. Touché, as Larry might have put it but did not.

Jacquie calls the project she conceived 'Operation Nag', truthfully enough. She insisted that the diaries of his various expeditions, though largely unreadable in their original form, were excellent raw material for a more polished first-person account by the adventurer who had become a newspaper celebrity. All she had to do was to convince Gerry that he could transfer onto paper the engaging storyteller who had led her through Belle Vue Zoo in Manchester, introducing her to its inhabitants as though they were guests at a party and telling of how and when he had met them and their relatives in places unknown to virtually everyone north of the Mediterranean. He refused even to try. 'I can't write, at least not like Larry' (*Ibid.*, p30).

He was persuaded to change his mind, at least according to Jacquie, by Larry, who arrived in Bournemouth in early 1951 with Eve. The timeline is accurate enough since Larry and Eve had decided to have their child in England at this point but there is no record of their supposed visit to Bournemouth.

The conversation between the two brothers, as reported by Jacquie, is hilarious, less in its own right than because of the effect it would have had on Larry several years after it was alleged to have taken place. Larry suggests that he should write 'a book' on those 'dreadful trips you go on', that the 'British simply love stories about fluffy animals and jungles, and it's so easy to do'. But no, Gerry won't have it. 'Remember, I've had no experience of serious writing. It's all right for you, you love it and you've been writing for years.' Or, as he might have added: look how you've ended up, respected but otherwise destitute.

Throughout the exchange there is a subtext: Larry saw himself as a proper writer and was happy to encourage his younger brother to produce something that might amuse those who were now exchanging books for television sets.

148

'I'm more than prepared to give you an introduction to my publishers, Fabers,' Larry advises in Jacquie's book. Larry treated Faber and its head Eliot as the literary nobility, to which figures only such as himself deserved access. If he had said this to Gerry it would have been to mock him. But he did not say it and Jacquie fabricated the comment to remind her brother-in-law that Gerry had indeed sent a manuscript of his first book and obtained a contract almost immediately from Faber, without Larry's help.

Gerry became a writer because of Jacquie. Before trying a book Gerry attempted a story for BBC Radio, provisionally entitled 'The Hunt for the Hairy Frog', based on his first visit to the Cameroons. Jacquie had already heard him read from his longhand diary records of the weird creatures he came across and while the substance of these seemed fascinating, she sensed that something was lacking, principally coherence. Suddenly the second-hand typewriter found for him by Jack Breeze transformed things. Weirdly he appeared able to put typed words on paper in a way that preserved the fluent, unforced manner of his oral accounts while adding the old-fashioned virtues of sentence structure and clarity. As each page came out of the machine, he handed it to Jacquie who was at one enraptured and critical: change that; shorten this passage; tell us more about the snake or the ape; expand on how the swamp felt hot, friendly yet a little frightening! Gerry found that he could type faster than a trained secretary, and went back through his first drafts, talked about them with Jacquie, and improved on them all the time.

In late summer 1951 they sent the first draft of the hairy frog story to the BBC Talks Department, explaining that a reading would last around ten to fifteen minutes. For almost two months the Corporation did not bother to acknowledge receipt of the script but in September a letter arrived from Mr T. B. Radley who stated that he had enjoyed the story and invited Gerry to call him by telephone at Broadcasting House. The discussion was a formality. Radley said he thought Gerry's work delightful and asked him to come to London for the weekend of Friday 7 to Sunday 9 December. A rehearsal took place on the Friday and on Sunday Gerry read the story live for the BBC Home Service, which would later become Radio 4. During the same year *The Goon Show* and *The Archers* were launched and Tony Hancock made his acting debut on the Light Programme. BBC Broadcasting was creating a new blend of popular culture comparable to the equally entertaining brand of writing soon to be epitomised by the likes of Kingsley Amis and Philip Larkin.

At the time the accurate measurement of listener numbers was dubious but letters arrived from all over the UK expressing delight in Gerry's melodic, picturesque presentation of a world that most could barely conceive of. Over the subsequent months into early 1952 Gerry wrote and did three more live BBC recitals of more stories on his escapades in Africa and South America. He was the talk of the land. But the BBC paid him around £15 per broadcast, which amounts to around £400 today, barely enough to keep oneself on the breadline.

He applied for work in the Uganda Game Department and the Khartoum Museum in Sudan, which kept a stock of dead but well-preserved wild animals. Failing in both instances he and Jacquie decided that his self-evident popularity as a storyteller might result in something close to an income: he would write a book.

The Overloaded Ark carries only Gerry's name on the spine and title page but in truth it was co-authored by him and Jacquie in the cramped attic room of 52 St Albans Avenue. Jack Breeze had found him a modern typewriter, a quieter version than the last that didn't waken the other guests when Gerry and Jacquie stayed up into the early hours in their attempt to present something that would interest a book publisher. The typescript, roughly 65,000 words, took them less than six weeks to complete and they sent it to Faber for the simple reason that they knew of them as Larry's publishers, had contact details from his correspondence with Louisa, and they had the address of no one else. The typescript went out in April and in early June Faber replied, stating that they loved it and inviting Gerry to their office in London to discuss the terms and conditions of a contract.

The offer by Faber was £25 on presentation of the manuscript, £25 on publication and 10 per cent royalties once the advances had been cleared by sales. It was a parsimonious offer even for a debut author but Gerry accepted it; Faber was a prestigious imprint which might offer him better prospects.

Nonetheless he wrote to his brother's agent Spencer Curtis Brown, who was appalled by Faber's contract. He went through it and found that it omitted terms and conditions related to sales of the book outside the UK and translations. Notably, he forced Faber to agree that US rights should be paid immediately to the author: £500. Today such an advance would amount to around £12,000, an extraordinary sum for a debut book. The fact that Curtis Brown could corner Faber into such an arrangement, and their apparent willingness to concede to his demand, testifies to their shared perception of the book as a bestseller.

Faber ruled that the book should be published on 31 July 1953, almost a year after they had accepted the manuscript. In normal circumstances a potential money-maker would have been rushed through production in six months but T. S. Eliot decided that it would be a publicity boost to bring out books by two brothers simultaneously. Larry's *Reflections on a Marine Venus* had recently been accepted. Both could be roughly classified as travel books – a welcome escape for those with no other means to put up with the post-war years – but in other respects they had nothing at all in common.

Larry's account of the eastern Mediterranean, Rhodes specifically, reflects a poet's intoxication with a landscape that bespeaks beauty and preserves a legacy of classical wisdom. It is the kind of book that those who thought themselves intellectuals would purchase, if only to reinforce this self-image.

Larry wrote to Theodore: 'Gerry and I will be cheek by jowl in Faber's Spring list – two Durrells where only one grew before' (5 January 1953, UCLA Archive). There is a detectable hint of irony and resignation, and later to Miller a year later. 'My youngest brother Gerry has scored a tremendous success with his first book and is making a deal of money. He collects wild animals for zoos and writes up his adventures afterwards. The one pays for the other; how marvellous to have one's career fixed at 25 or so and to be able to pay one's way' (5 January 1954). Much of the rest of the letter comprises his complaints about the onset of middle age ('now in my old age (42!)'), the difficulties of making a living from the vocation of writing, and the expense and bother of restoring his recently acquired house in Cyprus. Read in this context his apparent jubilation at his young sibling's sudden financial and literary achievements must be treated as disingenuous, to say the least.

The notices for Larry's book were politely respectful, treating it as part of a new hybrid genre which blended travel writing with an exploration of the culture and mythology of place. He was ranked alongside figures such as Gavin Maxwell, Laurens van der Post and his friend Patrick Leigh Fermor. Early sales were decent enough but during 1953 his royalties took him only a little beyond his £100 advance.

Gerry became a star overnight. The *Daily Mail* classed *The Overloaded Ark* as Book of the Month for August, following a celebratory review. It ignored Larry's book entirely, presumably because its largely working- and lower-middle-class readers preferred escapism to highbrow writing. The Book Society chose it as their 'Summer Choice' and by December the BBC had picked up on the arrival of a new popular cultural hero and selected his work as Book of the Week, with extracts read on five consecutive days on the Light Programme.

The reviewers were entranced *because* they were a little confused. Peter Quennell in the *Mail* admired Gerry's gift for 'discovering an apt phrase' alongside his talent for something more anarchic. Similarly, Nigel Nicolson in the *Daily Dispatch* observed that 'as a zoologist he is a modestly disguised expert', which left one wondering if he felt that he had hidden or faked his expertise. But Nicolson was impressed most by his talents as a writer: 'He has almost everything – clarity, great humour, a vivid style and an exact knowledge of how not to be dull without being flippant ... It is a splendid book.' Gavin Maxwell in the *New Statesman* admired his ability to 'communicate every detail of his experience with just the right degree of zest'. The common feature of the reviews – including ones by 'serious travel' writers such as van der Post (in the *Countryman*) and Maxwell – was that they detected in Gerry a talent for communicating his passionate commitment to the preservation of threatened species and his love for their environment along with something more disrespectful, almost juvenile.

By September *The Overloaded Ark* had sold more than twenty-eight thousand copies. At the time bestseller lists were not entirely reliable but he came close to the top of each available. His royalty cheque for that financial year was more than £3,500, roughly seven times the average UK salary.

Rationing of basic food items had gradually been reduced from 1948 onwards but it would not be until 1954 that limitations on the luxuries of sweets, sugar and good meats ended. For nine years after the end of the war in Europe Britain still felt as though it was being punished for standing up against Hitler and a mood of rebelliousness emerged in film and writing. The Ealing comedies were disrespectful of old values (heed *Passport to Pimlico* and *The Lavender Hill Mob*) and quite soon novelists such as John Wain with *Hurry on Down* (1953) and Kingsley Amis with *Lucky Jim* (1954) rejoiced in making fun of what were supposed to be hallowed social ideals. Gerry was part of this, one might even argue its initiator.

Gerry and Jacquie were very well off but rather than doing what most newlyweds might had done – such as buying a house – they planned new expeditions, this time to South America.

In December, shortly after *The Overloaded Ark* became the BBC Book of the Week, Larry wrote to his brother. 'We are now a circus act. Clad in sequinned tights, three hundred feet above the ring, you will fling yourself into space, while I, hanging by my knees, will attempt to focus my bleary eyes sufficiently quickly to catch you by the ankles as you sweep past' (December 1953, Jersey Archive). The jokey nonchalant manner is bogus. His true state of mind is evidenced in his correspondence with Miller. Aside from his specific references to Gerry's success the letters during this period bespeak a special kind of bitterness. After describing Cyprus's attraction for writers and artists he switches focus to the wives of British diplomats and army officers, all 'bored to tears'. He considers setting up a 'little bureau for them', given that he only has time at present to 'medicinally nibble at the fresh fruit lying about – just to sleep better' (20 November 1953). He makes it sound as if extramarital sex is as much about vengeance as lust.

By the time that Gerry was about to publish two more books – *Three Singles to Adventure* and *The Bafut Beagles*, both 1954 – within eighteen months of his debut work, Larry to Miller sounded even more dispirited. 'I'm sorry I have become such a rotten correspondent these days. I'm simply hoarding physical energy for my book which moves like a snail, paragraph by paragraph' (April 1954). Or, as he might have put it, it moves far more slowly than those which appear as speedily as their subjects: cheetahs or antelopes for example.

Eve had just left, following one of her brief visits to see Sappho. 'Everyone had the impression that she left me because of my bad treatment of her but in fact she simply had a bout of Judeo mystical schizophrenia. The Jews are extraordinary people – the extraordinary shallow hysteria and the enormous sexual charges given by race-continence and intermarrying. I am so glad I belong to the equivocal, sluttish uxorious Irish and not the Jews.' Antisemitism is bad enough but when directed against one's wife it becomes something worse: hatred for its own sake, motivated, but certainly not excused, by something particular to the hater. The spectacle of his brother becoming a cultural superstar while he toiled away at a book which was arduous because it was in his view superior by its nature to anything produced by Gerry turned Larry into a ghastly individual. The whole letter is driven by a subtext of bitterness. After presenting Eve and Jews as a whole as a subspecies he shifts focus. 'The English book-trade is so bad that one can't hope for any money from books any more and the advances offered one by English publishers are ludicrous.' He knew his generalisation was absurd and he might as well have closed the sentence with: 'except for writers like Gerry'.

With three books in press and another contract signed with the publisher Rupert Hart-Davis, Gerry and Jacquie set off from Tilbury Docks in November 1953 on a part-passenger, part-merchant ship for Buenos Aires. They were informed, somewhat vaguely by their travel agent, that the vessel would call at other ports in South America. Larry offered advice on how to convince the Argentine Embassy in London and the Foreign Office that their expedition should be classified as an 'official mission', specifically a project undertaken by experienced zoologists to ensure that endangered indigenous species in Argentina could be preserved with the assistance of British specialists.

They had enough money from *The Overloaded Ark* to book a cabin which their agent assured them was Tourist class. It would, Gerry informed Jacquie, be their belated honeymoon, a luxurious prelude to their adventure in the southern hemisphere, with meals served in their stylish stateroom, if they wished.

As Jacquie recorded in her memoir the cabin was more like a cell, without even a porthole, an 'overgrown coffin' with no fresh air, flickering electric lights and a one-above-the-other bunk bed. They shared a bath and lavatory with other passengers, a room which was left to its users to clean. The food – which was the same for all classes of passengers and crew – was ration-standard, the saloon bar stocked only beer and the whole ship was infested with cockroaches.

They docked at Buenos Aires on 19 December. Hart-Davis publishers had succeeded well in publicising their arrival for the local press. They expected to disembark and be greeted only by border authorities and so were shocked to find a group of photographers and English-speaking interviewers keen to question Gerry on the nature of his expedition. The Argentine press were inquisitive partly because they were bemused by who exactly Gerry was and why his arrival had been designated as an 'official mission'. The weekly magazine *Vea y Lea* presented him as a reformed, modern version of the 'old-style big game hunter' and was only capable of describing what he had become by quoting the Hart-Davis promotional material verbatim for English-speaking Argentines: 'He works for science ... looks for unknown animals which he takes back to England alive to *study their behaviour and breed them in captivity*.' The italicised phrase reflected their puzzlement. For them and their readers it was only possible to conceive of wild animals as creatures to be avoided, hunted to death or eaten.

Most papers concentrated on them as minor celebrities, a smartly attired couple about town, while sidelining any reference to the seemingly bizarre nature of the activities.

The popular daily *El Hogar* informed readers that Gerry had 'risked sudden death' by confronting 'strange beasts in the wilds of Africa', without explaining why he had done so. Instead, they concentrated on his captivating appearance: 'a bit dishevelled and on the lean side', but 'youthful ... with auburn hair and the bright clear eyes of a boy'. His wife, they reported, 'is small and slender with a charming fringe that looks like the last memento of childhood ... she looks like a little girl at her husband's side'.

Before they left England Larry had sent Gerry a note saying that they should not book a hotel in the Argentine capital but contact one Bebita

Ferreyra. She was of course the beautiful wife of Jorge. The Ferreyras had been Larry's hosts and patrons during his time in Argentina and Larry knew that Bebita would be alone in their luxurious Buenos Aires property when his brother and Jacquie arrived. As Gerry recorded in his diary, 'She was the nearest approach to a Greek goddess I have ever seen' (Jersey Archive, undated). Larry had been captivated by her and knew that his youngest brother would be too. Maybe, as senior Lothario, he was helping out his apprentice. Gerry commented, 'the most fantastic requests never ruffled her', without offering any detail on the nature of his entreaties.

He had promised to bring some of the threatened species of birds from Tierra del Fuego to Peter Scott at his Severn Wildfowl Trust but the Tierra visit was cancelled for unrecorded reasons.

Instead, they headed by hired car for the pampas around 'Los Ingleses' in the north of the country, so-called because much of the land there had been purchased and settled by British immigrant farmers in the nineteenth century. Memorably Gerry records his encounter with 'Eggbert', a baby *chajá*, a species of goose but much larger than most whose Spanish name comes from the noise they habitually make: 'great screamers'. Eggbert, probably only a week old, was around eight inches in length and according to Gerry's record 'the most ridiculous-looking and the most charming baby bird I had ever seen'. He survived the journey back to Scott's Wildfowl Trust and thrived, despite being the only one of the genus there.

Next, the Durrells crossed the border into Paraguay, without any clear perception of what they were looking for or what they'd find.

The area was alive with rare species of birds which feasted on the vast number of fish and freshwater amphibians with which the various swamps and rivers often seemed to boil; such was their density. Cages were filled with at least a dozen kind of carnivorous birds, many of which Gerry had never seen before and to which he could find no reference in his guidebooks. He foresaw news broadcasts, and celebrity on his return to the UK, the man who had introduced previously unknown creatures to the trusts and sanctuaries that awaited him. Uncharacteristically, the birds were not anthropomorphised with quirky names, unlike Pooh the baby crab-eating racoon, or Foxey the grey pampas fox. The one which garnered unalloyed affection from Gerry and Jacquie was a *Myrmecophaga tridactyla*, commonly known in English as the giant anteater. At full size the animal could be almost two metres in length but their new guest was tiny – even, as they calculated, for a baby of only a few weeks. She had, however, already acquired the habits of her seniors, being able to shift from insect-hunting on pasture and pampas to the various parts of trees where they would secure themselves from more savage carnivores. Gerry and Jacquie's trousers, shirt sleeves and coat became her tree trunks and branches. After she had shinned up Jacquie's left leg, Gerry removed her only to find that she had attached herself irremovably to the shoulder of this jacket. Hence, she was given her name: Sarah Huggersack.

Jacquie:

> Gerry simply adored her and she him, and he fussed over her feeling like a father with his first-born. Nothing was too good for her or too much trouble, and she soon realised it. She shared his bed at night ('she mustn't catch cold') and his every free moment ('it is essential that she feels loved; after all she would normally be clinging to her mother all day'). I got scant attention in those days so I contented myself with looking after the other animals. (*Beasts in My Bed*, pp60–61)

Her touch is light yet gently suggestive. Gerry, she implies, has a store of tenderness for animals that she can share but perhaps not quite equally.

She goes on to comment on how a film crew that had joined them in Argentina – which Gerry does not mention in his recollections – had blinded themselves to what she saw as a kind of sexless infidelity. Their so-called honeymoon caused him to fall in love with every new creature he encountered.

On an orange armadillo, which native Paraguay Indians had brought to their camp and which Gerry thought should share the marital bed with Sarah and Jacquie: '"I don't care who you share your bed with, Durrell, but I'm fussy," I said determinedly' (*Ibid.*, p61).

The only other being in South America who seemed capable of stirring Gerry's attention was Bebita Ferreyra, who, reports Jacquie, entered the room when they first arrived in Buenos Aires looking, for Gerry, 'far lovelier than her portrait' (*Ibid.*, p53). This was her description of his thoughts. She was not a mind reader but by the time she wrote *Beasts in My Bed* Jacquie was aware that her husband was a serial adulterer. To her credit, she attributes his inattention towards her, during their South American trip and later, to his love for animals. Bebita and Larry had slept together during his time in Argentina and it was he who asked her to welcome his young brother to the country. Pimping, it seemed, sidelined sibling rivalry over book sales.

Gerry and Jacquie had researched Paraguay as a location for numerous species of threatened animals but seemingly paid little attention to the chaotic politics of the place. Since 1940 various parties and military groups had overridden the flimsy democratic structure and attempted to seize control of the country. In May 1954 a coup d'état led by General Alfredo Stroessner and supported by most senior officers in the armed forces displaced the various political factions – from Communists to Neo-Nazis – that had competed for electoral gains during the previous decade.

The coup was largely unopposed but for the previous three decades Paraguay had gone persistently from one civil war to the next and it was suspected by those in the Western Foreign Services that left-wing paramilitaries, supplied with Soviet bloc arms, would organise guerrilla resistance units. In the end they did not and Stroessner, like a South American version of Franco, remained in power as a dictator until 1989. Nevertheless, Gerry's party received an emergency message from the British Embassy in Buenos Aires urging him to leave the country immediately.

By means still undisclosed he arranged for a light aircraft to land at a rough, single-runway field barely five miles away. There would, he was told, be room only for barely a fifth of his cages if the camera crew were also to travel. It took him a while to decide on whether leaving the humans would enable him to take a significantly larger number of animals – maybe even fifty per cent of those captured – and was persuaded eventually by Jacquie of the questionable morality of such a conclusion.

What happened next disturbed him even more: which would go and which would stay? By their nature the birds decided on freedom without pause but the other creatures upset him greatly. Rather than decide on which of the mammals should go or stay he arranged their cages in a circle around the campsite and opened the doors offering all the opportunity to return to the wild. None seemed inclined to go anywhere and Jacquie tells of how he had to rid himself of animals whose love for him was self-evident.

All we know for certain is that Cai the douroucouli monkey, Pooh the racoon, Foxey the pampas fox and, of course, Sarah Huggersack boarded the plane with their human fellow travellers.

The animals gathered in Argentina and Paraguay were stowed away in the forward deck of the *Paraguay Star* in Buenos Aires and in June the Durrells set sail for London. The *Star* offered them the comforts that were so conspicuously absent on their voyage out: they had their own bathroom, the food was as good as anything provided by Bebita and the captain presided over dances with free drink, though Gerry and Jacquie became the centre of attention as the only first-class passengers without clothes that might generously be called casual. They arrived at the Victoria Docks, London, in mid-July and dispatched their animals to various zoos and sanctuaries. Sarah Huggersack was destined for Paignton Zoo in Devon and the Durrells borrowed a van to take her there before setting off east along the coast for Bournemouth. Jacquie described them leaving her as 'heart-breaking'.

They returned to Margo's house, to a 'double' room which only qualified for the description because of the size of the bed. A letter from Hart-Davis awaited them, stating that in their absence *The Bafut Beagles* had gone into production and that Gerry would receive proofs within days, as he would a contract for *The Drunken Forest*, a memoir of his South American expedition which he had discussed with Hart-Davis but not thought about since. In Jacquie's account the prospect of more sales and therefore more commissions depressed him greatly. "'I do hope they're not going to do this every time I catch up with myself," he wailed, "otherwise I shall go mad. I suppose I'd better start on the one about this trip before you all start nagging me'" (*Ibid.*, p67).

Jacquie's comments on the relationship between Gerry and Larry is lightly sardonic. She asks her husband to adopt Larry's 'system', writing two thousand words and then allowing himself during the rest of the day to devote himself to 'other things', hinting at the insouciant and bohemian state of mind to which artists thought they were entitled.

> Durrell groaned. 'Believe me, I only wish I could, but the subtle difference between us is that he loves writing and I don't. To me it's simply a way to make money which enables me to do my animal work, nothing more. I'm not a serious writer in that sense, but merely a hack journalist who has the good fortune to be able to sell what he writes. (*Ibid.*, p68)

Sales figures for *Three Singles to Adventure*, and *The Bafut Beagles*, which came out on 15 October 1954, were outstanding. The *Scotsman* serialised the latter, while the BBC bought the rights to a fourteen-part radio adaptation of it for *Book at Bedtime*, plus arranging a dramatised version to be broadcast on New Year's Eve. Hart-Davis was overjoyed and invited Gerry and Jacquie to a dinner at the Savoy Hotel. Food rationing had only ceased a few months earlier, in July, but the Savoy had stored away rare items, unofficially for their regular and wealthier clients for the official cessation of restrictions. They had secured and frozen top-quality meat and poultry and had kept champagne and good Bordeaux reds from the late 1930s. Gerry could barely remember such culinary luxury and aside from treats in Argentina Jacquie had never come across anything like it. A month later the *Poetry Review* published an article on all of Gerry's books, praising him as a writer whose prose was infused with an 'innate poetry' which surpassed that of his brother's. There is no record of how Larry felt about this.

On 13 November 1954 Gerry arrived in London to deliver a lecture at the Royal Festival Hall, arranged by Hart-Davis. The event was published at the end of October and sold out within three days. Almost three thousand people wanted to hear Gerry Durrell talk of his adventures and his love for animals.

He was hysterically nervous. His anxiety about speaking in public was now multiplied gigantically by the prospect of an audience of more than 2500. Hart-Davis forced him to go to Savile Row for a bespoke dark blue suit, which increased his level of stress even further and on the night of his performance he emptied almost half a bottle of whisky before sauntering nervously onto the stage. Once there, however, he was transformed into a magically versatile performer. First, he spoke impromptu of his expeditions, and the audience laughed, but he quietened them by shifting to a diatribe against European culture in general and zoos in particular. Animals, he proclaimed, deserved the same respect as us, humans, and should never be discussed as a form of entertainment. Zoos must become a means of allowing creatures from elsewhere to regain a degree of freedom and self-regard. The audience, now silent, began to gasp in admiration as he uncovered massive blank sheets of paper and crayoned onto these beautiful cartoon versions of the creatures he'd come across in Africa and South America. It was as though he was bringing them to life on the stage and quite soon, he would.

He announced that he would now introduce two members of 'the opposite sex'. 'One I caught in the Chaco, Paraguay, and the other in Manchester. The first is called SARAH HUGGERSACK!,' and he was joined on the stage by the now almost adult anteater, seemingly oblivious to the spotlights and the expressions of surprise from the audience. From the other wing came Jacquie. 'The other one, ladies and gentlemen, is called ...' He pretended to forget her name, hesitated and declared, '... well, I married her.' They had borrowed Sarah from Paignton Zoo and Jacquie's recollection of the evening is as usual deliciously amusing.

> Sarah, who has arrived before us, was ensconced in the dressing-room just vacated by Sir Thomas Beecham, while we poor mortals were left to fend for ourselves ... [she] stole the show, running along the stage, playing with Gerry and honking madly. (*Ibid.*, p69)

She was so excited by the adulation showered on her that she resisted being taken back to her travelling box. News spread of the event and a week later she appeared with Gerry on BBC Television and, as Jacquie reported, 'captivated even the stoniest-hearted stage hand at the Television Centre. But, like most great stars, Sarah developed a temperament – being a star she needed to be appreciated' (*Ibid.*).

There is a touch of understatement here because Sarah's exposure to the newly expanding celebrity culture of screen and wireless along with live appearances before audiences who laughed and cheered at her antics caused her some trauma. It is self-evident from Jacquie's report that Gerry's credo of enabling wild animals to thrive in what amounted to their natural environment had been undermined by his own appetite for money. He was certainly not avaricious but his dedication to conservation had become self-defeating. He needed a regular income to fund his expeditions to Africa, South America and elsewhere and his only means of obtaining this was to promote his output of books via events such as the Royal Festival Hall appearance where Sarah was turned into a form of entertainment. She eventually recovered from her ordeal but spent several months in Paignton Zoo seemingly unable or unwilling to associate with other members of her species and in dread of humans who offered her food and attempted to clean her enclosure.

In Jacquie's memoir she switches immediately from their escapades with Sarah to their next trip abroad, this time involving encounters only with humans.

> Our trip to Cyprus was marred from the very beginning, and during the cocktail party that Larry gave to introduce us to Cypriot society, the first bomb was exploded. (*Ibid.*, p62)

On 24 October 1954, three weeks before appearing at the Royal Festival Hall, Gerry had written to his brother Larry in Cyprus announcing that he had plans to 'start a trust or organisation, with land', where various species of animals from across the globe would be allowed to range as freely as possible. It would encourage 'the breeding of those forms of animal life which are on the borders of extinction, and which without help of this sort cannot survive' (Jersey Archive). He wanted Larry to introduce him to three or four people who might be sufficiently sympathetic to his cause to raise, between them, around £10,000 to enable him to get the project started. He mentioned eminences with whom Larry, he believed, was closely associated, including Freya Stark, Igor Stravinsky and Osbert Lancaster.

None had indicated conspicuous interest in conservation or zoology and despite being eminent in their various fields they were not outstandingly rich. Indeed, Gerry had, from his first book onwards, earned more money year by year than any of his projected donors.

Gerry was certainly committed to his mission, yet he was also becoming a little delusional. For each of his public appearances, interviews in newspapers and other media and coverage on radio and television, he was asked for details of his background, particularly in relation to his interests in zoology and conservation. Initially newspapers had used the umbrella term 'scientist' to describe him while avoiding any reference to his training or qualifications. They could find nothing on record so Gerry worked hard on filling in the gaps, telling of his education in Greece and England – geographically authentic but suspect regarding his comments on specialisations and academic successes – along with his time at schools and universities in Switzerland, Italy and France, countries he'd only traversed on his way to Corfu. He supplemented this with accounts of his experiences as a member in British institutions involved in the study of animal ecology shortly before and during the war. Those who took these last claims seriously must have been entranced by him, given that he was only fourteen when war broke out.

Nonetheless, no one questioned the impressive self-image, and the mythology of Gerald Durrell caused some of the most eminent naturalists on the globe to respond to his enquiries and offer advice. In London he was the guest of Julian Huxley, previously the Director General of UNESCO and founder of the International Union for Conservation of Nature, and James Fisher, Britain's most celebrated ornithologist. He spent several days in France in the company of Jean Delacour, who had established a menagerie on the family estate in Normandy. He had been traumatised in the First World War, in which he had served, and in the Second World War when the Germans bombed his chateau to ruins. Delacour became convinced that animals were more innately decent and kind than their human counterparts. Gerry found in him an individual who had turned his own discordant instincts into a philosophy. Delacour had become a vegetarian mainly because he hated the idea of humans sustaining themselves at the expense of animals, and he swore never to have children. He did not wish to contribute to the dominance of man over other creatures.

All of Gerry's advisors were impressed by his plans, principally his vision of what we would now refer to as a safari park in a zone and climate that would accommodate species that found Europe disagreeable. His plan was to purchase large amounts of land in one of the Caribbean islands that was still part of the empire and where the indigenous population could barely earn enough money to keep themselves fed let alone buy tracts of land. His various mentors enthused with him about his objectives but were less helpful about how he might raise enough money to realise them.

Gerry and Jacquie arrived in Cyprus on 31 March 1955. The rationale for the visit remains unclear, though they were accompanied by a television crew seemingly to make films on local avian wildlife and, unusually for Gerry, the ways in which farmers and remote villagers irrigated fields and gardens. These were never completed and Gerry and Jacquie spent most of their time in the guest quarters of Larry's newly renovated house. There were numerous cocktail parties and the two brothers spent as much time as possible swimming in the shallow waters of a nearby bay accompanied by Sappho and Jacquie. Eve seemed always to be busy with other matters and hardly ever spent time with her husband. She would soon leave Larry for good but neither of them spoke to Gerry of their imminent marital breakdown. Sappho immediately formed an affectionate bond with her uncle who enjoyed carrying her on his shoulders into the sea, throwing her into the air and catching her gently before she plunged into the water. Jacquie later recalled that he afforded her as much care and affection as he would for a 'baby chimp', which was not a backhanded compliment given his unswerving love for vulnerable animals.

Gerry, again according to Jacquie, had also begun to talk with whoever would listen to him about how to purchase or at least make use of territories that were neither formed nor for that matter legally owned. Cyprus is the third largest island in the Mediterranean, not densely populated, and a considerable part of its landscape was in the mid-1950s uninhabited. The climate is subtropical and as Gerry familiarised himself with the place he was first reminded of the idyll of his childhood in Corfu and next caused to speculate on the island as a location for his home for threatened species. Quite soon, however, the possibility of the latter evaporated. Gerry and Jacquie's arrival coincided with the beginning of the insurrection by EMAK and EOKA, organisations committed to the liberation of Cyprus from Britain, though unclear about what its subsequent relationship with Greece and Turkey would be. A week after they began to tour the island bombs exploded in all of the main urban areas and soon afterwards British soldiers and policemen were ambushed and shot.

Gerry and Jacquie returned to London much sooner than they had first intended, on 12 June. Their plans made before and during the visit were largely abandoned yet the time with his brother had prompted for Gerry another money-making strategy for his home for threatened species. He had resurrected the Greek he had spoken on Corfu, and been reminded of his childhood on a different eastern Mediterranean island where his human companions would, he decided, become as quirky and bizarre as the animals he loved: *My Family and Other Animals* would soon be born.

On their return to England Gerry and Jacquie firstly rented a flat in the suburbs of North London, 70A Holden Road, Woodside Park. Soon after they moved in in late June 1955 Gerry underwent one of his recurrent bouts of hopelessness, brought on mainly by jaundice. It is thought that he contracted one of the many viruses that underlie the condition in Cyprus, and in his case heavy drinking worsened things. His skin turned yellow-orange; other symptoms included abdominal pains and aches in his muscles and joints. Confined to bed he was attended by Jacquie as his live-in nurse and the situation was not improved by complaints from his horrified landlord. Before arriving in London, they had 'fostered' two ailing young chimps from Whipsnade who were straining the resources of the zoo.

Rupert Hart-Davis was sending regular enquiries about the delivery date of his next book, yet another of his adventures in the wilds of a distant continent that guaranteed massive sales in the monochrome banality of mid-1950s Britain. But Gerry felt mentally as well as physically incapacitated. He wrote nothing, but according to Jacquie he became preoccupied with recollections. These had nothing to do with his post-war experiences as a self-made conservationist but went back to before the war, when he was a child. He had talked to his wife distractedly about his childhood in Corfu but now he spoke of nothing else, often drifting into what sounded like a deranged monologue. Names she recognised, largely those of his closest family members, were mixed in with those that sounded exotically foreign – such as Krajewsky and Petrogubski – and others seemingly drawn from a rude children's story: including Roger Widdle, Dodo and Puke. Jacquie mentions only the strain put on their marriage by her having to look after an invalid.

> After the fortnight was up, Sister Margaret drove up to London to convey a rather seedy Durrell back to the bosom of his family in Bournemouth. There, Durrell's enforced inactivity brought on a sudden urge to write ... In 1935 the entire Durrell family had moved *en masse* to the unsuspecting Greek island of Corfu. It was obvious from the way they spoke about it that this period was one of enchantment for the entire family ... Never have I known Gerry work as he did then; it seemed to pour out of him and it was all that poor Sophie [their typist] could do to keep pace with his output. Six weeks and 120,000 words later, Durrell collapsed gracefully. It was finished – and so, nearly, was he. (*Beasts in My Bed*, p71)

Gerry told his friend David Hughes that he set out 'consciously to manufacture a bestseller' and that he intended 'like a good cook' to magically blend three ingredients: the 'spellbinding landscape' of the island; his discovery in childhood of its 'wild denizens', both Greek and animal; and the bizarre conduct of the rest of his family during their time there (Botting, p227).

He went on to describe how he had to wrestle with this tripartite compound, the parts of which seemed to have declared independence from each other. First, his family appeared to be overrunning the draft, and then had to contend with the indigenous population, human and non-human, for control of the story, while the heat, the sea, the glorious sky and the colourful botanical backdrops cultivated a magnetic collage of their own. He confided in Hughes that the book's success was ensured by his failure to subdue this battle between its parts, which he had invented but could not control. Jacquie should be commended for her modesty and restraint given that in her memoir she moves straight from Gerry's state of exhaustion in completing the manuscript to their decision to spend Christmas and New Year on the moderately temperate Scilly Isles.

She says nothing of her role after Gerry reached Bournemouth but in the privately held unrevised typescript of *Intimate Relations* (revised version published by Collins in 1976) it is evident from her marginal notes that she worked as his editor. The original 'text' was by parts oral dictation and longhand draft and Jacquie made sure that what went to Sophie his typist was a coherent narrative.

When Rupert Hart-Davis received the draft of *My Family* in November 1955 he and two editors read it within three days, agreeing that it was the best thing Gerry had produced. Book production in the mid-1950s meant that even an agreed bestseller could not go from manuscript to binding with cover in less than seven months but Hart-Davis decided that it must be a Christmas book and postponed publication further until October 1956. He guessed that reviews post-publication and publicity would guarantee its purchase by those who wanted it for themselves or as a gift for others; an escape from incessantly bad winters to a sunlit Mediterranean paradise where the temperature allowed everyone to wander the beaches or swim twelve months of the year, at least in Gerry's account of the place.

Early proof copies were read by members of Gerry's family who found themselves confronted by rather unsettling, distorted mirror images. Botting records Louisa as stating that 'the awful thing about Gerald's book is that I'm beginning to believe it is all true, when it isn't' (*Ibid.*, p230). Larry, in his characteristically bookish manner, observed that 'He has successfully recreated his family with the devastatingly faithful eye of a thirteen-year-old… the best argument I know for keeping thirteen-year-olds at boarding schools and not letting them hang about the house' (*Ibid.*). In other words, he told the truth as a mischievous thirteen-year-old would, very falsely. Larry was showing a commendable amount of generosity, given that his youngest sibling had turned him into a grouchy failed novelist and exterminated his then wife Nancy much in the way that Stalin's henchmen would edit out images of his enemies from photographs. Margo was appalled at being presented as a feckless teenage nymphet and initially demanded that Gerry should rewrite the passages in which she appeared. She relented when her brother assured her that the entire family would benefit financially beyond their dreams when the book went to press.

He was correct, in a way. His earnings were extraordinary but no money went to anyone else.

Leslie, accompanied by forty-six-year-old Doris, had become a farm manager in Kenya and had written to the rest of the family of his comfortable colonial circumstances, with a large, well-furnished bungalow serviced by relatives of the indigenous Kenyans who worked for him on the farm. He presented himself as having recreated an African version of the family's time in the Indian Raj. In truth his situation became precarious soon after his arrival. The Mau Mau rebellion against British rule was at its most violent, particularly in rural areas where British landowners were seen as easy targets. Leslie began to visit Mombasa and Nairobi regularly, partly to avoid the rebels but also to set up fraudulent enterprises to deprive expatriate Britons of their savings. This would cause him to flee the country in 1968 and return to London. Gerry did not show him the pre-publication draft of *My Family and Other Animals* and there is no record of him having read it after it went to press. He did however later tell of having seen the mass coverage of a book apparently by his younger brother in week-old copies of British newspapers in Nairobi but he knew nothing of how he too had become a major literary character.

Gerry sent a copy of the draft to Theo Stephanides. The accompanying letter is lost but we know that Stephanides was the only real character other than close family members to feature prominently in the book. We can guess that Gerry asked Theo only to correct any errors regarding Corfiot spelling, ornithology and the detailed history of the place because those are the only topics he referred to in his reply. Not once did he comment on how the actual Durrells he had known so well twenty years before were barely recognisable in the book. With characteristic politeness he did not remark on how he too had become someone else, with mercurial and eccentric features of his personality added to those he recognised. Spiro existed, certainly, but Gerry remodelled him utterly, both for *My Family* and for the other two volumes of what would become a Corfu trilogy. He neither consulted him nor sent him a pre-publication draft or copy of the book. He had died in 1939 but before we assume that Gerry's fictionalisation of him was a memorial we should note that he did not bother to ask anyone if he was alive or dead.

On publication Gerry's book was met with unanimously celebratory reviews. The *Sunday Times* had never come across anything like it. 'Across the pages troop and gobble the bent, the bearded and the zany; talk and laughter, dismay and love, fill the villas ...' The humans are 'marvellously and most attractively crazy'. Kenneth Young in the *Daily Telegraph* confessed that when reading the book on a train he had to close it 'for fear my lowering fellow-Goths [northern Europeans] should think me unbalanced', because of his uncontrolled laughter. The BBC Light Programme summed up the mood of reviewers and ecstatic readers. 'They are ridiculous, illogical, at times infuriating but almost always adorable, and above all they are *real*.' The emphatic and hence italicised 'real' sums up the unstated but evident question that troubled all of those who reviewed the book: was it factual or fantasy? To this day his account of his family in Corfu is treated as a memoir. The numerous film and television adaptations have been based on the premise that while the actors are only theatrical versions of Gerry, Louisa, Lawrence et al., they are committed dutifully to representing their real-life authentic counterparts offered to the reading public in the book. Gerry used the framework of events shared between those who had experienced them – essentially the Durrells and others in Corfu in the 1930s – and turned these into what amounted to a novel.

Gerry's brother Larry had his first major novel, *Justine*, in preparation for publication when *My Family* came out. The first of the wildly celebrated *Alexandria Quartet*, it would be pored over by highbrow critics and academics for decades but *My Family* sold forty times more copies in 1956–7. *Justine* became a literary touchstone for the endurance of modernism but only sold two thousand copies in the UK and US during its first two years in print. *My Family* equalled Churchill's *History of the English-Speaking Peoples* as a bestseller and within six months Gerry and Jacquie had received over £3,000 in royalties.

Shortly before Christmas 1956 Gerry, Jacquie and a party of nine companions, including a film crew, set off from Southampton for the Cameroons on the SS *Tortuguero*. It was a banana boat but there were no other passengers and Jacquie recalled that it was like having their own 'private yacht'. She meant that Gerry had cashed in more than £2,500 from initial *My Family* income both to fund the expedition itself and to ensure that passage was as luxurious as possible, given the circumstances. The ship was loaded with decent wine that Hart-Davis had sent from his London club, plus twenty-five bottles of scotch. The celebrity couple secured for themselves a cabin larger than that of the captain and equipped it with a brand-new double bed of the kind that moderately wealthy people purchased to escape the discomforts of the furniture-spare immediate post-war years. There is no record of what happened to it after they disembarked in Africa on 7 January 1957.

They were mainly in pursuit of gorillas and shortly before departure Jacquie had given a tongue-in-cheek interview for the *Sunday Express*. In actuality they hoped to monitor and perhaps even film the breeding habits of the animals in the hope that the zoos which received the ones they might capture would be able to replicate the conditions and circumstances in which they found partners and fostered their young. Unfortunately, Jacquie was in a risqué mood and informed the reporter, following her serious account of the zoological rationale of the expedition, that 'we hope to find out if a gorilla beats his wife on a Saturday night but we shall be lucky if we see anything of their courting'. She did not expect to be quoted at all but her statement appeared verbatim under the headline 'Wife off to Film Love Life of the Gorilla'.

On landing they were met by a British colonial official who ordered them to attend a meeting at Government House in Buea, the then capital of the British Cameroons and the headquarters of the British administration. Independence was imminent despite the fact that France ran almost half of the country and hoped to continue with their policy of incorporating protectorates, such as French Cameroon, as part of a global French Republic. They had outlawed the pro-independence parties in 1955 with the result that a minor civil war broke out between pro-French elements and separatist guerrillas.

The various parts of Cameroon would not become fully autonomous until 1960–61 but when Gerry and Jacquie arrived the British were busily creating a framework they hoped would serve them well enough for trade and political influence in later years. They were anxious about Soviet interventions in countries that had recently shaken off imperial rule and the Foreign Office was keen to convince Cameroonian activists that after Britain left it would support and even finance the revival of pre-colonial culture as a preferred alternative to Marxism. This meant that Gerry was a problem. *The Bafut Beagles* (1954) focused partly on his 1949 expedition but its star character was Achirimbi II, 'Fon', the tenth king of Bafut. The British were concerned that as independence drew nearer press attention would be drawn to how this embodied hangover from the nineteenth century would be used as ammunition against the ideas of a new mutually respectful relationship between the ex-colonists and their one-time subjects. The 'Fon' in Gerry's book is almost a pantomime caricature of an African chieftain, speaking 'hilarious' pidgin English while cultivating an air of grandeur in his brightly coloured robes. His 'palace' is a rebuilt version of the single-storey building destroyed by the German administration at the end of the nineteenth century, a shambolic brick and straw structure where he entertained 'honoured guests'. In his ballroom tables and chairs used for dining and drinking would be cleared to make room for dancing, as the chickens and other domesticated wildlife looked on. He had at least eight wives though the exact number remains uncertain to this day and while polygamous sex occupied much of his leisure time he gave over a fair amount to the consumption of whisky and the local palm wine, *mimbo*. On the wall of the ballroom was a portrait of Her Majesty the Queen to whom Fon would offer a toast at the opening of his riotous celebrations.

As Jacquie later observed in *Beasts in My Bed* Gerry's portraits of him and indeed her would probably in later decades be treated as 'politically incorrect', but in her view they were authentic.

Despite attempts by officials in Buea to have him submit any copy of publishable material to them for scrutiny and even an offer to fund his return to Britain, Gerry, Jacquie and their crew pressed on, inspired by a letter from Fon of 25 January. 'I will be looking for you at any time you come here. How long you think to remain with me here, no objection ... Please pass my sincere greetings to your wife and tell her that I shall have a good chat with her when she comes here' (Jersey Archive).

In Bafut itself Fon welcomed them with a typically outrageous display of hospitality. Jacquie recalls that he had supplemented his picture of the Queen with others representing senior and minor members of the Royal Family from the middle of the reign of Victoria onwards. After the feast – no wine but impressive amounts of whisky – he danced with at least six of his wives, all clad in traditional African costume. Yet he seemed impatient and turned to Gerry. 'My friend, you remember dat European dance you done show me last de time you done come to Bafut? How you go call um – de conga? Well, I go show you something' (*Beasts in My Bed*, p86). He went on to present an African version of the conga involving himself, the six wives and more young ladies who had appeared as if by magic. The band played something that to Jacquie sounded like a hybrid version of European jazz and indigenous African call-and-response rhythms of pre-colonial music. It sounded, she said, faintly maniacal, as Fon and his female co-dancers performed a thoroughly entrancing version of the conga, circling the ballroom in a crazed energetic manner.

Soon Fon gave in to exhaustion, ordered his companions to sit on the floor and approached Jacquie and Gerry. 'Dis woman your wife get brain ... you be good wife for me.' He asked her to dance and Gerry insisted that she must. The experience was, she recalled, bizarre. She was five foot one and less than nine stone in weight while Fon stood at six foot three and weighed about sixteen stone. First, she feared that he would stamp or, worse, fall on her but he soon decided to lift and whirl her around like a child. His suggestion that she might be shared by him and Gerry as their co-wife seemed a bit like self-caricature but as the evening wore on it was apparent that what appeared ludicrous should be treated with cautionary seriousness: 'before I realized what was happening' recalled Jacquie, 'I was on the floor.' He praised *The Bafut Beagles*. 'Dis book you [Gerry] done write, I like um foine. You done make my name go for all the world' (*Beasts in My Bed,* p86). He added that he was, because of it, invited to meet the Queen during her visit to Nigeria a year earlier and she had asked him to sign her copy. It sounds mad but the Queen had indeed visited Lagos in January 1956.

This expedition into the Cameroons hinterland in 1957 involved several turning points, for Gerry and Jacquie in particular and for the world they had known during their relationship.

Following their initial warning from the British administration against a repeat of *The Bafut Beagles* it became evident that the various officials responsible for licensing their activities had been instructed to hamper them at every opportunity. The Conservator of Forests, who in the past had given Gerry a free hand in whatever he wished to do, now demanded a detailed account of how he would capture animals and spent ten days comparing these with a spuriously 'official' list of regulations. The Head of Customs was indeed named Pine Coffin despite later suspicion that Gerry had baptised him as such. Mr Coffin attempted to have Gerry arrested because, in his view, the firearms licences did not cover the calibre of rifles carried on the expedition. He also tried to confiscate film equipment that he claimed had been removed from Britain illegally. The fact that the crew possessed it was not sufficient proof that they owned it, apparently.

Before the party reached Fon they'd stayed over in Mamfe where Gerry appeared to have a nervous breakdown. This began with a row with Pious, who had been his devoted helper since he first visited the region eight years earlier. There was no obvious reason for the altercation but Gerry was drinking whisky heavily and the more drunk he became the more he seemed intent on alienating those closest to him. The Mamfe District Officer was one of the few British officials who did not attempt to make life difficult for him but nonetheless Gerry called him weak and demanded that they race each other around the unpaved rocky paths to see who would collapse first. Footwear was forbidden and although Gerry gained a considerable lead, he tore the soles of his feet to pieces on sharp stones. He was hospitalised, unable to stand or walk, for almost two weeks.

The youngest member of the party was called Bob Golding, only just nineteen. He was from Bristol, two years out of school but with enough self-taught expertise in zoology and conservationism to convince Gerry that he should come. He was in awe of his boss and sponsor and exhilarated by the experience itself; he had never before travelled beyond Europe. But what struck most in his recollection was the evident disaster of Jacquie and Gerry's relationship. 'There was no rapport between them, no shred of affection or compassion, no physical, emotional, even personal connection' (Botting, p246). Jacquie wrote to Louisa: 'Gerry has been ill and we will probably return to England sooner than planned. Things are not good at all and I'm not sure we'll be bringing animals back. He's not happy at all' (1957, otherwise undated, Jersey Archive). Jacquie later recalled that he actually entered a state of near suicidal depression, eating hardly anything but drinking whisky from morning onwards. She did not write to Louisa of this and nor did she in print or interviews suggest a particular reason for his dreadful decline. She did, however, recall that he felt that his love affair with the region was coming to an end, through no fault of his own. The British, she thought, were intent on presenting people such as her husband as inflexible colonists, while in fact Gerry 'got on terribly well with the native people. One of the greatest compliments he was paid was that he didn't behave like the English' (Botting, p248). She also remembered that during the last painful weeks of the 1957 expedition he would sit on upturned kerosene barrels with local men, smoking, sharing bottles of whisky, and insisting that the 'white men' would bring them nothing but improvement to their economy and infrastructure. His kind would no longer rule them but should be welcomed as their advisors and friends. The communists would turn them into ideologically programmed robots and the call by others to go back to the culture and practices of pre-colonial times was self-destructive. They listened because in effect he was speaking to them on behalf of his old friend Fon who was, as much as Gerry, confused and upset by what would soon occur in the country they both loved. Gerry's Fon, Achirimbi II, was not a colonial sycophant but from the post-war years onwards he had earned the contempt of other Fons of the region for his insistence that the British had done the area far more good than harm. His territory in British Cameroon shared borders with Nigeria and when both countries gained independence within months of each other in 1960–61 and he was given the option of affiliation to one or both he declared that it was the equivalent of choosing the 'fire or the deep sea'. His tribal ceremonies, ridiculous garments and intemperate lifestyle were, he knew, parodies of the way his predecessors had lived before the arrival of Christian missionaries in the mid-nineteenth century; as enchantingly unreal as the pomp of the British Royalty. But he enjoyed them nonetheless and encouraged his subjects to join him in as much debauchery as they could afford. All of this was made available by trade with Europe in oil, cocoa and coffee, an arrangement that improved educational and medical resources almost to the level of the poor regions of Europe.

Jacquie wrote that though 'Fon didn't have much time for Europeans in general', he enjoyed taking money from them and that 'he adored

Gerry'. Both men were misfits, not quite of their time nor of conventional creed but dedicated to something idiosyncratically their own.

Despite the setbacks of the visit, and on Gerry's part private catastrophes, they managed to fill more than a hundred cages of spectacularly varied species: Gaboon vipers, mice unknown in Europe, tiny sunbirds, Ringhal cobras a yard in length, African hawk-eagles and chimpanzees.

They hired six trucks to transport them three hundred miles to the coast where another banana boat, the SS *Nicoya*, would load their cargo for England. It was at this point that Jacquie seemed to diagnose the cause of Garry's malaise and come upon a solution. She and Sophie, Gerry's secretary, were sharing beers in a bar in Tiko where the ship was moored.

'Seems that we are always the mugs, doesn't it, Jacquie?' observed Sophie. 'Well let him do it next time, if there is one, that is.'(*Ibid.*, p94) By 'it' Sophie meant the expeditions. Jacquie later reflected on why the more he succeeded in his missions the more Gerry seemed to plummet further into despair and hopelessness, and she eventually concluded that the creatures he loved almost as children would always be given away. 'When we eventually reached England, I, in a fit of demented enthusiasm, had suggested to Durrell that we keep this collection and use it to blackmail the Bournemouth Council into giving us a suitable zoo site in the town. This had given Gerry a new lease of life' (*Beasts in My Bed*, p94).

7

Larry: Spying Again

In July 1954 Larry was summoned by letter to Government Lodge to meet the British Governor of Cyprus, Sir Robert Armitage. It was, he was told, an 'interview' but in effect Armitage simply offered him a post which he had neither heard of let alone applied for. After little more than an hour he descended the granite steps of the Lodge newly appointed as Director of the Information Services. George Wilkinson, Larry's old friend who with his wife Iris had cared for Sapphy, as she was now known, during Eve's illnesses, had been promised the job by a friend in the Foreign Service. After Larry left Cyprus in 1956 the two men never spoke again. The governor had not previously heard of Larry and the instruction to appoint him came from Burrows who was then Political Resident in the Persian Gulf and was particularly concerned with the relationship between Arab nations and the newly formed State of Israel. Cyprus had become a detention centre for Holocaust survivors up to the point that Israel was recognised by the UN in 1949 and arms dealers on the island had supplied guns and ammunition to Israel during the 1948 Arab–Israeli War. Through the 1950s there existed an unofficial alliance between Cyprus and Israel, mainly because each felt that they had been poorly treated by the British.

EOKA would become the most powerful guerrilla group on the island. Roughly six months after Larry's appointment it was involved in outright warfare against British troops and its objective was to unify Cyprus with Greece. At the same time, smaller nationalist groups were being supplied with arms from communist eastern Europe in the hope that they would establish a pro-Soviet outpost in the Mediterranean between Greece and Turkey. The island was a tinderbox of possibilities, involving its sympathies with Israel against the latter's antagonistic Arab neighbours and the tension between left- and right-wing elements in its struggle for independence.

It is no accident that shortly before his appointment Larry set aside *Justine* to prepare a manuscript of a James Bond-style novel, provisionally entitled *White Eagles Over Serbia*, in which MI6 hero Methuen is parachuted into Tito's Yugoslavia to help anti-communist partisans. Larry hoped to cash in on the fantasy of Cold War spying pioneered by Ian Fleming in *Casino Royale* a year before but his own book, published in 1957, anticipates the gritty realism of John le Carré's *The Spy Who Came in from the Cold* (1963). Both authors were fictionalising a world they knew from personal experience. It was a desperate money-making venture which, unlike Le Carré's, did not sell and once he had settled into his new post he found that the salary meant that he could now live well enough and concentrate on what he regarded as proper literature, *Justine*. For a while he had worked as a teacher at the Pancyprian Gymnasium; founded in 1812 and housed in a magnificent classical Greek building, effectively the Eton of the island. It was a training school for the University of Athens and those who had no taste for higher education wore their time there as a badge of esteem. Nonetheless it paid non-permanent members of staff such as Larry a pitiful amount and his new government post provided him with almost four times as much.

Larry's job was a replica of that in Belgrade. Ostensibly he was the intermediary between the British authorities and the press but more significantly he exploited his contacts, a network of figures connected to the island's turbulent politics, to feed intelligence to MI6 officers in the Government Lodge. Two of Larry's friends and contemporaries, George Seferis and Adamantios Diamantis, artists and writers both, were unsettled by his apparent conflict of affiliations. Diamantis wrote to Seferis on 24 August 1954 that, 'what a tragedy it is that when one realises that their [Larry's] love, enthusiasm and visions of Greek faith and life were only stimulating games ... that friendship and openness for them were nothing more than a ploy for systematic research and cool classification of ideas and feelings to be canned and served at the right moment' (*Allilographia, Letters*, Stigmi Press, Athens, 1985). Some might take this to imply that Larry was an unfaithful Grecophile, one who simply plundered its legacy for his fictionalised version of it, but forty years later Diamantis would state in an interview that 'Durrell was not a straight person' (MacNiven, p413). He believed that Larry was a spy (Theodora Pavlidou, 'Another Dark Side of Durrell', *Cyprus View* 2, 1991, pp4–8). He was, his erstwhile friends believed, passing on as much information as he could to the British authorities. He was not part of the diplomatic service, not quite: diplomats, as the campaign for independence became more intense in 1955, were treated as legitimate targets for guerrillas. Indeed, his boss Sir Robert Armitage survived with only slight injuries after a bomb – a bottle partly filled with homemade explosives – detonated under his seat at the theatre in April 1955. Larry was seen by most on the island as an expatriate aesthete, one who knew the cultures of the eastern Mediterranean intimately and who might therefore be sympathetic to the desire of the indigenous population, Greek and Turkish, for self-determination.

It was for this reason that Burrows had him appointed to his new post. He was a perfect sounding board for British Intelligence, a man who would be able mix safely enough and to diagnose the levels of support held by Cypriots for the various factions of the independence movement.

Eight months after Larry's appointment, EOKA began its most intensive period of armed struggle. From the end of March through to the end of June there were 204 serious incidents involving attempted and sometimes successful attacks against British forces and bombings of military barracks and government buildings. EOKA had conducted a far more murderous campaign against the British than their smaller communist/socialist counterparts and as a token of this Westminster decided that they would be the group with whom negotiations for peace would open. EOKA wanted *enosis*, the incorporation of the island within the Greek state, which in turn involved its alliance with western Europe and NATO.

Larry was forced to set aside much of the time he hoped to dedicate to writing because he was now busy conveying information to his employers on what he knew or could surmise regarding the popular support for EOKA's objectives.

Justine was completed shortly before he left Cyprus, and one has to wonder how his time there influenced the novel, particularly the

Gerald Durrell and his wife Jacquie stroking thirteen-year-old cheetah 'Prince' at London Zoo. November 1954. *Credit: Keystone / Stringer*

Gerald Durrell looks on as his wife Jacquie allows a red bill toucan to eat a grape from her mouth at London Zoo. November 1954. *Credit: Hulton Deutsch*

Lawrence Durrell and 'Two Kings of Ancient Cyprus'. 1958. *Credit: Bettmann*

Lulu, the chimp from Gerald Durrell's zoo, at the BBC Studios in Bristol. February 1961.
Credit: Mirrorpix

Lawrence Durrell at home with his wife Claude and daughter Sappho. 1961.
Credit: Hulton Deutsch

Lawrence Durrell. October 1961. *Credit: Evening Standard / Stringer*

Gerald Durrell and Jacquie Durrell in their new home, Les Augres Manor, on the island of Jersey, Channel Islands. March 1963.
Credit: Popperfoto

Lulu the chimp poses with 18-year-old Pat Waigh in the warm Jersey sunshine.
Credit: Keystone Pictures USA/ZUMAPRESS.com/Alamy Live News

Lawrence Durrell on the terrace of a brasserie with a friend in Paris. Circa 1970.
Credit: Raphael GAILLARDE

Lawrence Durrell on a French walkabout. January 1976.
Credit: Sophie Bassouls

Gerald Durrell holding his OBE award with Lee Durrell at an investiture ceremony at Buckingham Palace. February 1983.
Credit: United News/ Popperfoto

Lawrence Durrell,
late 1940s.
Credit: Bettmann

Les Augrès Manor,
former home of
Gerald Durrell and
present headquarters
of Durrell Wildlife
Conservation Trust.
Credit: Tim Graham

substantial revisions made during his final year on the island when the guerrilla campaign was at its height. The narrator is shifty and distrustful. He tells us much in terms of his impressions of feelings and individuals but hardly anything of how the former are caused or who exactly the latter are. It was praised as a new hall-of-mirrors extension of the modernist experiments of a generation earlier. But then again when he wrote it Larry was leading a double life, deceiving his Cyprus friends and pretending that a marriage long broken down might still be repaired. His refuge was a novel which blends obscurity with hazy imprecision.

In mid-August 1955 Eve left Larry for England and took Sappho with her. For the following year they would be offered accommodation by friends of his who pitied them. They had no sympathy for Larry. George Wilkinson, among others, had already written to mutual acquaintances on how badly Larry was treating Eve. Sappho recalled in her diary, later published in *Granta*, that her father was behaving much as he had in Belgrade: 'She had become frightened of his violence and had decided to leave. She was talking to herself in bed, saying that she would tell him tomorrow, and a voice in her head said, "You *won't*"' (*Granta*, Autumn 1991). Larry's old friend Maurice Cardiff was then head of the British Council in Cyprus and he offers an account in his memoir, *Friends Abroad: Memories of Lawrence Durrell, Freya Stark, Patrick Leigh Fermor, Peggy Guggenheim and Others* (Radcliffe Press, 1997, pp 29–30). According to Cardiff's wife Leonora, Eve complained to her that Larry was treating her like a figure he had invented for his ongoing novel, always attempting to 'psychoanalyse' her, not because he wanted to help her but as an experiment in how he could represent a fictional character as emotionally unhinged. One morning Larry was hosting a reception at Government Lodge for 'journalists covering' the uprising but Eve arrived first, sporting a black eye and a less conspicuous bruise to her cheekbone. Cardiff was there and asked about her injuries. 'Larry,' she replied, and when he arrived later he was wearing a silk scarf which failed to fully conceal the scratch marks on his neck where she had dug in her nails to protect herself against his blows. Larry later reported to Miller that Eve was in England 'with the kidnapped daughter', and that she was possessed by 'Jewish hysteria and religious mania… May she fry in a nice Jewish hell!' (24 December 1955, UCLA Archive).

Most of the expatriates who felt brave enough to leave their homes enjoyed late-night openings in a small club called The Cosmopolitan on the outskirts of Nicosia. Larry sometimes played jazz tunes on the piano and one evening he was introduced by his friends Dennis and Joan Wetherell-Pepper to Philip and Fay Nind. The former was a wealthy executive with Shell Oil and his wife Fay an artist whose work was displayed in London galleries. She was under five feet tall, which made Larry feel less self-conscious about his own height. Though pretty she was also insecure, feeling that her paintings were treated by the high-cultural establishment as an indulgence and that her husband had made use of his social rank to persuade galleries to offer her space on their walls. Larry, in a manner he had cultivated with other vulnerable women, made her feel confident and assured. Margo, when talking with MacNiven, said, 'Larry always ruined woman. He would build them up, make them dissatisfied with their husbands, discontented' (MacNiven, p416). Margo goes on to describe how Larry had developed a means of turning his shortness of stature into the opposite. His torso was average in size so he would make sure that when he wanted to make an impression he would arrive first at a venue and be seated and that anything reflective – a large window or a mirror – caught him from behind. Hence when he rose to greet his guest, he would lean forward confidently to take their hand or more often kiss them on the cheek while a version of him would simultaneously rise above both of them from his rear. Even Margo, who had known him since they were infants, was taken in by this. 'I never felt he was small,' she said. 'He was always the tallest in the room.'

Margo knew nothing of Fay Nind but her description of her brother's habit is a perfect account of how he turned his acquaintance with Fay into something more intimate. The Ninds' daughter Charlotte was around the same age as Sappho and he managed to arrange a driver to bring mother and daughter to Government Lodge where he would be waiting with Sappho in a car that was allocated to him as part of the job, an Opel Olympia Rekord open-top. It looked more like the kind of car that featured in American movies than the rather utilitarian models of the period and Larry did a fair imitation of Cary Grant in *To Catch a Thief* as he drove Fay and the two girls around the cliff-top roads of the island, stopping to captivate them with views of the sea, half-hidden fishing villages, and impressing Fay with his knowledge of the history of the place. She was particularly beguiled as they parked and walked through the Sanctuary of Aphrodite, the supposed birthplace of the goddess of sexual passion. He whispered stories to her as their daughters played innocently on the green meadows surrounding the ruins.

Their affair lasted until he left the island in 1956, even after he had met the woman who would become his third wife, Claude-Marie Forde. He met Claude-Marie in formal circumstances in January 1956 when she applied for the job as his secretary and assistant. Asking her if they had met before she answered yes; in Alexandria, at various social events. She was married with two children, both at boarding school in England. Her husband was a naval officer but, she ventured, it was doubtful that their marriage would survive too long after his return from London. Her manner and cosmopolitan, multi-ethnic background fascinated him. Born in Alexandria her father was a French banker and her Jewish mother a society beauty, and in her twenties, she had been recklessly nomadic, dividing her time between managing a pub in Cork and training as an electrician in the newly formed State of Israel. All of this bewitched Larry but her shining blonde hair and beautiful features caused him to become besotted. Decisively, she came in at only five feet tall.

A day after he offered her the job, she was headhunted by the Public Information Director of the Cyprus Broadcasting Service as head of the French Section. She was multilingual and her French was perfect. This suited Larry well since gossips could not now claim that he had hired her with an ulterior motive. They began meeting regularly for drinks and when he spoke to her of *Justine* she asked if she could read parts of the draft. She too was writing a novel, based on her time in Ireland. She had no proof of the truth of this but she intuited to Larry something of having returned to a long-forgotten point in her family legacy, somehow connected with the place. Larry could hardly contain himself. Liars both, they were besotted.

Shortly after the departure of Eve he had boarded up and locked Bellapaix and for a short period moved into a deserted mosque above a rarely used beach on the coast. The only other inhabitant was an elderly Turkish *hodja*, a term combining our notions of teacher and sage, said to have been banished there for a suspected case of rape and murder which never went to court. The old man was a devotee of Sufism, the Islamic brand of mysticism, of which he spoke to Larry. The latter was fascinated and spent his time, when alone, picking out parallels between his companion's comments and his new interest, specifically D. T. Suzuki's writings on Zen Buddhism.

Typically, Larry preferred a melange of vaguely related and half-digested concepts to anything specific and this is all he needed for the epiphany that occurred during his early meetings with Claude-Marie. It was as though she had followed him, ghost-like, from Alexandria, the setting of his ongoing novel, to the moment of its near conclusion. She was like many of the characters of *Justine*, multicultural by nature, neither one thing in particular nor anything else, but rather constantly fissiparous. Most of all she echoed Larry's weird and delusional claims about his Celtic roots, which he also hands over to the novel's narrator. At least Claude-Marie had lived there, albeit briefly. Eve was the model for the eponymous Justine, the 'true child of Alexandria' (*Justine*, p27). The narrator adds that 'we are the children of our landscape; it dictates behaviour and even thought in the measure to which we are responsive to it' (*Ibid.*, p41).

These were the characteristics that eventually alienated him from Eve, particularly her being tied to the suffocating monoculture of Middle Eastern minorities, Jews in particular. But Claude-Marie showed him that the exoticism that first attracted him to his wife could, in some women, cultivate audacity and recklessness.

They began an affair within a week of their first meeting. Somehow, he managed to meet her and Fay at different times in different bars.

He had now taken a house on Castellorizon and Claude-Marie had a flat on Archangel Michael Street. Fay's flat was on the other side of Nicosia and Larry busied himself with numerous schedules. The ones he cared for least were meetings with large numbers of the international press who had flocked to the island to cover the uprising. He was more concerned with how to manage visits to Fay at her place alongside what now appeared to be his cohabitation with Claude-Marie. The latter did not stay at his house every night but during the time that they could spend these together during the day Larry positioned their typewriters at separate ends of a long oak table. Both enjoyed the rhythm of their words hitting the page, his with revisions of *Justine* and hers with the novel based on her time in

Cork. Larry also put on the wall a detailed map of Alexandria, and Claude-Marie, who knew the city more intimately than he did, would correct him on the movements of his fictional characters through the metropolis. It was as if the novel he was writing had come to life.

Its keynotes are deceit, subterfuge and infidelity, and as Larry wove the lives of his characters around them in the book, he also acted them out in his double life with Fay and Claude-Marie. Indeed, there is evidence to show that the intensity of his feelings for each woman was stronger than one would expect of a mere Lothario. Less than a month after Eve had left him, he asked Fay to break with her husband and marry him. Four months after that he began his equally intense relationship with Claude-Marie. We will never know if he was simply playing the field, waiting to see which of the two women would be the first to exchange their marriages, and children, for a life with him – which in the end would be Claude-Marie. If this were the case he had sunk to an extraordinary depth of general and emotional opportunism, verging on sadism. Read *Justine*. All of the characters are irresolute and inconstant in terms of their relationships, but they are more than debauchees. They treat sex and infidelity as routes to an existential condition that is neither definable nor fully attainable. If one needs a lesson in how to distil personal foulness into an aesthetic enigma go to this book.

When the novel was published, *The New York Times* observed that 'The story is told by the "epiphany" method of James Joyce. Letting his memory range freely over many people, many incidents, many years, the narrator recounts only those significant "manifestations" which occur to him naturally ... No formal attempt is made at structure or even at rendering the story easy to follow' (25 August 1957). Perhaps Larry was intent on sustaining modernist experimentation but it might also be argued that he was using literature as a means of displacing his own less appetising temperamental characteristics. For him love and contempt, debauchery and fidelity, commitment and narcissism were constantly interchangeable and he shared this aspect of his personality with the characters and mood of the novel.

Consider its labyrinthine plot scheme. Darley (albeit unnamed at this point in the *Quartet*) is seduced by Justine, but he loves Melissa, the mistress of Cohen. Nessim is Justine's husband, while Pursewarden and Justine are lovers too. Clea might once have made love to Justine, and the latter, when much younger, was probably raped by Capodistria, the one-eyed money-lender and pederast. Nessim might have killed Capodistria on a hunting trip but we cannot be certain of this. The story concludes when the narrator returns to Alexandria after much of the internecine partner-swapping is concluded, and finds that Melissa has recently died and takes with him to an unnamed island her orphaned child who might have been fathered by Nessim, or might not.

That we cannot be certain of anything, aside from the fact that everyone seems obsessed with sex, meant that Larry would be treated as the quintessence of the psycho-sensualist brand of modernism, beginning with D. H. Lawrence, resurfacing with Larry's friend Miller and taking in the likes of Freud and Reich along the way. When we compare the book with Larry's life, however, something a little more sordid becomes apparent. Just as we have no proper idea of what actually goes on in the novel so its author was busy obscuring the truth of what he did and felt both from those involved and from himself.

Penelope Tremayne, poet and Red Cross volunteer, told Gordon Bowker of a conversation she had with Larry in midsummer 1956. He announced that he had sent the first part of his planned quartet to Alan Pringle, his editor at Faber, though he did not mention the title of what would be published as *Justine*.

> 'So,' I said, 'splendid, and what is it going to be?' 'Well,' he said, 'there's only one thing that really sells in the present day and that's pornography. But it's got to be thriller pornography – James Bond, if you can do it, he said.'

Tremayne knew nothing of his spy novel based, like Ian Fleming's, on a fantasised version of his own skirmishes with British Intelligence in various parts of the eastern Mediterranean. He added:

> I'm never going to be able to write that sort of stuff, so I'm going to write highbrow pornography and they'll swallow it.' (Bowker, p231)

This is as close as Larry comes to disclosing the true nature of the opening volume of *The Alexandria Quartet*. It was about subterfuge and espionage yet only in the sense that debauchees lied to and spied on each other in a sexual *danse macabre.*

Kingsley Martin, editor of the *New Statesman*, had visited Cyprus in 1956, met Larry at one of his press briefings and got to know him well over several drinks and supper gatherings during his ten days on the island. A year later he wrote an article on his time there for the magazine and concentrated on Larry, telling of how distraught he was at having to leave 'the house he had built with such passionate joy in Bellapaix, before his demi-paradise of love and friendship had been transformed into the saddest and most reluctant inferno of superstition and murder' (*New Statesman*, 27 July 1957).

We know from a letter to Miller in November that Larry left Bellapaix in late 1955. A few months before that he was sitting in a nearby bar when the manager, a Cypriot friend, suggested he should leave quietly by the back entrance. Three men had been seen in the street outside, one carrying what appeared to be a Sten gun, a crude but effective submachine gun supplied to partisans by Britain during the war and now circulating among EOKA members. Larry wondered if he was becoming paranoid but a week later, in early June, he found an incendiary bomb in his garage adjacent to the house. A few days afterwards when he, Claude-Marie and Penelope Tremayne were drinking cocktails on the Bellapaix veranda, three young men, whom he later described as slim teenagers, strode along the street, chatting in a seemingly unthreatening manner, until one of them hurled an object towards Larry and his companions. Fortunately for them it landed close to the house opposite and blew off the front door. To the surprise of both women Larry snatched a service revolver from a canvas bag under the table, fired several shots at the fleeing bombers and then raced across the street. His neighbour, whom he knew only slightly as the wife of a British administrator, stood covered in dust along with her two naked, screaming children. No one was harmed physically. Kingsley Martin's use of the term 'superstition' should not be treated as him trivialising Larry's dilemma. He was using it in the older sense of an unreasoning awe or fear of the unrevealed. Larry now carried his service revolver with him everywhere he went because beneath the often benign, even tranquil mood of the island seemed to lurk something unknown and deadly. That he had been issued with the sidearm testified to his work being undercover.

185

He told Tremayne that he had decided to leave Cyprus before the end of the summer.

> 'I'm going to live in the South of France, where the cigarettes are a shilling a packet and wine is sixpence a bottle, and I've enough in the kitty to live for a year like that.' (Bowker, p231)

'The book' he had described to her earlier 'will really sell'. He had decided to ask Claude-Marie to come with him, but he told no one else of this. Already he had found that many of his friends still in Cyprus were unsettled by her presence. She was too forthright and unconstrained for those who might claim to be bohemians but were in truth still bound by the conventions of middle-class Englishness. Joan and Dennis Wetherell-Pepper swung between the elitist diplomatic social network and the company of expatriate British artists and writers, their friend Larry in particular, who sought inspiration in the region. For them Claude-Marie was a little too impetuous. In truth what worried them and others was that their friend had found a woman who was too much like himself, a woman who would do much as she wished socially and sexually.

Larry hoped that his old friend Alan Thomas would offer him accommodation for a few days in England until he made plans for France, but he did not tell him that he might arrive with his new lover.

Typically, he kept as many balls in the air as he could. He arranged a meeting with Fay Nind, promised to stay in touch with her and more than hinted that when he was out of Cyprus, they might meet up again. At the same time, he made preliminary arrangements for Claude-Marie's two children to go to a boarding school just outside London.

In the end he booked two tickets on a flight to London from Cyprus, on 26 August 1956. He persuaded Penelope Tremayne to take over Bellapaix and asked her to look after his library. She said goodbye to Larry as he and Claude-Marie boarded the bus for the airport and he gave her the keys. As the vehicle began to move on, he assured her that as a Red Cross worker she would not be a legitimate target but added, 'just in case, you can have this too', and threw his revolver onto the road in front of her.

8

Animal Farm

Less than a year after Larry was forced out of Cyprus by assassins wielding submachine guns and planting bombs his brother Gerry and wife Jacquie became stars in a real-life version of the much-cherished Ealing comedies which amused British cinema audiences through the 1950s. Few of the films involved animals but Gerry's escapades would have provided a wonderful model for a production called *Kind Hearts and Marmosets*.

On 7 July 1957 the *Nicoya* docked at Liverpool and a week later the *Daily Telegraph* ran a piece announcing that 'Mr Gerald Durrell, 32, the writer-zoologist, hopes to start a zoo at Bournemouth', adding that 'Mr Durrell and his wife, Jacqueline, 27, have just returned from a seven-month expedition to the British Cameroons. They brought back 200 reptiles, 50 birds, 18 monkeys, 47 bush babies [and] a nine-month-old Chevrotain deer ...' They also brought with them 'Chumley 2', who replaced the now deceased Cholmondeley of the late 1940s and was officially named Cholmondeley St John Durrell.

As the *Telegraph* reported, Gerry hoped that Bournemouth Council would 'be sympathetic to the extent of letting us have some land'. They would not and Gerry contacted his mother and Margo, whose houses faced each other across St Albans Avenue, and asked if they would allow their gardens and interiors to become a temporary zoo until he found somewhere more spacious and permanent.

Margo's back garden was the larger open-air space and Gerry bought a massive second-hand marquee once used by a travelling circus, appropriately enough. Inside were placed a dizzying assembly of creatures chosen on the assumption that they were unlikely to fight with or attempt to eat each other in a relatively confined space. Species of squirrels, hares and rabbits unknown to Europe shared the enclosure with ostriches, gazelles, honey badgers and pangolins. The spacious garage was set aside mainly for birds, with a fabric of horizontal poles installed as perching facilities. Some creatures – mainly the overexcited chimps and baboons and the carnivorous eagles, hawks and vultures – were confined to cages. Reptiles had access to the pond at the rear of Louisa's house and those monkeys deemed sufficiently domesticated were allowed to roam the gardens on leashes and eventually offered the more comfortable situation of the houses themselves. Margo's paying guests were now dwindling in number but since her B and B was the cheapest in the area a further reduction persuaded them to tolerate brief encounters with hairy companions on the ground floor.

At first the immediate neighbours were appalled by what seemed to be an invasion by creatures from another planet. Few of the animals escaped but other residents of St Albans Avenue were unsettled by the constant barrage of growls, squeaks, grunts and whistles that issued from the Durrell menagerie. There were complaints to the council and letters to the local press. The former looked into bylaws to see if any had been breached but since the animals were not being exhibited or kept for any purpose other than as 'domestic pets' they were unable to act.

Soon, however, the popular press heard of this hilarious pantomime on the south coast and several reporters were dispatched to cover what seemed a welcome relief from the aftermath of the Suez Crisis and the ongoing conflict in Cyprus. Margo and Jacquie agreed to interviews for the *Women's Sunday Mirror*, on the assumption that this female-oriented annex to the popular *Daily* and *Sunday Mirror* would be less prone to mockery than its male-dominated counterparts.

The focus of the main interview with Jacquie was Chumley. She began by explaining that she and Gerry were conducting groundbreaking experiments regarding the myths and presuppositions of anthropomorphism. 'I'm mother to a chimp,' she said, going on to tell how that they had decided to treat Chumley as if he were a human toddler. They would carefully record his behavioural tendencies and most importantly see if he began to acquire habits and characteristics that were noticeably different from those of chimps raised among and by their own. They did not seriously expect that he would become linguistically competent but they wanted to see whether he would familiarise himself with and respond to routinely used phrases. On the surface this sounded like cutting-edge zoological research but the interview gradually drifted towards the farcical and the faintly bizarre, especially when Jacquie added that 'I have decided I would never have children – the life of an ordinary housewife did not seem right for me. Now I am mother to Cholmondeley – he just steals your affection.' Jacquie gave an account of the interview in *Beasts in My Bed*:

> His day was quite a simple one; he was awakened in the morning with a large cup of milky tea and then dressed in the exotic sweaters that my mother-in-law had knitted for him 'to keep the cold out, dear'. Then the rest of the day was spent in plaguing the inhabitants of the house ... At first he slept in Mrs Durrell's room, until we found that she did not read at night in case the light disturbed the furry monster. We quickly removed him to our own room, where he soon learnt to accept light, noise, cigarette smoke and anything else without detriment to his health or well-being. (p97)

In all of the interviews and accounts of this period by each of them the boundary between humans and Chumley as something else is eroded.

Jacquie goes on to describe how Chumley was 'befriended' by the son of one of the guests in Margo's B and B, John Hawker, of how the two youngsters loved playing with a wheelbarrow and that it usually ended up 'with poor John Hawker, red faced and puffing', pushing the wheelbarrow with Chumley as passenger. Reading the account, it is as though, at least to Jacquie, Chumley is a more quick-witted character than his new pal. Chumley also tormented golfers on a nearby course, picking up balls and hiding them in the bushes for the sake of it.

There is a passage in *Beasts in My Bed* in which Jacquie describes how Chumley had become angered by the attention that press coverage had generated. During 1957, Peter Scott, producer of the BBC programme *Look*, descended on Bournemouth as did the crew of the more prestigious weekly *Tonight*. The wish to 'interview' Chumley, or at least get some impression of him via his human intermediaries, was becoming the goal of many otherwise sane news outlets. Jacquie:

> It was my opinion that our dear chimp was by now so full of himself and his own importance, having appeared on television so many times ... that he had become pompous and was determined to let no one else have a chance. (*Beasts in My Bed*, pp98–9)

Chumley, it seemed, was a skilled operator on the new medium of television, unlike his father. 'Durrell was not happy in a television studio and if he was going to pursue any career in this particular medium, he would have to be skilled on location ...' (*Ibid.*) In other words, he regarded the wild as his natural environment, unlike Chumley, apparently. As usual Jacquie's prose is at once sharp yet unflustered and one has to wonder whether the role shifts between the two delightful creatures in her life, her husband and her adopted 'child', were a whimsy or an involuntary revelation.

It soon become apparent to Gerry that his various zoological projects were being treated by the popular media as a real-life sitcom with himself and Chumley in the starring roles. He began to write to councils on and around the south coast stating that he would be willing to rent or buy properties with land and outbuildings where he would establish a proper zoo or wildlife conservation area, as he now referred to his objective. He received only one reply, from Poole, barely five miles away. The borough council had, some years earlier, purchased Upton House on the shores of Poole Harbour. It was a graceful and spacious Georgian house, almost a stately home, with fifty-four acres of land and numerous stables. Its former residents, the Llewellin family, members of the minor aristocracy and according to records William Llewellin had 'gifted' the estate to the Borough of Poole in 1957. By then the property had been left uninhabited and untended for almost a decade.

Gerry put it to the borough council that they could continue as the owners provided they financed the restoration of the house and the conversion of outbuildings. He would fund the rehabilitation of the rest of the infrastructure, mostly the land, where the animals would exist in as close to a wild environment as possible, and he would be the leaseholder for a mutually agreed amount and for a specified period. Gerry pointed out that on his eventual departure the council would be left with a useful and valuable asset. They did not reject his proposal out of hand but stated that they would postpone a final decision on his terms until the New Year of 1958. In the meantime, he and Jacquie had to find shelter for the most vulnerable animals during the coldest midwinter months. Paignton Zoo agreed to take some but they were left with the prospect of the family properties in St Albans Avenue being so crammed with mammals, mostly chimps, as to have little space for human beings.

Eventually Gerry or Jacquie – it remains unclear which – came up with the idea of approaching J. J. Allen, the most prestigious local department store specialising in clothing and furniture for the middle classes, with a suggestion. Rather than mounting a relatively brief performance of Santa handing out gifts to the children of affluent customers they could introduce these kids to an otherworldly experience of the African and South American hinterlands. In the spacious basement youngsters would be allowed to wander past, even feed, caged creatures they'd probably never heard of before. Gerry even managed to create a taped soundtrack which might, for all the visitors knew, be an authentic replica of the background noises of the Cameroonian jungle. J. J. Allen agreed, even offered a modest payment to Gerry and all went well until shortly after Christmas when the store manager telephoned Louisa announcing that a disaster had occurred and that her son must drive there immediately to resolve matters.

Georgina, a baboon of about the same age and size as Chumley, had escaped from her cage and gone upstairs to the ground floor. When the manager phoned, she was rampaging through the immaculate window displays of suits, dresses, furniture and beds. Gerry, Jacquie and Margo arrived to find that a large crowd had gathered, along with a number of officers from the Bournemouth police. The latter had been summoned by the manager because he felt that various acts of bodily harm and criminal damage were being committed but the policemen were confused given that it was apparently not possible to arrest non-humans for such offences, at least not since the eighteenth century. Once again, we find that Gerry had blurred the boundary, though unintentionally, between animals and us. He confused things further by insisting that Margo, Jacquie and the constables stay outside while he entered the

191

building and calmed Georgina. He argued that he knew her better than the others, having rescued her from an African bar where she was required to dance for drinks or else receive a beating.

Unfortunately, one constable followed him through the main doors only to find that Georgina, more than half his size, had seized his leg in a display of what might have been affection, or something else. Gerry teased her away, took her downstairs, and in Jacquie's account we have:

> 'Cor, I thought I'd had it that time, sir,' the poor bobby said, mopping his brow.
>
> 'You behaved extremely well, and I want to thank you for your help.'
>
> 'No trouble at all sir,' he assured us, 'and it makes a change from teenagers, I must say.' (*Ibid.*, p101)

Believe it? No, nor do I, but it improves on something like the wearisome actuality of late-1950s Britain. The first *Carry On* film would be made a few months later.

By early spring 1958 Poole Council responded formally to Gerry's proposal. He must, they insisted, contribute £10,000 to the costs of restoration and upkeep of the property and grounds – roughly £200,000 today. In return, he would be granted the lease of Upton House for forty-nine years. They were vague regarding the exact amount which they would contribute towards the establishment of what Gerry had called the Wild Animal Preservation Trust. He had nowhere near enough to pay them this amount but during a visit to London to meet Rupert Hart-Davis he mentioned his dilemma and Hart-Davis offered to put up £10,000 as an 'advance' for the bestsellers that would result from their author's establishment of his own zoo.

However, it soon become evident that the repairs to the house and outbuildings, let alone the construction of open-plan enclosures, would send Gerry's costs well beyond the Hart-Davis advance, which he calculated would also eat up virtually all his royalty payments for the next ten years. These were his only regular source of income. Reluctantly, he withdrew from the provisional arrangement at Poole and, encouraged by Jacquie, tried to see if he could raise enough money by other means to retrieve the animals presently being kept by Paignton Zoo. They had planned another journey to Argentina in late 1958 and it would either be a matter of cancelling this or asking Paignton to keep his friends for good.

In the interim he had been visited in Bournemouth by Tom Salmon, a reporter for the BBC based in the south west. Local radio and television did not exist at the time and Salmon, only a year in his job, wanted to promote a series for his London bosses that was focused on the region. Gerry, who was now only just behind David Attenborough and Peter Scott as a newsworthy wildlife presenter, seemed ideal: conservation with a touch of comedy.

In spring 1957 when he was in the Cameroons BBC Radio had broadcast his pre-recorded six-part series called *Encounters with Animals*, which emphasised what was now Gerry's signature theme: that he treated animals with the same respect and regard as he did human beings. Salmon had read the often farcical accounts in the popular press of Gerry and Jacquie's new 'family', made up mainly of chimps, and suggested that he should do a series which offered a respectable quasi-scientific account of animal and human behaviour, involving how we and other species deal with long-term relationships, caring for our offspring, engaging in conflicts with competing groups, planning and building homes, etc.

Broadcasting House loved the proposal and commissioned a series called *Animal Attitudes* which would be recorded in summer 1958 and broadcast later that year. Jacquie prompted Gerry to contact Hart-Davis and suggest that the radio programmes could be the basis for a short book made up mostly of cut-and-paste rewrites of Gerry's account for both series. He agreed a contract almost immediately, knowing that Gerry's status as a media celebrity would guarantee sales. The typescript of *Encounters with Animals* arrived at the Hart-Davis office in late summer 1958 and was handed to the recently appointed junior editor David Hughes, who would remain a devoted friend of Gerry's for the rest of his life.

In his own account of Gerry, *Himself and Other Animals: A Portrait of Gerald Durrell* (1998), Hughes tells in his prologue of their first meeting:

> He looked young, blond, handsome, excited and nice, all to excess ... he gave me a hard blue stare of amusement and said, 'We're all going to lunch at Bertorelli's, if you'd care to join us.' That lunch at Bertorelli's was the first of countless meals. And meals counted. I quickly saw that

lunch and/or dinner, daily excuses to celebrate being alive ... must be for preference and never less than merry. (pp4–6)

The initial impression given by Gerry as the generous dissolute gradually shades into something darker as Hughes becomes a regular companion at their often day-long sessions of unrestraint. 'He appeared to believe, with so little done and so much to do, that self-indulgence alone offered any protection against despair' (*Ibid.*, p6).

People cast him as a rib-tickling ringmaster of the comic capers of animals, whereas the core of his life and work ... was his complex reaction, one moment furiously hopeful, the next in hopeless fury, to simple facts. These facts had made him bother. They had also cracked him up. The facts of the world disturbed his nights. His days were nagged by them. He had drunk too much on account of these facts. They had helped to cause a breakdown in his mid-forties. Facts had blackened his jokes. (*Ibid.*, p7)

Hughes goes on to tell how in the midst of jokey exchanges during their fifth bottle of wine Gerry would suddenly shift into a state of despondency and then hatred directed mostly against the 'establishment': career politicians, sanctimonious clergy, intellectuals of the left or right who felt they knew better than anyone else how to improve the world, etc. He seemed focused on his vocation as the protector of species that humankind knew little and cared nothing of: 'the hopeless fate of a particular species struck him on a moonlit night as we sat immersed in drink and laughter ... He thrust his thumbnail into my face. "It's that size," he said, "and it's as big in the scheme of things as you or me"' (*Ibid.*).

Hughes does not doubt his friend's commitment to conservation, but he also senses something close to masochism. 'Durrell's spirit functioned on discontent with himself ... He survived on his nerves' (*Ibid.*, p9). Throughout Hughes's portrait one finds in Gerry a loathing for mankind that is equal to the love he shows for our animal counterparts.

There is, however, a contrast between this and what actually went on during 1958. Larry wrote to Miller that, 'Brother Gerry has become a television star owing to a clever little ape he brought back from the

Congo which does everything but vote apparently' (late February 1958). Larry, now in France, was receiving regular accounts from his friends on his brother's antics with Chumley, which included them appearing as guests at the launch of a Hollywood-made film, on advertisements as the proud owners of everything from vacuum cleaners to cameras and as guests of honour at the WH Smith stand at the book fair in Olympia, surrounded by Gerry's most recent bestsellers. This took place a week after Larry wrote to Miller, and soon after that he sent a letter to the poet Richard Aldington. 'My beastly brother ... travels everywhere with a giant ape called Chumley ... I must admit it is a good way to call on one's publishers when asking for money. Our techniques are widely different.'

> I find that Fabers get awfully scared when I put imaginary titles to books. For a long time I convinced them that *Justine* was to be called 'Sex and the Secret Services' or 'Not Now Your Husband's Looking'. Gerry, who is cruder (with Hart-Davis one must be tougher I suppose), always threatens to write a life of Jesus. I expect they'll [Gerry and Jacquie] come down here and make my life a cicada-ridden mystery before long ...' (Early March 1958, Aldington Private Archive)

Larry is envious of Gerry's enormous success as a bestselling author but what annoys him more is his sibling's apparent guile as a writer who can blur the line between fantasy and truth. This, for Larry, was abundantly evident in *My Family* and now it seemed that Gerry was using an ape to persuade a reasonably respectable publisher to issue a limitless abundance of contracts.

Larry had heard tales of the Olympia Book Fair, particularly when Chumley had been invited to leave the WH Smith stand and attend a lunch at an adjoining hotel. Dressed in a Fair Isle pullover he joined Gerry at the main table and conducted himself impeccably, sharing side dishes with his patron-companion. The popular press and their photographers devoured the spectacle.

Hughes frequently tells of how Gerry detested the indignities forced upon animals by humans, especially in Africa, but his own tendency towards this can perhaps be excused by the financial dilemma he faced. He needed money to purchase buildings and land where he might allow threatened species autonomy and independence and to do so he must also, with the assistance of Chumley, feed the popular appetite for comic anthropomorphism. As Hughes discerned, his mission was often accompanied by bouts of depression verging on self-loathing.

He found in later summer that David Attenborough had been commissioned by the BBC to take with him to Paraguay a film crew for his already popular *Zoo Quest* television series. Feeling that his own trip would be overshadowed by this he called Attenborough and learned that his excursion would not overlap with his own trip to Patagonia.

Gerry and Jacquie now talked regularly of setting up a zoo on an island, partly as a form of escapism. The intransigence of the various councils they had dealt with on the mainland caused Gerry to reminisce about life in Corfu, especially the carefree fantasy he had created for *My Family*, when everyone did more or less as they wished. Gerry knew that the past was irrecoverable but the very notion of islands was enticing; they always seemed to have a kind of maverick self-reliance about them. Half seriously, Jacquie suggested the Channel Islands. The Queen was their head of state but they were not governed by the UK, and the climate, she guessed, was rather more French than English.

Her remark was little more than a joke but Gerry reported it to Hart-Davis during their meeting in London prior to his departure for South America. Ostensibly they had met to discuss plans for books and the formal cancellation of the loan for Poole, signed by each but now meaningless.

According to Jacquie, Gerry stressed that the prospect of buying a site on the Channel Islands was empty-headed. For one thing neither of them had visited the islands, and nor had they any contacts there.

'But I do,' said Rupert. 'An old army chum of mine lives there and I'm sure he'll do everything he can to help you. I'll write to him today. You never know, he might be able to pull something out of the hat for you.' (*Beasts in My Bed*, p105)

Gerry thought his publisher had joined the frivolity, adapting it to his own background of public school nepotism. The 'old army chum' might have been magicked from a novel by Powell or Waugh. But the next day

Gerry found that he was very real when Hart-Davis gave him the phone number of Major Hugh Fraser.

By the end of that week Hart-Davis had arranged flight tickets for Gerry and Jacquie from London Airport (now Heathrow) to Jersey. They were met by Fraser who drove them in his Bentley saloon through the tiny capital of the island north along roads that seemed hardly wide enough for two vehicles either side and which were hung over with rich late-summer greenery. They felt that they had found a place that combined the calm orderliness of the home counties with a faint touch of the tropical rainforests they'd known abroad. Until they reached it, they did not even know the name of their destination. Les Augrès Manor is little more than half a kilometre from the north coast of the island, and for the Durrells it seemed like they were entering another world. It was and is a beautiful building. Parts of it date from the late medieval period but the main house was built in the sixteenth century, added to and enlarged in the seventeenth and eighteenth, and reclothed according to taste in the nineteenth. It is a magnificent accumulation of competing and eclectic architectural habits.

At first Gerry thought that Fraser had brought him here simply to show him what was Jersey's finest country house. It was somewhere for a drink while they discussed the nature of the actual property and land thought suitable for his project; he expected to be shown some semi-derelict farm building and pasture elsewhere on the large estate of Les Augrès. But during aperitifs and a light lunch it became apparent that something staggering was about to occur.

Fraser explained that the upkeep of the property was becoming too difficult for him. Financially he might invest in it as a tourist destination given that with daily ferry and airline journeys from the mainland the more adventurous British lower-middle and working-class holidaymakers were flocking to the island. The scramble for the Spanish south coast would not begin until the early 1960s. It was not quite in the league of Chatsworth House which the Duke of Devonshire was turning into a profitable magnet for visitors but for those who wanted something special during their week in Jersey it would be an attractive prospect.

Fraser was part of the landed gentry and did not, as he explained to Gerry and Jacquie, wish to spend his sixties and seventies toiling over the preservation of a property he could no longer afford to live in. He had, however, come up with a plan after being first contacted by his friend Hart-Davis and then Gerry. He would rent the property to Gerry, which would enable him to use his savings to purchase a more modest house in the home counties without completely giving up Les Augrès. In return, Gerry would be able to finance his zoo by turning it into the tourist attraction that Fraser now saw as an avoidable burden. It would not only be a house and gardens which lower-order visitors could contemplate while feeling slightly alienated; with quiet satisfaction they could now wander proprietorially around the rooms which the minor aristocracy had treated as their private commonwealth. There would be something else too. The grandeur of the manor itself would be contrasted against other residences, spacious enough so that non-human guests would not feel entirely imprisoned.

On that day Fraser triggered and formulated the idea that would shape the rest of Gerry's life. Longleat, established in 1966, is treated as the first British zoo park: wrong. Over lunch in autumn 1958 Gerry, Jacquie and Fraser made plans for a zoo with open-air facilities that would surround another delightful country house that its owner could no longer afford to occupy.

When he returned to England Gerry discussed his plans with fellow conservationists, some of whom treating it as an act of madness. The ornithologist James Fisher and Peter Scott, founder of the Wildfowl Trust, saw the project as another example of their friend's endearing peculiarity. Fisher told him he 'might as well set up on Easter Island'. Who, he asked, is going to come to 'some remote bloody island in the English Channel' to visit a zoo. Both men agreed that the site, as Gerry described it, was perfect, if he was an indulgent millionaire, but he needed customers to cover the upkeep and in their experience zoos were served only by convenient access from urban centres on the mainland.

Sir Julian Huxley, one the founding members of the World Wildlife Fund, was also sceptical, initially. But Gerry explained to him what Fisher and Scott had overlooked, neither of whom having much interest in post-war tourist trends. Fraser, had, from personal experience, told of how Jersey, following the German occupation, had gone through a minor economic boom. Hotels were packed from late May to September and the quasi-independent statelet had reduced levies on alcohol, cigarettes and more luxurious items that remained overtaxed in the UK. The mild climate and pretty landscape added to the attraction of the place but after a few days many holidaymakers found that they had little to do. A beautiful old house only five miles from the capital, St Helier, and accessible from all of the other coastal resorts would become a tourist magnet from spring through to autumn. Following Gerry's peroration Huxley 'treated [the zoo project] with the infectious enthusiasm he showed for every new idea, great or small' (Botting, p266). The one unreserved celebrant of the move to the Channel Islands was Margo who might now reclaim several rooms of her guest house and her garden. Louisa was entranced but after being shown photographs by her son couldn't quite believe his promise that the whole family would one day take up residence in a stately home.

In September Gerry and Jacquie returned to Jersey to meet members of the States Assembly, notably Senator Krichefski, head of tourism. Gerry felt as if he had been transported to nirvana, the antithesis of his experience with local authorities in England. The Assembly granted him permission to found the zoo with unanimous enthusiasm and without reservations: they, like Fraser, foresaw the benefits to the tourist industry. Gerry adapted his plans for Poole to the ordinance survey map of the Les Augrès estate and assured the Assembly that the zoo would be open to the public by spring 1959.

The day after he signed the lease for the property and lands with Fraser, 18 October 1958, he flew to England and took the train to Plymouth to set sail, along with Jacquie, Sophie Cook, his secretary and now occasional mistress, and his mother – who was joining them for a holiday – for Buenos Aires.

The most significant moment of the expedition occurred during the second week when Jacquie was involved in a traffic accident in the Argentine capital. She fractured her skull, though the Argentine emergency doctors who first treated her seemed unable to diagnose the severity of the injury. Summer heat and disorientation worsened her condition and caused Gerry to book her onto a boat for England in February 1959 and to arrange treatment for her in a private London hospital. Despite the fact that their relationship had become precarious her departure prompted a surge of love and devotion in Gerry. The day before she left, he wrote her a letter and asked her to open it only when she was on board the ship. 'Did I mention that I love you? That I miss you? That I wish we were leaving tomorrow so I could be with you? Well, I do. Darling I am yours and only yours: not a very good bargain for you but there it is' (1959, otherwise undated, Jersey Archive).

Two months later Gerry would be in Buenos Aires awaiting a boat for himself, his film crew and his collection of creatures. He came across the man who would later outrank him as a zoologist-celebrity, David Attenborough. They had communicated before but this was their first meeting in person. Attenborough too had just concluded his expedition collecting endangered species in various parts of South America and despite having previously assured Gerry that their expeditions would not overlap the two men spent several days talking in the Argentine capital. Attenborough listened to Gerry's plans for a zoo in Jersey. It would not, Durrell explained, be a prison for animals deprived of the openness of their native environments. There would, for security, sometimes be cages, but where possible, open terrain would be made available to inhabitants.

Later Attenborough recalled that the comment from Gerry that struck him most was expression of distaste for nearly all British zoos, which condemned their creatures to 'life sentences'. He did not expect that animals should be returned to the wild but he found something sinister in the routine habit of 'preserving' them as a spectacle for those who knew nothing of their natural habitats. Instead, Gerry wanted to set a precedent by creating an open enclosure where rescued species could breed, care for their offspring and form a long-term legacy against the threat of extinction in nations where their continued existence might be threatened. The two men did not become close friends. They met on only two or three occasions thereafter. But for Attenborough Gerry's temerity and insight stayed with him.

The lease for Les Augrès was modest, less than a third of the £10,000 asked for by Poole, and Gerry divided the costs between the advance previously offered by Hart-Davis and his own funds from royalties.

The move of animals, cages and other equipment from St Albans Avenue to Jersey took place in January 1959, but Gerry had to dig deep into his savings for far more than the hiring of lorries for the

Southampton ferry. He needed staff, individuals with experience who were prepared to trade their skills for the pitiful salaries that Gerry could afford to pay them. Ken Smith had worked with him regularly since the second Cameroons expedition of 1949. He lived in Bournemouth and was then working at Paignton. As soon as Gerry announced the lease to the manor to him, he volunteered to manage the transportation exercise and said that if Gerry was happy to take him on, he would stay in Jersey as third-in-command to Gerry and Jacquie, dealing with the practicalities of hiring local tradesmen to convert buildings and so on. He also spoke to his wife Trudy who worked in the mammal section at Paignton about them both moving to Jersey. She agreed immediately and offered to tender her resignation if Gerry would take her on in the same role at Les Augrès. Neither of them discussed terms and conditions or wages; for them the project was a vocation which they would share with a man they greatly admired. Margo's eighteen-year-old son was caught in the frenzy. Gerry Breeze resigned from his job as his mother's B and B junior manager and said he too would commit himself to manual labour for the move and stay on in Jersey. He lasted almost two years, until the zoo went through one of its perpetual financial crises.

Smith took on the role of conservation-evangelist and did all he could to persuade other specialists that Gerry's venture was unique and important, completely different from the enclosure-exhibition principle that had dominated zoos on the mainland since the previous century. He was extraordinarily successful. Nick Blampied agreed to come over as vet, Nigel Hanlan – also of Paignton – became head of the reptile section, Timothy Carr took charge of birds, and eight more figures with experience in other zoos made themselves available for whatever work was necessary to transform the currently uninhabited estate into something the world had never seen before. Four of them – John Hartley, Betty Boizard, Quentin Bloxam and Jeremy Mallinson – signed up for five-month contracts, the assumed duration of the first summer that the zoo would be open to the public. They were all in their twenties but by 2000 each was still working at what was then called the Durrell Wildlife Conservation Trust, five years after the death of its founder.

9

France

In September 1956 Larry, Sappho and Claude-Marie arrived at Louisa's house in Bournemouth. She had never met her son's new partner before and only knew of her existence vaguely via comments about a woman Larry was 'seeing'. Even Gerry was surprised to find that the threesome now involved his niece and someone who was certainly not Eve, who was looking for a job in London in the expectation of an imminent divorce settlement. Gerry and Jacquie were about to set off on another expedition for the Cameroons.

Louisa had become used to her eldest son's musical-chairs style of relationships and welcomed Claude-Marie cordially. Claude-Marie, gregarious and easy-going, got on well with Louisa and indeed with Margo, and Larry's new family spent almost three weeks in Bournemouth.

Larry had been friendly with Alexis Ladas and his wife Diana in Alexandria during the war. They were now divorced and knowing Diana's family owned a number of properties in southern England he contacted her in London and was told that her holiday cottage in Wiltshire was now vacant. He could have it for a trifling rent. It was beautiful, roughly two centuries old with five rooms and on the edge of the charming village of Donhead St Andrew. It was named Stepping Stone Cottage after the trout stream that ran through the garden washing against the wall of the kitchen and rudimentary downstairs bathroom.

Larry had already completed *Justine* but it was in the cottage that he would finish *Bitter Lemons* and forge ahead with *White Eagles Over*

Serbia. It is difficult to imagine that the three books could have been written by the same person, let alone almost simultaneously.

Bitter Lemons won the Duff Cooper Prize in 1957 because the judges found it to be an outstanding work of autobiography which offered an unbiased insight into controversies within and surrounding Cypriot politics. Larry gave an unvarnished account of his time on the island as writer and diplomat, leaving out only his marital problems, Eve's mental illness and referring only briefly to Sappho. His other omission involved him not referring to his role as a pathfinder for the intelligence services. At the time the British government denied the existence of MI5 and MI6. *White Eagles* picks up on notes he made in Belgrade in 1952 and five years later the project seemed even more attractive, given that Ian Fleming's first four James Bond novels had appeared in quick succession and been bestsellers. To his credit Larry does not turn his hero Methuen into the epitome of male, and possibly female, fantasy that ensured the popularity of Bond. Methuen works for 'SoQ' ('Special Operations Q branch') and is dispatched to Yugoslavia to see if the anti-communist, quasi-royalist guerrillas (the eponymous White Eagles) who were waging a campaign against the Tito regime stand any chance of success. Principally he assists them in an attempt to smuggle King Peter's gold reserves out of the country as an investment for arms if or when there is a major uprising against Tito.

Methuen has a taste for womanising, opera and fly-fishing but aside from his temperamental singularity he comes across as a man with unique insights into the complexity of the Balkans in the early 1950s. He knows as much as would a figure who worked as an intermediary between the diplomatic corps and the intelligence services, as did his creator. Until le Carré this was the first novel to make use of a first-hand knowledge of the so-called 'trade-craft' of real spies and one senses that Larry is caught between how much he can give away and his obligation to make the autobiographical disclosures implausible. The ambush of the guerrillas by communists from which Methuen is the only survivor resembles the plot of a Cowboys and Indians B-movie, but this was not a case of Larry taking the novel downmarket towards the Fleming subgenre of adventurism. He needed to blend a true story – his own work in the Balkans with the intelligence services – into something utterly unconvincing.

Larry was reconfiguring his past as three very different narratives: *White Eagles* was a censored autobiography, *Bitter Lemons* a far more candid one, and *Justine* a dispersal of his memories across nothing at all resembling a coherent story. Claude-Marie too was hard at work in the cottage and at the close of 1956 her comedic fictional story of life in Cork, *Mrs O'*, was accepted for publication by Faber.

Perhaps Larry's experiments in looking back at his various selves were enlivened by the spectacle of his family, which seemed itself to have become a weird dramatisation of recent history. On his return from Cyprus to the Bournemouth houses owned by his mother and Margo he found that there were as many animal co-inhabitants – most of rare, exotic origin – as humans.

Gerry welcomed him and apologised for his forthcoming absences; he and Jacquie were about to set off again for the Cameroons. He had become the magnet of the British media – radio, television and newspapers – and was making regular visits to London for interviews. *My Family and Other Animals* was published on 11 October, three weeks after Larry, Claude-Marie and Sappho's arrival in Bournemouth, and was at the top of the bestseller list and receiving largely excellent reviews before their move to the Wiltshire cottage. Larry himself was more amused than unsettled by his youngest brother's rewriting of the Corfu years as what amounted to a work of fiction. Margo and to a lesser extent their mother were still fuming at his portraits of them as by parts whimsical and feckless. Much later Larry wrote to his brother from France shortly after he had married Claude-Marie in London. 'I recall that you did away with Nancy in *My Family*. A nice stroke, given my rate of exchange [of wives]. As you know, I'm trying again mostly for tax purposes' (Larry to Gerry, 1961, otherwise undated, Jersey Archive).

In the history of books, no other pair of siblings has produced such a spectacular range of cross-genre outputs – four volumes in total – over a period of a year, in which they variously recycled their closest family members, along with wives, lovers, friends, mentors et al.

Donhead St Andrew proved to be an excellent escape from distractions and Larry and Claude-Marie completed four books there between them, but he was becoming irritated by his long-time bête noire: Englishness. The village had one pub, The Castle, used mostly by farmworkers, and Larry enjoyed himself by getting moderately drunk in the company of men who might have featured largely unaltered in the novels of Hardy. This was the England he could put up with, rough and unpretentious sorts who were content with the land that kept them. It was the eastern Mediterranean without the weather but nonetheless Larry was still a snob. Sappho went to the local primary school and like most five-year-olds she imbibed the habits of her peers. Larry noticed that her accent had changed within two weeks; aitches were disappearing and her first-person pronouns sounded like 'oi'. She was becoming a West Country peasant girl. This was almost amusing but it reminded her father that being ordinary and unaffected was acceptable only if you were abroad, and as close to the Mediterranean as possible.

At the end of January 1957 Sappho was put on a train to London to be collected by her mother who had now found work and a flat in Marylebone. Larry sent a letter insisting that their daughter be enrolled in a private school, which he would pay for. Larry and Claude-Marie went south, taking the ferry to Paris. They took a room in a small, comfortable hotel in Montparnasse and Larry wrote to Richard Aldington, who was then in a house near Montpellier, asking if he knew of rentable properties in the south. Aldington was still dealing with the long-term repercussions of his controversial 1955 biography of T. E. Lawrence but despite this he offered Larry help; he could spare him a few weeks of property hunting.

Larry returned to London to do some interviews. *Justine* had caused a stir in the high-culture weeklies though not all were sure that it was *about* anything in particular, but he wanted to match Gerry as a media presence willing to talk about his recent controversial work. He returned to Paris in early February and was introduced to Claude-Marie's parents at their home in Boulevard des Invalides. Three days later the couple took the train south and met Aldington at the Hotel du Centre in Montpellier. News of responses to *Justine* continued to arrive, the most heartening being a broadcast by the acclaimed poet Christopher Middleton on BBC Radio who praised the novel as part of the resurgence and revitalisation of pre-war modernism.

Larry and Claude-Marie travelled by train and local buses through the villages in the Midi, mostly on the borders between Languedoc and Provence. Sommières gave them the impression of having been abandoned by time. Its history was vibrant but for several centuries things seemed to have stood still. Parts of it were Roman – the ancient bridge across the Vidourle river dated from that era as did the weir below it – and none of the buildings in the town itself were less than four hundred years old. Nimes and Montpellier were both less than thirty kilometres away and joined to the town by local railways. Claude-Marie, when not working on her next novel, would be able to commute to a job – she hoped to find work as the curator of something – while she and Larry could cut themselves off from the rest of the world in this idyllic backwater. Provence, to the east, had since the 1920s been a magnet for British and American expatriates but the central Languedoc region was the closest to unreconstructed rustic France as it was possible to find. The streets were narrow and cobblestoned, overlooked by an Albigensian castle; local farmers sold produce in the square twice a week and most villagers appeared to prefer wine or spirits in the local bars to anything resembling work. Twenty-five kilometres south was the sea and Larry felt as though he had returned to his beloved eastern Mediterranean.

He leased Villa Louis, a single-storey house above the river on the edge of the village. It was unassuming, some might even say ugly, its walls made of local limestone which had been poorly plastered over at different periods of its history by inhabitants who seemed unable to finish the job. There was a 'bathroom' with no running water which meant that Larry, Claude-Marie and eventually Sappho had to shower with the help of a watering can, bearable during the hot Languedoc summer but a form of torture in winter. The lavatory was outside. There was no flush but a pipe dispatched whatever they had released into the river via a 75-degree pipe. Larry modernised things over their first twelve months at the house but for three years he needed to store fresh water in a tank. Nothing was available via a mains pipe until the early 1960s.

In Britain, *Justine* received mixed reviews – most were puzzled and non-committal and the main weeklies ignored it. The New York publisher E. P. Dutton offered Larry a generous advance for a US edition and over the subsequent six months American reviewers celebrated the book almost unanimously, beginning in May when Kenneth Rexroth was impatient to advertise its 'grand complexity' and did a piece on an imported Faber copy for *The Nation*. This was followed by reviews in *The New York Times*, *Time* and *The Atlantic* (August–September) which can be justly described as ecstatic.

In July, Faber had received the first draft of the provisionally entitled 'Justine II', eventually to be called *Balthazar*, and on reading it T. S. Eliot offered him an advance of £500 and to publish the next book in the series – the equivalent of £10,000 today. In terms of money for two novels by a high-end publisher it was miserly, but Larry's weekly outgoings at Sommières were slight. The leasehold was £2 per week and they could pay for market vegetables, meat and table wine with what amounted to loose change. But he was paying Eve an informal pre-divorce allowance and in May 1957 Sappho was enrolled at Bedales School in Steep, Hampshire.

Since its foundation in 1893 Bedales had prided itself on its then unique status as a boarding school which was co-educational, non-denominational – there was no chapel, and it would even allow youngsters to declare themselves agnostic or atheist – and liberal-humanist in its view of what education was supposed to involve. Despite its credo of being outside the quintessential British tradition of the public school it was still the reserve of the left-leaning upper middle class who had enough money to ensure that their children were destined for positions of entitlement, usually via the ancient universities. At present the school charges about £46,000 per year, and in relative terms it was a similar amount in 1957, roughly £2,300. Earlier that same year Dutton had purchased *Bitter Lemons* for a US edition for a generous £200; *White Eagles Over Serbia* had brought in £100 again from Faber; in December the Duff Cooper Prize brought in another £200; Faber had paid Claude-Marie a £150 advance for *Mrs O'* and there were sundry payments for Larry's articles or reviews in highbrow UK weeklies and literary magazines, £100 at the most.

There are no precise records of by what means Larry met the expenses of sending Sappho to Bedales. There might have been some funds left in his late father's trust but these would have disappeared rapidly into the money pit of Eve's upkeep and Sappho's education. Guesswork suggests that Larry was prepared to live on the breadline to ensure a middle-class future for his daughter, irrespective of his well-cultivated persona as an unorthodox bohemian.

Claude-Marie had completed her second novel, *The Rum Go*, in 1957 – accepted by Faber in July – while typing up the 140,000-word draft of her husband's 'Justine II'/*Balthazar*. Also, during that same summer, she had secured a highly paid administrative/secretarial job in Sète, sixty kilometres southwest of Sommières and served only by unreliable buses taking more than two and a half hours across mountainous roads with numerous stops. She took a bed-sitting room in Sète for three days per week and her employer allowed her to spend four-day weekends with Larry. Without her income they would have been penniless.

In August 1957 Claude-Marie's children, Diana, aged eleven, and Barry, aged eight, came to stay in Villa Louis, followed soon afterwards by Sappho, and then Margo and her son Nicholas, aged twelve. There was still no indoor lavatory or shower but despite this being high summer guests were advised to bury faeces in the garden; this was thought to work well as fertiliser for the tomatoes and fruit growing close by. Most preferred this to standing in a queue for the open drain. They became accustomed to urinating wherever they wished so long as it was outdoors. Larry and Claude-Marie had purchased little furniture – two beds only. Others slept on cushions and blankets in various parts of the house. No one complained, given that even in the earlier hours of the morning the temperature rarely dropped below 20 degrees Celsius.

Letters from Larry and Claude-Marie to Louisa present the location as an idyll:

> The vegetable garden across the way is doing well and we are having some good salads and vegetables already, thanks to old Trintignac; this week twenty Leghorns will come in and we expect to be stiff with fresh eggs at no labour to ourselves. He's also planted some new vines so we should get some grapes this year. When the weather gets a little more settled you might like to come out for a fortnight. (1957, otherwise undated, Jersey Archive)

She did. Later that summer Claude-Marie wrote to her, beginning with 'Dear Mother'. Larry was away at a writers' conference in Edinburgh, the prospect of which had filled him with 'despair'.

> In his absence, he arranged for me and the children to stay in a dear little hotel about fifteen miles from Nimes on the river, here there is beautiful bathing and boating. Needless to say, we are thoroughly enjoying it. Sapphy 'shoots the rapids' in a way that will astonish her father on his return. The food is good and simple ... I am as pleased as a dog with two tails. (24 August 1957, Jersey Archive)

Life at Sommières was not quite the nirvana that they present but they were being kind to Louisa. Claude-Marie adds: 'Larry was very glad just before he left to hear from Leslie in the most encouraging terms, especially as he seems to have started painting again – and you know how L [Larry] felt that was his strong point.' Louisa had received a letter from Leslie, the black sheep now in Kenya, which he asked her to forward to his two brothers. Claude-Marie, on Larry's instruction, responded politely but neither Larry nor Gerry wrote to him directly at the address included in the letter to their mother.

In his letters to Miller and others Larry maintained that he would loathe 'Pudding Island' for the rest of his life but when an embossed envelope arrived informing him that he had won the Duff Cooper Prize his contempt for the place softened. It would be awarded to him at Buckingham Palace by Queen Elizabeth the Queen Mother. He was allowed to bring three members of his family and while he was not yet married to Claude-Marie, he chose her and his two children from his two ex-wives, Penny and Sappho. They had never met so there was the spectacle of an esteemed author introducing his daughters to each other and one, Penny, to his current partner. At the last minute he asked Claude-Marie if she would mind missing out on the ceremony itself. It would be covered by the press and he imagined scurrilous references to 'Mr Durrell, his daughters and his female French companion' (Jersey Archive). Also, he had introduced Penny to Claude-Marie only an hour before they were due to enter the palace gates. He had not seen the former since she was eight and now she was almost eighteen. She wore a stylish black velvet dress and looked older than the fifteen years that separated her from her father's new partner. She opened the conversation with Claude-Marie by asking 'Where exactly do you fit in?' though she knew, and Claude-Marie later recalled her first impression of her: 'ravishing ... an ice maiden.' (Jersey Archive). Shortly before the ceremony he wrote to Louisa: 'Hope you are well. I shall have to come to London 9th for one night only to have this cowbell strung round my neck. I shan't be able to make Bournemouth alas' (Jersey Archive).

Bitter Lemons is an admirable book but it dispels any doubts that Larry had been, during the events it depicts, an impartial observer. He claimed in the preface that it was not a 'political' book, yet sixty years of historical studies of the crisis disclose its biases. The British occupying administration in Cyprus is depicted as egalitarian but ill-advised in its dealings with an island already divided by Greek and Turkish loyalties. In truth it was one of the numerous last gasps of imperial decline, in this instance an attempt to maintain a UK military outpost close to east Mediterranean and Middle Eastern hotspots of potential Cold War conflict: the Suez Crisis of 1956 testified to this ambition. There are some hints towards his dealings with the murkier side of the administration, MI6, but the archived final draft shows that a good deal of heavy editing had been undertaken by a hand not his or the publisher's.

There are several rewritings of history in the book, most shamefully the figure of 'Panos', a schoolteacher with whom Larry claimed to have shared lodgings during his first weeks on the island. He was, according to Larry, murdered by EOKA for sympathising with the British. There is no official record of his death, let alone his existence, but the motive for Larry inventing both is clear enough. His story overlaps with the undoubtedly truthful one of Michalis Karaolis, an EOKA member who in August 1955 shot dead a Cyprus Special Branch Police Officer who was spying on insurrectionist groups. Karaolis was hanged by the British and riots followed in Cyprus and on mainland Greece. Larry's invention of the unfortunate Panos gave the impression that the British were battling justifiably against murderous terrorists such as Karaolis.

At the award ceremony Larry thanked the Queen Mother and played down direct involvement in the events depicted. This was, however, undermined by others who had chosen to attend, including Lord

Salisbury, a major figure in the old pro-empire Tory Party who had supported occupation of Cyprus, Sir Bernard Burrows, Larry's Foreign Office mentor who had recruited him to all of his overseas jobs, and other Foreign Office figures Larry had known during his career as a spectral gatherer of intelligence. Salisbury followed up Larry's speech with an ironic 'Hear! Hear!' which was followed by a round of applause by his associates.

Feeling almost destitute despite their earnings Larry and Claude-Marie spent almost a third of the £200 prize money in Paris on the way back to Sommières. Patrick Leigh Fermor had been given a luxurious rent-free apartment by Fox Movietone on the expectation that some of his books could be turned into films. Larry and Claude-Marie enjoyed a week there while Leigh Fermor was in England. They ate in outrageously priced restaurants – Michelin Guides to continental Europe were, post-rationing, becoming the means by which well-heeled gastronomes might feel truly free of the deprivations of the war and its aftermath. Larry and Claude-Marie visited as many recommended establishments as they could during their time in Paris.

Villa Louis was now beginning to feel more like a long-term refuge from the world beyond its village. Penelope Tremayne had moved back to England from Bellapaix but had taken care to arrange transport to Larry for its paintings, by him and others, and most of his library. She rented it out to another expatriate which supplemented Larry's uncertain income from his writing. The owner of Villa Louis wanted to move the Durrells out at the close of the six-month lease, but Claude-Marie made use of a lawyer friend of her employer to intimidate him into allowing them to stay on for a full year. They would be forced to leave in September 1958, but Larry treated the ramshackle house as the cradle for his emergence as the writer he wished himself to become. The first volume of *The Alexandria Quartet* had been partly completed in England but when he moved to France, he was unsure of its direction, even its nature and expanse. In January 1958 he completed the third volume, *Mountolive*, only eighteen months after Faber had received the first, *Justine*.

After he returned from Paris with Claude-Marie, Larry decided that *Mountolive* would not wind up his multi-faceted eastern Mediterranean odyssey. It would bring in a completely different figure, the eponymous diplomat, David Mountolive, to shift the sequence into a quasi-realistic mode, including a Coptic plot to supply Zionists with explosives and guns. But that, as *Clea* showed, would not be the end of things. Larry wrote to Miller in January 1958:

Just sent off [to Faber] the huge MOUNTOLIVE mss ... which I'll route via you as a curiosity. I wanted you to read *Balthazar* as it was counter-sprung and have a clue as to the form. This big novel is as tame and naturalistic in *form* as a Hardy; yet it is the fulcrum of the quartet and the rationale of the thing. With the fourth I can plunge back into the time-stream again as per *Justine*. You may yawn your head off over *Mountolive* and whisper 'Shucks'; we'll see.

This is as close as Larry ever came to offering an account of what he was attempting in the *Quartet*.

He did not need to explain to his friend and occasional mentor that the only significant alteration was the cameo appearance of Mountolive who existed only for the duration of his own volume, alongside most others who appeared in the rest. Larry apologises disingenuously to Miller for the displeasure that awaits him in *Mountolive* – 'yawn your head off ... whisper "shucks"' – because both men treated 'tame naturalistic form', conventional fiction, as aesthetically inferior. The reason for him using it is implied in his comment that he will in the concluding volume 'plunge back into the time-stream again'. The *Quartet* was as much a polemic for the avant-garde as a literary work in its own right. He wanted to show readers of *Mountolive* how much better the previous volumes had been. He wished to unsettle and disappoint them before the fourth. For devotees of high-art modernism, whom he and Miller regarded as their chosen acolytes, he was saying: look at what lowbrow readers might enjoy and know that it is not for us.

Through winter 1957–8 and spring 1958 Penny and Sappho got to know each other better as they regularly visited Villa Louis. They were guided to the British ferry ports by Eve and met at the French side of the Channel by Claude-Marie. Up until less than a year before that the half-sisters knew hardly anything of one another and had not met; Sappho was a six-year-old child, while Penny, physically and intellectually, was a precocious near adult, still only seventeen but for those who met her first seeming a clever, knowledgeable and very attractive twenty-something. Odd as it might seem Claude-Marie brought them together by joining them as one of a trio of outsiders. They had come together suddenly and their only common factor was their attachment to Larry, variously amused, discordant and devoted.

For example, on 11 May 1958 Larry and Claude-Marie collected Anaïs Nin at Nimes railway station and drove her north in their rickety, recently purchased Peugeot 203 to attend several literary events in Paris, including one involving Larry's French publisher Corrêa. Also they would meet up with Nin's husband Hugh Guiler, Diana and Yehudi Menuhin, the diplomat and orientalist Sir Walter Smart and his wife Amy, and the poet, physician and psychoanalyst Jean Fanchette.

In the midst of this Claude-Marie drove to Gare du Nord to collect Sappho, Penny and the latter's new ballet-school friend Jill Dawkins. The youngsters were treated as adults, introduced to the impressive figures in what amounted to Larry's loose salon of artists and thinkers. Seemingly, from later accounts, neither of the older girls nor the eminent intellectuals felt unsettled. The girls formed an alliance with Claude-Marie who was their companion but also their intermediary, enabling them to feel more self-assured.

After dinner at a Chinese restaurant with Jean Fanchette, Larry, Claude-Marie and the three girls drove south, though not directly to Sommières. First, they went to Lyon, the capital of French cuisine, then further east to Orange and Avignon and only then swung west along mountainous roads to Sommières. The excursions were unplanned, the kind of improvisation that Larry and Claude-Marie had attuned themselves to as a means of exploring and assimilating previously mysterious landscapes and destinations. For most who were not used to the habits of the couple, including Larry's daughters, the experience might have been unsettling but not Penny and Sappho.

The Alexandria Quartet often involves distasteful acts and incidents – murder, disfigurement, torture – but at its core is its author's fascination with how different perspectives change the apparently stable nature of what is real and actual. Some have treated this as an engagement with Western versus Eastern philosophy wrapped in ideas drawn from Einstein, Freud and others.

I believe the one humanising factor in the books was Claude-Marie. They were begun during his time in Cyprus but at that point *Justine* was an unfocused, directionless project. The theme that informs the books, that pulls them untidily together, is a sense of individuals separated by intimacy, something that made its way into the books in France. Again and again, the same figures and the same events are recycled in each volume; they are subtly and persistently altered but they never quite leave each other.

During the summer of 1958 Claude-Marie drove Sappho and Penny across southern France on excursions to Aigues-Mortes, Les Baux, Saint-Rémy and Avignon, taking them swimming in various beaches on the Mediterranean and in primitive wild rivers. Larry rarely accompanied them, but the threesome perceived their experiences from spectacularly varied angles and perspectives and spoke to Larry of them on their return to Sommières. The parallels between the world of his disparate loved ones – his family – and the lives of his inventions in the *Quartet* are striking. In the books and in life, each was magnetised by belonging to the same circle, yet at the same time their perceptions on what this meant were nuanced and blurred by their particular sense of life outside it. Darley steps in and out of narratives involving those who shape his life and emotional condition, mostly women. Larry, as he wrote in Sommières, involved himself in a domestic replica of the words on the page.

In mid-July 1958 Larry and Claude-Marie accepted that they would soon have to vacate Villa Louis. Its owner was implacable in his refusal to further renew the lease and his tenants were frustrated by having had to renovate a property they would never own. A village friend put them in touch with a retired farmer whose partly derelict house and outbuildings were in a wild area about twenty kilometres from Sommières. They followed directions as well as they could, with the road becoming gradually more impassable at intervals of around ten minutes. Eventually they came upon a small Cathar castle. It first seemed abandoned but as they drove closer, they noted movements around the ground-floor gateway, and exchanged waves to whoever lived there. They first thought that it was their closest inhabited building but never again encountered the figures who had waved. The Mazet Michel, their destination, was literally the end of the road. The track went no further. Like Villa Louis there was nothing resembling a modern bathroom but the building was served by a deep well which had a basic but serviceable electric pump. No one explained how or why such a modest dwelling had been connected to mains electricity, but timber poles carried a power line to the house across sixteen kilometres of rugged terrain from a junction with the high-voltage system. The main house was slightly smaller than the Villa Louis but there was an adjoining *mas*, previously a storage area for farm produce in decent enough condition to convert for guests. Decisively for Larry it also came with almost two square miles of olive trees and vines and twenty-two acres of rough pasture previously used for goats and sheep. Surrounding this was open scrubland where, he was told, the occupier had access to hunting. Hare, rabbits, quail, grouse and pheasant were in abundance; sometimes deer were sighted and *sanglier*, wild boar, which tasted like a cross between pork and strong mutton. He foresaw a tidying of the bedraggled olive groves and vines, the planting of a kitchen garden in the sheltered corner between the main house and the *mas*, the installation of a chicken shed, and pictured himself as the hunter bringing back game of various types to go with home-grown vegetables.

Larry took it on a three-year lease-rental agreement with an option to buy written into the contract and at the beginning of September he and Claude-Marie borrowed a lorry to move their belongings from Sommières to this neighbourless outstation where the temperature in spring and summer rarely dipped below 30 degrees Celsius at midday, where the skies were cloudless and rain came only in autumn to revive the otherwise parched landscape. It was in the midst of what is still claimed to be the sunniest region of mainland France.

Self-sufficiency was more a bohemian principle than a necessity, given that the Peugeot would enable them to visit striking-distance markets twice a week and money was beginning to roll in. Despite his distaste for downmarket travel writing, he was offered and accepted freelance work by *Holiday* magazine and, typically, a two-night visit to Grenoble, expenses paid, earned him $1,000; it took him half a day to write. By

November *Mountolive* had sold 10,000 copies in the UK, an impressive amount for a piece of 'highbrow' fiction, and its predecessors, *Justine* and *Balthazar*, were taking the prestigious house of Faber into the realm of bestseller culture. It was quite an improvement given the fact that in its first year the opening volume of the *Quartet* had been largely ignored. His advances for each book had now been surpassed by income from sales, and royalties from the first three books of the *Quartet* were making him close to £100 per month, almost £2,000 in today's terms.

There were drawbacks. After three weeks in the new house, he hired a builder and supposedly specialised electrician to do repair work while he and Claude-Marie planned to spend a further three first in Nimes with Aldington and then in Paris with Jean Fanchette and Anaïs Nin. Fanchette, only twenty-six years old, was becoming a trailblazing figure. He had already qualified as a medical physician in Paris and his poems had won him the Paul Valéry Prize in 1956. Shortly before Larry's arrival in the city Fanchette had founded the bilingual Anglo-French magazine *Two Cities*, designed to sustain the experimental writing that had thrived in London and Paris in the 1920s. Miller, Nin, William Burroughs, Yves Bonnefoy, William Golding and Larry were regular contributors. Nin described Fanchette as 'a handsome and dark young Mauritian'. It is difficult to conceive of a figure of such ethnicity and colour being feted and lionised in the other editorial centre of the journal, London, in 1958.

Larry and Claude-Marie returned to Languedoc excited by their experiences in the capital and expected to find their house at least partially refurbished. Instead, their builder had spent most of his time there drinking the wine they and the previous owner had stored. He had installed a new pump for the well but had not bothered to turn it off during his prolonged period of alcoholic oblivion and the house was flooded.

They made do; Larry took on another builder but did a good deal of basic manual work himself. At the same time, he was desperately trying to complete *Clea*. He was well ahead with it earlier in 1958 in Sommières but now he was worried about the very notion of an ending for the whole project. Aldington met him in Nimes and expressed his distress at the death earlier in the sequence of Scobie, a paedophile, homosexual and enthusiastic colonial policeman – and Larry promises that by the means of what would be called magic realism he would bring him back to life. Aldington also saw the treatment of Melissa by the male characters as unsavoury and unjust and demanded that his friend rectify matters as the narrative proceeded. His ability to treat Larry's inventions as real people was extraordinary, given that they dwelt in a fictional world that was governed largely of illogic and a carnival of mythmaking. But Aldington himself had for much of his life displayed a contempt for the consensus of what life in general involved. His notorious 1955 biography of T. E. Lawrence presented the then national hero as a liar, charlatan, egotist, terrible writer and closet homosexual. Some of the accusations were later substantiated but when he wrote the book he had made most of them up. His motive in the mid-1950s was to appal and offend the British establishment but he treated characters in books, even real ones such as Lawrence, as the property of the work's author who could turn them into whatever he wished. Larry loved the biography mainly because he too was keen to horrify the moral and cultural custodians of Pudding Island. Aldington's desire for Scobie to be kept alive in Larry's work came not from an affection for him; rather he saw him as a means of wounding those who wished to safeguard the class system and legacy of Victorian and Edwardian Englishness. And he was also slightly mad. Soon after their meeting he asked Larry to contribute money to the resurrection of the publishing house of Count Potocki, mostly as a means of promoting the far-right ideas of figures such as the pre-war fascist Oswald Mosley, who was now busily campaigning against immigration to Britain from South Asia and the Caribbean. Aldington was also a fan of the poet Roy Campbell, who had died in 1957. The latter had been an overt supporter of Franco during the Spanish Civil War and while Aldington was affiliated neither to the extreme right nor the left, he regularly sought to incite controversy and cause offence. At this point Larry himself had become largely apolitical but he craved eccentricity in extremes.

Henry Miller flew to France with his new wife Eve in 1959 and the couple met Larry and Claude-Marie in Paris in April. Miller opened the conversation with his friend by announcing that he expected the marriage to be brief and that he had already embarked on several adulterous relationships, all of which was overheard by Eve. He had brought with him his daughter Val from his previous marriage and the couples joined Fanchette and his new wife Martine, Gerald and Buffie Sykes, André and Odette Bay, Edward Mullins and others from the broad salon of literary Paris for a six-day pub crawl. Miller himself had become the equivalent of an anarchist-hedonist; he cared little for those closest to him nor for matters such as politics and the encroaching tensions of the Cold War. Bad behaviour was his enthusiasm and on one evening during the period in Paris he and Larry went out on their own. Miller was sixty-seven, twenty years older than his friend, but happily carried him upstairs and along streets from bar to bar, brothel to brothel. Larry was less than five foot three in height and slightly overweight. Most involved imagined themselves to be in the Paris of almost two generations before, the city of Hemingway, Fitzgerald, Dos Passos, Stein, Joyce and Pound. But the new expatriates were far more self-absorbed and narcissistic than their predecessors. For more than a year France had been going through a political crisis just as traumatic as the self-staged coup d'état of Louis-Napoléon Bonaparte of 1851. In May 1958 senior army officers attempting to suppress the Algerian Revolution staged a coup of their own against the Paris government. They threatened to take over France if the elected government of the Fourth Republic were not replaced by a regime which they felt was more likely to assure them victory in Algeria. A potential civil war was avoided by the return to power of de Gaulle whose military background appealed to the hard-right generals in Algeria but who also promised to assuage the various demands of communist factions in mainland France and to mediate between Muslim fundamentalists, the independence guerrilla movement, the FLN and the French colonial authorities in Algiers.

Scour the surviving correspondence between Larry and others, particularly Miller, during this period and you will not come across even a tangential reference to these events. MacNiven (p482) claims that Larry sometimes discussed them with Claude-Marie, Aldington and locals and apparently his principal fear was the rumour that if Algeria fell colonials of French origin would return to their homeland, where they would be treated sympathetically by whatever Paris administration was in power and settle in new towns of a similar climate and landscape to the one they had left, mainly the underpopulated inland areas of Occitanie, especially Languedoc. Larry was horrified by the prospect of concrete apartment blocks that were already springing up outside the centre of the capital. The wilderness of southern France was, he believed, his inspirational domain.

By the time that he, Miller and the other intemperate aesthetes hit the streets of Paris in 1959 de Gaulle had been in power for almost a year but the crisis was far from resolved. Extremism was rife, including groups of communists who treated the arrival of the new president as the establishment of a quasi-fascist dictatorship, and members of the right-wing paramilitary group the OAS, mostly veterans of the First Indochina War, who favoured a return to colonialism and a French authoritarian state.

During various periods in 1959 windows in Paris were smashed, cars set alight and sometimes banks were robbed by these groups but during their inebriated tour of the city centre Larry and Miller seemed not to notice.

10

Reunion at the Manor

In 1959 Gerry and Jacquie in Jersey faced a situation that made Larry's lifestyle in France seem both luxurious and risible. Larry inhabited a world of his own largely undisturbed by the concerns that drove others either to despair or the ordinariness of a regular income. Amazingly, despite producing books that the average reader would treat as incomprehensible they were purchased by a sufficient number of cultural dilettantes to guarantee him a decent if unexceptional income. He lived in a charming almost derelict farmhouse without the incursion of noise and only the companionship of those he knew would amuse him, and vice versa. Conversely, Gerry and Jacquie found themselves largely unable to sleep because of the fear of imminent financial ruin. True, they lay awake in an extraordinarily beautiful manor house, or to be more accurate shared its spacious first-floor apartments with Louisa who had recently moved from Bournemouth to help them out with the establishment of Jersey Zoo. Yet all this seemed borrowed and precarious.

There had been no paying visitors to cover the considerable expenses, mostly the pitiable salaries of those who had volunteered to help with the project. Larry had written to the wealthier residents of the island to see if they would sponsor what he described as a 'charity' that would gain honour for Jersey as a centre for conservation while eventually promoting its static economy. Some offered him support but the finance of the manor/zoo was going backwards. Gerry knew that the only means by which he could maintain his enterprise was to bring in more money from books. *A Zoo in My Luggage* had been contracted two years earlier but he completed it in early 1959 in less than six weeks. It sold more than 40,000 copies in two months, three times his brother's *Mountolive*. Within the next two years he published three more books: *Island Zoo* and *Look at Zoos* were based mainly on his experiences in Jersey, and *The Whispering Land* on the expeditions to Argentina. Each carried a £500 advance and went into the top ten in the bestseller lists. The royalties gained would have enabled a freelance writer to live luxuriously anywhere in the UK or mainland Europe but these monies disappeared into the financial black hole of Les Augrès.

The man who had never wanted to be a writer, who had no great interest in books, had overtaken his man-of-letters brother in terms of sales and celebrity status, but he was broke. He wrote to Larry in May 1960 telling him that he had decided to take Jacquie and Louisa to Corfu for six weeks. He hoped that the excursion would inspire him, given that his most successful and profitable book had been an account of the family's time there in the 1930s, albeit largely fabricated and fantasised. The weather was foul, treated by residents as the worst weeks of early summer in living memory. The sun was banished by low grey cloud and the sometimes welcome bouts of Mediterranean rain replaced by large frozen hailstones. On average the temperature was ten degrees Celsius lower than that of southern England. Gerry began to feel that fate was revenging itself upon the idyll created in *My Family*. Jacquie had made sure that what went to Sophie his typist was a coherent story and had served as her husband's muse by talking to him of the legend that unfolded on the pages. The writing of it had drawn them closer together than at any time during their marriage. For her Corfu was fixed in her mind as a sun-baked paradise, the sky and sea competing for the finest shades of sapphire. But now, as Gerry introduced her to it, dreariness seemed an understatement. Even the locals who had energised his account of the island shifted now between depression and absence, unable to fully comprehend such weather conditions and usually preferring to remain indoors. Then suddenly at the beginning of June the clouds broke and the magical brightness of Gerry's descriptions was restored.

They had taken a cottage called The Annexe, located on the other side of the valley from the two houses where he had spent his childhood. Both were now holiday homes of wealthy mainland Greek families and Gerry and Louisa thought it best not to tamper with memories and did not make themselves known to the new residents.

Following their return to Jersey they made arrangements for another revisitation of the past. Gerry invited Margo, Larry and Claude-Marie to a family Christmas at the manor. He also asked if Penny and Sappho would be available. Larry said that the former always spent Christmas and New Year with her mother but he would do his best to bring Sappho. Margo urged Gerry to contact Leslie. He refused but she did so on his behalf. Leslie was initially enthusiastic but soon followed this with a letter to his sister stating that his ongoing groundnut project meant that he must commit most of his time to his Kenyan farm. In truth his enterprise was already a failure and he was beginning a new career as a fraudster. The family would not learn of his record of swindling other expatriates until he fled the country much later. For the time being they treated him as the ghost not at the feast, despite Margo's attempts at reconciliation. They shared an awareness of his presence in Africa, without discussing it, and treated what he actually did as an acceptable mystery.

In the end Christmas – a long Christmas lasting from mid-December to mid-January – would involve Larry, Sappho and Claude-Marie, Gerry and Jacquie, Louisa, Margo and Margo's eldest, Gerry. Larry and Claude-Marie spent some time in London before taking a flight to Jersey and he appeared on the BBC *Tonight* programme, an invitation which reflected the acclaim with which the literary establishment in the UK, the US and most enthusiastically continental Europe had heaped upon the now complete *Alexandria Quartet*. Previously he felt that as a media celebrity he would always be overshadowed by Gerry, whose willingness to form a double act with animals had become part of the popular culture of the new age of television. Yet despite the fact that Larry's audience was largely the educated chattering classes – *Tonight* went out at 8 p.m. – his performance was informal, even diverting. He provided an account of the *Quartet* which was extraordinarily accessible, given that those who celebrated it would themselves have found it difficult to explain what it was about.

The following day Claude-Marie was suddenly taken ill and admitted to hospital. It was first thought that her ovaries might have to be removed but a closer examination indicated that antibiotics would remedy the infection. The ailment was less serious than first expected but one should note that even if something dreadful – even fatal – had been diagnosed, no one beyond Larry himself would have known of it. Several broadsheet newspapers covered his London visit, again because of his status as a British author of international repute. His partner, however, was never mentioned because officially she did not exist.

Larry enjoyed and cultivated his image as an unaffiliated cosmopolitan, a figure whose art was unconstrained by borders or parochialism. In his press releases he was always described as of Indian birth and Irish ancestry and as having spent his life in various part of the Mediterranean and the Middle East. England never featured and he gave the impression that he felt uncomfortable with a country that in his view was still inhibited by a class system and moral codes evolved during the reign of Victoria. At the same time, he was equally concerned that the press would suddenly turn its attention to his having what amounted to a permanent extramarital affair.

In France no one cared but the mildly ludicrous cover-up of the London visit followed the couple to Jersey. A week after their arrival a team from *Life* magazine appeared at Les Augrès Manor. For some time, Gerry had drawn the attention of the popular media in the US but *Life* covered a broad spectrum of issues from A-list movie stars to interviews with high-profile politicians and the serialisation of authors such as Hemingway. The prospect of a feature on the meeting of two brothers who matched one another in terms of global fame but who were utterly antithetical in what they represented and wrote was irresistible.

Larry's agent Juliet O'Hea of Curtis Brown arranged for the fee of $600 to be divided equally between the two men and each, supported by the rest of the family, insisted on a contingency. Claude-Marie would not appear in any of the photographs and nor would she be mentioned in the text. To her credit she understood this obsession with secrecy. Larry's divorce from Eve was being dealt with by his London solicitors and he did not want scandalous press coverage to compromise a mutually agreed financial settlement and his access to Sappho. Once reporters knew of

Claude-Marie it would not take them too long to uncover the full story of their relationship – that they had been living together permanently for the previous five years.

It was a pity that the *Life* team was so closely monitored by its subjects because an honest coverage of Christmas 1960 in Les Augrès would have been hilarious.

For different reasons Larry and Gerry had since the early 1950s been tormented by various forms of disquiet and stress. For the former, his marriages and extramarital relationships, his standing as a literary figure – by intervals overlooked and celebrated – alongside his occasional service as part-time intelligence officer who relied on the Foreign Office for a regular income turned his life into a hall of mirrors. At first he'd enjoyed the masquerade but less so now. Gerry's pursuit of a site for a zoo and his need for money had driven him to levels of success in an activity that he loathed and which defined his brother's existence: writing. His corollary activities as a popular celebrity often became an unintended parody of his mission as an environmentalist. As a result, both had gradually begun to rely on drink as a means of allaying their fears and sometimes moods of depression. When they met up in Jersey, they were by any medical practitioner's estimation alcoholics in that neither could cope with the daily tasks that faced them without a considerable amount of wine and spirits.

Following the departure of the *Life* team Gerry and Larry spent two days together in the grand ground floor of the manor and drank unremittingly. Larry was charmed by what seemed a burlesque caricature of his memories of Bournemouth. The various creatures that had made themselves comfortable in the gardens, sitting rooms and bedrooms of Louisa's and Margo's dull Edwardian houses now scuttled through a mansion, a modest version of Waugh's Brideshead.

Larry and Claude-Marie had sometimes spoken of Gerry and Jacquie's lack of children. Was it deliberate, a means of avoiding a delay in the conservation project? Or was it a medical problem? On the first day Claude-Marie thought she'd discovered something. While Larry was drinking with his brother she went into the kitchen and found Louisa with an infant in her arms, feeding it with a bottle. It was dressed in baby clothes but as she moved closer, she noticed that its hand and lower forearm were unusually hairy. It was a young male but it was the child of Lulu the chimpanzee. Claude-Marie later reflected that life on Jersey bore a resemblance, albeit a surreal one, to Larry's ensemble of misfits in France. The common feature was a determined sense of disconnection from the 'world that most human beings classified as normal' (undated note by Gerry in the Jersey Archive, quoting Claude-Marie).

Gerry cooked a very traditional Christmas dinner of turkey, roast potatoes and sprouts. It seemed like England, in its timeless, pedestrian conformity. As they settled down to eat, those present, excluding Louisa and Margo, felt that the two sides of the family had at last come to realise how they had by equal degrees become exceptional and renowned and in a slightly different sense equally bizarre.

During their time together during the week before Christmas Gerry and Larry had spoken intimately about their lives over the foregoing decade. They knew the facts, of course. Their publications and, especially in Gerry's case, travels had been well covered in newspapers, and sometimes via radio and television. Now, however, they spoke to each other openly about what they felt; Larry talked to his brother much as he had to Miller on how he hoped to leave his imprint on the modern novel and Gerry told of how he was determined to create a refuge for creatures that were in imminent danger of extinction.

In a fragment on the meeting written by Gerry when much later he was putting together notes for his memoir he wrote: 'In 1960 we spoke much. I of animals which I love, sometimes more than men and women. He of men and women who had infuriated him, caused him to inveigh against the European soul. These he would portray in his books, show them as they are. His problem, he said, was that our culture is rotten, flourishing in its decay. How could he contain this in the one thing he still treated as worthwhile, beautiful – literature? I answered that I would never improve on the beauty of animals or rescue them from their plight by writing about them' (Jersey Archive, undated).

Larry's divorce from Eve was finalised in February 1961 and in the following month he and Claude-Marie flew to London and married at the Chelsea Registry Office. On the licence they gave their names (Lawrence George Durrell and Claude-Marie Forde), their professions ('writers'), their ages (forty-nine and thirty-five), and declared that they shared the same address: the Basil Street Hotel, Chelsea.

Two months earlier at the manor, Gerry, Jacquie and Ken Smith had organised a post-New Year lunch and party for those who'd felt like outsiders during the family events. The savouries were made up of leftovers from the latter; stuffing, cold ham and sausage rolls mostly. But the dessert course was more generous and varied, including chocolate bars of different hues and flavours, sweet biscuits, mince pies and cream, cake with icing and colourful bowls of fruit.

The guests included Fernando, a *Leopardus jacobita* or Andean mountain cat, a species of puma small enough to render it relatively harmless to humans. Pedro the speckled bear was there but the majority of those present were apes and chimps, most prominently N'Pongo, Chumley and Lulu.

The spring of 1960, the zoo's first opening to the public, had been disastrous. Despite Gerry's optimistic proposal to the Jersey authorities that it would boost the tourist industry most visitors were locals, fascinated by the spectacle of exotica conveyed to what amounted to an offshore version of the home counties. Most were as beguiled by the presence of Gerry, bestselling author and media star, as they were by the creatures he had brought to their island. The keepers had set up a series of signs for enclosures and explanatory accounts of the various species kept within, their indigenous environment and at-risk situations. Yet many visitors went towards the doors of the main house and rang the bell, hoping to be entertained by Gerry who when the zoo was open to the public began to take refuge in a bedroom at the rear of the quarters. He would be there chasing deadlines for publishers in the hope of reducing the £20,000 of debt incurred over the previous year, partly from monies owed to the owner of the manor and to builders, and partly to cover the unpaid salaries of his employees who had been willing to put up with free food and accommodation in lieu of being paid. Today £20,000 is the equivalent of more than £390,000.

Astonishingly, his two new books for children, *Island Zoo* and *Look at Zoos*, reduced the debt by more than 15 per cent from advances, along with collateral fees from TV and radio appearances that accompanied publications. Almost 30 per cent more was taken from arrears by the build-up of royalty payments that became available at the end of the financial year in March 1961, due in part to the large number of his 1950s bestsellers going into print in French, Spanish and German. He had not cleared his debts and even though he could have almost halved his borrowings over about three months instead he made much of this windfall available to those who had worked at Les Augrès for almost nothing.

In early April Jacquie had a miscarriage. She did not even know she was pregnant and she'd experienced the same thing several years before. Much later she reflected, 'Gerry didn't want any children. We both felt the state of the world was such that we didn't want to bring anyone into it.' But she added that on the first occasion 'he even refused to speak to me for something like three weeks, addressing me, when he had to, through a third person' (Botting, pp296–7). One might compare Gerry's attitude to fatherhood – by parts embittered and conflicted – with his often tortured state when his animals were giving birth.

In spring 1961 Gerry felt exhausted and anxious. Writing had fatigued him and within a few months he knew that the zoo had to make a profit from visitors so he said to Jacquie and Louisa that they must take a short period away to prepare themselves for the summer season. Spain in late April would be warm and they could take the ferry from Jersey to France and stay at various auberges on the main roads They stayed overnight at Larry's Mazet and then crossed the border and went to Northern Spain.

Jacquie was overjoyed, but the trio spent only a three or four days in Spain. Larry sent a message to their hotel and invited them back into France where he would introduce them properly to life at the Mazet. Gerry was enchanted and told Jacquie he expected that the scent of herbs and wild flowers, and especially the sweet aroma of the olives, so resonant of the Mediterranean, would remind him of the Corfu years. They stayed for just over a week, coinciding with visits from Aldington, Fanchette, their respective partners, and the American painter Buffie Johnson. The annex was almost complete but the house was still overcrowded and Larry was overjoyed at being able to play host to members of his cultural salon while his closest family looked on. He certainly did not make Gerry, Jacquie and his mother feel excluded. Quite the opposite. He introduced his brother to his literary associates as the Durrell family's natural philosopher, a zoologist of global renown. Nonetheless, the latter listened in, fascinated, as Larry's friends talked of life itself as something that only mattered as material for artistic recycling. From politics to sex and death, everything seemed to feed an appetite for imaginative creativity. In his later notes for his memoir, he writes of the visit: 'A different universe, but in some ways, we are versions of each other. His zoo, like mine, is full of creatures who have little in common with humankind' (Jersey Archive, undated).

The hoped-for financial recovery during the summer of 1961 was a disappointment and even though Gerry's media profile drew in more visitors from outside Jersey he was outraged by their behaviour. His ideal of respecting the autonomy and behavioural dignity of animals seemed not to be shared by those who routinely fed sweets and sandwiches to primates. Even worse were those 'morons', as Gerry put it, who passed lipstick, lighted cigarettes and even razor blades through the wire to monkeys. A chinchilla died because an 'oaf' had emptied half a bottle of aspirin into the enclosure. The situation regarding income was much as it had been at the close of 1960 but this worried him little; he was seriously considering closing the zoo to the public because he felt that humans were inferior to the creatures he was attempting to help. In October 1961, after the zoo closed for the winter, Jacquie began to suffer severe stomach pains. At first, she thought she was pregnant once more but after admission to hospital in St Helier she was diagnosed as having a severe infection in her womb. She underwent a partial hysterectomy, sufficient to ensure that she would never conceive. Gerry visited her mornings and evenings during her ten days in a nursing home and when she returned to the manor he waited on her in a loving, solicitous manner. She recalled to Botting that he had never before shown such tenderness – 'I had a wonderful time' (p297) – and her reflections carry a nuance of her husband's devotion being shot through with a touch of private consolation on his part. The fraught question of whether they would have children would never again be addressed.

Conversely the pairs of species in the zoo matched for breeding were delighting their owner. Eleven births were recorded during autumn and early winter and Gerry was especially pleased by the coming of a six-inch-long son to Juan and Juanita, a pair of South American peccaries

– a species of wild pig – brought back from Argentina five years earlier. Juanita was much younger than her 'husband'. Juanita had on several occasions suffered severe ill-health when pregnant and failed to deliver a living child but this time they were successful. 'To look out of the kitchen window and see Juanita, her husband and baby playing a new game they have invented, fills me with pride' (Jersey Archive, undated). His pride and by implication joy came barely a month after he and his own wife learned that they would never have children.

For Gerry it seemed that the zoo could only be kept going as a charity, with him as the principal benefactor. In late 1961 he commuted regularly between Jersey and England to do BBC programmes, first for a transmission of the new TV series called *Look* on his experiences in South America and then, more profitably, as narrator and screenwriter of a series of his own called *Zoo Packet*, a light-hearted account of his attempts to set up a zoo in Bournemouth and on the establishment of the institution in Jersey. Payments were decent and regular, but the most profitable enterprise never went into production. Stanley Donen was one of Hollywood's most successful film directors during the 1950s. *On the Town, Singin' in the Rain* and *An American in Paris* had made vast amounts of money for their studios and stars. In 1960 he moved to England, started to look for enthralling British screenplays to sell to American studios, and persuaded Paramount to pay Hart-Davis £5,000 for the film rights to *My Family and Other Animals*. The movie was never made but 50 per cent of this generous payment went straight to Gerry.

Hart-Davis was delighted both with the money and the confirmation that his bestselling writer had a conspicuous international profile. This was reinforced early in the New Year when the Prime Minister Harold Macmillan invited Gerry and Jacquie to 10 Downing Street for lunch. The principal guest was Manuel Prado Ugarteche, President of Peru. While Gerry had not actually visited the country Ugarteche wished to show his appreciation for a man who cared so deeply for the threatened species of South America. Two days later he and Jacquie attended another lunch, this time in Buckingham Palace at the invitation of the Queen, who was hosting a banquet for Ahmadou Ahidjo, President of the Federal Republic of Cameroon, one of the more recent members of the Commonwealth. Ahidjo had asked the Foreign Office to ask Her

Majesty if Gerry could join them at the state banquet. At the event he introduced him as 'the finest and most distinguished English friend of our nation'. Jacquie too was invited and Gerry took quiet satisfaction in this act of one-upmanship. Five years earlier Larry had received the Duff Cooper Prize at the palace from the Queen Mother. Gerry and Jacquie shared the top table with the Queen and the Duke of Edinburgh.

Soon after his return Gerry received a longhand letter purportedly from Noël Coward then in Jamaica and assumed that Larry had asked one of his globe-trotting friends to do it as a hoax. The prose sounded like one of Coward's flamboyant dramatic personae and his praise for Gerry as a writer and conservationist went beyond hyperbole. But it turned out to be authentic and when he was in London later that year Coward invited Gerry and Jacquie to dinner at the Savoy. Gerry replied that they would be delighted but bashfully enquired about the dress code: dinner jacket, suit, casual? Coward answered: 'How about leopard-skin tights?' Gerry was never certain if the joke amounted to a kind invitation to Coward's world of self-caricature or if the great man saw him as a clown who'd made his name performing with animals. Gerry and Jacquie joined Coward and his partner Graham Payn on various occasions over the next ten years but while Jacquie was always amused by their companions' shifts between charm and cutting sarcasm Gerry could never decide on whether Coward did, as he regularly professed, admire his punishing endeavours or if he'd brought him in as the court jester.

In February 1962 Gerry and Jacquie set off by boat for their most ambitious expedition, to New Zealand, Australia and finally Malaya. Arriving in Auckland he began what would be his final letter to his mother. Louisa would die in 1964 but during the intervening two years she did not venture beyond the manor, her general health and mental condition gradually and inexorably declining. For some reason Gerry's letter to her from the southern hemisphere would remain unfinished and unsent. He brought it back to Jersey with him in autumn 1962 and one suspects that as reports came to him of Louisa's diminishing state, he refused to finish it much as one might the draft obituary of a loved and respected friend commissioned by a newspaper: its incompleteness would postpone their departure.

It is fifteen pages long and made up of accounts of everything that he could cram into what amounted to a brief travel memoir. The beginning is a description of the 'red carpet' greeting in Auckland where they are met by a member of the country's Wildlife Department and a week later taken by chauffeur-driven car to Wellington for a lunch with the entire New Zealand Cabinet. He had, briefly, seen something of how the landscape of the country was in a state of transformation and, as he reported to Louisa, he had said to government ministers: 'It's a bit like having a Rembrandt. Once it's destroyed, you can't replace it. If you had a Rembrandt, would you destroy it?' (Jersey Archive, undated). He was telling his mother of how the sheep farmers of New Zealand were allowing their most profitable export to make the natural landscape uninhabitable for indigenous species, especially rare birds.

Members of the Cabinet encouraged him to visit the bird sanctuary on the island of Kapiti about three miles offshore and roughly an hour from Wellington. At the time it was a bird sanctuary uninhabited by all but a couple of wardens and was home to rare species such as takahē, kōkako, saddleback, kākā, bellbird and the country's legendary flightless kiwi. Gerry was impressed but commented that the island was effectively a zoo, a small compensation for damage already done to the original home landscapes of much native wildlife.

This impression was reinforced by his visit to a pair of rocks called The Brothers reached from the shoreline by a crane. Here were more takahē, several pairs of rare fairy penguins and some colourful giant geckos, a species of the lizard he'd never come across before. In the letter he compared these animals to Napoleon on St Helena, 'an undignified exile'.

The Notornis Valley was New Zealand's most commendable attempt at a wildlife park. 'The valley is, of course, strictly protected, and no one is allowed to go in without permission,' Gerry wrote. Rare bats thrived, as did the tuatara, a reptile dating from the Triassic era and unique to New Zealand, along with odd-looking birds such as the kākāpō, a large flightless parrot. The valley contained a lake which Gerry and Jacquie visited in the hope of finding new animals that moved between land and water but saw nothing.

They were accompanied by a BBC film crew directed by Chris Parsons and the difference between Gerry's letter to Louisa in which he praised New Zealand and the screenplay of the film is striking. In the latter for example he describes Notornis as 'one of the most unpleasant bits of country I had ever been in.'

The so-called 'Ten Pound Poms' scheme set up after the war was still running, designed to encourage emigration from the UK to Australia and New Zealand. Britain was attempting to cement a closer relationship between the old country and what was left of the Anglophone empire and Gerry and Parsons shared a suspicion that they were expected to turn the wildlife films into advertisements.

Gerry and Jacquie found Australia more agreeable. The government kept its distance and allowed them to travel through the wilder parts of New South Wales and Victoria as they wished. Beyond the main cities there were areas with scattered populations and varied landscapes where mammals, reptiles and birds which pre-dated the arrival of British settlers still thrived. Jacquie fell in love with the country and even suggested that when Jersey entered another bout of financial catastrophe, as both expected, they should pack up and move to it. In the letter Gerry wrote, 'If ever I was compelled to settle down in one spot ... Australia is one of the few countries I have visited that I would choose' (Jersey Archive, undated).

They reached Singapore in July and went on to Malaya. In his later notes, he commented that in all three countries animals were losing a 'battle against public apathy and political and big business chicanery'. Unlike humans 'animals have no control over their future. They cannot ask for home rule, they cannot worry their MPs with their grievances, they cannot even get their unions to agree to a strike for better conditions. Their future and their very existence depends on us' (Jersey Archive, undated).

They separated from Parsons' crew who returned to London to edit the films and hoped to set out on their own for East Africa but in Kuala Lumpur they received a phone call from Jersey advising them to return as soon as possible. Louisa was seriously unwell. At least this was the message from Louisa's friend Betty Norton who had been asked to look after the manor and care for Gerry's mother in their absence. In truth there were no symptoms of a severe medical condition. Louisa was lonely and depressed. Her daughter was only an occasional visitor, Leslie had long disappeared, there was no certainty that Larry would visit in the near future and Gerry was clearly hungry for new expeditions. She felt as if she had, like the animals, been left to survive rather pointlessly in a place that was not remotely connected with her life or the friends she'd made following the family's move from Corfu to England. During the period of Gerry and Jacquie's trip to the Pacific she became more and more reclusive, remaining in her bedroom where food was brought to her by Betty along with bottles of gin which she demanded almost daily.

When Gerry and Jacquie arrived back in Jersey in September 1962 they were horrified. Louisa seemed to have been left to drink herself to death and the zoo itself was shambolic to say the least.

Over the summer it had been in the hands of Ken Smith and his wife Trudy but takings from visitors hardly paid the electricity bills. The buildings and cages were dilapidated and a large number of the once devoted staff members had returned to England. They had been dedicated to Gerry because they shared his principles. Now, however, the project seemed to lurch from one catastrophe to the next.

Trudy later claimed that they had done their best with the money and resources left for them by Gerry but Jacquie was enraged by what she saw as Ken and Trudy's feckless incompetence. Gerry refused to take sides but the mood of bitterness stewed for several months until the Smiths decided to leave in early 1963.

Gerry didn't want to close the zoo but he faced the prospect of another winter with little income, the costs of feeding and caring for 650 animals and wages for the remaining full- and part-time staff of almost forty. What they needed, Jacquie insisted, was not another expert in the natural sciences to keep the place afloat but a figure with practical experience in business, preferably accountancy. She did not, though, explain how such an individual could magically produce money for an institution that had for the time being no source of income.

They advertised the post locally and interviewed several applicants with entrepreneurial backgrounds in the island's tiny economy; all had run businesses which had gone bust. The final candidate, Catha Weller, was the only one who showed promise. She had worked in London in a successful advertising company and had recently moved to Jersey with her husband, also in advertising, who had been posted to his company's sub-office in St Helier; many British financial and advertising organisations were creating outstations in the Channel Islands as a partial escape route from the still swingeing tax regime that had been imposed after the war.

Catha's CV was impressive so Gerry and Jacquie found time to interview her on a Sunday morning. She enthralled them with her knowledge of microeconomics and they offered her the job on the spot. They were somewhat unsettled when during the informal chat over drinks she disclosed that she was a clairvoyant and had in a dream entered the very same room in which the interview had taken place. They could hardly withdraw the job offer and in any event a person with the gift of second sight was preferable to the collection of no-hopers they'd met during the previous week, just. Catha began work on 12 December 1962 and while not promising miracles she went through the accounts, details of expenditure and wages and all other available paperwork during Christmas and the New Year.

Through January and February, she imposed the harsh discipline of survival-at-all-costs, which she explained was an attempt to avoid cuts, especially redundancies, by bringing in a system of regimented efficiency and savings. Nothing unnecessary would ever be purchased in order to feed the animals and the suppliers of foodstuffs and hardware would be subjected to a practice of haggling.

The debts remained but losses via poor budgetary practice were curbed. Crucially Catha was instrumental in the transformation of the status of the institution from a zoo, in legal terms a business, to the Jersey Wildlife Preservation Trust (WPT), which was formally established on 6 July 1963. This was Gerry's ideological zenith, an institution dedicated to animal conservation rather than the presentation of them to human spectators.

Gerry knew James Platt slightly but Catha's husband Sam had a closer friendship with him from their time in London. Platt was a director of Shell International, the largest British private-sector business globally. Although Green politics was a minority interest in 1963 Platt was intrigued by the controversy in the US caused by

234

Rachel Carson's *Silent Spring* (1962), which was principally a warning against pesticides but brought into its target zone all industries that posed a threat to the natural environment. Platt foresaw problems for companies like Shell and this lay behind his offer to help with the WPT. He would invest in any future protests against the damage done by oil extraction, becoming the unpaid advisor to WPT with particular regard to finance. He and Catha became an effective team. As Jacquie later reflected, 'Gerry was a dreamer ... without Jimmy Platt we could never have done it' (Botting, p309).

Platt and Catha insisted to Gerry and Jacquie that even if the forthcoming spring and summer season was moderately profitable, in that they might clear outgoings for wages and myriad costs, the perpetual debt would be carried forward with only slight reductions nullified by interest payments. They would, he pointed out, be incessantly on the brink of bankruptcy and the only solution was to advertise their new status as a charity dedicated to the preservation and protection of rare, and often charmingly photographed, animals; as Jacquie put it, 'we should put out a massive begging bowl'.

Betty Boizard was a dedicated veteran from the zoo's first year and had diligently recorded correspondence from enthusiasts and devotees over the previous four years. Catha gave her the grandiose title of 'zoo secretary' and had her type letters to everyone who had wished the institution well, explaining its new status as an animal charity and offering them the chance to become 'non-profit shareholders'. Gerry signed every letter, almost two thousand in total, and small donations began to roll in. On Jersey itself, those who had settled as tax exiles donated almost £1,500 over February and March and the less well-heeled of the island almost equalled the amount over the same period. By the beginning of April donations amounted to nearly £14,000, almost £250,000 in today's money. The most generous donor was anonymous, a 'Mr X' of St Helier who wrote a cheque for the Trust in his real name for £2,000. This soon had to be paid from the Trust to the island's exchequer when he was exposed as a swindler and imprisoned for six years in a mainland gaol.

Gerry realised that reducing the long-standing debt would not be enough to enable the Trust to survive let alone expand. He took out a private £20,000 bank loan which he secured against a promise from Hart-Davis to repay it in lieu of all of his advances and royalties for the forthcoming five years. In a private note Gerry observed:

> Toucans – they have that sad soulful expression that leads me to believe they are the reincarnation of bank managers, for every bank manager I have possessed has always looked like that when trying to tell me that my overdraft was slightly bigger than the polar ice cap. (Jersey Archive, undated)

The organisation was through spring and summer 1963 taking on a semblance of professionalism and efficiency, dressed with something close to an aristocratic demeanour. The first four trustees were James Platt, Lady Coutanche, wife of the ex-Bailiff of Jersey, Sir Giles Guthrie, BT, OBE, DSC, senior merchant banker and now resident of the island, and George Francis Child-Villiers, 9th Earl of Jersey.

On 6 July 1963 a ceremony took place in the Royal Court, essentially the parliament building, where the Jersey Wildlife Preservation Trust was initiated as part of the island's financial and legal infrastructure though no one aside from the black-gowned officials knew quite what this meant. Nevertheless, Gerry, Jacquie, Catha, Jeremy Mallinson and several others from the Trust repaired to the nearby eighteenth-century pub, the Cock and Bottle, where they spent the rest of the day.

The first explicit sign that Gerry and Jacquie's marriage was moving towards the rocks came in a letter she wrote to Alan and Ella Thomas (24 July 1963; correspondence kept privately by the former). The Durrells had taken a short holiday with Larry and Claude-Marie in the Mazet in the Languedoc. The period there, though little more than a week, reinforced for her the peculiar relationship between the brothers. Ostensibly the zoologist and the novelist who was now the favourite of the European intelligentsia adopted different lifestyles but in truth each spent much of their time writing. And here was the problem. For Larry it was his vocation and he chose to put words to page in an environment that freed him from distractions; specifically, he turned a small spare room in the Mazet into his private study. Gerry, however, seemed intent on revenge against an activity he loathed. He wanted to spend his days planning the future of the Trust and looking after the animals in its care but he faced the obligation of having to turn out bestsellers to ensure its financial survival. Jacquie wrote to the Thomases that, 'I am not looking forward to our return. Gerry has turned the manor into his office, his bar, his chamber of egomania and self-regard.' He wrote his books on the kitchen table and when he took a break sat at the dining table in the main reception area drinking as much as he could with visitors there on official business, along with employees who had no other things to do.

Jacquie described the zoo to the Thomases as his 'Frankenstein's monster'. He 'never went out' to cocktail parties and other events organised on the island by those who were involved in publicising the Trust and raising money on its behalf.

Things came to a head on 24 January the following year when Louisa, aged seventy-eight, died in her sleep. Of the three brothers Gerry had been the closest to her and her loss seemed to affect him greatly.

She was cremated in Bournemouth after a church service. Larry flew over and Margo attended but Leslie was absent, as were Jacquie and Claude-Marie, though Alan Thomas was present. Gerry had what appeared to be a nervous breakdown when the priest was proclaiming the funeral rites and had to be helped out of the church by Thomas. He sat on a bench and wept, refusing to return. Jacquie was interviewed by Botting long after the marriage broke down. 'He never came to terms with it, he was utterly unable to accept it, he could not even grieve for her ... As a child his life was so idyllic, especially in Corfu, that he came to believe that life would always be like that, and that when it wasn't, when something untoward occurred, he just couldn't cope. He would run away from problems, and just drink, or take drugs such as tranquillisers, or combinations of both' (Botting, pp316–17). Late in his life, after his brother's death, Gerry concocted an interview between Larry and a journalist from a highbrow French newspaper.

Lawrence Durrell: Why do you keep asking me questions about my
    brother? I hardly knew him socially, though I knew the secret of his
    enormous physical stamina. He was suckled by my mother until
    the age of 41 [close to Louisa's death] which makes him unique.

Journalist: How do you know that?

Lawrence Durrell: He has said so himself in his autobiography.

Journalist: But he hasn't written his autobiography. (Jersey Archive, undated)

In his unpublished notes for a memoir Gerry offered an account of his relationship with Louisa which reinforces and explains Jacquie's observations on the effect on him of her death. He tells of how she had guided and formed his personality, presenting her as a benign, faintly anarchic figure, a woman who loved every one of her children greatly while refusing to force them to do anything in particular. She was, however, a fan of quirky individuals. In its way, it is a credible explanation for the eccentricities of Gerry, Larry, Margo and Leslie who most certainly went their own ways.

> It is curious – and something you don't realise at the time – but my mother allowed us to *be*. She worried over us, she advised us (when we asked) and the advice always with 'but anyway dear, you must do what you think best'. It was, I suppose, a form of indoctrination, a form of guidance. She opened new doors on problems that allowed new exploration of the ways in which you might – or might not – deal with them. Simple things now engrained in me without a recollection of how they got there. I was never lectured, never scolded ...

He explains how, because of Louisa,

> In India, I saw, heard and felt and smelt with great intensity. The colours stirred me as they were illuminated by the sunshine. Back in England of course I experienced the same sensations but they were bland, subdued, the difference between eating a curry and a blancmange. When I got to Corfu the sun injected me and all my senses came to full life again. Corfu town – sea smell – olive groves – sun smell. (Misc. 17, Jersey Archive, undated)

A few days after the funeral the family solicitor arrived at the zoo with Louisa's will. Much of the money from the Bournemouth properties had been 'invested' in the zoo as soon as she moved permanently to Jersey and aside from that her collection of Christian and Buddhist paraphernalia dating mostly from her days in India was all that was left. But Gerry, Jacquie and Margo were surprised by the single significant endowment. Following the publication of *My Family and Other Animals*, his most profitable book, the volume that made him famous, he had given all the rights to his mother. This chimes with Jacquie's observations of him being unable to cope with the less agreeable aspect of adulthood. Corfu was his childhood idyll; Louisa epitomised the otherworldliness of those years and he never truly wished to dispatch either to an irrecoverable past. His book had made them timeless so he thought it appropriate that she would be part of its destiny. He did not seriously imagine that she would cash in on adaptations or translations – she had without reservation signed over the Donen adaptation money to him – but bringing her into its legacy was an expression of thanks for his infancy, despite him having made most of it up.

There was, therefore, some surprise when the solicitor announced that Louisa had bequeathed the rights to Jacquie. She had spoken to no one about her reason for doing this but the fact that she had made the will eighteen months before her death is significant. Like Jacquie and others, she too saw that Gerry was becoming more obsessed with the zoo and gradually destroyed by it. Jacquie wrote to Larry and Claude-Marie, 'Visitors daily in and out till one feels like screaming. The place is a mad house, and most of the people coming and going are opportunists, all wanting something and promising what they'll never give' (12 October 1963, Jersey Archive).

When he wasn't writing Gerry was welcoming to the old house dozens of people who professed interest and even promised donations. But most were rubberneckers, quite a few from Jersey, drawn to the place because of Gerry's growing reputation as an unquestioning host. He was becoming an alcoholic and was overjoyed to share his bottles of beer and whisky with whoever cared to walk in.

Louisa's handing over of the book rights was neither malicious nor irresponsible. She knew that her favourite son could no longer cope and she felt it appropriate that the woman he loved should take over as curator of his most cherished memories. Neither Gerry nor Jacquie had disclosed to her that their relationship was gradually becoming consigned to oblivion.

In April 1964 they joined Larry and Claude-Marie for a week's holiday on Corfu. It was Jacquie's idea and she had written to France to ask if her brother-in-law and his wife could find the time to come. It seemed an act of madness since the Trust was going through one of its perennial bouts of disarray that came with the turn of the financial year. A lioness was seriously unwell, which distressed Gerry and signalled large bills from the vet. But the signing over of *My Family* to her had caused him to become freakish. He became by parts saddened and overjoyed, and Jacquie thought that a return to his spiritual home might help to repair his mental clutter. She was wrong and he wrote to Alan and Ella Thomas on their return. 'Since our return we have had a right basin-full ... I am afraid that we have lost all sense of time and everything else' (May 2, 1964; correspondence privately held by A. and E. Thomas, undated; quoted by Botting, p319). Both knew that his frame of reference was beyond the running of the zoo. Jacquie had written to them regularly on her difficulties with Gerry's increasingly erratic behavioural habits.

As they struggled through the summer she returned again to an overseas expedition as a potential solution to their problems and by coincidence Chris Parsons telephoned to see if they would be interested in doing another series of films. Gerry responded enthusiastically and insisted on Sierra Leone, seemingly for no other reason that it would involve a revisitation of his experiences the Cameroons.

Jacquie argued that to sell films and books they needed original discoveries and proposed that Guyana, Middle America and various islands in the Caribbean contained species of mammal and birds of which Europeans knew little. Gerry refused to countenance the idea and seemed set on repeating journeys of his past. Parsons accepted that he was the magnet for TV viewers and in January 1965 began arrangements for a trip and filming in West Africa. Jacquie booked herself a cabin on a boat to Argentina and made arrangements to travel from there by train, car and ship to Guyana and then Jamaica. Two women who had helped establish the zoo, Hope Platt and Ann Peters, agreed to go with her. She did not plan to collect animals and there would be no accompanying film crew but she had contacted Hart-Davis suggesting a book; something that went beyond wildlife and covered the culture and society of Latin America and the Caribbean. In the end this came to nothing and the true reason for her journey was as a means of emphasising an irreversible state. They were moving in very different directions.

During his period in Africa Gerry sent Jacquie thirty letters. On average they were a thousand words in length and while the style is hyperbolic it would be unfair to treat them as exaggerations of his frame of mind. Typically:

> Darling, I wish you had come on this trip. I wish it for a great variety of personal reasons ... Darling, life's so bloody short, let's try not to be parted again, either mentally or physically. I know I'm difficult to live with and very demanding, but I will try and reform. The trouble is that when I feel you drifting away from me I get so hurt and angry that I get bloody minded and this makes you drift still further ... I miss you terribly ... Darling, I miss you like Hell. What I miss most is that I can't talk to you ... I love you so much, and I can't wait to hold you and kiss you again. I am dirty, love-sick and full of faults. But I love you and, if ever one human being can possess another, you have me ... To say that I miss you is stupid, it's rather like saying: 'Isn't it curious, the sun fell out of the sky yesterday...do you find it dark?' ... My love for you has increased to the extent where it is not just a feeling but a physical pain, rather like walking round with a few red-hot coals under your ribs ... With you – and without anything else – I have the whole world. Without you I am nothing. (Extracts from eight of Gerry's thirty letters to Jacquie, early 1965, Jersey Archive)

Jacquie replied to him twice, affectionately and patiently; she seemed to be calming him and she certainly did not come close to his mood of passionate fervour.

She returned to England in early spring 1965 two months before he was due to arrive. In the interim he persuaded her to sail to Freetown, Sierra Leone, and spend the closing period of his African visit with him. He explained that he had been injured while sitting on the back of a Land Rover used by the film crew. The driver had hit a bump on an unpaved road and he'd been thrown to the ground. He had two broken ribs and was unable to walk with sticks because of damage to his lower back. He begged her to come because she only, he argued, could enable him to return home without further medical attention, implying that the magic of their earlier relationship might reinvigorate him.

This did not go as he had hoped in that they bickered during the remaining period in Sierra Leone. She was particularly displeased by his having turned the trip into an exercise in animal collection rather than sticking to its ostensible purpose of making a film series and making notes for a book. He had captured almost one hundred creatures, including ten rare monkeys and four young leopards. It went without saying that while this would enable him to expand the zoo it would also put further strain on its ever-dwindling expense account.

David Hughes did not witness the Sierra Leone visit but from the recollections of Parsons and others directly involved, Jacquie included, he judges it as the nadir in Gerry's battle between gusto and despair. Parsons said that he had become a caricature of the man who could once mix the zeal of animal conservation with entertainment. 'The humour goes sour on him under strain. The thought-out comic lines don't work, even on a commentary track, because all the fuss and bother makes him self-conscious' (Parsons quoted in Hughes, p180).

The man Jacquie rejoined in Freetown harbour reinforced the difference between the way he looked when they first met and now. At the beginning of the 1950s he could have been a film actor. He had thick beautiful brown hair, sometimes slicked back, but often allowed to grow wild; he dressed liked a playboy and was athletically built. Now he was around four stone heavier, bearded, his hair still unkempt but this time suggesting neglect. His cheeks had the bloodspots that signal extreme and regular alcohol intake.

In Jersey Gerry got back to work on the book about his journey to New Zealand, Australia and the Far East. The television programme on the expedition shown two years earlier had attracted an impressive audience so he gave his volume the same title, *Two in the Bush*. It was at this point that Jacquie announced that she too would become a writer and began *Beasts in My Bed*. Almost eight years later the secretary of the Trust, Judy Mackrell, talked with her of the book and Jacquie disclosed that her publisher forced the title on her despite her insistence that they should go with her original choice, 'My Life with an Animal'. That the marriage lasted amazed those closest to them. Few if any were prone to blame one or the other for the long-running catastrophe but it was clear enough to all that what had begun as a quirkily romantic attraction of opposites descended into a *danse macabre*. Year by year they became further aware of their often infuriating, irreconcilable differences yet at the same time neither seemed willing to admit that they should give up on something they loathed.

David Hughes's *Himself and Other Animals* (1997) is treated by most who knew Gerry as authentic, affectionate, if not entirely unbiased. Its only failing is that Jacquie features as someone who exists on the borderline of the 'portrait'. In truth, she was her husband's inspiration; she fuelled his journey from obscurity to fame by embodying, every day of their time together, all that he loved and hated.

When they met in Manchester it was not only class difference that intrigued them. She saw the post-war Labour government as the best thing that had happened in Britain in recorded history. Jacquie read Marx but was alert to warnings from writers such as Orwell that the Soviet workers' paradise in the East was as tyrannical as fascism. She was committed to the advancement of moderate democratic socialism as the best opportunity for civilised mankind. Gerry on the other hand held human beings in contempt. He saw them as having overreached themselves. According to Jacquie: 'I think Gerry's real interest in politics ... springs from his concern for man as an animal – he is deeply involved in any aspect of the evolution of man as an animal ... We always call stupid anything that we can't understand, don't we? ... He's incapable of realising, for instance, that "the working man" ... is locked in this bitter struggle with what he considers his lifelong enemy' (Jacquie quoted in Hughes, p136). Her point is that Gerry regarded human beings as aberrations. Animals do not burden themselves with anything like the deadly self-obsession and ideological malice that have become quintessential features of the history of humanity. She diagnoses his weird myopic view of the world as the result of his colonial background. 'Gerry can't see, having never been involved, never having been compelled to work on that level [of the working classes], that they are constantly fighting for their existence and are resentful ... of anyone who is not a manual labourer' (*Ibid.*). In her view Gerry had opted for a kind of reverse-anthropomorphism, judging the failures of humans in terms of his idealised notion of the animal universe.

'When Gerry meets a human being, he loves that human being. But in general, he is infuriated by their asking for another pound a week ... Gerry's a biologist, he should realise that they [humans] want the strata, just as an animal wants his territory at the expense of others' (*Ibid.*). He lived, she believed, in a fantasy world where relations between animals marked an apogee of perfection and he was horrified by the apparent inability of his own species to recognise their loss. 'The trouble is that he gets society thrown at him morning noon and night on television, and he will insist on watching. No wonder he gets irritable' (*Ibid.*, p137).

It hardly needs saying that his most famous book epitomises his desire to make humans more like animals. In *My Family* he was not merely improving on the heedless, chaotic state of his family life in Corfu, though that was a factor. He was turning those he knew during his childhood into figures governed by intuition rather than logic: the animals of his fantasy world.

Conservationists are difficult to categorise in terms of a temperament that matches their vocation. Sir David Attenborough comes close enough to being the archetype: intellectually accomplished, from a middle-class liberal family, and willing to give up the advantages of his background to become an ascetic evangelist for animal welfare. Alternatively, we come across Dian Fossey, a primatologist who treated gorillas as superior to the humans who occupied the same parts of the continent, Africa, where she spent most of her life: she was a pro-animal racist. Gerry was in a class of his own. The familial legacy of colonial India followed later by life in the southern England instilled in him a desire for unaccountable indulgency. He never asked a great deal of his animals but the humans who accompanied him on his expeditions and worked for him in Jersey he regarded as natural subordinates. While Fossey lived with and tried to imitate the behaviour of gorillas in the wild Gerry preferred the manner of an Edwardian gentleman and his favoured repast shifted between French haute cuisine and the traditional British fare offered in London gentleman's clubs. Such dishes would be difficult to prepare in the wilds of Africa but in desperation he made do with any spirit available and stout, which remained popular around what was left of the empire and the new commonwealth.

The question of who the real Gerald Durrell was became a matter for discussion in editorial meetings at the *Daily Mail* in early 1966. The TV series on the Sierra Leone expedition, *Catch Me a Colobus*, was attracting a large number of viewers while *My Family and Other Animals* featured on the O-level English curriculum alongside Shakespeare, Dickens and Chaucer. On live television interviews Gerry appeared to be halfway between zealous and comedic, committed to the preservation of threatened species but a natural entertainer too and unprinted rumour had it from those who had accompanied him abroad and socialised with him at home that he drank not merely to have a good time but as a means of numbing some form of distress which neither he nor anyone else could make sense of. As Jacquie observed, Louisa's death seemed to make alcohol more a necessity than an indulgence.

A *Mail* reporter was dispatched to Jersey in June 1966, with Gerry and Jacquie's reserved approval. The intended article/interview was never published because it was impossible to drag anything coherent from the notes and tapes. Often, he mumbled almost incomprehensibly and then he would shift into states of rage, targeting his anger against those who read his books and watched the TV series but who in his view blinded themselves to the real issues. Did they not realise, he asked the reporter, that the *Daily Mail*, 'or some other worthless rag', had been put together from the pulp of rainforests and that the creatures for whom this was once their home would soon be extinct because of a policy of 'extermination', and what about the tins of baked beans that most people fed their kids on these days? These horrible fast foods had come to their table because greedy multinationals had planted thousands of acres of land in Central and South America with quick-grow topsoil and fertilised it with chemicals that poisoned the natural habitat of everything from snakes to voles.

He then went through some thick files and spread letters in front of the unfortunate Fleet Street correspondent. 'They ask,' he said, 'what the point of all this is,' and he waved his hand towards the zoo, 'and I wonder, what's the point of *you*?' He reserved particular contempt for a television viewer who had declared it against 'God's law to shut up little creatures in cages', and claimed that Gerry himself deserved to be in a cage for what he had done. Gerry observed that even if he was inclined to reply to such letters, he would be lost for words given the abject stupidity of his correspondents.

He was no doubt sincere enough in his anger with the media and the general public in their misunderstanding of his mission to preserve as much as possible from the destructive presences of humans, but Jacquie's comments to Hughes tell us a little more: 'He is deeply involved in any aspect of the evolution of man as an animal ... He just despairs of us all' (Hughes, p136). She meant that in his view the human race was well behind its animal counterparts in terms of collective enlightenment, which was why no one seemed able to comprehend the nature of his calling.

Jacquie knew that her husband was coming close to a kind of mental burnout that could not be explained nor remedied in terms of the twin pressures of being misunderstood by his audience and the obligation of keeping the zoo afloat from his writings, an activity he loathed. Something more disturbing and inscrutable was plaguing him and the only time he seemed to come close to contentment was when he talked of his childhood in Corfu, or more specifically the version of it that he had magically reinvented for *My Family*. In early summer 1965 they had employed a young woman from St Helier called Doreen Evans as his personal assistant, secretary and typist. During the interview he had asked if she would be prepared, in emergency, to breastfeed a baby hedgehog. She replied, without hesitation, that 'certainly, in principle, but I doubt the youngster would benefit given that I'll not be its mother'. Gerry was impressed by her humour and by her seemingly instinctive recognition of animals and humans as part of the same tribe.

Doreen was excellent at her job but she also served as Jacquie's spy, willing to talk with her confidentially about Gerry's various states of mind. Initially she was taken on to type up *Two in the Bush* in a small office at the top of the house and he would join her for long periods, correcting parts of his longhand draft in advance and sometimes dictating new passages to her. It worked so well that she was employed on a semi-permanent basis to work with Gerry on forthcoming books and more importantly to report back to Jacquie on his moods: often he would pause from the work at hand and just speak to her distractedly on whatever troubled him. This was how Jacquie came to realise that his memories of Corfu had become as much an obsession as a sentimental recollection and leaving aside what a psychologist might have thought she came up with a plan.

She and Doreen would drive their large Vauxhall estate through France and Italy and then take the ferry from Venice to Greece. The two women deliberately planned a slow and gentle progress through continental Europe. Aside from the fact that Gerry couldn't drive they wanted him to feel as though he was taking the Grand Tour of the Continent enjoyed by minor aristocrats more than a hundred years before; savouring its cultural delights while savouring just as much the wines, spirits and meals available at each of the hostelries arrived at every day of their journey.

Jacquie felt that this weird form of time travel might in some way assuage what seemed to be his concern with being a son of the empire while wishing he were someone else. He would at least have two women who cared for him during this journey towards his childhood. Their destination was Corfu.

The cure worked, at least according to Doreen's account of their time on the island. They rented a large nineteenth-century house and within days Gerry seemed to become someone else, or at least be at ease with who he was. He still wrote and dictated to her but in an unencumbered, placid way, sometimes pausing to stroll through the nearby olive groves or along the beach. The three of them would have lunch and supper together every day, either in a local bar where service was slow but wine continually available, or in the house. Gerry, Doreen found, was a superb cook, not a thing he'd shown any inclination to do on Jersey, producing chicken or fish stews and pies or his favourite, prawn Provençal. Even Jacquie had never come across his talent for producing such delicious meals. She would play classical music on her gramophone, or sometimes jazz, and the tensions that Doreen intuited and reported to Jacquie while in Jersey seemed miraculously to have disappeared.

Things shifted back towards abnormal when Gerry and Jacquie had to be present in person at the annual fundraising ball for all sponsors of the Trust in Jersey. By this time the event had become the most prestigious on the island. Everyone who aspired to the new-money aristocracy of the place had become donors to Gerry's zoo, and the ball required dinner jackets for men and magnificently competitive dresses for women.

Gerry, somewhat restored to good humour by the Corfu trip, appeared in unconventional attire; his beard had disappeared, he had 'blacked up' his face, and dressed as much like the Fon as available clothing would allow. The day before, however, he had concluded a plan to remove himself once more from the island. Larry had made enough money to purchase a well-appointed century-old bourgeois villa in the town of Sommières and it is still unclear whether he offered the lease on the Mazet to his brother or if Gerry asked for it. In any event Gerry became leaseholder of a remote property in Languedoc at the point when Les Augrès was about to plummet towards yet another financial catastrophe.

Instead of spending the early spring there, where the local climate is a considerable improvement on the Channel Islands and England, Gerry responded quickly to a phone message left by his long-term BBC filmmaking associate Chris Parsons. Parsons wanted to adapt *My Family and Other Animals* as a television series. It would, he explained, be screened on BBC2 which was about to become Britain's first colour TV outlet, an excellent means of capturing the natural beauty of the place. He proposed to call it 'The Garden of the Gods', and without hesitation Gerry and Jacquie arranged to meet Parsons, his crew and the team of actors he had elected for the principal roles, on Corfu in May 1967. Inevitably, Gerry wondered who would play him as a youngster and who might suit the roles of Louisa, Larry, Margo and Leslie. He was therefore surprised to find that when he met Parsons in the hotel only the film crew were present. Gerry asked, 'Where is the cast?' and Parsons was dumbfounded, only realising soon afterwards that they had completely different conceptions of the project. It was, Parsons explained to him, a documentary and the only 'performer' would be Gerald Durrell, playing himself in middle age and sometimes referring back to his childhood years on the island.

Parsons remembered that the film was not as good as it ought to have been because of the 'running battle' in the background between Gerry and Jacquie. She disclosed to Parsons that before leaving Jersey her husband had been plagued by what seemed to be regular bouts of angina: pains in his left arm, chest and jaw, breathlessness when ascending stairs. He saw a general practitioner who confirmed that the symptoms suggested the early state of coronary heart disease, and Jacquie diagnosed the principal cause as his latest bout of speculative madness. At an informal meeting of donors and investors following the ball on Jersey Gerry had announced his newly formulated 'ten-year plan', involving the conversion of old barns and stables, the erection of a new building – including veterinary surgeries – and the purchase of adjoining land for the creation of areas where species could live as if in the wild. He estimated the cost at around £200,000, approximately £3m today.

His audience were at once impressed and unsettled. The project was exhilarating but he appeared to be asking them for the gigantic amount that would bring it to life without even hinting at repayment and they were not that generous. Gerry was living in a fantasy world, or so Jacquie thought, treating other humans as versions of himself, prepared to give up everything for animal conservation, and his health was suffering because of his detachment from reality.

Further evidence of the latter can be found in a book he wrote without a contract. Shortly before he set off to film *The Garden of the Gods* in Corfu, he sent his agent Curtis Brown the typescript of *Rosy Is My Relative*. It is the only self-confessed full-length novel he produced that was not aimed at children and his agent wrote back saying that it was both substandard and even worse than that a divergence from the type of books that had guaranteed him fame and income. He replied, insisting that either they do their best to place it with a good publisher or he'd drop them and they'd lose the profitable 15 per cent on his advances. He had switched from Hart-Davis to Collins with *Two in the Bush*. They paid more than his previous outlet and seemed less concerned with continuity than getting into print anything their new celebrity author offered them. Curtis Brown sent it to Collins and they accepted it immediately. It went into print in 1968, though with few reviews; probably because hardly anyone knew what to make of it.

Rosy is an elephant bequeathed to Adrian Rookwhistle by his reprobate uncle, and the 'My Relative' of the title tells us much of the book and its author. Rosy and Adrian share various aspects of Gerry's temperament. She loves alcohol and is by her nature rebellious and disinclined to obey the rules imposed on her by human beings. He loves her because she embodies everything he aspires to. As an animal she has no concern with the customs and restrictions of middle-class Englishness. Together they rampage through various parts of southern England, notably a meeting of the Monkspepper Hunt and the stately home of Lady Fenneltree. Adrian and Rosy collude in their author's private fantasy, a state of mind in which wild animals can only be appreciated when accepted as the equals of humankind.

Before Gerry and Jacquie left Corfu for Jersey, he received an invitation to dinner at the Palace of St Michael and St George in Corfu town, previously the headquarters of the British High Commission. Now it was the occasional residence of King Constantine of Greece and his wife Anne-Marie who would, according to the invitation, be the Durrells' hosts for the evening. Also present would be Prince George of Hanover, his wife Princess Sophie of Greece and Denmark, and Prince Juan Carlos who would eventually succeed General Franco as the Spanish head of state. Gerry first assumed that it was a practical joke but when he telephoned the palace an official stated that the invitation was indeed authentic. Constantine and Anne-Marie had contacted him because they too were avid conservationists. The evening was bizarre to say the least, with Gerry picking up on the diatribe he had delivered to the *Daily Mail* reporter and his royal hosts treating him as something close to a saint. Constantine offered him free use of his private aeroplane the following year so that he could travel wherever he wished across the Greek mainland and the islands, to monitor and where possible preserve the threatened wildlife of the nation. Drink flowed in enormous quantities and once more Gerry seemed to have crossed the boundary between the actual and the fantastic. The real world intervened when soon afterwards the army coup abolished the Greek monarchy for good. One can appreciate how all of this reinforced Gerry's sense of life, his own in particular, as a cabinet of anomalies.

Following the Durrells' return to Jersey in September 1967 an old colleague from Whipsnade drew Gerry's attention to something to which most conservationists had paid no attention. Indeed, Gerry himself had never heard of the teporingo, one of the smallest rabbits in the world, which dwelt exclusively on the arid slopes of the largely extinct volcanoes around Mexico City. Most of the local population had no time for it. It was too tiny to merit the effort of hunting and stewing and its function seemed to be only that of target practice for men with shotguns who wanted to hone their skills for taking down larger animals. This, along with the expansion of the urban area of the Mexican capital, meant that it was soon likely to become extinct.

Because of who he was Gerry became infatuated with the teporingo. Few, if any, cared about it and this excited his lifetime mission: find a home for those non-humans apparently without hosts or sympathisers. Much of the money raised for his ambitious programme for the zoo went into the funding of a trip to Mexico and the expedition depressed Gerry greatly. He found that his initial contacts, the Mexican rangers who looked after what had become a National Park around the capital, knew where most of the teporingos existed and bred because they were so poorly paid that they shot the little creatures en masse and cooked them five or six at a time in large pots over open fires as part of their basic diet. Further confirmation that human beings were the enemies of hopeless, peaceful animals drove Gerry into a state of deep melancholy.

He captured only four, each female. Later, a friend in Mexico sent him two males. They bred but each of their descendants died and Gerry faced the likely prospect of having failed to preserve a species from extinction.

For what remained of 1968 Gerry worked on his next book, *Birds, Beasts and Relatives*. He completed it the following year and Curtis Brown were delighted. It was a continuation of his bestseller *My Family and Other Animals* and in it Gerry's ability to turn truth and recollection into fantasy is further evident. Larry becomes even more the marginal, failed novelist than he was in the first volume. The fact that he shared a different house with Nancy is once again excised and Gerry's eldest brother becomes something of a parasite unable to create a life for himself beyond the family home. Margo is yet more feckless and batty and only Louisa seems to have acquired something admirable: generous contentedness would be the best description.

As Gerry was completing it, he received a letter from a solicitor in south Devon stating that his brother Leslie was begging for his assistance. Several women, mostly middle-aged and elderly widows based around Mombasa in Kenya, had been lured into an investment scheme devised by Leslie. They were ex-colonials and desperate to find a way of securing their assets against the corrupt and acquisitive regime of Jomo Kenyatta. Leslie turned out to be a fraud, able to steal even more than the local government. His schemes proved catastrophic both for his victims and himself. He made, or rather stole, a good deal of money but lost it as rapidly as he'd emptied it from the accounts of his victims and in late 1968 he returned to England bankrupt, a Kenyan arrest warrant pending, and with Doris in a state of despondency. Leslie wrote to his brother to ask if he could provide him with financial assistance. The British police, apparently, had no interest in charges brought against him in Kenya but he was technically on the run, as well as penniless. Gerry replied that he would not 'get you out of whatever mess you have got yourself into' (Jersey Archive, 1968, otherwise undated) and demanded that Leslie not communicate with him again.

Leslie and Doris found a flat close to Marble Arch, a basement where they could live as caretakers for the wealthy couple who owned the Victorian house above them. News of the 'third brother' of Gerry's classic book reached the *Guardian* who sent their journalist Lee Langley to visit Leslie to ask about his associations with the famous family. To his credit Leslie held back the fact that neither of his brothers would now speak to him and that only Margo, out of desperate pity, sometimes came to see him. At one point he asked her to contact Gerry on his behalf to see if basic lodgings might be found for him and Doris at Jersey Zoo. In return both would take on whatever basic jobs – manual labour such as cleaning, even painting and decorating – where necessary to keep the institution in good order. They would not, he added, expect wages. Food and drink would do. He impressed on Margo his wish to become reunited with the family. Gerry refused even to provide his sister with a reply. All of this was happening while the Leslie of *My Family* volume two was being reinvented by Gerry as the same eccentric but charismatic figure of the first book.

11

Larry in Hell

The house bought by Larry and Claude-Marie in Sommières in 1966 was called La Maison de Mme Tartes. No one in the locality seemed to have knowledge of Mme Tartes. Clearly, she was married at some point but there were no ancestors in or around Sommières and she was rich. The building dated from the mid-nineteenth century and while the French never favoured the nouveau-Gothic style of Victorian British architecture it was a strange mixture of the Romanesque and decorative extravagance. He described it to Miller as 'rambling, ugly', 'not a chateau' but the sort of home enjoyed by well-off bourgeoisie sorts – doctors, lawyers and notaries. The ceilings were high, and the interior was decorated in a loud, charmless manner. Claude-Marie had provided most of the £6,000 for the purchase and went on to pay for redecoration, decent furniture and bathrooms that improved on the originals. What appealed to Larry were the spacious gardens of around two acres, planted with trees that were as old as the house.

He was working on his first post-*Alexandria Quartet* novel, *Tunc*, and continually abandoning first drafts. He did not revise his initial texts, sometimes as long as 50,000 words, but rather threw them away, sometimes burned them, and began again as if what he had previously attempted had to be sent to oblivion. The novel that was eventually published by Faber in 1968 is his most controversial. Even those who applauded him as the heroic standard bearer for experiment were perplexed by it. It is oversaturated in erudition even by Larry's usual standards, and as for a narrative the principal character Charlock is bounced between lurid sexual experiences and encounters with an assembly of other figures – once more based largely in the eastern Mediterranean – who are unflaggingly unappetising and enigmatic. Throw in a cocktail of necrophilia, sadism, rent boys and, bizarrely, science fiction, and you have a novel that could lay claim to being unique, though sadly not readable.

One might take a charitable view of it given that while he went through its various drafts Larry's own life followed a storyline that was variously horrifying and chaotic.

In July 1966 builders were still involved with the renovation of the new house and Larry and Claude-Marie hired a live-in housekeeper, Marcelle, to look after the place for most of the summer. They bought a second-hand Volkswagen camper van and set off on a journey across southern France, through northern Italy and then by ferry to mainland Greece and Corfu. Sometimes they slept in the van but just as frequently found an auberge for decently cooked food and a bathroom.

Once in Corfu they rented a house in Palaiokastritsa and had agreed to meet up with Horst and Frances von Maltitz. Horst was an academic historian of minor aristocratic German background and his early 1970s study of the rise of the Nazis would become widely respected. Larry had known Frances since the mid-1950s and one day while the two of them were swimming at an island beach, they came across a small sailing boat occupied by Peter Bird and his wife Joan. Larry knew them too, given that Peter had served as Group Captain in the RAF during the war and thereafter worked in the Foreign Service where their paths often crossed. Joan was tall, dark-haired and head-turningly enchanting and Frances later told MacNiven that she and her husband were convinced that the encounter with the Birds was unlikely to be coincidental.

There was, she said, something false and disingenuous in Larry's expression of surprise, returned by Joan Bird. During the subsequent two weeks the three couples spent most days in each other's company with Larry playing master of ceremonies, sometimes telling stories of his time on the island during his first marriage, mocking other members of the literati, especially critics hostile to his work, caricaturing his closest friend Miller as an almost feral lecher, and then switching to apparently improvised limericks on everything from politicians to the various races that the end of the empire had caused to return to primitive fecklessness. Most present had witnessed these aspects of Larry before but now, escalated, they seemed designed to test their restraint. The von Maltitzes often retired to their own house as soon as they could while Peter Bird paid polite attention to Claude-Marie until she too elected to go to bed rather than listen to her husband. Only Joan indulged him, laughing at everything he said. Often he would arrange to show her walks along the coast which few seemed to know of, and it was apparent to Frances that the two of them were involved in an exercise in exclusion. They wanted to spend as much time alone with each other as possible and she had little doubt that they were having an affair.

Claude-Marie said nothing of her own suspicions, but they were evident in her mood. She seemed more and more vulnerable and would drink brandy at breakfast time. Larry would join her but while she appeared to be anaesthetising herself for the day ahead, he gave the impression of rehearsing for further indulgences.

An equally bizarre feature of the Corfu visit was that it overlapped with Gerry and Jacquie's time there. They had arrived at the end of May but were still present when Larry and Claude-Marie arrived. Gerry wanted time away from Jersey – a regular inclination despite the foundation being his lifelong objective – and this time he was trying to absorb some of the atmosphere of his childhood idyll for his revisitation of *My Family and Other Animals* in *Birds, Beasts and Relatives*. There were certainly parallels. In the second volume his eldest brother is once more reinvented as the ambitious but not very successful novelist, unmarried and still living with the family. There is no evidence that Gerry and Larry communicated with each other during this period and no record that they knew of their presence, barely ten miles apart, on the island that had such a formative influence on each of their lives. I have found no correspondence between them on their simultaneous visits, but it seems absurd to assume that they were ignorant of each other's close proximity. One can only speculate on why they did not arrange to meet.

Larry telephoned Gerry in late October inviting him to Sommières for Christmas. It would, he promised, be a 'real English' event, like Gerry's in Les Augrès in 1960, with roast turkey and beef, mince pies, classic steamed pudding and Melton Mowbray pork pies imported by Alan and Ella Thomas, Larry's English friends, who had agreed to come, as had Catha Aldington, daughter of Richard, along with Mary Mollo and her husband Henry. Larry had known Mary since the early 1950s. Tellingly, for Gerry, Theodore Stephanides would travel over from Corfu. Theodore had spent numerous evenings with Gerry in Corfu earlier that year, once again playing the role of sage and proxy uncle that Gerry had created for him in *My Family* and which he was reviving for the sequel. Larry during the same period on the island stayed out of contact with the long-term family friend. For the more cynical it might appear that Larry was, at least for a few weeks, separating himself from Gerry, Jacquie and others he was so close to. This might seem odd were it not for the von Maltitzes' suspicions that Larry had planned the visit specifically to set up an 'inadvertent' encounter with Joan Bird.

Claude-Marie put an enormous amount of effort into preparing the house for their guests. She even had Marcelle touch up some of the painting and decorating done by the builders over the summer and measured all the beds available to ensure that Alan Thomas would not be bent double by the head and foot boards. At six foot three he was by far the tallest person in the group. Claude-Marie had always been a generous host but now she appeared to be preparing herself for something precipitous, even conclusive.

She had had breathing problems and a bad cough for several months and while the Sommières general practitioner suggested that she might have contracted a virus of some sort, her condition worsened so severely within a matter of days that Larry telephoned all of their guests on 9 December to apologise that Christmas was cancelled.

Larry persuaded his wife to come with him by train to a private clinic in Geneva and had Diana Forde, her daughter from her first marriage and then resident in the city, to make emergency arrangements. Claude-Marie spent three weeks there on penicillin but it soon became evident that antibiotics would be ineffective as a means of dealing with what was cancer. She died of pulmonary cancer on New Year's Day, 1967. Larry had her cremated in Geneva and purchased a plot near the church in Sommières where he intended to bury her ashes.

The cremation was a secular ceremony and Larry seemed reluctant to inform everyone close to her that it was taking place. Two days before her death her daughter Diana was told to contact Sappho and order her to fly from London to Geneva as soon as possible. She was appalled and replied, 'It's not her mother who is dying', meaning that her brother Barry must also be summoned. Larry did not reply but Diana telephoned her brother, and he arrived roughly twenty-four hours after their mother's death. Penny had been as attached to Claude-Marie as had Sappho and her two biological children but Diana had difficulty finding a telephone number for her. Shortly after Larry cancelled the Christmas celebrations, Penny had telephoned him and left a message saying that she was about to marry her boyfriend, the actor Peter Ellis Jones. It was not exactly an invitation to the event at a London registrar's office, but Larry did not bother even to reply let alone explain that Claude-Marie had become ill. He made no effort to contact his eldest daughter and she only learned of her stepmother's death via press reports in mid-January. No members of the family were present at the interment of Claude-Marie's ashes in a tiny plot in the Sommières churchyard. Hers were, supposedly, the first cremated remains to be buried there, crematoria being all but non-existent in the more remote parts of the country. There is no record of whether an official, either secular or ecclesiastical, or anyone else was present and the burial itself is a matter for speculation given that Larry later stated to a number of figures that he kept the ashes in an urn in the house.

Over the next twelve months Larry entered a state of obsession and derangement. Some would attribute this to grief, others might not.

In her diaries, written later in the 1970s, Sappho stated that her father became obsessed with her. As I have stated above, some passages were published in *Granta* but much remains privately archived. From *Granta* we have a paragraph on how Larry insisted that she must go alone with him to the spot where he had buried Claude-Marie's ashes.

We went to visit the tomb and found dogroses and Venus' mirror on Claude's grave. On the way back, in the strange light, he began to improvise a Poe-like story very badly to demonstrate how the Languedoc lent itself to this. (*Granta*, Autumn 1991)

Larry spent much of the year following his wife's death in pursuit of sex. Margaret McCall, a filmmaker and actress, had contacted him suggesting an adaption of one of his novels for a movie set on a Greek island, vaguely though not specifically based on parts of the *Alexandria Quartet*. He invited her to Sommières and insisted that they must drive to Corfu in the Volkswagen camper van that he and Claude-Marie had used for the same route a year earlier. Despite his numerous attempts to seduce her she resisted his advances and as soon as they arrived in Greece opted to return to the United States rather than endure the presence of a persistent lecher.

He remained in Corfu for much of the early summer, working on drafts of *Tunc* and at the same time making notes in a diary entitled 'The Vampire Book'. The latter – largely chaotic and incoherent – was never published but there are self-evident parallels between his bizarre private inspirations and the work he would eventually send to Faber. He made enquiries to numerous people about the nature of necromancy, specifically on whether a deceased person, properly embalmed, would remain sexually attractive to those who had known them when alive. In her diary Sappho refers to parallels between her teenage experiences and Nabokov's *Lolita* (1955) (*Granta*, p68), calling herself a 'nymphet' and insinuating that the novel's trio of Humbert, Dolores/Lolita and her late mother Charlotte, resemble, respectively, Larry, herself and Claude-Marie. She implies that her father had turned her into a version of Claude-Marie and wanted to have sex with her as a resurrected version of his late wife.

In September Larry went to Paris to meet up with Miller and his new wife, Hiroko (Hoki) Tokuda, a pianist and jazz singer born in Japan. She was thirty-eight, he seventy-eight and they went through a bizarre prenuptial agreement formalising their relationship as marital but not sexual. By this point Miller, while still reasonably fit, was incapable of having sexual intercourse and he insisted to Hoki that their marriage would be passionate and physical but only in the sense that such liaisons occurred in fiction.

In Paris Hoki was immediately attracted to Larry, eleven years younger than her husband, flirted with him ostentatiously and the two of them had sex within three days of this first meeting. It was a one-night stand but the following year Larry visited Miller and Hoki in their Los Angeles house and slept with her every night during his two-and-a-half-week stay.

They were joined in Paris in September 1967 by Joan and Peter Bird. Larry persuaded the former to have sex with him again, but she rejected his suggestion that he should cease to use condoms and that they should try to conceive. She thought he had become unbalanced. While her husband was aware of her occasional infidelities – they were a liberal, indulgent couple – the notion of her becoming pregnant by another man while she remained married to Peter struck her as grotesque.

An equally outlandish addition to the Paris assembly was Alan Thomas. Seven months before, at the end of February, his wife Ella had 'disappeared'. No body was ever recovered but evidence suggested that she had drowned herself in the sea close to their house on the south coast of England. Thomas adored Larry and had taken on the role of his bibliographer. He believed his hero would be awarded the Nobel Prize for Literature and thought it his duty to leave a comprehensive record of everything he had ever written or stated in interviews.

While he was pursuing his studious scholarly work on Larry, something seemed to turn him into a version of the man he idolised. At the beginning he was reluctant even to speak of Ella and what might have happened to her. Like most self-restrained Englishmen of his class, he had no taste for the macabre, particularly when it involved those closest to him. At the same time, however, he ventured to discuss with Larry aspects of necromancy that seemed to inform so much of *Tunc*, drafts of which had been shown to him.

In February 1968 Larry set off on his first visit to Miller and Hoki in Los Angeles but before flying to America he stayed over with Alan in his rather forbidding house in 16 Hobury Street, Chelsea. It was a late Georgian residence which might have been magnificent were it not for Alan's obsessive concern with changing nothing of it from the moment that his wife closed the front door never to return. Not only were photographs of them, and a painting of Ella, left undisturbed, the surfaces of the elegant antique furniture seemed not to have been dusted. The place resembled a mixture of Dickens's *Bleak House* and something far more noir and unearthly.

After Ella's disappearance Alan had employed Shirley Celentano as his secretary and assistant for his work on Larry's writings. She had a degree from New York University, was in her late twenties and was a tall, slim brunette with sharply defined cheekbones and an elegant slightly aquiline nose. Initially Alan succeeding in making himself indifferent to her charm and beauty, at least until the arrival of Larry. His friend convinced him that sex was not an insult to loss but rather an emotional, even moral, restorative. You cannot, he convinced him, bring shame to a past you adored by investing in new desires. He told him of his recent sexual experiences, especially with Hoki, and how they 'sanctified [my] loss of Claude-Marie' (Jersey Archive, 1968, otherwise undated).

Alan and Shirley began a relationship almost immediately afterwards. When later, Alan read the published version of *Tunc*, he took against it. It seemed to him to be a lascivious manifesto for what Larry had done and persuaded him to do after each of them had lost their wives; literature as narcissistic self-justification. Thereafter the two men remained on reasonably good terms but certainly not as close friends.

In Los Angeles Larry had sex with Hoki, sometimes noisily, while Henry slept alone next door and neither man thought it necessary to unsettle their long-term attachment by discussing Larry's replacement of him as her intimate partner. The marriage was unconsummated by mutual consent and none of the three individuals involved appeared to regard matters as upsetting or unorthodox.

On 22 June 1968, Larry wrote to Henry from Sommières telling him of his experience during the transatlantic flight and then in Paris during the following days.

> Well, I was on an Air France plane for London when a very pretty hostess saw I was reading Eluard's poems and said she was a friend of his. The plane was empty, she found some champagne and sat by me to talk about Picasso's early days, Montmartre etc. Clever, warm-hearted, spontaneous, candid.

Diane Deriaz was forty-two but looked no older than thirty, partly because of her extraordinary physical fitness. During her early years she had worked as a trapeze artist and circus acrobat. A famous portrait of her by Man Ray done in 1961 catches her breathtaking beauty.

She dined with Larry in Paris and told him, without boasting, of her friendships with many of the major artists and writers who had risen to prominence as the next generation of modernism. He asked her to come to Sommières, not in a tedious role as secretary or PA, but as a muse. She was, she explained, about to be retired by Air France because of their ageist policies and although he told Miller that 'we had no love affair' in Paris, things changed a month later when she arrived at Larry's house. 'Oh dear, I must be an awful fool but it isn't possible not to like this woman quite hard!' he reported to Miller. She agreed to stay and their relationship was brief but passionate. 'She's only had one lifelong lover and he died the same week as Claude.' This, perhaps, was Larry folding a thread of guilt into his fascination with mysticism.

Since the dawn of modernism, the notion of 'difficulty' has been prized by advocates of experimental writing. The maxim seems to be that if a work is accessible, even enjoyable, then it fails to meet the principal criterion of great literature. That is, making the common reader feel like a fool for not being able to understand it. By this standard *Tunc* (1968), and indeed its immediate sequel, *Nunquam* (1970), are works of true genius.

It would be improper to attempt a summary of the work since Larry was clearly determined to prohibit anyone from doing this. In desperation we must allow that the principal character is Felix Charlock and that Charlock has a problem with women. His girlfriend Iolanthe is an occasional prostitute, and as usual with Larry her exotic eastern European background and lasciviousness beguile him. Benedicta, whom he actually marries, is heir to the mysterious organisation called Merlin, which might, or might not, be connected with espionage or early computer science. Merlin could well have affiliations with Soviet Russia or not: we never know for sure.

Ruling out the possibility of Larry having gone mad the only explanation for his creation of this literary calamity is his trauma following the death of Claude-Marie, which occurred when *Tunc* was at an early stage. He loved her, certainly, but this did not curtail his lifelong tendency towards adultery and nor did it prevent him from pursuing women, often successfully, within months of her death. Hence we have a literary character, Charlock, whose sex life and emotional commitments are conflicted and inexplicable, aside from the suggestion that Merlin, or 'The Firm', absolves him of responsibility for what he does and makes him unable to understand the consequences of his actions. The two novels were Larry's means of displacing his feelings of guilt into a messy world in which Charlock was neither accountable nor responsible for anything he did.

In September 1968 Larry drove to Nimes to meet Miller and Hoki. Their time in the city was by parts ludicrous and sad. Henry, ever the sexual optimist, urged him to start an affair promptly, despite the fact that his own marriage to Hoki was formally asexual.

The place seemed full of fans of Henry, mostly women who wanted him to talk of how his books had earned the scorn of the social and cultural establishment, a coded suggestion that they should discuss sex. Larry's relationship with Diane Deriaz was now over and his friend urged or rather promised that he must 'find a woman soon', implying that he would be happy to act as pimp. Embarrassment was avoided when in the lobby of their hotel they met up unexpectedly with Simone Perier, actress, writer and society beauty. Henry knew her well, Larry less so but with the encouragement of the former she and Larry spent the night together. The following evening, she was replaced in Larry's bed by Hoki, with her husband's full knowledge and quiet approval. The morning after that the two men visited the Roman Arena, placed their hands behind their ears with their index fingers pointing forward and pretended to be bulls fighting each other. Their exhibition of macho rivalry was rather absurd given their age and Henry's impotence.

After spending a few days in Paris with Larry, Henry and Hoki returned to the US. Larry remained in the city with his friends Nadia and Alex Blokh, who had a house close to where Larry had lived with Nancy three decades earlier. His memories came with a mixture of nostalgia and sadness, and this might have contributed to his subsequent responses to letters from Hoki.

She bombarded him with urgent enquiries about their next meeting, sometimes speculating on how they might go even further with their erotic adventures but most frequently indicating her obsession with his paunch.

The matter of weight might seem trivial but for Larry it went to the core of his private obsession with vanity and sexuality, something that he separated from his profile as a gnostic modernist. Hoki complained to Miller that Larry was not replying to her letters, and it became apparent that he was uncomfortable both with his image as a Lothario and Hoki's preoccupation with his obesity as what attracted her to him. He had found a woman who was good-looking and sexually adventurous, but he hated the fact she was drawn to him because he was a middle-aged debauchee. Miller, twenty years older than Larry, had retained the build of an athlete. In letters to her mother Sappho referred to her father's 'barrel belly' and several years earlier Claude-Marie's daughter Diana had written to her maternal grandmother of how Larry had become 'mad' with dieting.

> The table is being laid now ... Larry is on a diet. He eats one meal a day (lettuce) and has a glass of [illegible], an American food substitute for the other. I tasted it and it's just like baby food – repulsive. He spends the time between making sure his weight doesn't go down by disposing of remarkable quantities of alcohol.
>
> I can hear him crunching at his lettuce now ... (27 July 1961, Jersey Archive)

Diana was fourteen at the time and clearly had a precocious talent for drollery.

12

Gerry's Hopelessness

In 1968 the problems they faced while filming in Corfu the previous year now seemed a utopia. Gerry had been distressed by Parsons' *Garden of the Gods* (1968) because the film was a documentary, designed to tell the true story of what the family had experienced in Corfu in the 1930s and Gerry's psychological mindset was shaped by his book, a fantasy which he treated as authentic. Any other version would have ruined his image of life as a youngster whose love of wildlife informed all of his adulthood.

But now the mythology might come magically to life because in May he had been approached by the actor Albert Finney and producer Michael Medwin who had formed the company Memorial Enterprises specifically to dramatise Gerry's book. Finney was the driving force of the project. He had made his name eight years earlier as Arthur Seaton, the rough-house working-class focus of *Saturday Night and Sunday Morning*, and had since dedicated himself to producing kitchen sink dramas.

He saw *My Family and Other Animals* as a variation on the anti-establishment works by figures such as Kingsley Amis, John Braine, David Storey and Alan Sillitoe. The latter tended towards satirical comic realism promoting contrariness in preference to the mantras of class, faith and patriotism that had endured since the eighteenth century. The Durrells of Gerry's book came across as classless, a family who had exchanged the obdurate conventions of post-war England for the primitivism of the eastern Mediterranean.

This at least was his impression until he met Gerry in Corfu to discuss the nature of the adaptation. They disagreed on virtually everything, principally Finney's plan to turn the expatriate family of Gerry's book into uneducated working-class reprobates who had rebelled against the misery of Britain between the wars by simply abandoning the place. He wanted to present them as unreasoned anarchists, too indifferent to affiliate to political beliefs and too lazy to be full-blown hedonists. Gerry hated his plan, principally because it ignored his message promoting his own love for animals as an intuitive ideal. Things worsened when Peter Bull, a friend of Larry's since before the war and now a filmmaker, joined the group as a potential producer and fundraiser. He was accompanied soon afterwards by Larry himself and as the brothers talked of their background, first in India and later in England and Corfu, Finney became aware that he had completely misinterpreted the book. Something of Gerry's public school mannerisms had already unsettled him but he now realised that the real Durrells behind the creations of *My Family* were unapologetic embodiments of empire and the Raj. It dawned on him that the family in Corfu had tried to recreate a redoubt of privilege not available to the lower middle classes in England, with a considerably better climate..

Finney had purchased the film rights for £500, the equivalent of around £7,000 today, and Gerry was grateful for one more contribution to the hungry money pit of the zoo. The actor-director returned to London after two months and sold them on to EMI for the same amount. The film never went into production.

What happened next can only be described, at least for Gerry, as an experience in agonising time travel. Following the departure of Finney Larry stayed and the two brothers talked of their recent lives and feelings of hopelessness. Gerry confessed that he and Jacquie now seemed to live in different worlds despite sharing the same bed, usually, and presenting themselves to the television and press as the daring adventurers of the 1950s. Larry was, he said, incapable of coming to terms with the death of Claude-Marie and felt ashamed by using debauchery as a cure for his loss. The fact that both of them had gained roughly three stone in weight since the mid-1960s and had started to begin drinking at around ten o'clock every morning caused them to reflect miserably on their histories.

They had taken on Louisa's habits on Corfu during the 1930s. She, like her sons, seemed unable to cope with a past that had bequeathed her an unwelcome present.

Things were not improved by the arrival of Margo who stayed with her siblings for most of the summer. She was delighted by the prospect of reliving the Durrell heyday of the 1930s. After hunting down Theodore Stephanides, whom her brothers had studiously avoided, she invited the doctor over for several dinners and then asked the frightful Aunt Prue to fly over from England and join them for a family reunion. Margo even suggested that they should invite Leslie and pay his fare; he was still bankrupt and keeping himself as a hotel porter. She seemed to imagine that a miraculous revisitation of the 1930s was possible. Gerry and Larry treated the prospect with horror; the former even admitted that his chimerical representation of Corfu of the 1930s had done more harm than good, at least for the people, the real people, involved – Leslie in particular.

The documentary film *The Garden of the Gods*, based on Gerry's book, was shown at the casino in Corfu town. It was attended by military figures from the so-called Regime of the Colonels which had turned Greece into a totalitarian state similar to Spain under Franco. Like the Spanish dictator they had a sentimental attachment to their country unpolluted by such modern vulgarities as democracy and secularism. With them was the sister of Prince Philip, Duke of Edinburgh, and other members of sometimes displaced European royal families. Prince Michael of Kent, a distant cousin of the British Queen Elizabeth, was also present. Gerry was distressed because, once more, the inspiration for all of his writing – the preservation of rare and threatened species – had been thrown back at him in an utter misinterpretation, this time the quasi-Romantic image of the past as preferable to the present, cultivated by the aristocracy and hard-right conservatives.

For no apparent reason Gerry's recent past appeared to be queuing up to remind him of issues he was trying to disown. David Hughes was now a trusted friend and had been trying to convince him that he could be authorised as his biographer though not in the conventional sense – he did not wish him dead before beginning the book – but rather as a Boswell to his Samuel Johnson. Eventually Gerry agreed but in 1968 he did not wish for a confessor. His various projects – principally the zoo and the seemingly endless procession of books he must write to keep it going – were becoming unendurable. His marriage to Jacquie was a disaster but he did not have the courage to bring it to a close.

Hughes visited Larry in France to ask if he would go further than helping out with the planned project – he had already agreed in principle to do interviews – and consider including himself in a book that covered and contrasted the lives of the two brothers. Larry was even more appalled than his brother had been. The prospect of opening up to Hughes on his distant past let alone what had recently happened to him, principally his attempt to ameliorate the loss of Claude-Marie by having sex with as many women as possible, was horrifying. There were some things he cared not to admit to himself, and he was about to be confronted with a real-life performance of what he'd already decided to keep from Hughes. Margaret McCall arrived at Sommières when Hughes was there, without warning, and explained to Larry that she had forgiven him for his behaviour, much of which he could hardly recall aside from trying to seduce her, and that did not make her an exception to the rule. Hughes himself was married to Mai Zetterling, the beautiful Swedish actress, and she appeared in Sommières several days after he did. Again, she had not been invited and the reason for her visit was unclear, except that she seemed magnetised by Larry while largely ignoring her husband. The events in Corfu that year mostly involved Gerry once more revisiting his past – a dramatised film version of *My Family* which was doomed following the departure of Finney, and the ceremonial showing of *The Garden of the Gods* – yet at the same time Larry was confronted almost daily by people from his own previous experiences. Alan Thomas, whose wife Ella had disappeared around the time of Claude-Marie's death, arrived in exuberant mood with his new spouse Shirley, ten years younger than him and luminously pretty. Larry wrote, 'So many friends have died, so many have come back to life ... I feel ringed with graves and ghosts' (Jersey Archive, letter apparently unposted but addressed to Miller). When Xan Fielding drove unexpectedly to the Sommières house with his wife from their nearby rented villa Larry was astonished and bewildered. Fielding, Special Operations Executive hero, had during the war made a habit of appearing apparently from nowhere and for Larry now seemed to have magicked himself into a noir comedy where Larry's various remembrances, many unwelcome, were intent on tracking him down. During all of this Hughes, and his alluring wife, remained in one of the spare bedrooms and made themselves known to the other guests, unwitting spectres at the feast. Briefly, Larry was tempted by the captivating, and welcoming, presence of Mai Zetterling but eventually advised Hughes that he would be best to talk with Gerry of his ideas. Hughes's volume on his friend did not appear until 1997, two years after Gerry's death, not authorised as a biography but made up of recollections of conversations and meetings.

Larry had difficulties with the influx of old friends but for Gerry the effect of the same was even more striking. In Corfu he, Jacquie, Doreen Evans and Margo borrowed a Mercedes from a military officer who had attended the screening at the casino and tried to find parts of the island that Gerry treasured in his memories of it. First, they went to Afra, the magnificent estate of the Curcumelli family, aristocrats who had held positions of eminence in Venice and other regions of northern Italy and who, like many others of their background, treated Corfu as an exotic extension of their heritage. The house had been built in the eighteenth century but the family traded on the questionable rumour that some of its stones had been taken from Roman ruins. The owner, Marie Curcumelli, was in her seventies and had known the Durrells, albeit only occasionally, during the 1930s.

In the summer of 1968, she greeted Gerry as a hero, mainly because in *My Family and Other Animals* he had charmed and improved upon the past. The Durrells and Doreen were invited to stay at the Curcumelli estate for as long as they wished. She and others from her class had chosen to remain on Corfu because it seemed a closely guarded means of avoiding the modern world. The pink Venetian façade of her mansion, her olive and wine groves, Renaissance-style garden and richly decorated interior were real enough but the only people allowed to enjoy and appreciate them were her personal friends, on this occasion Gerry included. The ordinary people of Corfu entered it only as artisans or servants and whatever they got up to or endured elsewhere was of no concern to her. Gerry had offered the likes of the Curcumellis a conscience-salving cartoon version of this world: ordinary Corfiots in

My Family were charming and innocuous, simple and intuitively wise. Spiro was the naughty peasant, Theodore his sagacious counterpart.

Marie Curcumelli adored the book because it legitimised her view of humanity as made up of different species, varying from divinely ordained authority to subjection and naivety. The former should be kind towards the latter but not pretend that the two groups belonged in the same place. The parallels between this and Gerry's obsession with protecting threatened species is striking. He loved animals but despite the tactile affection for the likes of Chumley the chimp their 'friendship' was an extreme case of anthropomorphism as theatre. Treating creatures as a junior, respected form of humanity is not too far from regarding supposedly inferior humans as honourable animals, as did aristocrats such as the Curcumellis.

Sir Giles Guthrie, Baronet, belonged to the same class, albeit its Anglo-Saxon version. He learned to fly in his privately owned Tiger Moth in 1932, aged sixteen and as a pupil at Eton. He exchanged the plane for a more sophisticated Percival Vega Gull during his first year at Magdalene College, Cambridge, in 1934, and went on to serve in the Fleet Air Arm during the Second World War. Like many of his class in the early twentieth century he saw aircraft as the modern equivalent of horses ridden for sport and warfare by his predecessors the knights cavaliers.

When he first met Gerry, in early 1968, he had just retired as Managing Director of BOAC, Britain's only international airline. He had sold his home-counties house and bought a manor close to and even more grand than Les Augrès and soon after his arrival became a financial sponsor for the zoo.

Guthrie contacted Gerry in midsummer stating that he and his wife Lady Rhona had booked a flight from London to Corfu. They wanted to purchase a small but well-furnished property to use when winters in Jersey offered large helpings of wind and rain. His inspiration, he added, was Gerry's *My Family* but he offered this coda with some irony. He knew that the book was fantasy, but Guthrie like Gerry had little time for the difference between illusion and actuality. The latter was the predicament of ordinary folks. Sir Giles was advised by Gerry to visit the three Mannisse brothers (addresses withheld until the Guthrie's arrival) who lived in a remote but extraordinarily beautiful villa and were gifted with magical powers. Anything you wished they, with a nod, from Gerry, could provide: from a basket of lilies, fruits and asparagus to a pardon for any crime the Guthries might care to commit on the island, murder included. Marie Aspioti was very real – a poetry-magazine publisher and journalist who lived in a mansion slightly more modest than the Curcumellis' – but in his letter to Guthrie Gerry turned her into the 'White Queen' alluded to in his writings as someone too superb to be ordinarily human. There was, he advised him, a bandit called Christos – pure invention but a fictional cousin of Leslie's equally unreal friend of *My Family*. Spiro's son – another perversion of the truth because he hardly knew the real son Lillis – could magically repair anything from broken-down cars to leaky plumbing, and the best cook on the island was Vassili, with 'a face like a camel', living at an unspecified address. Closing, he provided Guthrie with an 'Admiralty Chart' from the days of the British occupation, marked it with places of outstanding beauty and those best to avoid, and advised that Lady Rhona should row them around the island in a boat that he could arrange to hire as a means of introducing them to its 'grandeur' (Gerry to Sir Giles Guthrie, Jersey Archive, 1968, otherwise undated).

The Guthries assumed that his letter was a joke, a self-caricature of the daydream in which Gerry had starred in 1956. But sadly, for those with him at the time, it was evident that he had wandered unwittingly across the boundary between the actual and the fantastic.

While Gerry, Jacquie and Doreen were driving around the island they came upon Palaiokastritsa. It was one of the most remote and beautiful parts of the coast, a place he had known as a child and visited later when he returned to what he saw as his spiritual home. There had been an ancient, partly ruined monastery, a few fisherman's cottages, a tiny inn and a white sand beach. Now, however, concrete mixers and cranes were busily constructing two modern hotels. Jacquie in her notes for *Beasts in My Bed* records that Gerry could not endure the spectacle. He returned to the car, lay in the back seat and wept unconsolably. '[He] realises it will never be what it was. That's why I loathe Corfu – for what it does to him now' (Jersey Archive, undated).

In truth, Palaiokastritsa and other parts of the island were dealing as fastidiously as possible with the indigenous topography of architecture and landscape in response to the increasing desire for tourist accommodation, at least in comparison with the brutal transformations of the southern Spanish coast. Nonetheless Gerry wrote to the Greek Prime Minister, the strongman officer Georgios Papadopoulos, announcing himself as a figure with a vested interest in the culture of the nation. He called what was happening in Corfu a 'rape' of the island and demanded that the Athens government must 'give more power to the people on the spot, who are as worried as I am at the all too rapid and tasteless development of the island' (Jersey Archive, copy of original letter, dispatched 1968, otherwise undated).

This confirmed that Gerry existed in a parallel world. The leaders of the military regime which ran Greece until 1974 were anti-communist authoritarians though not as oppressive as the governments close by in Soviet-controlled Middle Europe. The Greek colonels were economic pragmatists who realised that the country would never compete with northern Europe in terms of industrial productivity and could barely hope to break even in terms of the export of exotic foodstuffs and wine. Tourism was the only way to rescue the economy as a whole and at a more local level to provide ordinary people with a regular income. The colonels recognised that the Greek proletariat were largely rural peasants who might be attracted to socialism as preferable to the annual struggle to feed themselves from the land. Hence, they sponsored the building of more airports and the construction of hotels such as those Gerry had witnessed: ordinary Corfiots would have regular jobs. Gerry received no reply to his letter.

Everyone who encountered Gerry during the summer of 1968 later reported that he appeared to be undergoing a nervous breakdown. He socialised but would only speak of his obsessive concern with the apparent vandalism of the island – as he once put it, a 'Greek version of Brighton'. Despite his letter to the Athens government being ignored he spent hours every evening composing similar entreaties to persons in authority, begging them to halt what amounted to the transformation of the island which the majority of its population welcomed. When he was not appealing to those closest to him or writing to others he wept incessantly and on average drank a bottle of whisky a day.

He and Jacquie returned to Jersey following a brief stopover in Basel Zoo where the director Ernst Lang found it difficult to discuss with Gerry the practicalities of zookeeping, the supposed reason for the visit.

In Jersey Jacquie insisted that Gerry must visit Dr Hunter, the local GP. He was at first reluctant but then opened up to her.

> And at last, he told me what was wrong with him. He suffered these terribly black moods, he felt suicidal. I said, 'Why on earth didn't you tell me? I had no idea it had got to this pitch.' I personally thought that what he needed was a total break from the Zoo for perhaps two years ... The doctor, when I told him, was all for leaving it until ... I said, 'If you wait that long, mate, he'll probably hang himself.' (Hughes, pp139–40)

Hunter referred Gerry to the private hospital The Priory in London, run by a psychiatrist called Dr Flood who seemed to believe that all forms of mental disorder were the result of various kinds of excess, addiction or overindulgence. Jacquie reported their opening conversation to Botting (p349) as a kind of noir comedy. 'He's just an alcoholic,' was Flood's first observation, to which she replied that she was fully aware that he drank too much, like a large number of others they knew. And that he, like the rest, his brother included, were far more depressed without strong drink than with it.

Flood now seemed confused and shifted from assertions to questions. 'Well, he's been having affairs, I suppose?' No, she replied, he has not. 'Well, then you've been having an affair.' Wrong again, she said, and waited for his next choice from what appeared to be the *Reader's Digest* guide to mental imbalance. But he seemed to have exhausted his options.

Jacquie said that her husband had gone into gradual but inexorable decline since the death of his mother, but Flood showed no interest in this. He spoke to Gerry only twice afterwards, prescribed regular doses of tranquilisers and confined him to his own room. If the drugs were intended to 'dry out' Gerry as a substitute to whisky or an anxiety depressant it seems odd that Flood allowed daily deliveries to his room of generous packages of bottled ale and various types of spirits. After three weeks Jacquie removed her doped-up husband from The Priory and flew with him back to Jersey. He spent almost twelve months taking a version of the drugs prescribed by Flood and his state of mind is evident from a letter he sent to Alan Thomas in early February 1969 (Jersey Archive, otherwise undated). He reported that for most of the time he wandered around 'in a state of euphoria', but from the rest of his report his notion of 'euphoria' was completely different from the standard definition. He was stupefied certainly but very unhappy with what the medication had done to him. 'I sometimes wake at night to find myself standing in the middle of the bedroom and wonder what the hell I am there for.'

Opinions differ on the cause of his breakdown. Jacquie, ever the pragmatist, put it down to a combination of overwork, stress and his inability to cope with his mother's death. Flood went for a combination of alcoholism and adultery on his or Jacquie's part, and Margo settled for a failed love story. She had never really got on with Jacquie and decided that Ann Peters, her brother's occasional secretary since the early 1960s, was besotted with him and he, secretly, with her. 'He'd have done better to have married her,' she told Botting (p348). The most astute comment came from Larry. Jacquie wrote to him explaining that for the time being his brother might have problems replying to letters given that only the combination of drugs and whisky were keeping at bay his threats to commit suicide. He replied that he understood and that he too was experiencing bouts of depression and closed with a brief, enigmatic note: 'Corfu, I expect' (Jersey Archive, 1969, otherwise undated).

We can never be absolutely certain of what he meant but there is a probable interpretation. Both men had treated the island during the 1930s as paradise, though for different reasons. The imminent outbreak of the Second World War had sent them to other places, geographically and emotionally, but they had brought with them the things that had delighted them on Corfu and which would configure their temperaments thereafter. For Larry it was his fiction, an escape from the less satisfactory features of his life. There, Gerry grew to love animals more than he did human beings and in 1968 he found that the latter had apparently savaged the Edenic bliss of his childhood. Stress, overwork and writing to pour more and more money into the upkeep of Jersey Zoo picked away at his sense of stability but the summer of 1968 in the island that meant everything to him pitched him over the edge.

Obviously, Jacquie did not take seriously Larry's comment as a warning against the island's resonances because she replied to him on 18 March 1969, reporting that Gerry seemed to be improving and announced that in April she and Saranne Calthorpe, one of the Trust's most hardworking fundraisers, would accompany him on a three-month recuperative journey away from Jersey: to Corfu.

On their return in late July Gerry seemed not to have improved and Jacquie suggested that they should revisit Australia, where he had been captivated by mammals and birds seemingly unique to the place. Jacquie, intelligent and witty as she was, seemed struck by a form of emotional short-sightedness. Along with Saranne she also asked Ann Peters to accompany them, first to London where they hosted a dinner at Bertorelli's and then to Gothenburg to board a cargo ship for Sydney.

Margo was correct about Ann Peters' obsession with her brother but it was unrequited. She was unaware that something more impassioned was taking place between Saranne and Gerry. Saranne was good-looking, with shoulder-length chocolate-brown hair. Also, she embodied various aspects of the Durrell mythology. She had been born in Dublin into a minor Ascendency family, which meant that Larry's delusion of their family as Irish aristocrats, shared by Gerry, might now come close to predestination. Dividing her time between working as an air hostess for Mercury Airlines and modelling for high-class magazines she had attracted the attention of one of the pilots who proposed to her on their first date. The pilot's full name and title was Peter Gough Calthorpe, 10th Baron Calthorpe. The estate of the family included manor houses and large amounts of land in Norfolk and Warwickshire. Saranne's inclination to spend a good deal of her time at Jersey Zoo and to accompany Gerry on the visit to Australia reflected the state of her marriage. In 1971, a year after they returned from the southern hemisphere, the divorce was finalised.

During Christmas 1969 and New Year 1970 the trio were in North Queensland, one of the hottest locations in the Australian high summer, Britain's midwinter. Gerry was struck by how the ordinary people of

Queensland were devoted to preserving the parts of their environment and native species therein now threatened by urban and industrial developments that seemed likely to turn the wild north coast into a version of southern cities such as Sydney, Adelaide and Melbourne. They told him that each time they put their case to the federal government in Canberra they were silenced by a collective resolution that Australia must shed its junior colonial status and become a major player among the emerging economies of the Pacific. Urbanisation and a production economy were the only way forward.

Gerry hoped that his own reputation as a preservationist would have some effect when he drafted and dispatched complaints to the Australian Prime Minister, John Gorton. The reply was polite and facile, but Gerry felt energised, able to exchange his recent self-destructive phase for his traditional role as zoological partisan.

On Christmas Day Gerry, Jacquie, Ann and Saranne hired a boat and set off for one of the coral islands on the Great Barrier Reef. They took with them a traditional British lunch/dinner of turkey, roast potatoes, stuffing and sprouts, along with several bottles of champagne in buckets of ice.

Before the meal they planned to go scuba diving. Ann and Saranne had chosen devastatingly skimpy costumes to wear under their breathing apparatuses but as Jacquie later observed, 'he [Gerry] had other things on his mind' (Jersey Archive, undated). These 'things' were the astoundingly beautiful community of plants and fish that turned the shallow seabed 'more colourful than a Matisse … more intricate than the Bayeux tapestries, structurally much more beautiful than the Acropolis' (Jersey Archive, 1969–70, otherwise undated).

The day was bizarre. Three women who worshipped Gerry had been made inconspicuous by the magnificence of the seabed and its inhabitants. Jacquie was fully aware that her two female companions had designs on her husband but with droll relief accepted that something of the Gerry of old had returned: the scenery and its non-human lifeforms concerned him far more than sex.

They returned to Jersey in May 1970 and on his first visit to London Gerry, newly enthused, lunched with his publisher and suggested a new book, based on his visit to the southern hemisphere: 'Bonking Round Oz with 'Three Sheilas'. The title was invented, with rough irony, by Jacquie and as she'd observed he'd 'had other things on his mind'.

Over the next year Gerry took on the mood and habits of an unfocused itinerant. For more than six months he spent his time both at the Mazet, a distance from Larry's house, or at various resorts on the French Mediterranean coast. After a week at one of the last he pitched up at Sommières, prompting Larry to report to Miller that 'My brother turned up with an entourage of females. He travels with a permanent seraglio like a Turkish potentate' (4 October 1970). Larry's portrait of Gerry was shot through with genial envy. Saranne Calthorpe was now making it clear that she was available to him, sitting close to him at dinners, offering to accompany him to bed if he was feeling exhausted by entertaining and hosting his own and Larry's guests, dancing closely with him if music was played. Jacquie never commented explicitly on what happened but Anne Valentine, a young American assistant to Gerry, later informed Hughes that quite often Gerry and Jacquie slept in different rooms while the one supposedly used by Saranne was empty. After Australia Ann Peters knew that she had been displaced by Saranne, did not visit France at all and in Jersey moved politely into the background.

Between the first lengthy period in France and May 1971 Gerry, Jacquie and Saranne paid only brief, expedient visits to the zoo, the most important of these being exchanges on the purchase of the manor, enclosures and grounds as the sole possessions of the Trust. Major Fraser, still the owner, said that he would accept £120,000, over £1.5m today – in terms of general purchasing power. Add to that the recent inflation in property prices, especially on the Channel Islands, and £4m is more accurate. A public appeal brought in £25,000, and Gerry committed the same amount from recent royalty income and a handsome advance on his new book of short stories, *Fillets of Plaice*. Jersey States Assembly voted unanimously to offer Gerry a £60,000 loan at 1 per cent interest to secure the purchase. They thought it a secure investment in the island's prosperity as a magnet not just for British tourists but on the international market, especially wealthy visitors committed to animal conservation. The remaining £10,000 came from individual donations by islanders who had already put money into the project and wanted to see Les Augrès, now with a global reputation as an animal sanctuary and study centre, as synonymous with a transformed image of the island, previously best known for its occupation by the Nazis and as a tax haven.

The purchase itself went through without much ceremony. Gerry left the details to Sir Giles Guthrie, Financial Advisor to the Trust, while he, with Saranne and Jacquie, returned to southeast France to spend as long as he could with Larry. Gerry wanted to buy the Mazet but though it was cheap in comparison with ordinary British properties – roughly £4,000 – Gerry had used up all of his resources on the purchase of Les Augrès. Larry wanted his brother to have it but lowering the price even further would have left him severely out of pocket given the money he'd spent making it habitable. Instead they agreed to continue the lease agreement.

Gerry was committed to the development of the Trust yet at the same time the longer he spent in Jersey the more he felt that the persistent queue of responsibilities and the constant edge-of-the-cliff problems with finance would drive him once more towards a nervous breakdown. He wanted the Mazet as his ever-available escape route. The telephone there was now disconnected and while Larry would receive messages for him there was no instrument on a desk or by his bedside that would demand his immediate response.

The brothers were drawn to each other for several reasons. The age difference that had distanced them for much of their early lives had now been all but eradicated, mostly because of their similar attachment to dissolute lifestyles. Neither took any exercise and though they sometimes tortured themselves with dietary regimes that lasted less than a month they made up for it by returning to rich, fatty food with a vengeance. And they drank, often wine and then spirits from breakfast onwards, so while Larry was twelve years older than Gerry an accumulation of corpulence made them look like twins. Something else bound them together: a perverse notion of being with two women simultaneously. Larry's brief sexual relationships following Claude-Marie's death had been numerous but he informed his brother that he was performing a kind of sexual ghastly dance of death, pretending that these women were versions of the one he had lost: 'they were Claude-Marie resurrected, he said, back in his bed' (Jersey Archive, undated). The most recent was Fiddle Viracola, a beautiful Italian-American actress, twenty-six years younger than him; and not too much older than his daughter Penelope. The equivalent for

277

Gerry was Saranne. He insinuates in the Jersey Archive notes that they were having a sexual relationship but it involved for him an element of temporary release. He regarded Jacquie as a woman from whom he would never willingly separate: 'She [Jacquie] is me, and always will be, though I wish we were different people' (Jersey Archive, undated). His relationship with Saranne was the realisation of male fantasy: erotic, surreptitious and unconditional. In 1971 Saranne had been appointed as chief fundraiser for the Zoo at a committee meeting of all involved with the Trust. Gerry announced that she deserved the post because she was 'the sexiest bitch on the island' and that her contract would include a codicil that she must remain 'single' while she held the position. Her relationship with Calthorpe had been precarious for some time, and at the time of appointment a divorce decree nisi was in place given that they hardly ever met; they were still married but only on paper. In late summer 1971 Saranne announced to Gerry that her divorce had been finalised and that she now met the full conditions of her contract. She added, whimsically, that her status might change again before too long. Tony Lort-Phillips was a native of Jersey, from a military family, minor gentry, who owned an impressive eighteenth-century manor just outside Saint-Aubin. She had, she disclosed, been seeing him discreetly on the occasions that she, Gerry and Jacquie had returned to the Zoo from their now regular visits to France. Lort-Phillips had worked for the Trust irregularly around the time that Saranne had been taken on by Gerry and the triangular relationship between the latter, Jacquie and her – which had been the cause of gossip among those in France and on Jersey, most of whom thought it unwholesome – was now disclosed as a quartet.

Gerry exploded with rage and the account of what he said given to Botting by Jacquie is by parts irrational and hilarious. 'From the very outset of this affair,' he bellowed, not making it clear if he meant the 'affair' with Lort-Phillips, himself or her arrangement with the Trust, 'you have behaved with a crass stupidity which I had hoped was only a temporary manifestation due to your private life ... As you say, happiness tends to make one incoherent – so does imbecility. I would be glad if you send your letter of resignation direct to Lord Jersey' (Botting, p367).

She did so and married Lort-Phillips a month later. The marriage lasted only two years, after which she remained on Jersey living on what was left of the settlements from her two divorces while seemingly attempting to drink herself to death. She wrote off two cars by driving them into the granite walls on the island's narrow country roads. Those who'd known her when she'd worked at the Trust put it to Gerry that a job of some sort might help her turn over a new leaf. He refused even to consider it and she died prematurely from alcohol-related illnesses in a St Helier nursing home. The episode further reinforced Gerry's own admissions that he felt more sympathetic towards suffering animals than to their human counterparts.

From midsummer 1971 to early 1973 the Trust became the hub for factional exchanges between parties who thought they knew the best direction for it.

In August 1971 Lord Jersey announced to all with senior managerial and financial interest in the institution that he was about to call a meeting to discuss policies which would both reform the governance of the zoo and ensure that the Trust maintained financial viability and a global reputation as a centre of excellence in conservation. In September he issued what amounted to an agenda for discussion or more accurately a manifesto of his own which left few options for debate or opposition.

Gerry was too busy with projects collateral to the zoo itself to pay much attention to Lord Jersey's demand for reorganisation. His collection of short fiction *Fillets of Plaice* was finding sympathetic reviewers and moving towards the top of the bestseller list. The chronology of the stories is in truth a dramatised autobiography opening with Corfu and taking the reader to England in the 1940s. It is not as farcical as *My Family* but he reserves a doughty lightness of touch for episodes that are shameless borrowings from his own experiences, and the parallels between his and Larry's early novels are difficult to ignore. Except that Gerry seems to be implying that while he can rival his brother as a fiction writer his own imprint of reader-friendly unshowiness discloses their differences too.

During the same period the film director Christopher Miles announced to Gerry that he had found a sufficient number of financial backers to hire front-line stars for a cinema adaptation of *My Family*, which would be shot on Corfu. For Mother he had contacted Maggie Smith, Joan Greenwood, Audrey Hepburn and even Ingrid Bergman.

Michael York was interested in playing Larry. No child star had as yet been found for the role of Gerry but as author he would be brought in as 'special advisor'. Filming was set to begin in early summer 1972 and Gerry was overjoyed. Once more he could revisit the location and the story which had informed virtually all aspects of his adult life. By the early New Year the TUC announced that anyone who worked on the project, actors included, would be branded as blacklegs and prevented from taking up further work in the movies or the theatre. All British unions were united in a boycott of anything which could be treated as cooperation with a country they classified as a military dictatorship. Interestingly, the states within the Soviet bloc were excused this sanction. The film came to nothing.

Appalled, Gerry distracted himself by trying to complete the long-delayed *Catch Me a Colobus*, important to him because while it has no chronological or narrative backbone it involved accounts of his travels and experiences with wildlife which were far from random. He used each to illustrate the essential principles regarding the environment and wildlife. Shortly afterwards he became, almost simultaneously, a Fellow of the Royal Society of Literature, a recognition of the esteem in which he was held by the most influential figures in the British literary establishment, and a Fellow of the Institute of Biology. Only C. P. Snow had attained equal recognition as an eminent figure in the arts and sciences.

At a meeting of Trustees Lord Jersey asserted that the zoo centred on Gerald Durrell, 'the author, and his books, and the TV personality and his films and appearances, and the zoo is linked to him in the public eye and in the minds of Trust members ... [and] we must do nothing to break the impression that this is Gerry Durrell's private zoo, and that the animals are all his pets' (Jersey Archive, September 1971). Gerry was by equal degrees flattered and horrified. Despite his frequent claims that writing, television and other platforms to fame were but necessary evils, a means of pulling the Trust back from its routine drifts towards financial disaster, he had begun to crave his status as a celebrity. But while Lord Jersey praised the Trust as 'a very important specialist zoo' he also made it clear that Gerry's role in it was now that of ceremonial head, the equivalent of constitutional monarch or a university Chancellor; decorative rather than executive.

The meeting that Lord Jersey hoped would follow his memorandum mutated into a long-term series of exchanges between interested parties. On 1 May 1972, for example, the Trust hosted the First World Conference on Breeding Endangered Species in Captivity. More than three hundred conservationists, mainly from western Europe and North America, gathered to address questions on the morality and pragmatics of capturing animals in the hope that monitored breeding would assist in the preservation of their often endangered counterparts in the wild. Sir Peter Scott gave the opening Plenary Lecture followed by Gerry. The latter made a measured, impressive case that the 'captive breeding of an endangered species should [not] take the place of conservation of that species in its natural habitat'. Rather, he contended, the immense amount of scientific expertise at hand, in the audience he was addressing, should concentrate on gathering data which disclosed levels of danger of extinction and devise methodologies which would determine if or how 'captive breeding' was the only and final resort. Persistently, he stressed that such a 'worthwhile undertaking' was the exclusive objective of 'this Trust'. His rationale was convincing but at the same time it was evident that his message contained a subtext. Lord Jersey was being informed that Gerry was still the controlling presence of the Trust, not merely its figurehead.

Nonetheless his presentation of himself as pure scientist and conservationist had already been undermined. Before the conference began the Gorilla Breeding Complex was opened by David Niven, one of the most glamorous of the male film stars of the post-war period. Reporters and photographers from national newspapers worldwide flocked to the island and Niven came up with his usual combination of the suave gentleman and something more salacious. He declared its two most prominent apes, Nandi and Jambo, officially 'married' and immediately afterwards they began to have sex. 'Wherever I go this sort of thing happens,' Niven declared. The press corps were overjoyed and Gerry sat with his head in his hands.

At the end of May another dignitary arrived to be shown around the zoo by Gerry and Jacquie. Princess Anne's visit to Jersey was supposed to be one of the routine excursions to less significant parts of the realm by junior members of the royal family: among her official duties was a trip to the island's new sewage works. In 1971 she had become BBC

Sports Personality of the Year for her successes in equestrian events and apart from her dedication to horses she, like her elder brother Charles, professed a commitment to animal preservation. A visit to the Trust was not on her official schedule but she insisted that transport and security must be arranged for a full day there. Frisky, an exuberant multicoloured mandrill from mid-Africa, approached the bars of his cage, turned and made a proud display of his genitals and gaping anus to Gerry, Jacquie and Her Royal Highness. Gerry asked Princess Anne if she would not 'love to have a behind like that?' 'No,' she answered, 'I don't think I would,' but despite his seemingly inappropriate suggestion the faint ghost of a smile crossed her face. Two weeks later she agreed enthusiastically to become Patron of the Trust.

In September and October Lord Jersey and Sir Giles Guthrie referred the Trustees to the former's recommendations of a year earlier: that Gerry should remain as nominal head while professional accountants and managers should be brought in to restructure the organisation and financial state of the Trust. They argued, brutally but undeniably, that Gerry spent more than two thirds of each year away from Jersey, returning mainly to appear at events which attracted media coverage, such as the recent visits by David Niven and Princess Anne. Gerry replied that both men were 'mendacious' and 'treacherous' in their attempts to 'disenfranchise' him as the 'originator' and 'true inspiration' for the zoo. Eventually by 1973 a compromise was agreed with Gerry attaining the rank of Director General while most practical duties were discharged by committees established by Sir Giles and Lord Jersey. Gerry made do with a title that sounded supervisory but was in truth ceremonial.

Sir Giles and Lord Jersey were correct in their assertion that Gerry felt more content travelling or spending time in the Mazet than he did on Jersey, except on those occasions when he was welcoming famous guests. In 1974, for example, Niven arranged a reception by Princess Grace of Monaco for Gerry and Jacquie in the Palace of the Principality, and a month later Princess Grace visited the zoo. Jersey was swamped with journalists and film crew still hungry for reports on the activities of the princess, previously Grace Kelly the most beautiful actress in Hollywood. Gerry lapped it up, much as he did equally well-publicised visits by James Stewart and Katharine Hepburn in 1975.

Between August and late November 1973 Jacquie joined him during his tours of the United States. He spoke at several meetings of environmental activists and scientists, most convened in his honour, and felt flattered and terrified. In Chicago University he faced an audience of two thousand, far more than could be raised for politicians of the time or cultural and social activists such as Gore Vidal or Norman Mailer. He drank almost half a bottle of Scotch before feeling brave enough to appear on stage. Similarly colossal gatherings faced him in San Francisco and Los Angeles and he required equal amounts of strong spirits to be able take them on. Unsteady as he was, his speeches were greeted with a blend of laughter and affection. America unsettled him but so did the prospect of returning to Jersey where he would find himself struggling to establish what status he actually held. He spent much of 1974 treading water. The zoo was now made up of almost eight hundred animals but while he welcomed this expansion as proof that he would be able to continue to bring in, breed and then release vast numbers of threatened species, the enormity of the place depressed him. When the zoo was first opened, he knew most of his creature guests by name, had indeed named them himself when he welcomed them in and brought them to Jersey as security for the survival of their species. Now, aside from the apes who had sex in front of David Niven and those who'd made other conspicuous displays for the press, he felt they were strangers.

Gerry and Jacquie's divorce did not reach court until spring 1979. The grounds were 'irreconcilable breakdown' and the events of the previous five years provided ample evidence for this but at the same time it is difficult to ascertain the exact dates of their separation, let alone its ultimate cause. In spring 1975 Gerry, Jacquie, David Hughes, the Trust secretary Judy Mackrell and another administrative employee at the zoo, Sue Bateman, went to France. Larry had decided against selling the Mazet to his brother, an arrangement informally agreed on in the lease but left ambiguous. Larry was having tax problems with money owed on advances and royalties for books going back a decade and while a cash amount from Gerry would have been welcome, he knew that he would make more by putting the property on the open market. Languedoc was by the mid-1970s becoming an attractive alternative to the expensive Côte d'Azur and Provence regions for expatriates. As if to demonstrate to Larry that he could have come up with the asking price Gerry bought a house in Le Tignet in the Alpes-Maritimes, further inland from Grasse, where wealthy celebrities and business people outnumbered the indigenous Provençal population.

During the period when Gerry and his four companions, Jacquie included, worked hard in redistributing the furniture and pictures from the Mazet in the new property, 'La Chèvre Blanche', there was a meltdown in friendships and relationships, caused, according to those prepared to talk of it later, by Gerry's state of mind: simultaneously morose, vindictive and self-destructive. During the six months before leaving for France he had, on doctor's orders, been off spirits, though maintaining a regular intake of wine. Hughes told Botting that unless Gerry and Jacquie were asleep, in different rooms, the 'verbal violence' between them was incessant. Hughes had broken up with his wife Mai Zetterling less than a year earlier and witnessing the death rattle of a relationship that had lasted a quarter of a century unsettled him. Following Gerry's example, he took refuge in strong drink and then attempted to seduce Sue Bateman. Judy Mackrell felt herself cast as a bit-player in a later-twentieth-century Jacobean drama and tried to spend as much time as possible in the garden or the nearby village. Gerry, seeing himself bizarrely as the conscience of the group, ordered Hughes to leave immediately. He took an expensive flight back to London from Marseille at his own expense and never again laid eyes on Jacquie. Judy Mackrell put it to Gerry as politely as possible that while she loved the zoo it would be impossible for her to stay in post if the environment in France was maintained after their return to Jersey. 'Fine,' he replied. 'You're sacked!'

Jacquie told Botting that when they returned to Jersey during the summer 'I told him that I could no longer tolerate his behaviour ... and proposed to go away on my own,' which sounds like a declaration of her immediate or at least imminent departure, but by Christmas she was still in the manor. She was, however, planning a journey of her own to Australia to do research into the roles played by women in the conservation movement there. She was declaring her independence without severing her links with the establishment she had played a major role in establishing. She wanted to do a book on women who had, like herself, committed themselves to zoology and conservation but whose profiles were obscured by better-known male environmentalists. Curtis Brown had already expressed an interest. Gerry saw it as a deliberate rebuke to his eminence. He could not, of course, prevent her from going. She had legitimate access to the Trust's travel budget. But once she left, he entered a state of rage.

He left Jersey before she returned, despairing of how he would respond to her account of the project, and decamped to a hotel in Bournemouth for no other reason that, aside from Corfu, the place resonated with memories of his life before Jacquie. In March he flew to Mauritius to investigate reports that the island's forest and wildlife were being subjected to a policy of mass destruction. Since independence from the UK in 1968 the key features of the economy, small farms and sugar plantations, had gone into serious decline and various governments had attempted to introduce something resembling production industries and resorts that might attract tourists from Europe and the Americas. The result was mass deforestation and the extinction of several rare species of birds and mammals. His attempt to distract himself from the state of his marriage depressed him even further. He returned to Jersey in May to find that all of Jacquie's clothes and private possessions had been removed. She had, according to Trust employees, packed all of them into their co-owned Mercedes and taken the ferry for England, though no one seemed to recall exactly when she had left. She had spoken to none of the staff, many of whom were close friends, and not left a note for Gerry.

In June he left again for Bournemouth where a week later Jacquie joined him briefly for their final meeting, lasting only a few hours. She recalled for Botting that he seemed 'well balanced', at least in comparison with the mood swings between drunken rage and depression of the previous year. He apologised for his recent behaviour, pledged to introduce her to previously unexplored regions during his forthcoming journey to Russia, or anywhere else if she preferred, and repeated his earlier promise that if she chose to leave, he would divide everything equally between them, including the contents of the various bank accounts relating to the Trust and the properties they owned and leased in Jersey and France. She would, he concluded, have forty-eight hours to make up her mind. She already had, but one aspect of his promise of equanimity prompted her to act quickly. She drove immediately to a solicitor in London whom she had already informed of the state of things and explained that she did not trust her husband's promise to split everything fifty-fifty if the marriage ended. There was nothing to confirm this on paper and she needed advice on how she could make a claim to what she felt was due to her. Her lawyer told her that it would involve a lengthy court case. She was likely to win a fair amount, given that Gerry could not prove she was primarily responsible for the breakdown of the marriage. This was much as she expected, as was Gerry's reaction when she telephoned him and stated that she was certainly not coming back. He shed his 'balanced' persona and 'absolutely exploded', promising that he would be 'as bloody and obstructive as he could' (Botting, p412).

Four years later the court determined that she must be granted a £7,000 per annum index-linked maintenance award, roughly £33,000 today. Since inflation in 1979 was in double figures Gerry seemed to face considerable losses. Jacquie recalled that the case, resembling that of Dickens's *Jarndyce v Jarndyce*, went on for so long because Gerry was from the beginning determined 'not to give me anything' (*Ibid.*, p413). As a condition of his offering her the maintenance fund he insisted that she must agree to have her name excised from the annals of the Trust. He went further and demanded that the books he'd written about their experiences and excursions should be recalled and revised with any reference to Jacquie excluded from the texts. His publishers told him that legally and financially this would be impossible, but for the next two years he ordered his staff to go through the accounts and reports on the zoo and the Trust and with meticulous attention to detail cross out or by any other means obliterate reference to Jacquie. He was confident that his institution would be recognised as an early point of reference in the cause of animal conservation. He expected it to be written about and he wanted Jacquie to disappear from any chronicle of its development, despite the fact that without her he would never have created the zoo on Jersey.

She said later, 'I willingly sacrificed all I ever held dear – family, career and health – for twenty-eight of the cream years of my life, in return for which I got hurtful abuse and financial neglect. I was deprived of my rightful place in the annals of the zoo and Trust and treated as if I had never existed' (*Ibid.*, p414).

13

Ghislaine, Among Others

While working on *Nunquam* (1970), the second part of *The Revolt of Aphrodite*, following *Tunc* (1968), Larry experimented with poetry drafts that can only be described as morbidly pornographic. The descriptions of sex are informed by equally detailed accounts of sadism and death and he seemed unable to dissociate lust from decay and the termination of life. Typically:

> From a winter of vampires, he selects one,
> Takes her to a dark house, undresses her:
> …
> A transaction where the words themselves
> Begin to bleed … ('A Winter of Vampires', *Collected Poems*, 1980, p306)

In the novel Iolanthe dies and is revived by computer technology, which was prescient given that at the close of the 1960s computer science was still very primitive. In an abandoned draft, however, he considered a more crude revival of her corpse, with the techniques of embalming used not only to improve her appearance but as a means of reinvigorating her internal organs. Larry asked Nadia Blokh, based in Geneva, to look into how chemicals might create more than the appearance of mortal existence, but rather restore life itself. She assumed that he was in an extended stage of deranged grief at the loss of Claude-Marie and sent him an account of how the various techniques and materials of embalming worked – principally how blood was replaced by chemicals – and pointed out as diplomatically as possible that death was irreversible. In the poems that made up *The Red Limbo Lingo*, published as an epilogue to *The Revolt of Aphrodite* but written at the same time as his composition of the novels, blood, crucifixion and most insistently vampirism compete for prominence as themes. The poems themselves are too densely incoherent to be summarised – they resemble the most impenetrable verse of Ezra Pound – but one is left with the impression that vampirism horrifies and captivates him. In the first instance he seems to see it as a transparent, pagan version of the blood rituals of Christianity while at the same time it comes across as a feral relative of male lust: an untamed, irrational desire for the body and its constituent portions.

Iolanthe's resurrection was clearly tied into Larry's difficulty in accepting that Claude-Marie would never ever return, but there was a more psychologically macabre aspect of it too. Almost immediately after Claude-Marie's death he set out on a rampant pursuit of virtually every woman who was flattered by his eminence. This might be seen as a form of emotional denial: displacing his grief by turning himself into an emotionless sexual animal. By 1970 he had started to behave more like the figure of the vampire poem, selecting, undressing and possessing women in a manner that shifted between masochism and diabolism.

On 27 February 1970, Larry's fifty-eighth birthday, he received a letter from Miller telling him that he and Hoki had separated. He replied, expressing his regrets, but privately he was relieved. He knew that a visit to America was likely later that year, following the publication of *Nunquam*, and he dreaded a return to the arrangement of cuckolding his friend, with Miller's approval. The novel was launched by Faber in London at the beginning of March. Larry had flown there from Marseille to do radio and newspaper interviews. As usual the reviewers seemed to have read two different books; the acolytes of experiment praised it, while champions of post-war level-headedness saw the novel as another specimen of elitist self-indulgence. By this time Larry was used to this and rather enjoyed polarising opinion.

On 17 March he flew to New York for more public relations work. Miller had arranged for his publisher to book him into the Algonquin

Hotel, an establishment famed since the 1920s for its magnetic attraction for writers, actors and artists. The day after his arrival he was summoned to the reception to meet his guide for the next few weeks of book signings, interviews, dinner parties and drink-fuelled jazz concerts. As stated Fiddle Viracola was a beautiful film actress and singer, aged thirty-three. Miller knew her and had arranged her assignment: 'pimp' he wrote in the margin of an unpublished letter to Larry later that year. Fiddle and Larry slept together the night they met. Their relationship, such as it was, lasted around a year. She visited Sommières several times and in April she wrote to Miller to report that her first week in Larry's house was 'a perfect experience'. Six months later, in September 1970, he drove her around the various parts of France that enraptured him the most, mainly because of memories of his time with Claude-Marie. On 14 September, in Paris, he declared that he wanted to marry her but he was too old. There is no record of her reply but the day afterwards she flew back to New York. They would meet again and have sex on at least four occasions until their final encounter in the Bronx in 1986. Read *Nunquam* and you will find, if not quite stories, then a persistent tension between presence and absence as sexual tropes.

Less than a year after his contradictory declaration of marriage to Fiddle, in mid-August 1971, Larry travelled to Geneva, primarily to meet up with Denis de Rougemont, a Swiss philosopher who specialised in Christian anti-totalitarianism; Larry was particularly drawn to him because of his knowledge of the Gnostics and the Templars, non-conformist religious sects whose heresies were, he felt, a spiritual counterpart to his unorthodox fiction. He also wished to see some physicians who specialised in skin disorders. For the previous three years he had suffered from severe bouts of eczema. His general practitioner had advised him that while alcohol was not the cause of the condition, the consequent dehydration made it worse. Larry visited a Dr Kiefer, a dermatologist who promised to help him but was equally flattered by being consulted by a writer of international prestige. Kiefer invited him to a dinner party, where he met his wife, Claude: intelligent, pretty, with bright blonde hair that reminded him of her departed namesake. She visited Larry on the afternoon of the day following the party at his hotel and they began an affair. They arranged to meet next at Lake Orta, which

Larry had chosen because it was the place that Nietzsche used to meet the woman who obsessed him, Lou Salomé. Nietzsche by this point was showing early symptoms of a psychological disorder and within hours of meeting Salomé, insisted that they must marry. She refused but he pursued her to various locations across Europe, pledging that they would find happiness together and that their relationship would have a collateral beneficial effect on the ills that beset the Western world.

Larry had occasionally seen himself as a twentieth-century version of Nietzsche, both as a non-conformist radical – he often repeated the philosophical mantra 'all gods are dead' – and as a man whose courageous intellect had sometimes taken him to the brink of insanity. At Orta he asked Claude to see herself as Salomé and him as Nietzsche, and proposed marriage. She displayed commendable calm and did her best to restore him to a rational state. Many women would have taken the easy way out and ended things then but Claude Kiefer was fascinated by Larry, the unbalanced yet charming eccentric.

In mid-February 1972 the Vidourle river in Sommières flooded, filling Larry's cellar, which was stacked with wine bottles, with filthy water and damaging books on the lower shelves in his library. He called Claude and she arrived the following day, arranged for local jobbing builders to do what they could with the building and drove him in his own Peugeot to the Hôtel d'Europe in Avignon where she insisted that he stayed in bed and drank responsibly. Next, she took him to a villa owned by a friend of hers in the Vaucluse and restored his composure by ensuring they had regular sex.

Grateful and sexually obsessed, Larry promised her another liaison at Lake Orta, and on 2 May for a week rented a boathouse on the lake near Sacro Monte, which his research suggested was as close as possible to where Nietzsche courted Lou Salomé. By this point Claude's husband was aware that her regular journeys to unspecified points outside Switzerland had nothing to do with interests in history and culture. Ironically, while she was primarily interested in sex, Larry was equally obsessed with his fantasy regarding Nietzsche's infatuation with Lou. The latter energised his best-known philosophical work of fiction, *Thus Spoke Zarathustra*, in which the eponymous character, based on a ninth-century BC Iranian prophet and poet, declares that nothing, especially gods, exists beyond the tactile world. Nietzsche's despair at his rejection by Lou informs his work – he dedicated the book 'von Orta an', 'from Orta onwards' – and Larry persuaded Claude to act out with him the courtship of the couple from almost a century before. She thought it amusing and preposterous, given that unlike their predecessors they *were* having sex, enthusiastically. But for Larry this was the point. For decades he had extrapolated into his fiction aspects of his life that in various ways fascinated, unsettled and appalled him but he was always cautiously selective, creating in the fictional account something he'd usually managed to lie about or avoid. He now became even more unaccountable. After Claude returned to Geneva Larry stayed on in the boathouse and made notes and short draft passages which would eventually from the basis of *Monsieur* (1974), the opening volume of his final sequence of novels, *The Avignon Quintet*. Much of his interest in gnosticism feeds into the novel but just as pertinently we find parallels between its structure and Larry's experiences before and during its composition, particularly his sex life. There are five different narrators who compete for attention and cause the reader to wonder whether which, if any, of the stories is true. The 'narrative', if one can credit it with the title, involves a cocktail of failed marriage, infidelity, deaths of wives, female partners undergoing treatment for mental illness and in one case suicide. The predominant theme involves all of the male figures drifting from front stage to the background and by implication absolving themselves of responsibility for what happens to the women. In short, it is an unrepentant escapist version of the life of its author. Lawrence Durrell inhabits the book persistently while renouncing responsibility for anything that occurs in it.

Larry's relationship with Claude continued for at least seven years on intermittent occasions. The final record of their meeting alone is in October 1978 when, once more, both took trains to Lake Orta and stayed in the boathouse that had become a memorial to earlier trysts.

The summer after his first Orta liaison with Claude, July 1972, Larry visited Catha Aldington in her home in Saintes-Maries-de-la-Mer, a seaside fishing port in the Camargue as yet undisturbed by visitors or property-hunting expatriates. Catha's other guest was her friend Ghislaine de Boysson, whom Larry had met briefly seven years earlier.

Ghislaine was a minor celebrity. A friend of Aristotle Onassis and his wife Jackie, the widow of John F. Kennedy, photographs of her had decorated society magazines during the late 1950s and 1960s; she epitomised the slim, sensual elegance of the finest models of the period and the stars of the post-war golden age of Hollywood. She was not trained as an actress but she could easily be mistaken for a dark-haired version of Grace Kelly. The mutual attraction between her and Larry was evident to Catha and to all with whom they mixed during the next year. She visited Sommières on a number of occasions while Larry was also arranging meetings with Claude Kiefer. He invited her there for Christmas, 1972. Gerry and Jacquie were present too and Jacquie later commented that Ghislaine 'lusted after' her brother-in-law in a manner that was conspicuous and, for some, embarrassing.

During the early years of Larry and Ghislaine's relationship he was also seeing a number of other women among whom Fiddle and Claude were the prominent examples. In later interviews with biographers and others Ghislaine never mentions them and since she was transparent regarding other unsavoury aspects of her time with Larry one must assume that her omission was due to ignorance rather than politeness. We can add to the list the filmmaker Margaret McCall whom Larry had alienated with his lascivious overtures during the late 1960s. By 1970 they were working together notably on a BBC film called *Lawrence Durrell's Paris*. Their friendship was neither platonic nor purely professional in that they shared the same bedroom during her visits to Sommières. In July 1971, for example, she moved into the house for five weeks. This time they were not planning or working on a film and Larry made a point of informing everyone, especially the women in his life, that he was busy with the early draft of *Monsieur* and would not for a while be a good host. In late December 1971 Larry and McCall flew to California to celebrate Miller's eightieth birthday and in January on the way back stayed over in Dublin. Richard Pine, a junior lecturer, wanted to interview him before an audience at Trinity College. By this point Larry's work was drawing much attention in universities, especially among doctoral researchers and early-career academics who involved themselves in European critical theory where the boundaries between philosophy and literary writing were being eroded. Larry's status as a novelist who treated fiction as a means of investigating aspects of existentialism and arcane religious/mystical cults was seen as gold dust for the new enthusiasts embodied by Pine. He managed to persuade Trinity to pay for Larry's travel and accommodation expenses, which were considerable since he insisted on first-class air tickets from the US to Dublin and then on to Paris, and four days in the most luxurious suite in the Shelbourne, the city's most prestigious hotel. Everything was covered for himself and his 'companion', which caused consternation at the Shelbourne when Larry refused to sign in Margaret McCall as 'Mrs Durrell'. In Ireland much was then still accountable to the moral codes of Catholicism. Larry told them to shut up and hand over the room key, which they did.

The day after the Trinity event Pine drove them into the Wicklow mountains for a cold-weather picnic, involving sandwiches and whiskey, and then showed them the Martello tower where Joyce had lived and which featured in *Ulysses*. On the journey back into central Dublin Larry and Margaret argued over their future. She refused to divorce her husband and he insulted her by claiming that taking her on as a long-term partner was both flattering and generous. She would, he informed her, soon be 'too old' to attract anyone.

This was a turning point in their relationship but not its conclusion. They continued to meet after Larry's first liaison with Ghislaine later that year. In April 1972, for example, they met in Paris where Margaret found that Larry was also having an affair with a young woman who worked at the Department of Antiquities at the Sorbonne. No one is sure of her real name but she is referred to in surviving documents as 'Buttons'; thirty years old, petite and attractive, according to Larry who taunted Margaret by saying, 'Look at her, she's just a child!' He began his affair with Ghislaine two months later, in June 1972, albeit tentatively; but he would not stop seeing Margaret McCall until the following year.

Larry and Ghislaine made their affair public in April 1973 when he took her to London for the launch of *The Black Book*. It had first appeared in Paris in 1938 and while Faber offered to bring it out in London, they also demanded the expurgation of the passages on sex. Larry refused, insisting that arousal, fornication and perversion are its predominant themes. It was produced by Villa Seurat and the launch itself took place at Hatchards bookshop in Piccadilly, which was bursting with his admirers. He signed more than 240 copies. Larry gave a short speech admitting with pride that the book had been inspired by his friend Henry Miller's *Tropic of Cancer* and noting that like D. H. Lawrence he had been denied freedom of publication in the UK because the English establishment had an institutionalised aversion to talking about sex. He was interviewed by *The Times* and the novel was widely reviewed, mostly with approval. Larry had kept his private life a secret from the press but Ghislaine was self-evidently his new partner and there were whispers and speculation, especially among journalists.

At the end of April Larry and Ghislaine flew direct from London to Cannes for the film festival. He was on one of the judging panels along with Sydney Pollack and Ingrid Bergman and was interviewed by Robin Livio for *Film Français*: 'To love is to understand one another, and to understand is to imagine everything ... Sexuality is as fragile as life itself, and twice as interesting' (*Bulletin of the Cannes International Festival* 11 May 1973). This piece of gnomic gibberish was typical of his comments on life and writing but since it was about sex, and this was 1973, no one complained that it didn't make sense. Robin, an appealing twenty-three-old brunette, was fascinated. 'The only thing which has added value and a spiritual density is that tragic episode in everyone's life: love,' he said and asked her if she would come with him to the next film he was appointed to judge, followed by 'a fuck'. She politely declined and after too many drinks that night when he was dining out with Ghislaine, the pair disagreed over something seemingly innocuous – the artistic status of film, according to witnesses – and he stood up, leaned over the table and slapped his partner hard across her cheek. He was, she knew, impulsive – one of the reasons she was attracted to him – but she did not think him capable of violence. Indeed, this was the first time she had witnessed a man hitting a woman, and she was the victim. Next morning, she did a decent job of covering the bruise with make-up and booked an afternoon train to Paris.

He begged her not to leave, burst into tears and apologised, explaining that what he had done was caused by the stress of being among so many celebrities at the festival, that he loved her; and he asked her to marry him. She was convinced by his account of things and did not board the train. Two days afterwards she agreed to be his wife and only later did she realise that Larry was perpetually violent. He would hit her once a week on average. We know from what he did to Nancy and Eve that he was a habitual domestic abuser but aside from the initial instance of assault, for which she accepted his explanation, Ghislaine had no warning that she was walking into an unremitting nightmare.

She moved into the house in Sommières where during the summer and autumn of 1973 she got to know her fiancé. He was struggling with the final draft of *Monsieur*, which was his excuse for his increasingly foul behaviour. He would begin the day with a flask of coffee and move onto wine by 11 a.m., drinking through the afternoon, and if work was particularly difficult sometimes help himself to a private store of laudanum – no one knew from whom he'd acquired it. Towards Ghislaine he was irritable and intemperate, criticising her for preparing meals he did not enjoy or for wearing dresses he felt would draw the attention of lustful young men in the town. Often he slapped her and, forbearingly, she suggested that they might postpone the marriage but he insisted, 'No, no, darling, you see, when I am your husband, I will be absolutely different' (Bowker, p352). She didn't believe him. As a token to her of his integrity he arranged their marriage in early November, but by late October Ghislaine was becoming more and more unsettled by the nature of their relationship and by the man to whom she had committed herself. On the day of the ceremony, 8 November, France was riven with strikes by private and public sector workers – even bistros and restaurants were closed in most areas – and that morning he ordered Ghislaine to 'put on a nice dress because we are going to be married tonight'. He had not mentioned this to her previously. The local *mairie* was open until 6 p.m. and they arrived ten minutes before it closed. The witnesses, arranged by Larry, were a local prostitute and a drunk who was suffering from withdrawal symptoms and persuaded to come to the ceremony in exchange for a bottle of whisky from Larry's stock. Larry asked both witnesses back to the house afterwards. The drunk persistently questioned Ghislaine on her sexual preferences and the prostitute offered a detailed account of her own adventures with fee-paying customers. Ghislaine later reflected that her wedding day was like appearing as a character in one of her husband's novels.

Following the departure of their guests their married life began with his demand that she return to Paris the following day, clear all her possessions from her flat and arrange for them to be transported to Sommières. She reported to him by phone that she could carry several packing cases but that it was impractical to bring south with her larger items such as furniture. He ordered her to have them removed by an auctioneer and sold. She owned the flat, in the fashionable Quai Voltaire, and Larry added that he expected her to put it on the market before she left the Paris. He did not explain to her his peremptory orders but it was clear to her that she faced the prospect of having her previous life erased, of becoming part of the dominion of Lawrence Durrell. The day after the phone call involving the furniture he called again, stating that, 'you are my wife now, and don't be angry'. He had, he confessed, invited a woman he had met at the Cannes Festival to the Sommières house for sex but that, 'she said I stank and wouldn't sleep with me'. He was lying, partly. It was hardly credible that someone would accept his invitation to the house, fully aware of what he had in mind, and then turn him down. A woman was present at Cannes, his previous lover Claude Kiefer, and they did have sex, though how he achieved this without the knowledge of Ghislaine is mystifying. Ghislaine became aware that he was a philanderer and a poor liar when she looked at the new volume of poems, *Vega*, published several months before their marriage but prior to which Larry had said nothing and kept hidden in a drawer. It was dedicated to Claude Kiefer. Before this she had not heard of her but following discreet enquires among mutual acquaintances she began to unravel Larry's web of fabrications.

A few weeks after the wedding Gerry and Jacquie came to see them in the Sommières house. Jacquie demanded that she should warn Ghislaine of what she must expect during her marriage but Gerry asked his wife to allow him to speak to her first. Ghislaine was already becoming aware of his violent tendencies but Jacquie knew from her husband that he, Larry, could supplement domestic violence with serial philandering. Gerry took Ghislaine for a walk in the garden, stated that he was sad that they had not spent time together previously and then blurted out, 'I was going to tell you not to marry Larry.' He offered no explanation for why he thought his brother an unsuitable partner and fled back to the house through the French windows.

Within a few weeks Gerry's belated scrap of advice began to make sense. Larry was trying to complete *Monsieur* and as ever he maintained his bizarre routine, with sunrise coffee followed by late morning wine. As a compensation for his indulgences he'd limit himself to tomatoes and lettuce and then a yoga session followed by a swim in the recently installed pool. He'd dress in baggy, ill-fitting khaki shorts, plus sunglasses and either a beret or a hat that seemed to have come from the wardrobe room of an Ealing comedy. By three he would be listening to something on his gramophone – usually Mozart – and until the early evening he would continue to write, having exchanged the wine for whisky. Supper was rarely more substantial than lunch. For several decades he had been trying manically to reduce his extensive paunch and now his forty-inch waist made him appear almost comically oval rather than just obese.

Before their marriage Ghislaine had found his eccentricities endearing but soon she felt that a subtle change had occurred. She was present but not quite there, more an observer than a participant in their relationship. One day she asked him, amicably enough, why he wore funny hats when swimming. He answered, 'When you have a nose like mine it's better to have a funny hat on your head because it distracts people from your nose' (Bowker, p355). His tone was neither self-deprecating nor genial. Rather, he made it clear that what he wore, or did, was none of her business. She would join him for supper and drinks but he seemed to tolerate rather than enjoy her company. Their conversation rarely seemed to extend beyond him asking for her to pass him condiments or the bottle.

She put up with it because she had never lived with a writer before and assumed that self-absorption was a precondition for the completion of a major literary work; nor had she experienced life in a remote place with a domestic abuser. But his behaviour in the house was symptomatic of something more disconcerting. Despite being busy he did sometimes invite friends from Paris to stay for a night or two. Usually, they too were writers and while he expected Ghislaine to cook their meals and present herself as charming and amusing, she usually felt more like a hired courtesan than co-host and wife. Her suspicion that his insistence that she empty and sell her Paris flat indicated a desire to both possess and expropriate her was reinforced when he refused to allow her to invite her own friends to the house. One, known in accounts only as Mathilde, did arrive from Paris and was so badly insulted by Larry – followed by his attempt to fondle her – that she packed and left in the early hours of the morning. Most significantly, when her marriage to Larry became widely known, *Elle* contacted Ghislaine and offered her a contract to act as their correspondent in Montpellier and for other parts of the flourishing western Mediterranean coast. Larry could not have prevented her from accepting the offer – this was the late twentieth century – but he objected so vehemently that she turned them down in the hope of maintaining a relatively peaceful existence.

In late 1973 Larry and Ghislaine flew to Los Angeles where he was to serve as Visiting Professor at the California Institute of Technology (Caltech). The name of the institute is misleading in that it is not exclusively dedicated to the sciences. It is the West Coast counterpart to the prestigious Massachusetts Institute of Technology. Both prided themselves on bringing a rigorous empirical approach to all disciplines from the pure sciences to linguistics and literature. Caltech could boast twelve Nobel Prize winners from its alumni, Einstein included. The Durrells were greeted at the campus in Pasadena by a group of Larry's friends and admirers, with a crate of chilled champagne, albeit the Californian version. Miller was present, along with his new, if occasional, girlfriend, the Chinese-American actress Lisa Lu, whom he shared with her husband Shelling Hwong. Miller lived within driving distance of the campus, which was one of the reasons why Larry accepted the invitation. He was on a full professorial salary and his teaching duties were light; but 26 December 1974 would be Miller's eighty-third birthday and Larry wanted to spend a three-month unbroken period in the company of his old friend.

The Head of English, J. Kent Clark, had been responsible for issuing the invitation to Larry. Following champagne with Miller and others, Clark took them for dinner at Myako's, a Japanese restaurant of great repute, and then introduced them to their accommodation. The Athenaeum Club was an ornate tribute to Spanish colonial architecture, built by Caltech to house its most distinguished staff, visiting and permanent. At each wing were three storeys of suites reserved for the most distinguished residents. Larry and Ghislaine were introduced to no. 20 on the first floor, which was made up of two spacious rooms, one for entertaining and relaxing, with its own fireplace and giving onto a spacious balcony overlooking well-watered lawns surrounded by olive and palm trees. There was a spacious bedroom but the bathroom next door was shared with the adjacent suite. Clark grandly announced that no. 20 was unofficially referred to as the 'Einstein Suite'; the great man had occupied it for almost six months. Larry, puzzled, asked if they were also expected to share a kitchen, and Clark explained that the Athenaeum was founded on the Oxbridge principle of collegiality, albeit with wives allowed. Residents were expected to take meals in the ground-floor restaurant, in formal attire; suits and ties for men, smart dresses for women. This, like High Table in old universities, was designed to encourage members of the intellectual elite to share ideas. Larry was appalled at the prospect of becoming what amounted to a member of a public school for middle-aged high-flyers and ordered Ghislaine to visit the nearest hardware store, purchase a medium-sized barbeque with enough bags of coal to keep them going for the foreseeable future and have it delivered discreetly and carried up the stairs to their rooms. He installed it on the balcony and spent the following week cooking steak and chops and preparing salads, accompanied by bottles of wine and bourbon from other nearby outlets. There were numerous complaints from other residents, mostly about the smoke and the smell, and Clark was forced to inform his guest that he was going against the rules of the club. Larry gave notice of his imminent departure. For the only period during their relationship Ghislaine took control and contacted a man she'd known during her time as a model and actress, the acclaimed film director William Wyler. Wyler offered them use of his luxurious summer house in nearby Malibu. Initially Larry had bought a dilapidated VW Beetle for basic transport but now he had joined the Hollywood aristocracy he splashed out on a three-year-old open-top Ford Mustang, the most conspicuously aggressive sports car in America. Larry enjoyed arriving for his brief seminars on modern literature in a car that was deafeningly loud and for a short while their marriage became something like a mutually enjoyed party. But things would soon return to the unpleasantly normal.

During one of Larry and Ghislaine's visits to Miller's house the couple had an argument, seemingly on the state of the novel. After Miller had gone to bed, following his doctor's instruction to sleep as much as possible subsequent to his recent heart operation, Larry leaned over the table and hit Ghislaine hard with the back of his hand, this time behind her ear trying not to leave evidence on her face. He hoped to get away with it but Anthony, Miller's son, was staying over and saw what he'd done. Anthony informed his father of it the next morning and Miller told Larry that if he ever did anything like it again, he would no longer be welcome in the house. According to Ghislaine Larry apologised to him though showing no hint of remorse for what he had done to her.

Soon afterwards Ghislaine was telephoned by William Wyler's daughter Cathy, whom she'd known since both of them worked in the movies and who was instrumental in securing the house in Malibu. Cathy was flying over from New York and, without inviting herself, suggested that it would be wonderful for them to meet up at her father's house; she would, she added, love to be introduced to Ghislaine's famous husband. Larry informed her that, 'I don't want to meet your fucking friend!', leaving Ghislaine to come up with a convincing explanation for them being somewhere else during Cathy's visit. Ghislaine was reminded by this of the same authoritarian routine in Sommières: he seemed to treat her as his possession and denied her any sense of a life of her own.

Had she seen the letters he wrote to his friends and heard his comments to them during the stay in America and following their return to France, her suspicions would have been confirmed. 'This marriage is going to end in a mess ... Ghislaine is driving me mad with fruitful irritation' (MacNiven, p607). To Mary Mollo he said, 'She's stupid ... And she likes money' (*Ibid.*).

In California Larry and Ghislaine celebrated his sixty-second birthday with a party at the Malibu house, the other guests being Anaïs Nin and Miller. The three old friends talked incessantly into the early hours of their experiences in Paris and the Mediterranean before and after the Second World War and Ghislaine felt like the lackey, treated with politeness but largely ignored.

Shortly before their departure Professor Clark told her there was a regulation that Visiting Professors could only bring with them a female partner if they could show proof of being married. She found that the official invitation to Caltech had been issued soon before he had proposed marriage to her. He could have gone alone but he hated travelling by himself, especially in aeroplanes, and the prospect of living without a woman – especially one who had been turned into a servant – for so long was equally off-putting. She was his passport to three months with his oldest friend. He would probably have preferred to take Claude Kiefer or Margaret McCall, just for the thrill of it; each was married to someone else. Ghislaine said nothing of this to him.

Following their return to Sommières she found it increasingly difficult to tolerate his appalling behaviour. In late summer 1974 he was working hard on *Livia*, the second volume of *The Avignon Quintet*, having dispatched *Monsieur* to Faber earlier in the year. One evening he and Ghislaine ate supper together, this being the first time he had spoken to her since the day before. He offered her an account of his childhood and early life, perhaps as an explanation for his tortured, sometimes violent adult state. Indian servants, he reported, had forced him to drink the warm blood of freshly killed chickens, and one had once locked him in a cupboard for a day and his parents had either not noticed or condoned this. At chapel in the school in Darjeeling the representation of a crucified Christ had dripped with blood, supplied from lambs, chickens, cattle or whatever else the native Indian butchers could find to supply their Christian masters. At school he was bullied, he told her, because he was short and a low-life colonial who was not Black but tainted by association. He was lying but once she began to show sympathy, he overturned the dining table which was too light to seriously injure her but which propelled her towards the wall. She was dizzy but after about an hour she went upstairs to find him snoring; she bit the index finger of his right hand with which he held his pen. He woke, enraged, and gave her the worst beating of her life. Luckily, for him, they had no visitors for the subsequent two weeks. Even those closest to him would have felt that the bruises on her face and arms would have merited a report to the police.

Later that summer Sappho arrived with her boyfriend Simon. She had recently graduated from York University and secured a junior editorial post with a publisher in London, without asking for assistance from her father. She announced to Larry that her true ambition was to become, like him, a literary writer and she brought him some drafts of short stories. She did not seek paternal approval, just the opportunity to discuss her work with a man who was both creative and opinionated. He read it and summed up its qualities, at least his opinion: 'It is shit.' He treated Simon as the equivalent of a squatter, someone he could not remove from the house but whose presence in it enraged him. He did not speak a word to him and nor did he reply to his polite verbal interjections, such as his attempt to introduce himself. Ghislaine did her best to make the young couple feel welcome. She thought Sappho highly intelligent and was impressed by her apparent indifference to what others saw as self-evident: her generous spirit and her beauty. Larry seemed to treat her as an unavoidable irritation. She was his daughter but given that he insulted her regularly he clearly did not wish her to stay long in the house. She told Ghislaine, 'You must leave! He is going to kill you' (Bowker, pp361–2).

After Sappho and Simon left, Larry announced to Ghislaine that Claude-Marie was looking down on them, explaining that despite having claimed to have buried Claude-Marie's ashes in the Sommières churchyard he had kept them on a shelf which overlooked their bed in the master bedroom. She can 'see us having sex', he said. Ghislaine now felt that she'd come upon an even more bizarre, macabre element of her husband than she had previously feared might exist. He suggested that he would properly bury the ashes in the garden between the French windows and the pool so they might 'greet her' when they went for a swim. Though having no faith herself Ghislaine persuaded him to place his late wife's remains in a place that was respected for its grace and spirituality. He took the silver container to the churchyard of Saint-Julien de Montredon, a quiet hamlet with an ancient Romanesque church. The grave containing her ashes remains unmarked, and it is still uncertain whether the silver container he claimed to have put there contained Claude-Marie's ashes or if he had faked the entire exercise.

In October 1974, the couple went to London for the launch of *Monsieur*. His standing as a writer who could claim the attention of those beyond the high-cultural elite was evident in his invitation to be interviewed by Michael Parkinson on his enormously popular TV show.

Parkinson's guests ranged from the footballer George Best through actors such as Bob Hope and Olivia Newton-John to ex-Beatles Paul McCartney and John Lennon and high-ranking politicians, including former prime minister Harold Wilson. Parkinson was a notoriously thorough researcher, capable of catching his interviewees off-guard on a live broadcast. For Larry he picked up a sentence from a recent newspaper interview in which Larry had referred to Ghislaine as a 'pig'. It seems that some knowledge of Larry as a domestic abuser was already in the public realm in that Parkinson was trying to draw him on how he treated women, though there is no record of who he had spoken to. Larry had done his homework too and explained to Parkinson that the word 'pigsney' was a commonly used term of affection by a man for his sweetheart. It had lost currency in the sixteenth century but Shakespeare had used it and it was frequently abbreviated to 'pig'. His light-hearted erudition was convincing enough, but he was lying. The word had died out before Shakespeare's time and there is no record of it being used in an abbreviated form.

The relationship endured, just, and they were divorced in 1979, though after 1974 Ghislaine chose to spend long periods in Paris. She had not, despite his orders, sold her apartment and there was enough of the original furniture to make it habitable. She was his fourth and last wife and probably the most accommodating and tolerant of them all. Even after their break-up she maintained in interviews that she had always loved him. During the final eighteen months, when she returned to Sommières from Paris to attempt to repair their relationship, Larry took her presence as an excuse to become even more foul than he had been previously. He slapped her routinely but he was too drunk to do serious harm. Often, he went into what appeared to be spasms. He claimed that he was epileptic and that he had been from childhood. Again, he was lying. He was drinking so much that quite often he was unable to remain on a chair, let alone stand up, and he needed a convincing medical explanation for his writhing on the floor.

14

Gerry: A New Life

During the three years following Jacquie's departure in 1975 Gerry's annual income and financial assets fell to around 30 percent of their previous average, and the latter already tended towards the precarious. Jacquie was neither appropriating nor demanding reparations for the break-up; these would not be settled until their divorce in 1979. Rather, it soon became clear that while she held no executive post nor even drew a salary from the Trust, she had been the steadying, pragmatic counterpart to Gerry's state of incautious disarray. He was obliged to spend even more time doing talks for the media and even after-dinner performances to raise enough merely to ensure that the permanent members of staff were paid their wages. Plans to expand the zoo, in terms of building enclosures and the acquisition of new inhabitants, came to a halt. He could afford neither.

In 1976 his agents Curtis Brown put out feelers to American universities, zoos and related organisations involved in conservation, enquiring about their interest in further lectures and talks from one of their clients, one of the most celebrated environmentalists in the world. There were dozens of replies and the agency went into business-mode: how much would they pay? The rewards for a day or two with the renowned Gerald Durrell were generous indeed. Curtis Brown were not simply doing Gerry a favour. They knew that all American institutions could make use of massive amounts of private sponsorship and that if Gerry spent a few months there he could earn far more than would come from touring the interview circuit in Britain and Europe. They wanted one of their bestselling authors to have more time to write, and calculated that an American tour would make enough money for him to support himself afterwards while he produced another book.

It was a shrewd move and at the end of an exhausting two-month schedule Gerry found himself at Duke University in North Carolina, a classy, private research university founded by non-conformist Protestants in 1838. The university was acclaimed for its commitment to zoological science both as an academic discipline and a reforming enterprise. It housed a zoo which held America's most prized collection of rare primates, notably lemurs. Gerry's host was Margot Rockefeller, who in 1970 founded the Maine Coast Heritage Trust, a conservation organisation based on the same principles as Gerry's Jersey project, except that it had access to seemingly unlimited funding from American sponsors whose pockets were deep, sometimes amounting to routine donations of half a million dollars. Gerry did a brief informal talk and was greeted at a dinner party as a hero.

At this event he met Lee McGeorge and an account of their encounter is in Gerry's notes in the Jersey Archive. It reminds one of the kind of romantic novel produced by Joanna Trollope. The style is respectable, even intelligent, but at the same time we feel that the boundary between decent writing and delusional fantasy is being eroded.

He feels alienated by the professors who talk 'polysyllabically' and 'gazing around the room desperately' he sees 'a young woman who was sitting on what used to be called a pouf, nursing her drink and looking remarkably attractive'. He notes that her fingers are ringless.

'Hullo,' I said, 'I'm Gerald Durrell.'
'I know,' she said. 'I'm Lee McGeorge.' (Jersey Archive, undated, and
    quoted by Botting, p417)

These notes are undated but he did not begin making them until the end of the 1980s, thirteen years after he met Lee. In the interim the story of what happened at Duke University became part of Gerry's standard repertoire for media appearances and talks, especially once they had married and Lee had become a senior figure at the Jersey Trust and an author and presenter in her own right. For example, Pat Ferns, a TV producer Gerry had worked with before, approached Jeremy Isaacs, the head of the recently established British TV network Channel 4. The latter was intent on turning Channel 4 into a radical alternative to the staid BBC and the mass-market commercial ITV; serious but sometimes a little outrageous. Gerry and Lee, argued Ferns, would be an ideal double act for a series on environmental issues presented by a quirky, idiosyncratic couple who were devoted to saving threatened species – Isaacs was convinced and *Ark on the Move* went into production in late 1980 and was televised in 1982. During production Gerry and Lee wanted to give prominence to the autobiographical, even romantic element of their enterprise; to talk about how they met and the progress of their courtship; and to give the impression that their love for each other mirrored and energised their dedication to animals. Ferns was cautiously indulgent but Isaacs was aghast. It struck him as a picturesque version of *Born Free*. The script which Gerry and Lee would share as narrators of their story unsettled him particularly, and the passage on their meeting in America, quoted by Botting, is a verbatim extract from it. This does not prove that they made it up, but it raises suspicions.

Lee McGeorge had, at the time of their meeting, just begun to write up her PhD at Duke. She had already done preliminary research in Madagascar on the social and cognitive behaviour of local mammals, notably lemurs, which would be the focus of her dissertation. She was twenty-seven and Gerry fifty-two. After the drinks reception the academics and their partners set off for a formal dinner at a nearby restaurant and though Gerry was the star guest he accepted Lee's offer of a lift in her ageing, battered car and the two of them spent the rest of the evening at a table of their own talking to each other but remaining separate from the rest of the party. Lee had not been invited. At around 2 a.m. she drove him to his hotel and they exchanged phone numbers and addresses.

Next morning Gerry made a transatlantic call to Dr Alison Jolly, an eminent zoologist who worked regularly in Madagascar, and asked her if she knew of or had met Lee McGeorge. He was not suspicious of her account of her research – all was on record for interested parties – but he had drunk a vast amount of alcohol and needed some verification for what now seemed, in part, a delusion. Lee was very pretty, his recollection was clear enough on that, but he needed to reassure himself that he had spoken for several hours to a woman as dedicated to the preservation of rare species and as erudite as he was – Jolly stated that she was one of the brightest graduate students in animal behaviour that she knew of, who probably had a promising career ahead as an academic.

Two days later he wrote to her announcing that she was 'so ravishing, refreshing and intelligent that you seduced me'. 'You are,' he added, 'one of the most beautiful and intelligent girls I have met ... should it ever happen (God forbid) that your love life comes unstuck and you think a trip to Europe to stay with me would not be too repulsive [you are] the sort of person I need. I don't just mean for obvious reasons, but I have a hell of a lot I want to do and places I want to go to and I need an assistant' (April 1977, otherwise undated, Jersey Archive; quoted by Botting, pp419). The collage of worshipping hyperbole ('refreshing, intelligent, beautiful' etc.), sexual inuendo ('the sort of person I need [not] for obvious reasons') and staid professionalism ('I need an assistant') would set the tone for his letters to her during the subsequent two years and, from what others have recalled, of their one-to-one exchanges too. It is clear enough that his respect for her as a zoologist was genuine but it is equally evident that his enthusiasm for a working partnership would not have been so eager had she been plain, his own age or male.

Lee has written about and been interviewed on her involvement with Gerry and the Trust and while she makes it clear that she had until his death remained fully committed to working with Gerry and thereafter as effective CEO of the Trust, she is guarded about their emotional relationship. To this extent she could be describing her love for an elderly relative to whose work and principles she too has committed herself rather than the man she married.

There is no record of a reply from her to his earliest letter but soon afterwards he wrote again inviting her as a guest to a ceremony at Yale on 16 May where he would receive an Honorary Doctorate in Humane Letters. Again, she seems not to have responded by letter but it is evident that shortly before the ceremony he telephoned her, promised that he would pay her fare to the university, and more, but she did not attend. His letter to her of 23 May suggests that he was willing to up the odds.

'As I told you on the phone, we [at the Trust] had a tiny windfall, the spending of which is up to my discretion' (Jersey Archive). This was untrue. No such 'windfall' – by which he seemed to mean a donation – had come. However, he stated that it could be used legitimately as the salary for someone with expertise in animal communication. 'I would like you to suggest areas of research which we could profitably put into operation … If you decide to come, I hope by that time that I will have some interesting material on the whales and a rather fascinating paper on the frequencies of bird cries.' (Botting, p421)

It was a double bribe. He was offering her a job at what was now a prestigious centre of animal research – at the time she was living on a piffling hourly wage as an instructor, doing teaching that tenured professors wished to avoid – and cleverly he also suggested that by doing her research in Jersey she would come up with 'fascinating' academic papers as a route back into academia. He had, he told her, discovered groundbreaking research material on whales. Gerry had never read let alone written an academic paper.

For the subsequent six months he bombarded her with similarly embarrassing outbursts of love and infatuation. They met briefly during his October visit to the States but the first surviving response from her was written on 26 November. She cannot 'reply with some suitably pompous soliloquy to your push on the state of my mind and the plans for my life', and goes onto flatter him as a 'marvellous man' who she'd 'like to spend a lot of time with', but only in terms of their shared interests. Anything other would be, 'Wrong for me in that I've found a person whom I'd marry'; she could hardly expect him to 'wait for me while I'm off being your friend and lover for a few years' (Botting, pp424–6). His name is Lincoln – we never learn if this is his first name or his surname in the letters or from other documents – but, she adds, she is so committed to him that she'll endure his 'ever-present' divorced wife and his child.

She was honest enough, while Gerry's claim that for him Lee was a matchless unrivalled individual was disingenuous to say the least.

Within a month of his return from the first US visit, when he met Lee, he began a casual sexual relationship with a woman in her early forties. She was married to one of Jersey's wealthier tax exiles who was more than twenty years her senior and happy enough to allow her to seek occasional pleasures elsewhere. He was also a generous donor to the Trust and Gerry benefitted from his largesse in more ways than one. Her name is recorded in various documents in the Jersey Archive but citation in print is forbidden. Gerry would soon write to Lee of the Mazet in France which he still hoped to purchase from his brother. 'The rivers like green satin ... and every village and cottage covered with roses' (20 June 1977, Jersey Archive). 'I love France,' he declares and promises that if they become a couple, she can share his delight. He does not, however, fully explain the sentence: 'I have never seen France so lovely as we drove down' (*Ibid.*, Jersey Archive). The 'we' included his forty-something lover.

Later that same summer he received a letter from Alexandra Mayhew, a zoology graduate aged twenty-three. The Mayhews and Durrells had been friendly since the 1930s when the latter had lived on Corfu, and Alexandra had now written to her 'uncle' Gerry for a reference. She included her CV and details of her application for an editorial job on a zoology magazine in London. Gerry said he'd be happy to help her but added that if she was committed to conservation why wouldn't she fly to Jersey where, if she were inclined, a job at the Trust awaited her. She had included with her various documents a recent photograph: Alexandra was a finely attractive brunette with angular cheekbones and the figure of an athlete. She accepted his invitation but arrived with her boyfriend. At first Gerry was dismayed and in an interview with Botting she told of how her host arranged that the boyfriend stayed in a separate bedroom and he had Alexandra largely to himself. 'He used to bring me up a tray in bed ... and one day he said, "Oh, you ought to get rid of that awful man. You're wasted on him. You should come back and marry me." He was serious. I was young and attractive ... He had only met Lee once ... it didn't seem that it was going anywhere' (Botting, p423) – or at least that was what he told her. During Alexandra's time in Jersey Gerry had composed several letters to Lee begging her to come to him.

During 1977 Gerry had been making and then postponing plans for a visit to Assam in north-eastern India to study endangered mammals, particularly the pygmy hog. In several of his letters to Lee he proposed that she should accompany him and once more suggested that her academic prospects would be improved by research findings for papers she might co-author with an eminent conservationist, him.

What happened next resembled an emotionally comedic version of musical chairs. With commendable politeness Lee advised him that the expedition had no relevance to her ongoing doctoral research but soon afterwards visited Jersey and agreed to take seriously, at least in theory, his marriage proposal. An amoebic bug caused Gerry to postpone the visit to India until spring 1978. Without Lee's knowledge Alexandra accompanied him there as his research assistant on the understanding that he would desist from attempts to seduce her. He agreed to the codicil but continued to make advances to her throughout their expedition, eventually successfully. At the same time, he sent regular letters to Lee. Such as:

> I love you deeply ... you are the most wonderful thing that has ever happened to me ... I feel like a man who has succeeded in capturing a rainbow – filled with a sense of awe and delight. (Letter from Gerry then in Assam, undated, Jersey Archive)

It is evident from their correspondence during his time in India that she was weighing up the difference between a future with Lincoln and Gerry's marvellous offerings.

> I am still living with Lincoln. The clean surgical cut required to break off the relationship was too painful for both of us ... I know what you must be feeling now – to see that the girl you love and will marry is living with someone else. God, how could I do it to you?... I can hardly wait 'til end May when you come over – the present phase of my life will be done and my new, marvellous life will begin. (Jersey Archive, spring 1978, otherwise undated)

She begins her next letter with her writing: 'How I wish I were sitting with you on the veranda overlooking the Brahmaputra' (21 March 1978, Jersey Archive).

Gerry replied not with a letter but a telegram dispatched soon after he received the letter of 21 March. He accuses her of 'AUDACITY' and insists that he will not 'CONDONE' her 'PUERILE UNINTELLIGENT AND ADOLESCENT AFFAIR' [with Lincoln]. He will not 'BOTHER

[to] CONTACT YOU AGAIN ... NOTHING YOU CAN SAY WILL ALTER MY VIEWS ON YOUR STUPIDITY BUT WOULD REMIND YOU OF OLD MAXIM ABOUT NOT BEING ABLE TO HAVE YOUR CAKE AND EAT IT' (30 March 1978, Jersey Archive).

We do not know why he responded to her as he did, but we can surmise that she wrote another letter to him after 21 March which displeased him. As is evident below, while much of their correspondence from this period survives in the Jersey Archive there are omissions.

In the letter drafted the day after she received his telegram, she is equally blunt.

It is now very clear to me that the woman you want to marry must in fact be subservient to you, a puppet to you, for the moment she takes any action that you perceive crosses you, she is out on her ear. (31 March 1978, Jersey Archive)

She knew nothing of Jacquie but her observations on Gerry are shrewd and perceptive. The woman from whom he would be divorced in 1979 had stood up to him from the moment they met, which meant that their relationship went into slow, inexorable decline from its first year onwards. 'Don't worry, my dear,' Lee continues, 'puppets and slaves are a dime a dozen and I'm sure you'll find yours soon ... you've lost me.' She does not expect or wish for a response, and this would appear to mark the end of something that had not quite begun. Or it would have done had she posted the signed letter. She did not but it is deposited in the Jersey Archive. Whether the one there is the original from 1979 or one she composed later is not clear. She spoke to her mother and father for the first time of her dilemma, especially whether she could remain with Lincoln or accept Gerry's marriage proposal. Lee did not leave any record of the exchange but it is known that Hal and Harriet McGeorge did not approve of her relationship with Lincoln. They were less concerned with morality than Lee's prospects with a man whose professional future would be as precarious as hers.

In place of the original letter, which she left folded and unposted, she sent a very different one to Jersey calculating that it would arrive around the time that Gerry returned from India.

We met and you asked me to marry you, and, after much painful consideration over the uncertainty of my future with Lincoln, the man I love, and the certainty of the future with you, the man I adore, but do not love, I said yes. (Undated but thought to have arrived in Jersey early April 1978, Jersey Archive)

From Gerry's response on 11 April, he appears to take this as an unequivocal acceptance of his proposal though he could have been forgiven for feeling puzzled, especially by the past-tense phrase, 'I said yes.' To herself, presumably, given that prior to this she had persistently turned him down, on paper and in person. Also, she implies that she has decided to drop Lincoln, 'the man I love', because their future involves 'uncertainty'. She will settle for 'the certainty of the future' with 'the man I adore'. In several letters Gerry drops reassuring hints about his resources. 'Don't worry, we are far from broke ... last year I spent my entire (£56,000) income like water' (21 July 1978, Jersey Archive). In today's terms this comes to around £260,000. This was meant to impress her though his admission that he was so incautious with money management might have been unsettling. In any event he was lying. His personal allowance from the Trust was nowhere close to this amount and much of his royalty income remained allocated to unexpected expenses for the upkeep of the zoo.

In his letter of 11 April, he seems to accept that her decision involves as much pragmatism as passion. 'If it wasn't exactly a love match from your point of view it was at least a business arrangement if you like' (Jersey Archive). Nonetheless he is certain that in time love will replace expediency, perceiving their courtship and engagement as something idealised in the nineteenth century, going so far as to claim that he would not attempt to have pre-marital sex with her because he regarded their long-term relationship as something far more significant than disposable pleasure.

The exact date of their marriage would depend on how long it took to finalise his divorce from Jacquie, whom he portrayed in the letter as someone whose 'constant nagging' and 'total lack of love both mental and physical' led him to alcoholism, a nervous breakdown and 'feeling unclean ... feeling that I had contracted some fearful disease'.

By this point he was planning renovations for the Mazet and buying furniture.

In haste I send you coloured photographs of what we can do in our new bed. Mon Dieu! The mind boggles. Please read the instructions carefully. I don't want you pleading ignorance at the last moment. If the bed breaks within a year (so the shop informed me without a smile) we can claim a new one ... I wish you were in it and I wish I was crossing the room and sliding between the sheets and then ... (27 April 1978, Jersey Archive)

Nothing remains of the photographs which indicate 'what we can do', but his letter of 2 May offers some clues. He promises that:

I am going to stuff you like a Strasbourg Goose, except I won't nail your feet to the floor. Maybe I'll just nail you to the bed. Or nail us both to the bed ... I hope by now you have had the instructions about the bed ... DO NOT PRACTISE THEM WITH ANYONE ELSE BUT ME. I don't mind if you're a bit rusty.

Gerry and Lee were married on 24 May 1979. Gerry's divorce from Jacquie had been settled only three months earlier but he foresaw no further potential complications and arranged the build-up to the ceremony as a symphony, with related movements progressing towards a grand conclusion. Earlier, in November 1978, Lee had performed brilliantly during the three-hour grilling of the oral examination for her doctorate on animal communication. Gerry waited outside the examination room and congratulated her. He was confident that she would succeed and throughout their time together insisted that her name would be prefaced by 'Dr' in all official documentation relating to the Trust. An hour after the oral examination, when her parents had escorted Lee and Gerry to a nearby restaurant, he presented her with first-class air tickets to London, where a private plane would take them to Jersey. There she would meet her fiancé's brother Larry and sister Margo along with those who had worked with him to set up the zoo and the Trust, notably Jeremy Mallinson and John Hartley. They would spend a 'family' Christmas in Les Augrès, though it was not for three years that Lee learned that the fourth sibling Leslie existed. Gerry wished to impress her with the day-long gut-bursting extravagances enjoyed by British gentry during the nineteenth century. An array of crab, lobster and trout was followed by main courses of goose, Scottish beef and roast potatoes. Growing up in America Lee had never encountered the denouement, a vast, dark-brown Christmas pudding served with flaming brandy and then covered in room-temperature cream.

Gerry's next surprise was a train journey from northern France to Spain. Fleur and Tom Cowles, American arts patrons, had donated money to the zoo on several occasions. They found an apartment in Madrid and a Renaissance palace about 150 miles away in Trujillo. Gerry had persuaded them to leave both properties open for him and his fiancée during the New Year and for most of January. Following that Gerry escorted Lee on trips through Monserrat, Antigua, Panama, Costa Rica and other parts of Central America and the Caribbean until they flew north to Memphis where a judge, a friend of Lee's parents, married them. Jeremy Mallinson was best man, Lee wore a dress similar to Scarlett O'Hara's white gown in *Gone with the Wind*, and music was provided by a small band playing flutes and guitars.

Almost three years later Larry wrote to Gerry about the Mazet, specifically his brother's reluctance to finalise any legal arrangement on ownership. Since their marriage Gerry and Lee had treated the property as their private holiday home despite it still being in Larry's name. The delays have 'irritated me as I was hoping not to be taxed for a *residence secondaire*, but of course owing to the delay I have had to declare the Mazet as still mine' (Larry to Gerry, 6 March 1982, Jersey Archive). At the end of January, he had been less courteous. Margo had, he learned, ordered that some correspondence for Gerry, notably from Larry, should be 'suppressed', 'on the grounds that he must not be disturbed when he is worried ... Do you realise that if I die tomorrow I have not one scrap of paper from you explaining what you are doing in the Mazet except squatting? You are always farting and fumbling about your heirs. What about mine!?' (Larry to Gerry, 29 January 1982, Jersey Archive). On the surface the brothers treated each other with tactful respect, but beneath there had been tensions since the 1960s when both had become global celebrities. Neither of their biographers explains why Larry did not attend Gerry and Lee's wedding. Certainly, the journey from southeast France to Memphis might seem arduous but he was already in the US. Larry had flown to Tennessee and, having drunk a fair amount of bourbon, argued with the groom the day before the ceremony. The initial topic of their exchange was the Mazet but there is circumstantial evidence that the property was the tip of a iceberg of deeper antagonism. Later he apologised to Lee. 'I hope by now that you have forgiven my defection from the actual ceremony and are settling in comfortably as Mrs Durrell' (28 May 1979, Jersey Archive). When he wrote this he was still in America and one has to wonder why he did not say sorry to her in person. Shortly afterwards Gerry entered a comment in his private notebook, 'My brother could, out of his nimble and mercurial mind, make statements which you knew to be untrue, but they were produced with such a wealth of convincing detail that you came close to believing them' (Jersey Archive). Obviously he did not treat his brother's apologies as sincere.

The Mazet might seem a slight issue in the relationship between the brothers but it exaggerated and aggravated the tensions between them. For Gerry it was his means of escape from the monetary catastrophe at the zoo. It reminded him of Corfu and his childhood, a place where nature was his main companion and he was answerable to little more than his surroundings. Writing to Lee's parents he often called the place Eden, implying that it freed him and his new wife from the turmoils of the modern, fallen world.

Following his return to France Larry sent his brother and Lee a sardonic note on the church nearby.

> As requested, I have planted candles before the saint for you both – he gave me rather a curt nod in acknowledgement but I think it will be ok ... when I came out of the church I found I had got a parking ticket on the car. (Jersey Archive, 1979, otherwise undated)

Given Larry's taste for profane mysticism it is difficult to decide whether this was piece of protective self-caricature or if he was mocking his sibling's treatment of the area as the source of paradisiacal bliss.

Around a year after he married Lee Gerry reported to her parents on their idyll:

> My wife is very much Lady of the Mazet ... The gardener Jacques comes to look after the olives and pruning ... [He] looks like Lon Chaney and his wife like an extra from *Bride of Frankenstein* ... Jacques tried to stamp out a colony of stick insects ... Lee, outraged by his lack of biological training, went and got a book with illustrations of a stick insect in it. 'If you see one,' said your daughter, 'don't kill it!' Jacques, apparently, retreated in shame. Jacques, like most French peasants, believes that if a living creature is edible it has no right to clutter up the planet. (Jersey Archive, 1980, otherwise undated)

Soon after in his notebook Gerry wrote,

> Mazet – when the wind fills its lungs and winds itself around the house and gleefully plunges down the chimenay [*sic*] to make the fire flare up in a rage, it is then that you know that the grand mistral has started. The wondrous malevolent wind.

Larry hated the mistral and the impatient bitterness in his letters to Gerry regarding a final transaction are not entirely prompted by money. He regarded his brother as having requisitioned part of his French demesne as his private fantasy.

Throughout 1979 and up to 1983 Larry bombarded Gerry with letters. 'Please bring your birth certificates we both have to sign up for the Mazet before the lawyer to make your hold on it firm and true' (1 February 1979, Jersey Archive). 'A quick line to ask if you are having serious 2nd thoughts about the Mazet. I was proposing to offer it to you at 30 million francs for 6 or 7 years.' Buyers in Zurich, he added, had already offered much more. In one of his last letters to Miller before his friend's death he wrote that, 'my brother, delusionist, is trying to turn Herault into the Corfu of his childhood' (Miller, private correspondence, August 1979).

It is intriguing to compare Larry's diagnosis with comments made by Gerry soon after he and Lee began to use the Mazet regularly.

When you travel about the world in search of animals you do not follow the well-worn trail of the tourist. You do not check in at the local Hilton. You do not have ice in your drinks, nor get your shoes polished ... by sticking to the tourist trails you are less likely to meet fascinating animals, both human and otherwise. It is rather like going to France and sticking to the autoroutes, all you see is the other man's exhaust pipe. I have heard people say proudly when in Provence, 'Made it down here in fourteen hours flat. How's that for going, eh? Of course the wife's a bit peaky ...' [He calls this man Percy and states this his own journey down to the Mazet took four days.] I had experienced many things that Percy had missed. He had, for example, missed seeing the dog with a wooden leg being attacked by a much larger member of the canine tribe, fighting it and, moreover, routing it, in spite of the fact that its wooden leg had fallen off in the first round, and so had to battle on only three. Percy had missed an enchanting small snail on the banks of a silver ribbon of river forcing its way through green wings of watercress, a farm run by an old widower and his charming 18-year-old daughter. We drank cider under his plane trees, discussed the sex lives of gastropods, then ate something that his daughter had cooked in parsley, butter, garlic and armagnac. (Jersey Archive, undated)

I think Larry's dismissal of him as a delusionist is wrong: transparent neophyte would be more accurate.

15

Larry: His Closing Chapter

Larry and Ghislaine's divorce proceedings began formally in late 1977. He later wrote to Miller that despite his having made a 'fearful and costly mistake ... G is all right and full of charm – and will have no nasty deal with me' (August 1978), but by September when he was faced with the figures demanded by Ghislaine and her lawyers he flew into a rage. According to Bowker from his interview with her, Larry burst into tears and said to her, 'I'm not crying about divorcing you. It's the alimony that I'm going to have to pay that I'm crying about.' She reported that she laughed uncontrollably (Bowker, p380). No record is available of the annual payments and other arrangements that were demanded and eventually agreed to but it is known that Larry bought a new comfortable flat in a delightful building on the Paris Left Bank and installed her as sole owner. In correspondence with Miller the two men shared reflections on how a break-up seemed to stir a special level of bitterness in women. Miller recalled Hoki's 'black lustreless eye' that followed him throughout their divorce proceedings and Larry bettered this; 'when money is discussed, [Ghislaine's] eye becomes black and dry as the anus of Time's dog!' (10 September 1977, Miller private estate).

Soon afterwards a kind of relief was offered to him in the form of a generously funded documentary film produced and directed by Peter Adam. It would be called *Spirit of Place: Lawrence Durrell's Egypt* and be aimed at a well-read yet considerable audience who treated *The Alexandria Quartet* as a modern classic and who would, as Adam shrewdly predicted, be magnetised by a cinematic tour of Egypt and other parts of the eastern Mediterranean in the presence of the author himself. Larry, Adam, the photographer Colin Waldeck and a crew of twenty others set off from London by air for Cairo on 7 October 1977.

Larry found modern Egypt vulgar and westernised, much less attractive than the place that had inspired his early serious fiction. He loathed the replacement of horse-drawn vehicles by motor cars, at least for use by the indigenous population. When he was there cars were the form of transportation for those who gazed with despotic romanticism on the people stuck with carts, mules and camels. The once magnificent Cecil Hotel in Alexandria where Larry had frequently stayed, dined and had sex was now swept of its nineteenth-century finery and resembled an airport departure lounge of 1970s tastelessness. He was cheered up by what seemed a version of the *Quartet* brought to life. He and Adam were invited to the grand house in Alexandria of Dr Adham El Naqeeb, previously married to the ex-queen of Egypt; the monarchy was abolished in 1952. Naqeeb chose his other guests carefully. Most were dedicated acolytes of Larry who saw him as hauling their country and culture into the Western intellectual hierarchy, even if they hadn't read his books. For Larry his host came across as a pimp, in that a large number of his fellow guests were women under thirty who were happy to make themselves available to him. He reported to Miller that he slept with one on the night of and after the party and referred to her in the letter as the new 'Justine'.

He returned to Sommières in mid-November and found to his horror that Ghislaine had moved back in. She announced that she would remain there until the 27th, the planned official date of their divorce which also involved the transfer to her of the deeds for the Paris flat and the beginning of perpetual monthly bank transfers of his alimony payments. It seemed that she was engaged in a sadistic ritual, celebrating her triumph simply by being there. Divorce proceedings would drag on for a further eighteen months and during this period Ghislaine continually made her presence felt.

He was busy completing *Livia*, the second volume of what would become *The Avignon Quintet*. It was published by Faber in 1978 and has been a magnet for academic speculation in essays and chapters that match the novel as pretentious, overwritten and ludicrous. I will not attempt to summarise the work – such would be the equivalent of trying to nail jelly to a wall – but some of its features are worth one's attention. It seems to be a prequel to *Monsieur* but aside from that other factors stand out. Notably the character Lord Galen, a Jewish financier and friend of the Egyptian Prince Hassad, who is convinced that Hitler will live up to his promise to find a homeland for Jews in the Middle East. Galen eventually becomes sceptical regarding the intentions of the Nazis but with benefit of post-war hindsight he stands out as particularly callous antisemitic stereotype: a rich Jew who is obsessively concerned with making as much money as possible and only at the last minute does he realise that his greed has blinded him to an ideology intent on the extermination of members of his race.

Larry didn't like Jews but he spread his antisemitic net even wider than that. Prince Hassad, obviously a Muslim and an Arab, is shown too to be a naive delusional fool, whose cultural and religious legacy prevents him from recognising the true evil of Nazism. In short Jews and Muslims have a good deal in common. They are trapped in a legacy of self-destructive solipsism.

The only group of people who are able to excuse themselves from the impending fate of Europe, involving political extremism and mass murder, are the novelist Aubrey Blanford and his friends who have no wish to associate themselves with the turmoil of the continent. They prefer drink and sex to anything resembling an engagement with politics or, God forbid, national affiliation. The parallels with Larry himself are self-evident and in the novel he seems to propose his ideological mantra: dissipation and unaccountability are preferable to involvement.

In mid-June 1978 Gerry and Lee spent a month at the Mazet, in separate bedrooms. Despite his lewd hypotheses on what they would get up to in the double bed in letters of the same period Gerry was committed to his promise that their sexual relationship would only begin following their marriage but their presence in Larry's previous home, along with the fact that Ghislaine had promised to pay brief visits to the Sommières house until the divorce was finalised, depressed Larry greatly. Gerry and Lee would spend high summer in the Mazet every year until the former's death and while the brothers did their best to maintain an amicable relationship Larry felt tortured by the annual spectacle of his sibling and his young wife in an apparently perpetual state of bliss.

In September Larry sought relief in a trip to Paris where he would sign copies of *Livia* at various bookshops. Professor Keith Brown of the University of Oslo introduced himself to him and insisted on discussing the 'architecture' of the novels in *The Alexandria Quartet*. Brown was confident that Larry's work would equal Joyce's as a magnet for academics committed to the exegesis of 'difficult' literature. Larry was bored beyond what he previously felt endurable but a miraculous opportunity for release appeared before him when the two men went for a walk along the banks of the Seine. Larry wrote to Miller that he wished to throw himself in but suddenly he recognised a slim woman in a trench coat who was walking towards them. She was the young 'Justine' of his recent visit to Alexandria. Her name remains a secret but she provided Larry with a delicious opportunity to release himself from Brown. She was, he explained to the academic, his niece who he had promised to look after in the city. Later that night, he claimed, they had sex.

Two weeks later in early October he telephoned Claude Kiefer and discussed with her the continuation of their relationship. We do not know what was agreed, or otherwise, but a week after that they met at their old trysting place on Lake Orta and shared a room for several days in the boathouse. There is no record of them ever meeting there or anywhere else again. On his return to France, he arranged to meet up in Paris with the young woman from Alexandria and wrote to Miller that, 'I have been having an extraordinary adventure with a 19-year-old Christian-Canadian Arab ... an angel of light and love' (5 November 1978, Miller private estate).

Later that month he arranged a meeting with Ian MacNiven, who had been in contact with him since the early 1970s. MacNiven wanted to do his biography but Larry was uncertain about the extent to which anyone might be prevented from writing one without his permission. Much correspondence and manuscript material was already deposited in several university archives and there were dozens, hundreds, of people he knew who could be contacted for interviews, and it was likely that those who had most against him would be the more enthusiastic witnesses. Larry promised MacNiven that he would become his authorised biographer after his death. In return, and in the interim, MacNiven would act as his unofficial bodyguard and do his best to disrupt attempts by unlicensed freelancers to write deliberately controversial accounts of him while he was alive.

Larry spent Christmas at Les Augrès with Gerry and Lee, engaged but living in separate bedrooms. Margo joined them and completed the compendium of anachronistic misfits and eccentrics. She reported that Leslie, now working as a barman in a downmarket London pub, had written to her asking if she might try to persuade the two famous brothers of the clan to readmit him to the family circle, pleading that accommodation, even work, in Jersey or France would save him from destitution. Gerry and Larry stated that it was up to her to continue to communicate with him, but they would not.

Larry flew to Paris for the New Year and on New Year's Eve spent the afternoon in La Coupole, then and now one of the most luxurious brasseries in the city, drinking champagne. His guest was Ghislaine whom he had telephoned at her apartment before he flew in. She said later that he told her that he wished to see if some of the 'magic' of their early relationship had survived their break-up and ongoing divorce. As if choreographing a piece of fiction, he had also called Buttons, now thirty-five, and invited her to La Coupole for around 6 p.m., roughly four hours and two bottles of Bollinger after the arrival of Ghislaine. He greeted her with a kiss on the lips and proudly informed Ghislaine that he had booked suite no. 13 – his favourite number – at the nearby Hôtel Le Royal where he and Buttons would spent the night.

His affair with Buttons would continue until May. He insisted on staying at no. 13 in the Hôtel Le Royal but never invited her to Sommières. His ostensible reason was that while their passionate liaisons in Paris energised him, he needed to keep his house largely to himself. He was working on *Constance*, the third volume of *The Avignon Quintet*, and 'sex in the novel cannot overlap with sex in the world' (9 February 1979, Miller private estate). He was lying. Catching the train south from Paris in late January a twenty-year-old concert pianist called Françoise (surname unrecorded) had introduced herself to him at the Gare de Lyon. She was, she announced, from Angers but was heading south to see friends in Provence. Larry would be changing trains in Marseille and after spending several hours talking about his novels, which she adored and had read in English, she accepted his invitation to take a train west to the Languedoc. 'I AM AFRAID IT IS A MIXTURE OF AGE AND ALCOHOL WHICH I AM SLOWLY BRINGING TO HEEL,' he wrote to Miller. 'A RATHER WEARY HEART ... I HAVE BEEN STRAINING BY TRYING TO MAKE LOVE TOO MUCH ... SOME OF THESE CHILDREN DON'T KNOW HOW TO COME OFF AND HAVE TO BE SHOWN!' (16 February 1979, Miller private estate). These 'children', he reported to his friend, were not just Buttons and Françoise; two other young women in their late teens, literary studies students at Montpellier University, visited Sommières regularly, sometimes simultaneously. The chastened atmosphere of Jersey over Christmas must have seemed like a different universe.

According to *Granta* Sappho began therapy on 5 April with a psychoanalyst Patrick Casement in London, which focused on her relationship with her father. She had not lived with him permanently since her childhood but she complained that her occasional visits now amounted to bouts of torture. He had, as long as she could remember, drank excessively and visited on her mother derisory comments and even, she claimed, sometimes resorted to violence. Now he would store up an extreme version of his personality for her visits to Sommières. The psychoanalyst asked if he had ever beaten her. She answered that sometimes he had but that he had done worse than that. Even when she and her mother lived with him in France, he would subject each of them to the spectacle of his adulterous liaisons with young women, some in their teens. Now, claimed Sappho, he would repeat the exercise with cruel precision; during her most recent visit he had, she reported, had noisy sex with two students who seemed younger than her. As if to ensure that these memories would endure, his subsequent letters to her in London would be folded around letters to him from his various lovers, with vividly erotic content.

Shortly after her first session of therapy she recorded in her diary that she had had a miscarriage and five months later in September asked her psychoanalyst to have her admitted to a mental hospital. She was, she recorded in her notes, having a nervous breakdown involving ineradicable visions of her father having sex, and contemplated suicide as her only form of release. Two weeks later in October she drafted her will stating her wish to be buried in a churchyard near Bedales School, which she attended when Eve lived nearby. She also records in her diary notes on books that she read on the recorded history and effects of incest.

She visited Larry at Sommières in December but he barely spoke to her, spending most of his time alone in his study struggling with the recalcitrant draft of *Constance*. He encouraged her to leave by the 15th so that he could make arrangements to visit Paris for Christmas where he stayed, yet again, in the Hôtel Le Royal in room 13. This time his fellow guest is a thirty-one-year-old French woman, a psychiatrist called Nicole, barely a year older than Sappho. Her surname is unknown but he continued to see her until April 1980, now producing more than a thousand words a day for his previously deadlocked novel. The eponymous Constance is during this same period turned into a psychoanalyst, and Livia from the previous novel commits suicide. Sappho claimed in her journal that she was the model for Livia.

On 7 June 1980 Henry Miller died at the age of eighty-eight. At the same time Larry fell ill with asthma and when Fiddle Viracola called him to arrange accommodation when he attended Miller's funeral, he screamed at her down the phone that, 'I don't want to go! There's going to be a bunch of bums hanging about. I know what my relationship with him is!' (MacNiven, p646). He hated the idea of there being hordes of literary writers – 'coat-trailers' he called them – and academics making a claim on the legacy of a man with whom he felt he had a unique relationship. He did not attend and refused to be interviewed or quoted for commemorations of him. The asthma lasted until 1981 and was complicated by arthritis. Larry claimed that the cause was the loss of a vital, irreplaceable part of himself.

In September 1980 Sappho married Simon Tompsett at Islington Town Hall, with two secretaries as witnesses. Neither of her parents attended. Larry and Eve suspected that Simon was a gold digger but Larry hated the prospect of his daughter becoming a squatter and gave her £5,000 to help purchase a flat in southeast London, then still an affordable area. They found a small dilapidated terraced house in Clapham for just over £10,000 and Larry's £5,000 plus the difference from Tompsett's family enabled them to buy it for cash. It needed a few more thousand to make it habitable. In late September Larry visited London for the launch of his *Collected Poems, 1931–1974* and *A Smile in the Mind's Eye*, a memoir or, as Larry put, it a 'spiritual journey' with his mentor in Zen Buddhism Jolan Chang, exploring the parallels between this Eastern philosophy, yoga, cooking, poetry, Petrarch and Nietzsche. Its impact in Britain, then experiencing its first year of Thatcherism, was modest. Sappho and Simon had just moved into their new home though neither was invited to Larry's book launches. Nonetheless Sappho phoned Larry in France shortly before he flew to England offering him accommodation in their spare room. He thanked her but stated rather curtly that he had arranged to stay with friends he'd met in France. In truth he spent much of his time over a hundred miles outside London at the run-down Somerset house of Miller's close friend Alfred Perlès, despite the fact that he and Perlès' wife Anne held each other in mutual contempt. In London Larry arranged an appointment with the consultant Raymond Mills with whom he'd become friends in Rhodes. Mills confirmed his suspicion that he was indeed suffering from asthma but that his frequent and severe bouts of shortness of breath were not caused exclusively by the condition. Obesity and heavy drinking were part of the problem.

He arrived back in Paris in early October and woke Buttons in her flat at just after 6 a.m. before she was due to set off for work. There was time enough for sex, though somewhat laboured on his part. He wrote to Perlès: 'I'm lucky – must not become gateux with it' (3 October, Larry to Perlès; privately held by Perlès family). By 'gateux' he meant to become stupid under the influence of extreme excitement or adoration. He took the train back to Sommières and entered once more his struggle to complete *Constance*.

In February 1981 Larry began to feel that the joints in his arms, legs, hips and virtually everywhere else were gradually seizing up. For almost a month he could not use his hands to type or write with a pen and his casual knowledge of Taoism convinced him that he had fractured the ideal symbiotic relationship between the body, the natural world and the mind. The latter, Larry felt, had been disrupted by *Constance*, an intellectual exercise that he had come to loathe. He felt that the book returned his feelings of hatred which had resulted in his mental and physical ruin while his local GP suggested that his condition was the result of aspirin overdoses. He gulped the pills throughout the day to offset the effects of alcoholism, specifically hangovers that involved acute headaches along with other devastating pains. In effect he was poisoning himself twice over.

At the end of February Sappho arrived at Sommières unannounced and stayed only two days. Her father was reluctant to acknowledge her presence, let alone speak to her.

On 1 April Larry delivered a talk on his life and work at the Centre Pompidou and such was his esteem within the French intelligentsia that it went out live on the French state television news broadcast at 1 p.m. Several hundred people attended and as the audience dispersed Larry walked towards the exit with his interviewer and was greeted by a lone figure waiting at the door. 'Would you care to join me for champagne?' she asked him. 'After that, you deserve the best.' Ghislaine then introduced herself to the interviewer as Larry's wife, leaving him to explain that they were divorced. However, he felt unable to tell her to leave and the three of them spent an uncomfortable two hours in a nearby brasserie. Clearly, she was taking revenge against him for the similar prank in New Year 1978 when he gave the impression that the two of them would spend the day at Le Coupole drinking champagne only to substitute her for Buttons halfway through.

On his return to Sommières Larry completed the first draft of *Constance*, though he would continue with revisions until he dispatched it to Faber in March 1982. Several key figures from the first two volumes of the *Quintet* reappear but they, along with new ones, notably the eponymous Constance, are placed in a radically different context: the occupation of France and much of the rest of Europe by the Nazis.

Some critics have mused on Larry's treatment of Nazism as like gnosticism – an anti-Judeo-Christian cult, but founded perversely on an adoration of evil: positive gnosticism is based on a worship of health-giving sex. (See Bowker, p395, for example.)

Others might treat it as a perverse celebration of the atrocious. Apart from the killing of Constance's husband Sam, von Esslin – an aristocratic, Catholic German General – is blinded, Blanford is paralysed from the waist down and Constance's sister Livia (of the earlier novel) loses an eye in a failed suicide attempt. Eventually she succeeds in hanging herself. The reason, it seems, is that she had an incestuous affair with her brother Hilary who is guillotined in front of her. Constance and her lover Affad attempt to achieve a state of quasi-mystical transcendence through vaguely gnostic sexual practice. This fails because each is unable to surrender a sense of control and Larry implies a parallel with the post-war execution of Nancy Quiminal of Avignon who was the lover of a senior Nazi.

In October 1982 it was shortlisted for the Booker Prize. Here I must confess a private insight. My 'Moral Tutor' at Oxford, John Carey, was the Chair of the Booker Committee. 'God,' he asked me, 'how can anyone turn Nazism into pornography?' The book which won the Prize did the opposite – Thomas Keneally's *Schindler's Ark*.

Six weeks before the Booker decision Leslie Durrell died from a heart attack in a Notting Hill pub, on 13 August. He and his wife Doris had spent their early years in London working as live-in caretakers for a wealthy couple but later took on a similar but less agreeable position in a block of insalubrious flats near Marble Arch. He was cremated in Bournemouth and while Margo had visited the couple when she could, she was recovering from an operation and unable to attend the funeral. Gerry and Larry refused even to speak of the loss let alone mourn their sibling. There are suggestions that Doris had left Leslie a few years before his death. She was not at the cremation and we know nothing more of her than that she died in London in 1990. Her son Michael had stayed in Kenya following his mother and stepfather's shameful departure. Apart from the single letter Gerry sent to Leslie in 1968 stating that he wished to have no further contact with him after he fled Kenya having swindled a number of wealthy expatriates, neither Gerry nor Larry acknowledged their brother's existence after he and Doris moved to Africa in 1952. Nor did they show any interest in the fate of Anthony, Leslie's son from his affair with Maria Condos, the Greek maid who had come with the Durrell family from Corfu to England. Maria, who had loved him greatly, did not learn of his death. Margo would have informed her but knew that such a gesture was pointless given that Maria was in an NHS hospice suffering from advanced Alzheimer's. The only occasion on which Leslie came close to meeting one of his brothers in person was in 1977 after he obtained Larry's address from Margo. He travelled to Sommières by various forms of public transport and Margo had telephoned Larry asking him to receive his brother hospitably. Despite the chaotic state of their marriage Ghislaine was in residence and he asked her to meet his brother at the door after instructing her to inform him that Monsieur Durrell was absent and would not be receiving messages let alone uninvited guests. Why exactly the two famous Durrells treated their brother with such contempt will remain a mystery. They left no record, written or oral, of what it was about Leslie that caused them to shun him. He was something of a scoundrel, certainly, but neither of his brothers was perfect. In all probability they were anxious that direct association with him would draw press attention and cast an unwelcome shadow across their respective profiles.

1983 was a year of ominous prefigurings. In January Sappho was admitted to hospital following a nervous breakdown. For some reason, still unexplained, Simon was not at their house and could not be contacted and Penny, her half-sister, moved in to take care of the property and to visit her in hospital. Penny contacted Larry but he replied that he was too busy with the fourth novel in *The Avignon Quintet*, *Sebastian*, to come to London. Close to its completion he sent Gerry what amounts to a confessional letter on how it and the previous volumes of the *Quintet* came into being through his perpetual habits of predatory sexuality. 'The [*Quintet*] is EN FIN done and I feel as free as I was at twenty. What a lot of girls it has taken me to write [it]. What potions have I drunk of sirens' tears' (Larry to Gerry, 6 March 1982, Jersey Archive). One can only wonder at what Ghislaine, Margaret McCall, Claude Kiefer, Buttons, Françoise and others would have felt about their unwitting contribution to the literary canon. It took a further ten months to polish it into a final draft which he sent to Faber at the beginning of 1983 and in March set off for a period of relaxation in Corfu. He hoped to stay with his old friends Peter and Joan Bird but despite Peter's attempts to persuade his wife that he would be a tolerable guest she refused to admit him to the house. He had been with them on the island during the previous summer and his drinking – beginning with spirits at breakfast – had forced Joan to throw him out. Had he simply become unconscious she could have put up with him but as each day went on, drink drove him further into rants against various political and religious affiliations – Jews in particular – and vivid descriptions of his recent sexual experiences with young women. She did not wish to risk another version of this and Larry had to book a small suite at the Club Mediterranée.

Following his return, he received news from Gerry of the death of Theodore Stephanides in England at the age of eighty-seven. He and Gerry were devastated. In his letter Gerry told of how Theodore had ordered the hospital matron to instruct consultants to use his eyes and any other organs for transplants, with a codicil that they must be 'absolutely certain that I'm dead'. 'So, he ends, not on a bang or a whimper but a Victorian joke,' Gerry added (Jersey Archive, undated).

Eight weeks later, on 8 June, Nancy Myers Durrell Hodgkin died of cancer aged seventy-one in Milton Abbas, Dorset. Her two daughters, Penny and Joanna, were present, along with her husband Edwin Hodgkin, and Margo. Larry did not know she was unwell, mainly because of his habit of ceasing to communicate with ex-partners and ex-wives and his reluctance to allow children or others to act as intermediaries. Nonetheless those who encountered Larry over the next few months found that he was clearly distraught.

As a compensation, for himself, he committed himself to the completion of *The Avignon Quintet*. He had sent *Sebastian*, volume four, to Faber in February and it came out to mixed reviews in late September. In October Sappho attempted to commit suicide with an overdose of sleeping pills. She seemed to change her mind in that she called her mother Eve and asked her to dial 999 for an ambulance before she lost consciousness. Her stomach was pumped and she survived, but only just.

Larry's life with women changed significantly in February 1984 because of Françoise Kestman, a pretty woman in her forties of mixed French and Slavic heritage. For two years she and her partner had owned and run a bar and restaurant in Sommières until in 1983 he had left in the night with as much of the previous year's takings as he could fit into his bag. Like most other small-business people in France, they dealt as much as they could in cash to avoid the state taxes, seemingly designed to ruin virtually all private enterprise.

Larry had taken drinks in her bar and got to know her well. She offered to become 'femme de ménage' at his house for a small wage, enough to keep her five children who still lived above the bar. She would become his cook, maid and 'protector', making sure that prying journalists would get no further than the forbidding steel gates to the house.

Larry's health was causing a concern for all around him. At a book launch in Paris in April 1984 he collapsed and appeared to be undergoing a potentially fatal cardiovascular arrest but came around after about ten minutes. He had already been diagnosed as suffering from hepatitis and was eventually told that unless he gave up drink, he would have barely six months to live. He did not go on the wagon but for a year until May 1985 he tried to limit himself to wine. After that he returned to drinking a bottle of whisky a day on average.

Three months earlier friends of Sappho had found her hanging from a beam in the attic bedroom of the house she co-owned with Simon.

I have already referred to Sappho's collection of notes that appeared in *Granta* 37, Autumn, 1991, specifically passages in which she recalls Larry's violent behaviour towards her mother Eve when she, Sappho, was an infant. Far more controversial were the coded and cryptic claims she made about her later relationship with her father, during and after his marriage to Claude-Marie.

> Since Claude died his traditional pattern of *wife = whore/stupid/bitch* and *me = Virgin/wise* has disintegrated. Because none of the women he has had since Claude died ever measured up to her, he has been placing more and more of the wife's role on me and he is *always* aggressive towards wives ... He is a master in the art of psychological destruction. He knows just where to hit. (*Granta*, Autumn 1991)

She added: 'I feel very threatened by the fact that my father is sleeping with women who are my age or younger. I feel he is committing a form of mental incest and that it is a message to me as his favourite daughter' (*Ibid.*). Sappho used the term 'mental incest' ambiguously, suggesting both that he is doing with women of her age what he has not, physically, done with her, while implying that he replicates his incestuous relationship with her by sleeping with young women, girls, of her age. In the bag of papers that Sappho left with her friend and executor Barbara Robson were letters which included descriptions of their sexual activities. They were not published in *Granta* but Robson testified to their existence.

Following the passage in the journal where she tells of how her father took her on a night-time visit to Claude-Marie's grave Sappho shifts back to when she seems to have been in her early teens, and tells an exchange:

> He: I'm not interested in you as a woman. Right at this moment. I can feel my blood withdrawing from my skin and shrinking into my centres, and a little bit of warm companionship helps ... Come on, unlace a bit.
> She: I'm level. As the situation stands or falls I see I have no choice ...
> (*Ibid.*)

Some have remarked that the discontinuities and fragmented frame of reference of the journal, often clouding the difference between the actual and the fantastic/mythological, testify to Sappho's mentally disturbed condition and cast doubts on the veracity of her claims about Larry's behaviour.

However, a very different inference can be drawn from it. Sappho had writerly ambitions – in the bag of papers she gave to Robson was a play of hers about Emily Brontë, for example – and she saw her father as by equal degrees her inspiration and her hindrance. In the journal:

> I know that, *rationally*, he would like me to stand up and create, but that there is something in him which would 'kill' me if I did – would knock what I did. I will always have his ego between me and the world, and my surroundings will be as dry as dust. (*Ibid.*)

Often, she shifts from the particulars of her relationship with her father to descriptions of states, locations they shared.

> Shuttered balconies swarming with rats, and old women whose hair is full of the blood of ticks. Peeling walls leaning drunkenly to east and west of their true centre of gravity. The black ribbon of flies attaching itself to the lips and eyes ...

These are Larry's words, from *Justine*, not Sappho's, but in her journal, she demonstrates that she is her father's equal in the creation of scenarios by parts squalid, horrifying and apocalyptic. Notable among these is her description of 'Mudu's house' in the Po Valley, 'arbitrary and unknown'. 'Mudu (Modo, Prince of Darkness) belongs to that category of country lesbians ... pert, shrewd, fixing you with an eye that has all the sharpness and flatness of a cod' (*Granta*, Autumn 1991).

Sappho had read all of her father's more challenging and controversial novels, including *The Alexandria Quartet* and those parts of *The Avignon Quintet* completed before she died, and she was fully aware of how he saw fiction as a means of usurping the actual world rather than an imitation of it. She knew too that she, like many women in his life, her mother included, had become part of the raw material of his process, recycling real life as his private universe of words. Hence her otherwise gnomic comment on how, 'I will always have his ego between me and the world' becomes transparent: she, and others, would always be subject to his authoritarian writerly presence.

Her journal is her testimony to the effect of being his daughter. She creates a replica – in idiom, style and mythological frame – of his major novels. This version will be hers, not his. Her most striking statement is: 'I seem to suffer from the hypochondriac obsession that I will die early and that he wants me to die before him' (*Ibid.*). The sentence and the journal itself prefigures her suicide; both were her means of escaping his controlling persona.

Was Sappho's childhood quite so bizarre as she states in those parts of the journal that take us back to her early years?

There is an unpublished letter by her step-sister Diana Forde, Claude-Marie's daughter from her first marriage, written when she, aged about fifteen, and her brother Barry spent a summer holiday with Larry and Sappho in the south of France (letter from Diana to her maternal grandmother, 29 July 1961, Jersey Archive). Mostly it is a light-hearted account of swimming, attempts to read French magazines, food and the glorious weather but sometimes it shifts towards the utterly macabre. She writes of 'the night we spent at the Mazet and I kept seeing lunatics peeping in the windows'.

A few nights later 'I woke up and had to make a perilous journey to the loo. I saw three mad women in Sappho's room (she sleeps with the door open, so does Barry) and two treacherous orderlies in Barry's room ...'

> I got into the bathroom and nearly died of shock when I saw a whole lot of surgical instruments (bloodstained) on the window sill and a pile of gory cotton wool and operating gowns in the basin. I couldn't get at the paper because there was a skeleton with a hole in its skull in the way. I couldn't sleep so I opened [my] book to read ...

There is no evidence that Diana made up these accounts to shock or amuse her grandmother. Her tone and mood remain consistent throughout the letter. Indeed, the paragraph following the above quote opens with: 'We spend our time swimming, sunbathing, playing or playing snakes and ladders. Yesterday afternoon we had a limerick competition which we all won.'

For some time, Larry had kept a notebook which was devoted to necrophilia, gory births and executions, dissections of dead and living humans and vampirism. He referred to Sommières property as the 'Vampire House'. Many of Larry's novels, especially in the *Quintet*, feed on such themes. Diana's letter suggests that they were inspired by something more substantive than his ghoulish imagination. It seems clear enough that Larry was a ghastly sexual pervert who involved his family in his abnormal practices.

In February 1985 Sappho was buried at Trent Park Cemetery in Cockfosters. Larry was not there but he went to a memorial service a few days later in St Luke's Church, Chelsea, on 9 February.

Thereafter he seemed perpetually exiled from his previous self. He never again had a sexual relationship, though Françoise Kestman made herself available if he were so inclined. While he continued to commit himself obsessively to the completion of the *Quintet*, he seemed to have little time for non-fictional individuals, irrespective of his earlier association with them.

In June 1985 the French 'fisc', the tax service, served Larry with a writ for £250,000 of what they calculated to be unpaid taxes. This, on top of

Sappho's death, plummeted him into a state of desolation and melancholy much worse than any he had previously experienced. He felt that he was being assailed by vengeful forces intent on making his life intolerable. He appealed against the fisc ruling on the ground that he had never deliberately withheld payment of taxes for monies earned outside France and that their calculation of interest owed on his tax burden, amounting to more than 50 per cent of the total, was inaccurate and capricious: why, his lawyer argued, had they imposed an extraordinary charge on an amount which neither Larry nor the tax service knew was owed? Larry himself considered suicide. He told Françoise that he felt that he had killed his most vulnerable child by predicting, perhaps encouraging, a fictional version of her to decide to kill herself. The judgement by *le fisc* to take most of his money was what he deserved. He would, he added, finish the job himself. Françoise persuaded him that he was not to blame for what Sappho did and that the tax nightmare could be resolved.

It was she who convinced him to accept an invitation to Pennsylvania State University for April 1986. It was to be an enormous conference attended by at least a hundred academics from Europe and the US, and as many graduate students and non-academic writers. Larry was being recognised as a contemporary genius. Despite his misgivings, he went, only to find that during his various podium discussions the French tax authorities had ruled against his appeal. He phoned his lawyer who advised that the only option was via the *viager* system, the handing over of assets to the state as an alternative to cash payment. He offered them the Sommières house, again on the instruction of his lawyer. The latter advised him that the state system was so inefficient and slow-moving that even if they accepted his offer, with the codicil that he should remain in the top floor as rent-free resident, it would probably take at least six years for them to make a decision. Larry was seventy-four at the time so he thought that such a delaying tactic would be worthwhile. It was a shrewd decision because while the French revenue officials debated the issue Larry took instruction from his London agent – who had consulted a clever solicitor – that to confuse the French even more and probably evade tax completely Larry should become an official resident of the UK with the status of a 'tourist' in France carrying a British passport. Thanks to EEC regulations he would now be subject only to the tax regime of his home country, which under Margaret Thatcher had become hospitable to the decently well-off. On 1 June 1987 Larry became fully British and the French authorities gave up in their pursuit of his monies and resources. The famous lady with the handbag had, along with Pudding Island, rescued Larry from penury.

In January 1984 he had sent a draft of *Quinx*, the concluding volume of *The Avignon Quintet*, to Faber only to have his editor return it with requests for revisions. Larry's fiction was the quintessence of the afterlife of modernism. Faber, for so many years run by T. S. Eliot, treated him as their vanguard of experimental difficulty, the man who produced books that most found unreadable and which guaranteed his publisher's status as the cornerstone of literary elitism. This time, however, he seemed to have crossed the boundary of inaccessibility.

This was understandable because while Françoise tried to limit his access to strong alcohol her French liberal temperament prevented her from locking up his bottles of spirits, and by the mid-1980s he was drinking more whisky than the locals did wine. By June 1984 he produced a version that Faber accepted and it was published on 20 May 1985. By 7 July it was listed at number three on the fiction bestseller list in the *Sunday Telegraph*, quite an achievement given that it is astonishing that sane individuals would wish to read it. Many of the characters from the previous four volumes appear, even those who are not 'real' but inventions of Blanford the novelist. Their activities in Europe during the aftermath of the Second World War are ludicrous and rather disquieting, given our knowledge of what the conflict inflicted on the continent. We have an ex-Nazi double agent Smirgel who might know something of the hidden Templar treasure that fascinates everyone. And then there's our old friend Lord Galen, Jewish aristocrat, who has spent most of his albeit fictional existence in pursuit of the treasure. Constance returns, as does the now completely blind General von Esslin, and one question presides: why? Narrative timelines shift aimlessly sometimes to the present day, the 1980s, and just as the work seems to edge towards an old-fashioned notion of a conclusion, with the Templar treasure seemingly about to be discovered, Blanford 'thought that if he ever wrote the scene he would say: "It was at this precise moment that reality prime rushed to the aid of fiction and the totally unpredictable began to take place!"' Some readers

335

might pretend to understand this but it's plain sailing compared with when Constance explains both to her fellow characters and the reader that 'We exist in five-skanda form, aggregates, parcels, lots, congeries. They cohere to form a human being when you come together and create the old force-field quinx, the five-sided being ...' To which the single appropriate response is, 'But I only asked for the salt.'

In early March 1986 he visited London, encouraged by his agent Anthea Morton-Saner and Faber, to sustain the early momentum of sales and courageous readership of *Quinx*. He did interviews with the *Telegraph*, *Guardian* and *Sunday Independent* and appeared on BBC Radio 4's *Woman's Hour* and the BBC World Service's *Meridian*. As usual he seemed intent on shocking, appalling and confusing listeners and readers. For *Woman's Hour* he declared that feminists were intent on proving that men 'weren't up to it', meaning sex, and derided Thatcherite Britain for impoverishing human sensibility and sexuality by replacing empathy and the intellect with false consumerism (*Woman's Hour*, March 1986). A year later he would exchange his French residency for British citizenship as a means of avoiding Gallic taxation. For the first week he stayed at the Morton-Saner house but when they had to bring in builders he moved into the prestigious and expensive Lansdowne Club in Mayfair. He enjoyed the massive indoor heated pool and after a swim on his second day decided to sample the widely recommended range of Irish and Scotch whiskies in the bar. At the entrance he was informed that members must wear a tie for admission. Larry asked the attendant if there was a spare bow tie behind the bar, which apparently there was. Further problems arose when he said that he would be happy to put it on and leave his rather damp dressing gown at the door. He was wearing nothing else but his baggy shorts. The next day he checked out, returned to France and never again visited England.

On 15 April he flew to New York, first for a party thrown in his honour in the city by Viking Penguin to publicise the launch of the US edition of *Quinx*, and then on to the fourth and so far biggest conference of the International Lawrence Durrell Society, made up almost exclusively of academics, at Pennsylvania State University. Larry, reluctantly, did a talk on his life and work, without notes or preparation. It was perpetually digressive in that there was no central theme from which it might digress. The delegates loved it because it struck a chord for their elitist sensibilities: like his novels it was impenetrable. It was published in *On Miracle Ground* (1990), a collection of academic essays from that conference and others. In print it makes sense, almost, because the editor of the volume Michael Begnal, Professor of English at Penn State, rewrote it.

How he really felt about becoming an icon of the academic establishment is evident in an interview he gave for *Le Matin*.

> They analyse a poem like a kitchen implement. I was reassured, they called me the new Einstein. Each character from *The Quartet* and *The Quintet* produced its own fan club. (*Le Matin*, 6 June 1986)

He found them absurd but he was polite enough to keep quiet until after his return to France.

Collections of Larry's work and unpublished writings, notably his correspondence with Miller (1988), would continue to appear. There remains an appetite, especially within academia and in the literary intelligentsia, for a clearer perception of this enigmatic figure. But over the subsequent four years he would only complete one new book, his reflections on the life and landscape of southern France, *Caesar's Vast Ghost: Aspects of Provence*. He finished a draft in 1987 but Faber was disappointed and returned it for revision. It would not go into print until shortly before his death in 1990.

Françoise became his carer and often his proxy. In August 1987 he was invited to attend the opening of the Buddhist Temple at Kagyu-Ling (actually the Chateau de Plaige in Burgundy) as guest of honour. He declined their invitation to give a talk and was only able to attend because Françoise drove him there and helped him to his room. Similarly, she drove him to Lyon and took care of him for the performance of the French version of his 1963 play *An Irish Faustus*.

In March 1988 Gerry and Lee were in the Mazet and the latter drove her husband to Sommières with a casserole and some wine. Larry was grateful but the meeting horrified both of them. They seemed to have become mirror images of each other, depressingly obese and hardly able to move around without discomfort. A month later Larry suffered a seizure far worse than anything before. The French GP diagnosed epilepsy, while referring him to a neurologist, but the fits continued and Christophe, Françoise's eldest son, was installed in the top floor of the house. He was much stronger than his mother and judged able to move Larry to a safe position following another collapse.

During the winter of 1988–9 Françoise contacted Larry's closest friends and relatives and encouraged them to visit him in an attempt to bring him out of what seemed a deepening state of melancholia. Penny and her new husband John Hope came, as did the Birds, his painter friend from the 1950s Barbara Robinson, and his long-serving physician Raymond Mills. Gerry and Lee spent Christmas at the Mazet and invited Larry and Françoise over for dinner. He declined and the brothers never met again.

In October 1989 Larry was awarded the Grand Prix Littéraire Jacques Audiberti. He refused to go to the ceremony and it was accepted on his behalf by Françoise and his agent Morton-Saner.

His old friend Jean Fanchette managed to see him in June 1990, despite his having become a recluse, and reported to his then authorised biographer Ian MacNiven that he was 'drinking himself to death'. Thereafter few if any people reported on his state of health or mind because hardly any were allowed into the house. On 24 September he lowered the drawbridge for Peter and Joan Bird and Raymond Mills. They took him to lunch at a nearby restaurant but have little recollection of their exchanges. His speech was incoherent and slurred.

In early October Françoise phoned Penny, stating that she should come to Sommières urgently. She stayed for three weeks during which Françoise on 6 November agreed to marry Larry. He had proposed to her five times over the previous three years. On the 7th Françoise's brother found him dead in the bathroom having suffered a cerebral haemorrhage.

He was cremated at Orange and aside from Françoise and her son Christophe only Penny of his immediate family was present. Françoise took his ashes back to Sommières but there is no record of where they were scattered or buried. There is a note in the Jersey Archive where Gerry states that 'I always considered my elder brother to be a somewhat inconsiderate man ... This is borne out by the fact that I was in the middle of a highly important animal-collecting expedition in Madagascar in an area that had neither plane, fax, phones, nor even decent roads, when Larry chose to die ... it was too late for me to comfort his ... former wives [and] his numerous lamenting girlfriends ... around the world.'

A month after the funeral Gerry, back in Jersey, received a reminder of the bizarre and insalubrious aspects of bohemian London to which his brother had introduced him after the war. It was addressed to 'The Duke of Angwantibo, of Les Augrès Manor [Gerry]',

Your Grace,
His Majesty the King is in Africa at present but I feel sure that he
    would wish to express to you his condolences on [the loss of] the
    Duke of Cervantes Pequeña [Larry] ...
I beg to remain His Majesty's servant and yours truly
The Reverend Baron Montalk

The 'King' was Count Geoffrey Potocki de Montalk, poet, visionary, pornographer and pretender to the Polish throne, who had welcomed the Durrell brothers to his court of equally eccentric aesthetes in Soho and Bloomsbury, notably John Gawsworth who is also mentioned in the letter of condolence. Gerry behaved as if he had been greeted by a ghost and asked Lee to reply with a brief and innocuous letter of thanks.

16

The Real Gerry

The Garden of the Gods (1978) was the final volume of the Corfu trilogy which began with *My Family and Other Animals*. Some reviews (such as that in the *Boston Globe*) received it well but at the same time implied that Gerry was testing his appeal as a stand-up comic, still able to amuse his audience but only by improvising on a long-repeated story. The familiar cast of Mother, Margo, Leslie, Lawrence, Spiro and Theodore are asked to perform in slightly different comic scenarios and Nancy, Lawrence's first wife, still no longer exists. New, entirely fictitious members of the cast are brought in: Lumis Bean, Harry Bunny, Prince Jeejeebuoy and Count Rossignol appear like farcical, exotic figures from a 'Carry On Corfu' film. The *Washington Post* reviewer said that he could not laugh aloud, 'though I could see I was expected to'.

Gerry still had ambitions to produce fiction comparable to his brother's. In 1979 he submitted to Collins a collection of short stories, *The Picnic and Suchlike Pandemonium*, and his editor, Philip Ziegler, reported to the editorial committee that, 'Of course we want to publish it', but that it was below 'his top standards', such that they saw 'a downhill trend in Gerry's sales' (April 1979, otherwise undated, Jersey Archive). Gerry was sent this note by his new agent Felicity Bryan and replied, 'Is it time I started looking for another publisher?' (6 April 1979, Jersey Archive). She told him that he should not, but his morale was damaged.

His cultural nadir was his appearance in 1979 on *Zodiac and Co*, a series made on a shoestring for Channel TV, the regional Channel Islands branch of the ITV commercial network. It was hoped that the format could be sold nationwide but the audience on the islands was so slight that it folded within a year. An astrologer, a palmist and a graphologist were asked to disclose the identity of an anonymous 'star', from only their gender, date of birth, handwriting and palmprints. It came close to being a parody of itself and his agent informed him bluntly that before taking on anything similar he must send them details.

Jeremy Mallinson, his longest-serving colleague at the zoo, told Botting that, 'Lee was undoubtedly Gerry's saviour', in terms of his health, and his career as a writer and zoologist. 'He had been in hell, and if that had gone on I think he would have died of a kind of slow suicide' (Botting, p471).

She came close to arriving too late. Their first major collaboration was the BBC documentary *The Edge of Extinction*. Shot in 1979 and televised in July 1980 it prefigures today's protests by the likes of Extinction Rebellion and Just Stop Oil. Contemporary campaigners argue that all forms of life – animal and plant life included – are facing imminent apocalypse but Gerry and Lee were just as vehement in their insistence that many non-human species were being systematically extinguished for commercial gain.

It was begun in the Wild Animal Park in San Diego, California, and finished in Les Augrès. Following their return from the US and on the way to the zoo from Jersey Airport Gerry complained of severe chest pains which soon afterwards his GP diagnosed as something worse than angina. It was, he said, a 'minor heart attack', he prescribed doses of blood-thinning medicines and insisted that he must reduce his weight from fourteen to twelve stone and drastically minimise his alcohol intake. Lee, shrewd beyond her years, was aware that any attempt to impose a regime of dietary restrictions and near-teetotalism on a man who had spent his life in love with the finest foods and drinks would be counter-productive. He would retaliate by overindulging, secretly if necessary, so she adopted a method of offering him what he most wished for, while politely, and humorously when she could, reminding him that she wanted to spend as long with him as possible.

She had already arranged for them go to the Mazet for the autumn with her parents Harriet and Hal and her sister Hat would fly in to

Paris and take the train south. Lee attempted to create an atmosphere reminiscent of Corfu during his childhood, where he would do much as he wished but without overindulging in things that might shorten his life. Local friends, most shared between him and his brother, called in, including Yehudi Menuhin and his wife Diana, the sculptress Elisabeth Frink and the painter Tony Daniells. Each had been a regular guest of Larry, nearby, but by the close of summer 1979 the latter had become something of a recluse, at least from those with whom he was not having affairs: Claude Kiefer, still; Buttons, intermittently; and the thirty-one-year-old otherwise Paris-based psychiatrist named Nicole. Gerry and Larry rarely communicated while Gerry was in southern France with his new wife. They lived barely twenty kilometres apart.

When Gerry and Lee returned to Jersey at the end of November 1979, they were met by Mrs Boizard, a veteran from the foundation of the zoo who informed them that their neighbour Leonard de Feu was about to put his house on the market. It was not as grand as the manor but was a wonderful farmhouse, even older, with a worker's cottage, outbuildings and eight acres. The Trust was doing well and Gerry made de Feu an offer which he immediately accepted. Les Noyers, as it was called, would become part of the Trust, a study centre for conservationists and zoologists. It would never in its own right offer degree qualifications but it was treated by several universities in the UK and the US as a research hub; doctoral students from prestigious universities would use it as a base for their research. Dr David Waugh, eminent zoo biologist and conservationist, was appointed to a role as proxy Vice Chancellor.

Gerry and Lee arranged to go to Mauritius in January 1981 and they arrived on the island of Madagascar in March. Gerry felt like he had revived the energy and anger of the 1950s. First, he came upon the 'beautiful and endearing' cousin of standard lemurs, and in the jungle, he heard the yowling cry of the indri, 'musical and beautiful' (Jersey Archive). When he found them, they reminded him of Australia; part koala bear, part kangaroo. They were fluffy, friendly with tangerine-coloured eyes and willing to sit alongside their human companions. The visit was funded and sponsored by Jeremy Isaacs for a Channel 4 series and while the money from that was useful Gerry wanted to take various species back to Jersey. They did not have the equipment and certainly not the funds to move even the smallest creatures. The recollections of the 1950s now became a waking nightmare. Deforestation was destroying the native environment of the animals he'd seen and he could do nothing about it.

Over the next three years Gerry and Lee would make visits to Panama, Belize and South Africa. Again, resources were insufficient for them to collect threatened species and return them to Jersey and the main purpose of such excursions was to make notes for the largest publishing project they would co-research and write. Dorling Kindersley was set up as a book packager in 1974 but by 1980 were expanding into the publishing industry as a brand for glossy-paged, beautifully illustrated volumes on everything from gardening and cooking to its main market, travel and environmental writing. Its new commissioning editor, Joss Pearson, approached Gerry with an idea to do a book called *The Amateur Naturalist*. The selling point would be that one of the most prestigious naturalists/zoologists of his generation, along with his photogenic young wife, would educate those with an appetite for knowledge of the globe's living creatures and plant life, the subtext being that those interested in the ideals of Greenpeace and of conservation in general would have a comprehensive reference guide shot through with polemical writing by Gerry and Lee. The advance of £30,000 was good from a relatively small house, and even more convincing was a contractual guarantee that the first print run would be at least 160,000 which if it sold out would provide Gerry and Lee with over £100,000 in royalties.

The couple signed immediately and toiled strenuously over the volume during every spare minute they had over the next three years. It sold out in 1983 and the subsequent Channel 4 adaptation in September 1983, involving Gerry and Lee as the star presenters, was praised exuberantly by every reviewer. The keynote was that Gerald Durrell was the messiah for those who were only just becoming aware that the natural world had been all but brought to its knees by almost two centuries of industrialisation and exploitation.

The couple's final foreign trip was to Madagascar in 1990 in search of still-wild members of the aye-aye species of primates. It is a long-fingered nocturnal creature that could be a small monkey but resembles a squirrel just as much. Gerry had loved them from a distance for decades and feared that tree-felling and local tribal belief that they were creatures of the devil would soon amount to their extinction. He wanted to bring a breeding couple back to Jersey but was himself stricken by seizures and chest pains which cut short his journey. Lee was reluctant to return to Jersey so soon from the region where she had done her most important work as an undergraduate and doctoral researcher. She felt that more time there would earn her greater respect as a zoologist in her own right rather than, as some had whispered, the pretty ambitious twenty-something who had married for fame. She saw herself producing academic papers for esteemed journals and becoming the diligent scientific counterpart to Gerry's self-taught showmanship.

He insisted that she should remain on the island, assuring her that at the worst he was having bouts of angina and that his GP had already suggested that a stent, which did not even require an operation, would solve things. It would be a period of tedium which he felt he could best deal with alone.

What actually happened was that he decided to begin his long-promised purely autobiographical memoir. It would be completely different from the part-fictionalised accounts of Corfu, the rarefied, rhapsodic stories of his attempts to rescue endangered species and the other contemporaneous notes on his thoughts and experiences. This time he would be brutally transparent about his feelings, shortcomings and less appealing idiosyncrasies.

The surviving documents are fascinating in that we are offered a rare insight into the mind of a writer who is struggling with his focus and objectives. Often he will draw up a Table of Contents which will be a chronological account of his life from his earliest memories of India to Jersey in the present day. In the more substantive drafts, however, he finds it difficult, often impossible, to fix upon particulars either recollected or documented. Instead he will drift towards timeless philosophical reflections. Early on he has a go at an account of what Corfu was really like:

> I remember the curve of a wrist, the glint of a smile, a wart, a blackhead, an old hand twisted and misshapen with arthritis ... patting my shaggy blonde head while toothless gums beamed glisteningly ...
> (Jersey Archive, undated)

Before we learn more about this figure Gerry gives up on description and shifts to contemplation:

> I have no way of knowing who we are, every one of us is a shrouded ship that passes in the night and berths alongside briefly and we do not know what cargo it carries, its destination or what crew ... (*Ibid.*)

In short, we should give up even pretending to know the true nature of other individuals. This does not lead him to a state of despair, because there is an alternative realm of awareness and comprehension.

> Don't ever think that magic is simply someone taking a rabbit out of a hat. Our ancestors believed in magic and were right for the wrong reasons – for the most part they believed magic was evil, not for good.
>
> But the magic that lies all about you from your own body to that of an elephant, a fly's wing as intricate as anything that lets the sunlight into Chartres Cathedral, to the magic of a surging sea ... to a teacup of water teaming with a myriad of life forms as extraordinary as anything you could find by exploring the man-made, man-inhabited cities of the world – *that* is magic.
>
> Anyone who goes through life unastounded by everything he sees is not alive. (*Ibid.*)

He continues:

> We are losing our hearing, plugged in as we are to Sony Walkmans, thus losing the beautiful babble of bird song, the crooning of a beehive, the whisper of wind in leaves, as suggestive as a rumour. Long ago, it seems, we all became blind. I have seen people walk through a forest and be unaware of the magic table of a mushroom. (*Ibid.*)

His model of the history of humanity is unconventional, with him postulating evolution as our failed relationship with animals. For him, primitive humans missed wonderful opportunities when they moved ineradicably closer to the present state of 'civilisation'. 'Imagine the astonishment of an eskimo presented suddenly with a giraffe, a mountain dwelling tribe being suddenly confronted with a blue whale or a backwoods farmer being introduced to a duckbilled platypus?' His point is that as humans acquired more technical and intellectual sophistication they alienated themselves from a global community where the boundary between *Homo sapiens* and other species was negligible, and he goes on to compare the gains of modern civilisation with what we fail to appreciate.

> Imagine the blue whale as an enormous underwater cathedral filled with its song and as intricately designed as any man-made edifice. Look at the grace and eloquence of a giraffe, so much more beautiful than the Eiffel Tower or the leaning tower of Pisa, or indeed any of these man-made Freudian erections. They are far more precious than any man-made painting, sculpture or building on which we bestow such reverence. Of course, we should be interested in our own beginnings, the ladder from sperm to sperm, ova to ova, bone to bone, until the skull was filled with tumultuous ideas that went beyond the necessity of pursuing another animal to survive. As soon as other animals became food they became inferior.
>
> It seems to me that no one is taught about the incredible mechanism we live in. People seem unaware of taste, touch, smell and the use of the ear ... (*Ibid.*)

Throughout, Gerry seems to resent the necessity of having to share his story with other human beings. Even when he reflects upon general notions of our condition he becomes impatient with fellow members of his species. He half records a dialogue with a figure from his past and then considers the existential nature of conversation.

> That's how conversations start, like rivers. At first a teaspoon of an idea, throbbing out of the ground, meandering slowly and gaily, a glint here, a ripple there, but then it develops into a great and powerful thing ... (*Ibid.*)

The vehicle of his figurative concept of conversation, a river, is effective enough, but soon it takes over from and completely replaces the human aspect of the description, speech:

> Water pulsing out of the earth like a glittering severed artery ... it grows and growing gives half of itself back to the earth from which it sprang and then proceeds, in its way changing, enlarging, carrying in its tumultuous way the droppings of fish and mammal and bird, spreading web-like, it creates an apron or shawl of vegetation around it ... (*Ibid.*)

This portrait of the river in the natural world is sublime and meticulous and it runs on for about a further five hundred words, but Gerry has expelled from it all traces of humanity. A little later he becomes evangelical, arguing that we ruin children by obliging them to intellectualise their world.

> We send kids to school but we don't encourage them to explore and astonish themselves by reading a rich honeycomb harvest around them, opening up the senses of their mind, titillating the imagination into growth. (*Ibid.*)

Early in the various drafts he comments that,

> Having been brought up in an unconventional way I feel it fascinating that while I was exploring and wondering at the ways of animals, the animals reminded me that I had to explore and understand this extraordinary zoo of humans. I found animals only more complex because of their talk ... something I had yet to get a glimmering of in humans. (*Ibid.*)

He goes on to explain that he believed that the orality of animal 'language' is as laden with signifiers and nuances as ours, but is enriched by a supplementary range of meanings imparted intuitively, especially in erotic exchanges.

> ... they [animals] became the world and so I had difficulty in distinguishing the flirting of a joyful Goldfinch from a lead-on of a

human maiden, except that the human maiden is more ponderous and lacks wings. (*Ibid.*)

On of the most striking passages is 'Miscellaneous 16'.

Dear Mrs ...

As you will know from the moment I met you, I fell deeply, desperately, inconsolably, irrevocably and inexpressibly in love with you. Up until this moment – gentleman that I am – my lips have had to be sealed and I have to conceal the tremendous hot flushes that flood my veins like Niagara at the mere thought of you. But now there is a ray of hope. My wife (who has more faults than you can shake a stick at) is deserting me [for] Madagascar to live it up with a lemur or tortoise or some such ... My lawyers tell me this is good grounds for a divorce. (*Ibid.*)

There is no evidence that Lee saw the notes of the 'Miscellanies'. When Gerry composed them Lee was in Africa and Madagascar and the seemingly anonymous 'Dear Mrs' is revealed in a handwritten fragment stored in the Archive separately from the typed draft. In this she is referred to as 'Mrs A. Shepherd'. Avril Shepherd was married to David, a renowned wildlife artist who Gerry and Lee had known for more than a decade. She was blonde and as glamorous as a film star. We do not know if she and Gerry had an affair but he seems to have done so with Araminta Whitley, wife of Edward Whitley. Gerry had mentored Edward Whitley in his ambition to become a campaigner and writer on environmental issues. In the draft he created for Araminta several exotic personae bearing versions of her name. He fantasised about her in notebooks and at the same time that he composed 'Misc. 16' he wrote her a poem, which concludes:

Girls beguiling, smiles so winning
Girls who like a bit of sinning.
But in all the places that I've bin ta
None compare with Araminta

A page and a half later in 'Misc. 18' Gerry offers up a very short story.

Dark hair, huge glistening eyes, like chestnuts newly polished, a face composed and gently supported by bone structure as beautiful as a coral reef. A most moist wide and gentle, a loving mouth. A body as eloquent as a teenage birch tree. Brown hands like starfish ... I longed to know her, to have the privilege of taking her into a secret garden full of night jasmine, tangerine and flowering creatures that would attempt to emulate her beauty but could only enhance it. She was pure Garden of Eden ... The waiter brought the bill and I paid. As I passed the table of this lovely, delicate paragon I heard her say – loud as a conch shell being blown, 'You stupid twat, I can't think why I ever married you. Your balls are as big as warm eggs and as much use.' I have never felt the same about women since.

There is no indication that this is informed by specific autobiographical experience, though Jacquie was sometimes prone to raucous language. Rather the narrative is framed by Gerry's gradually acquired existential postulation. The description of her is ridden with animal and natural imagery and her uniqueness seems to derive from her having closed a gap between the environment and the human condition. She ruins this epiphany not because of her gender but as a result of being a person, something at odds with the world of creatures and plants that have a special dignity in their alienation from language, foul or otherwise. The notion of human language as a token of human inferiority is returned to several times in the Miscellanies, and women are the worst transgressors. 'Why is it that we have the misfortune to marry women. Why don't we marry trees which have the virtue of not talking back' (Misc. 32, Jersey Archive).

Light a fire so trees who have given you so much delight while they lived can produce in their cremation a picture gallery for your delight ... Trees are loving immobile friends, giving you a pageant throughout their lives from wonderful to when they take off their clothes and let you see them naked and beautiful ... Trees are like women, we cannot live without them. The ... advantage of a tree is that you can move away from it if it blossoms too much or becomes too shady. Alas, this seldom happens to the opposite sex, who, being mobile, tend to follow you pleading for this, that or the other – trees don't do that, sweet things, they know their place. (Misc. 30, Jersey Archive)

A few pages later Gerry shifts from discursive prose to a dialogue between himself and an unnamed woman. The woman opens:

You could watch me in a mirror. In a mirror you would be unobtainable, a reflection. What makes you think I am obtainable now? You are warm. I can touch you. I am cold and not to be touched.

She turned her green eyes on him and they were without expression.

You may be able to turn your eyes on and off like green fountains but you can't quench the rest of you. Don't empty your eyes at me like that – you disappear, the real you, you hide somewhere under your hair.

Men over seventy watched her with pleasure as men who could no longer swim admired a water lily on the pool's mirrored surface.

The dwarfs loved her frankly and in abundance but there was always a tiny spark of wistfulness in their eyes. (January 1995, otherwise undated, Jersey Archive)

Gerry was just 'over seventy' when he wrote this. The woman is a blend of the chimerical and the actual, but mostly she reminds us of all the other figures that magnetise Gerry's attempts in the draft to make sense of his life. They are sensual but do not quite share Gerry's world; part human, part animal.

The most compelling passage involves the tension between his greatest love, the instinctive non-linguistic world of plants and animals, and the thing that defines us as humans, our ability to make sense of the world through language.

I have always said I dislike writing, which I suppose is not strictly true. What I do not enjoy is the self-inflicted discipline of writing. What I do enjoy – not always but sometimes – is the juxtaposition of words or the amalgamation of sentences to create, as it were, an effect ... I think painters get the same feeling when they shade one colour into another and find it true and pleasing ... [But] the author is a lonely soul, like an albatross. He does not know if his carefully constructed sentence actually portrays (in my case) the furry intimacy of a bird-eating spider, the throbbing thimble of incandescent colour of a Hummingbird ... He has a looming shadow always over his shoulder – the knowledge that he can write fifty thousand words and not be certain that anyone will ... understand what he is trying to say. (Misc. 32, Jersey Archive)

This is as close as we have to the spiritual mandate of Gerald Durrell. He has kept himself and maintained his career as an environmentalist by writing books about animals, or rather his relationship with them, and he turns a quiet loathing upon himself for having done so because the proper experience of the 'furry intimacy of the bird eating spider', the 'incandescent colour of a Hummingbird' must exclude verbal description. 'To know them you must see, even feel them.'

Larry is rarely mentioned but one must consider the astonishing difference between those two brothers, one of whom was addicted to creating in fiction alternative worlds to the one he inhabited and the other who detested having to sustain his love affair with nature by an enslavement to the written word. He is not mentioned directly but in the autobiography notes Gerry continues with a fictional account of an interview he'd begun earlier, between his late brother and a French journalist.

Lawrence Durrell: My brother (I wish you'd stop asking me about him: it's really *de trop*) is not really a scientist at all. He is a showman. He is to science what the *Reader's Digest* is to Holy Writ – his version is made readable to the many; science is something else, and he is well aware of the fact. So what has he done? With immense cunning he has actually trapped and married a real scientist, beautiful, the most brilliant of the younger American scientists, with everything including a prose style. In English we call this being 'home and dry'.

Journalist: I wonder how that would translate into my language – home and dry? (Jersey Archive, undated)

Gerry and Lee's most formidable expedition had taken place more than five years before this in 1984, involving two back-to-back separate visits to the Soviet Union totalling almost nine months. The Cold War was at a crossroads with Thatcher and Reagan shifting between robust speeches against Soviet authoritarianism and quieter gestures when Gorbachev came to power in 1985 which would eventually contribute to the collapse of the Soviet bloc at the close of the 1980s.

When Gerry and Lee set off for Moscow in October 1984 their visit was part of an East–West rapprochement that had been nursed into being by meetings initiated by Reagan, Thatcher and Gorbachev in 1982 and cultivated by the diplomatic services of each country during the following years. Both sides wanted closer cultural ties which, they hoped, would embed political peace-making, involving arms treaties and the opening of borders. The Durrells were part of this though they remained largely unaware of their role as pawns in a global negotiation. They went to the most remote parts of Russia: the red-hot desert of Turkmenistan (44 degrees Celsius when they arrived there in May 1985), the black treeless landscape of Siberia, the windswept freezing regions close to the Arctic Ocean and the mountains that formed the Russian borders with Afghanistan and China.

They came upon species that they had previously never heard of, and the Soviet authorities assured them that the State had secured the survival of all of its native animals. Gerry's attempts to take photographs were monitored and censored and there was certainly no option of the most peculiar and rare species of birds and mammals finding a future in Jersey.

Durrell in Russia, co-authored with Lee, appeared in 1986, but it was a heavily revised version of what actually happened during their time in the Soviet Union. Their editor at Simon & Schuster advised Gerry and Lee that turning the book into a diatribe against a regime that managed and distorted the truth about its conservation policies just as much as it did about its treatment of human citizens would cause reviewers to treat it as a right-wing anti-communist pamphlet. Gerry's signature modus, he reminded them, was as defender of animals against humans, irrespective of the ideological position of the latter. As his copious notes on the expedition showed, he was captivated by the vast undisturbed landscapes they visited while seeming oblivious to being the honoured guest of a repressive one-party state. Some thought the book was censored because it said hardly anything of what it was like to live in the Soviet Union but in truth its omission of what the Russian people experienced was a reflection of Gerry's temperament and mindset: for him people didn't matter.

Since the 1960s Gerry had been treated as one of the world's most celebrated campaigning conservationists and in the 1980s the British establishment had installed him as a cultural trophy. Following his 1982 lunch with the Queen at Windsor, along with the President of the Cameroons, he became a regular guest of members of the royal family. The Queen Mother entertained him and Lee twice, later in the 1980s encouraged by his most enthusiastic fan from the Windsors, Princess Anne. For example, he wrote to Lee's parents on the opening of a conference on wildlife preservation on 13 May 1992: 'We were so lucky to get Annie Girl (our Patron) to open it. She made a wonderful speech and set the seal of importance on what we and other zoos are doing' (Jersey Archive).

He sounds confident enough but eight months later in December 1992 his friend in London Sarah Kennedy invited him and Lee to her Notting Hill flat for early-evening drinks. The couple were offered a choice of wines but Gerry went for a decent bottle of malt whisky he had seen on her sideboard; Lee chose a white Sancerre. The three chatted in an amiable, directionless way until the downstairs doorbell rang and Kennedy excused herself. There were noises on the stairs. She opened the sitting-room door to admit Sir David Attenborough and Desmond Morris and laid the table for supper. Each was a person of considerable eminence for similar reasons but they could not be regarded as friends and she said later that she had decided to entertain Britain's, perhaps the world's, three most important naturalists because the previous year when she had taken lunch with Gerry he seemed to her worryingly breathless and self-evidently agitated by his discomfort. For Botting Kennedy added that, 'I had to do it, because I knew instinctively that it would be the last time these three would all be together' (Botting, p572). She suspected that quite soon Gerry would be dead.

In 1993 Gerry decided that he and Lee should spend as much time as possible in the Mazet where he would again try to make progress with the memoir now provisionally entitled 'Myself and Other Animals: A Sort of Autobiography'. It would, he decided, be the most authentic and candid account of his life. Alexandra Mayhew, who had worked for him before, was brought in by Lee to type his dictated account. Lee did not know that she and Gerry had had a short relationship when she was considering whether to leave Lincoln almost fifteen years earlier. Alexandra, still good-looking, was now divorced. Gerry and Lee no longer had sex and while she was not happy with the prospect of him spending time in private with another woman she decided that all he capable of was an extramarital fantasy as a means of literary stimulation. We know nothing of whether Alexandra and Gerry reignited the spark of their brief liaison but it seems likely that her presence – along with Avril Shepherd and Araminta Whitley – inspired his creation of the sensual other women, excluding Lee, who patrol the draft.

What we have of the project is by parts beautiful and tragic. As is evident above his prose is built upon anger and elegance but in the end he would not connect the often sublime parts. Gerry would spend whole days in a state of silent discontentment, often staring at the wall and finally resorting to mammoth glasses of whisky to project him out of his state of enervation. But drink made him worse. He would regularly have seizures and his ability to walk any distance was a major problem. In November 1993 he and Lee flew to London to launch the final part of his four-volume books for children, the so-called 'Puppy Tales'. He returned to France in December and abandoned drafts of the autobiography because of intense pains in his stomach. He wrote to Lee's parents that, 'The pain became so intense that I simply could not work, could not think and was driving Lee mad' (January 1994, otherwise undated, Jersey Archive). He was admitted to Nimes hospital for four days and scans showed that he had cirrhosis of the liver, complicated by a large tumour.

Lee telephoned doctors who had treated him in Jersey and London, and Dr Guy O'Keeffe arranged for him to be admitted to the private Cromwell Road Hospital in West London for further tests. After several weeks of careful scrutiny O'Keeffe pronounced that there was only one option. A liver transplant would reverse the cirrhosis, provided that he gave up drink, but there was no guarantee that the tumour had not spread to other parts of his body.

Jeremy Mallinson wrote to Jacquie and told her what was happening to her ex-husband. She replied:

What a dreadful business, and I feel for Lee. I would like to see Gerry as and when, for I feel very strongly that it is time to settle our misunderstandings and enter a new phase. If you can explain this to Lee I would be so grateful. Basically I just want to tell Gerry that I remember our time together with affection and gratitude. (24 March 1994, Jersey Archive)

The meeting did not take place. There is no evidence that Gerry refused to see his ex-wife; more likely the severity of his condition and the procession of emergency treatments made it impossible.

At the end of March Gerry had received a phone call from the Liver Unit at King's College Hospital stating that a liver of the correct blood group was available. Two days later, on 27 March, Gerry arrived at the hospital for his transplant. Staff were a little surprised to find that he was drunk but the procedure was completed on the morning of 1 April.

He came off the ventilator after two days, was moved to the private patients' wing and asked if there was anything he would like. He wanted a tape recorder to return to his memoir, plus a very large brandy. The nurse was stunned by the latter request, given that his liver had been ruined by alcoholism. 'Exactly!' he replied. 'And now I've got a new liver.'

In mid-April he was moved to a luxurious private room in Cromwell Hospital. While he was in hospital Sir David Attenborough opened the new enclosures for orangutans in Jersey and gave a speech:

There are some people who argue that there is no justification for zoos ... LET THEM COME HERE!

Gerry was receiving chemotherapy in an attempt to eradicate cancer cells that had spread from his liver. He was also being dosed with steroids to bring him back from his increasingly emaciated state.

In September Gerry's private healthcare service BUPA decided that, in the opinion of a physician they had hired to examine his condition, he would soon be dead. They cited a brutal subclause in their policy and terminated it. On 25 September he was moved back to King's College Hospital and by early November it was agreed that he would be more content in Jersey and he and Lee flew on an ambulance plane to St Helier hospital.

Twice she managed to drive him to the zoo but it was unlikely that he was aware of his surroundings. He could make little sense of what was said to him and could barely speak. On 27 January 1995, he was asked how he felt and his answer – 'Bloody awful!' – was his last recorded utterance. Three days later, on 30 January, he died of septicaemia.

On 9 March 1995 Gerry's ashes were buried beneath a marble plinth in the garden of Les Augrès. Six weeks earlier, shortly before the cremation, an informal goodbye was arranged by Lee at the St Helier undertakers. Margo was there, with her son Gerry and granddaughter Tracy, as was Larry's daughter Penny and Lee's sister Hat. The small room was crowded. At least thirty of Gerry's associates and employees from the zoo and veterans of his various overseas expeditions found their way in or queued outside.

Following her return to Bournemouth Margo wrote:

My Dear Lee,
    I feel that Gerry's little farewell gathering was perfect. He would have approved. But he is still with us. I feel safe!
    Margo x (6 February 1995, Jersey Archive)

Margo, the last of the siblings, died in Bournemouth on 16 January 2007.

SELECT BIBLIOGRAPHY

BOOKS BY LAWRENCE DURRELL

Novels

Pied Piper of Lovers, Cassell, London, 1935

Panic Spring, Faber & Faber, London, 1936 (under the pseudonym Charles Norden)

The Black Book: An Agon, Obelisk Press, Paris, 1938; Faber & Faber, London, 1973

Cefalu, Editions Poetry London, 1947; as *The Dark Labyrinth*, Ace Books, London, 1958; Faber & Faber, London 1961

White Eagles Over Serbia, Faber & Faber, London, 1957

Justine, Faber & Faber, London, 1957

Balthazar, Faber & Faber, London, 1958

Mountolive, Faber & Faber, London, 1958

Clea, Faber & Faber, London, 1960

Tunc: A Novel, Faber & Faber, London, 1968

Nunquam: A Novel, Faber & Faber, London, 1970

Monsieur: or, The Prince of Darkness, Faber & Faber, London, 1974

Livia: or, Buried Alive, Faber & Faber, London, 1978

Constance: or, Solitary Practices, Faber & Faber, London, 1982

Sebastian: or, Ruling Passions, Faber & Faber, London, 1983

Quinx: or, The Ripper's Tale, Faber & Faber, London, 1985

Travel books

Prospero's Cell: A Guide to the Landscape and Manners of the Island of Corcyra, Faber & Faber, London, 1945

Reflections on a Marine Venus, Faber & Faber, London, 1953

Bitter Lemons, Faber & Faber, London, 1957

Spirit of Place: Letters and Essays on Travel, Faber & Faber, London, 1969

Sicilian Carousel, Faber & Faber, London, 1977

The Greek Islands, Faber & Faber, London, 1978

Caesar's Vast Ghost: Aspects of Provence, Faber & Faber, London, 1990

Plays
Sappho: A Play in Verse, Faber & Faber, London, 1952
An Irish Faustus: A Morality in Nine Scenes, Faber & Faber, London, 1963
Acte: A Play, Faber & Faber, London, 1964

Poetry
A Private Country, Faber & Faber, London, 1943
Cities, Plains and People, Faber & Faber, London, 1946
On Seeming to Presume, Faber & Faber, London, 1948
The Tree of Idleness, Faber & Faber, London, 1955
Selected Poems, Faber & Faber, London, 1956
Collected Poems, Faber & Faber, London, 1960
Selected Poems, 1935–1963, Faber & Faber, London, 1964
The Ikons, Faber & Faber, London, 1966
Collected Poems, 1931–1974 (revised), Faber & Faber, London, 1968
The Red Limbo Lingo: A Poetry Notebook, Faber & Faber, London, 1971
Vega and Other Poems, Faber & Faber, London, 1973
Selected Poems (selected and introduced by Alan Ross), Faber & Faber,
    London, 1977
Collected Poems, 1931–1974 (edited by James A. Brigham), Faber & Faber,
    London, 1980

Essays
A Key to Modern Poetry, Peter Nevill, London, 1952
Blue Thirst, Capra Press, Santa Barbara, 1975

Comic stories
Esprit de Corps: Sketches from Diplomatic Life, Faber & Faber, London, 1957
Stiff Upper Lip, Faber & Faber, London, 1958
Sauve Qui Peut, Faber & Faber, London, 1966

Other
The Big Supposer. A Dialogue with Marc Alyn, Abelard-Schuman, New York, 1973

BOOKS BY GERALD DURRELL
Autobiographical
The Overloaded Ark, Faber & Faber, London, 1953
Three Singles to Adventure, Rupert Hart-Davis, London, 1954
The Bafut Beagles, Rupert Hart-Davis, London, 1954

The New Noah, Rupert Hart-Davis, London, 1955

The Drunken Forest, Rupert Hart-Davis, London, 1956

My Family and Other Animals, Rupert Hart-Davis, London, 1956

Encounters with Animals, Rupert Hart-Davis, London, 1958

A Zoo in My Luggage, Rupert Hart-Davis, London, 1960

The Whispering Land, Rupert Hart-Davis, London, 1961

Menagerie Manor, Rupert Hart-Davis, London, 1964

Two in the Bush, Collins, London, 1966

Birds, Beasts and Relatives, Collins, London, 1969

Fillets of Plaice, Collins, London, 1971

Catch me a Colobus, Collins, London, 1972

Beasts in My Belfry, Collins, London, 1973

The Stationary Ark, Collins, London, 1976

Golden Bats and Pink Pigeons: A Journey to the Flora and Fauna of a Unique Island, Collins, London, 1977

The Garden of the Gods, Collins, London, 1978

The Picnic and Suchlike Pandemonium (partly openly fictional), Collins, London, 1979

Ark on the Move, Collins, London, 1982

How to Shoot an Amateur Naturalist, Collins, London, 1984

Durrell in Russia (with Lee Durrell), MacDonald, London, 1986

The Ark's Anniversary, Collins, London, 1990

Marrying Off Mother and Other Stories (partly openly fictional), HarperCollins, London, 1991

The Aye-Aye and I: A Rescue Journey to Save the World's Most Intriguing Creatures from Extinction, HarperCollins, London, 1992

Myself and Other Animals, Penguin Random House, London, 2024

Documentary

Island Zoo: The Animals a Famous Collector Couldn't Part with, Collins, London, 1961

Look at Zoos, Hamish Hamilton, London, 1961

A Practical Guide for the Amateur Naturalist (with Lee Durrell), Hamish Hamilton, London, 1982

Fiction (mostly for children)

The Donkey Rustlers, Collins, London, 1968

Rosy Is My Relative, Collins, London, 1968

The Talking Parcel, Collins, London, 1974
The Mockery Bird, Collins, London, 1981
The Fantastic Flying Journey, Conran Octopus, London, 1987
The Fantastic Dinosaur Adventure, Conran Octopus, London, 1989
Keeper, Michael O'Mara Books, London 1990
Toby the Tortoise, Michael O'Mara Books, London, 1991
Puppy Tales, four volumes, Scott Ltd, London, 1993

BOOKS RELATED TO THE DURRELLS

Botting, Douglas, *Gerald Durrell: The Authorised Biography,* London, HarperCollins, 1999
Bowker, Gordon, *Through the Dark Labyrinth: A Biography of Lawrence Durrell*, London, Sinclair-Stevenson, 1996
Durrell, Jacquie, *Beasts in My Bed*, London, Collins, 1967
Durrell, Margaret, *Whatever Happened to Margo?* London, Andre Deutsch, 1995
Haag, Michael, *The Durrells of Corfu*, London, Profile Books, 2017
Hodgkin, Joanna, *Amateurs in Eden: The Story of a Bohemian Marriage: Nancy and Lawrence Durrell*, London, Virago, 2012
Hughes, David, *Himself and Other Animals: A Portrait of Gerald Durrell*, London, Pimlico, 1998
MacNiven, Ian S., (ed.) *The Durrell-Miller Letters: 1935–80*, London, Faber & Faber, 1988
MacNiven, Ian S., *Lawrence Durrell: A Biography*, London, Faber & Faber, 1998
Stephanides, Theodore, *Autumn Gleanings: Corfu Memoirs and Poems*, Corfu, The Durrell School of Corfu, 2011

INDEX